EXAM CRAM

The LSAT Cram Sheet

This Cram Sheet contains the distilled, key facts about the Law School Admission Test (LSAT). Review this information last thing before entering the test room, paying special attention to those areas where you feel you need the most review. You can transfer any of the facts onto a blank piece of paper before beginning the exam.

READING COMPREHENSION IN GENERAL

➤ You may be asked to spot "gotchas" that greatly strengthen or undermine the point of the article.

➤ Arguments that praise a point may say "the unassailable truth is" or "there is no doubt that."

➤ Arguments to undermine points may say "the argument is weakened by the fact that," or "the bald assertion is made."

➤ There are four kinds of questions that comprise the vast majority of questions in this section:

  ➤ Primary idea: Determine what most accurately summarizes the passage's central idea.

  ➤ Author bias or "attitude": Determine which way the author's biases or attitudes lie by the way they try to persuade you or present information.

  ➤ Refining meaning: Clarify an ambiguous passage, narrow the meaning of a word, or supply a definition for an expression or local colloquialism.

  ➤ Furthering implications or drawing conclusions: You'll be given a selection of facts or arguments that you can choose from to draw a specific point out of the reading passage. These facts or arguments typically are used to do one of two things to the passage: strengthen the main argument, or weaken it.

When faced with these types of questions, you'll need to keep two things in mind. First, be aware of the context of the entire passage. Second, if you're down to two likely choices for your answer, the correct answer will be the one that captures the passage's ideas with the most accuracy and detail.

TIME MANAGEMENT

➤ When you open the Reading Comprehension section, resist the temptation to run through the passage.

➤ Similarly, don't read and re-read the passage. Unless the passage contains truly atrocious or dense writing, a single pass will allow you to retain most of the information of note.

➤ You do not need to remember the passage in great detail in order to answer questions about it. One trick that the LSAT writers will employ on occasion is to give you a large number of details, or a blizzard of facts that will slow down the unwary and panic the uninitiated.

➤ If it makes you feel more secure to read the questions first, go ahead. Some people report that seeing the questions gives them a good "heads up" as to what to watch for.

FOCUS

➤ Focus is a way to manage or eliminate the anxiety of the unknown. Remember that the LSAT is not testing you on your knowledge of arcane subject matter. Narrow your focus on the passages so that you pick out facts and premises for arguments.

UNDERSTANDING BY CONTEXT

➤ You can understand any word from its surrounding context. Whenever running into unfamiliar material, back off and read the contextual material surrounding the word or phrase.

➤ Even if you think the use of the word is inappropriate, remember: The testers aren't picking the best writing for you to read; they are picking items that require a second glance and a period of thought.

ANALYTICAL REASONING IN GENERAL

➤ Throughout the section, the difficulty of the logic games presented will vary randomly, but there are two general rules:

➤The initial game that opens the section will not be the most difficult one.

➤The final one or two logic games are typically more complex than the others.

TIME MANAGEMENT

➤ A simple game could take you 6–7 minutes, while more complex games require a solid 10-minute investment of your time.

➤ You will not be able to rush on any question—there are no "easy questions" that take significantly less time than others.

➤ Keep a steady place and don't allot more than 10 minutes to any one logic game; then you will be fine. Of course, the amount of time that you spend on any logic game depends upon how complex or simple it is.

ADDITIONAL TIPS TO HANDLE ANALYTICAL REASONING

➤ If you're stuck on one game, it may be best to skip it and return if you can. However, don't skip more than one game.

Trying to skip over no more than one game will reduce the chance that you'll be left with blind guessing over a large number of remaining questions and give you a better chance for a higher score.

There is no single question type that is inherently much more difficult or time consuming than other types. You will not benefit if you plan to skip every question of a given type.

➤ Diagramming out the question will be useful in this section, so remember that the LSAT includes a couple pages of scratch paper in the back of the test booklet. You can also use the space provided at the bottom of each page of the Analytical Reasoning section.

➤ The key to an effective diagram is to keep it neat. If you make a mistake, it's best to cross out the diagram and redo it; simply scratching out names or writing on top of incorrect answers will likely confuse you at a critical time.

LOGICAL REASONING IN GENERAL

➤ Logical Reasoning won't subject you to the same amount of time pressure as the other two sections (no diagramming or heavy reading). Therefore, your goal should be to complete the entire section.

➤ Keep your eyes out for "weasel phrases" that subtly over- or under-play a statement. For example, the phrases "never," "cannot," or "always" can be subtly weakened with the words "almost," "potentially," "possibly," and "allegedly."

➤ In the context of the LSAT, "logical" does not equal "true." It's not unheard of for the LSAT creators to compose arguments that are logical, but manifestly untrue. Remember, even if you're absolutely certain that the statements presented are erroneous, treat them as if they exist in their own universe. Your job is to determine whether the statements properly support and follow each other.

ELIMINATING ANSWER OPTIONS

➤ Almost always, at least one answer out of the possible choices for a question can be eliminated immediately because it matches one of these conditions:

   ➤ The answer does not apply to the situation.

   ➤ The answer describes a nonexistent issue, an invalid option, or an imaginary state.

   ➤ The answer may be eliminated because of information in the question itself.

After you eliminate all answers that are obviously wrong, you can apply your retained knowledge to eliminate further answers. Look for items that sound correct but refer to actions, commands, or features that are not present or not available in the situation that the question describes.

EXAM CRAM™

LSAT

Michael Bellomo

que®
CERTIFICATION

LSAT Exam Cram

International Standard Book Number: 0-7897-3414-1

Library of Congress Catalog Card Number: 2005925366

Printed in the United States of America

First Printing: August 2005

08   07   06   05   4   3   2   1

Trademarks

Warning and Disclaimer

Bulk Sales

Que Publishing offers excellent discounts on this book when ordered in quantity for bulk purchases or special sales. For more information, please contact

U.S. Corporate and Government Sales
1-800-382-3419
corpsales@pearsontechgroup.com

For sales outside the U.S., please contact

International Sales
international@pearsoned.com

Publisher
Paul Boger

Executive Editor
Jeff Riley

Acquisitions Editor
Carol Ackerman

Development Editor
Sean Dixon

Managing Editor
Charlotte Clapp

Project Editor
Mandie Frank

Production Editor
Benjamin Berg

Indexer
Chris Barrick

Proofreader
Paula Lowell

Technical Editors
Jason Evans of
Advantage Education

Jeff Johnson

Publishing Coordinator
Pamalee Nelson

Multimedia Developer
Dan Scherf

Designer
Gary Adair

Page Layout
Kelly Maish

This book is dedicated to Laura Presnell, who inspired so many of the questions listed throughout this book. TCFYOG.

❧

--Michael Bellomo

About the Author

Michael Bellomo holds a Juris Doctor in Law from the University of California, San Francisco; an M.B.A. from the University of California at Irvine; and a Black Belt certification in Six Sigma project management. In the course of his career, Michael has worked with The Knowledge Labs, a think tank in Irvine, California, and with ARES Corporation, a project and risk management firm that works with the Department of Defense and NASA. He was the narrator for a multimedia presentation sent to Congress on the development of NASA's Orbital Space Plane. Currently, he serves with ARES Corporation as their Contracts and Proposals Counsel.

Michael has written 13 books in the areas of science, technology, and business. His works have been published in Italian, Portuguese, Chinese, French, Dutch, German, Russian, and Japanese. His latest book, *Microbe: Are We Ready for the Next Plague?* is about stopping bioterrorism attacks against the U.S. and will be published in June 2005. He lives in Los Angeles, California.

About the Technical Editors

Advantage Education provides educational services to students, educators, and business professionals, specializing in standardized test preparation for tests such as ACT, SAT, PSAT, GRE, GMAT, and LSAT, as well as MBE Bar Review and law school tutoring for selected courses. Training is delivered via live instruction in select locations throughout the U.S., and via Personal Distance Learning over the Internet. Our instructors and personal tutors are experts with a wealth of relevant experience who have scored in the 99th percentile on their respective exams. Since 1997, thousands have succeeded by putting their trust in Advantage Education. Jason Evans, as an Advantage Education instructor, teaches LSAT and PreLaw Preparation, Bar Exam Preparation, and ACT and SAT Preparation. He graduated Summa Cum Laude from Michigan State University on a full academic scholarship, based in part on his LSAT score, which was the highest score received on the Michigan bar exam in 2003.

Jeff Johnson holds a B.B.A. in Finance from the University of Texas at Austin and two Master's Degrees from Harvard University. He made 98th percentile on the LSAT (44 out of 48) but decided ultimately to pursue a dual Master's Program at Harvard and pursue a business career. He is currently an executive with Science Applications International Corporation (SAIC), a Fortune 500 Company with HQ in San Diego, CA.

Acknowledgments

I would like to thank my tirelessly patient editor Carol Ackerman and two people who helped with the process of bringing this book from concept to reality: Joel Elad and Jeff Johnson. My thanks also go out to Donald Ayre and Bruce Chiriatti for our long-ago discussions that led to additional material for the exams.

And of course, I would like to acknowledge the superb work of two people who immensely improved the quality of the written and the audio portions of this book: Carol Traver of the Chrysippus Corporation and Sean Graham of the Atlantis Group.

We Want to Hear from You!

As the reader of this book, *you* are our most important critic and commentator. We value your opinion and want to know what we're doing right, what we could do better, what areas you'd like to see us publish in, and any other words of wisdom you're willing to pass our way.

As an executive editor for Que Publishing, I welcome your comments. You can email or write me directly to let me know what you did or didn't like about this book--as well as what we can do to make our books better.

Please note that I cannot help you with technical problems related to the topic of this book. We do have a User Services group, however, where I will forward specific technical questions related to the book.

When you write, please be sure to include this book's title and author as well as your name, email address, and phone number. I will carefully review your comments and share them with the author and editors who worked on the book.

Email: feedback@quepublishing.com

Mail: Jeff Riley
         Executive Editor
         Que Publishing
         800 East 96th Street
         Indianapolis, IN 46240 USA

For more information about this book or another Que Certification title, visit our website at www.examcram.com. Type the ISBN (excluding hyphens) or the title of a book in the Search field to find the page you're looking for.

Contents at a Glance

Table of Contents

Introduction

Why You Need to Become an Expert at the LSAT

If you are seriously thinking about applying for admission to one of the vast majority of law schools in the country, you need to become extremely familiar with the LSAT, or Law School Admissions Test. Essentially, if you plan to go into the legal field, there is no getting around the fact that you'll have to take the LSAT. The test is required for admission to all 202 law schools that are members of the Law School Admission Council (LSAC).

Although inclusion within the ranks of the LSAC is not necessarily a guarantee of quality, the vast majority of the legal programs in the U.S. are part of the LSAC. All law schools approved by the American Bar Association are LSAC members.

Therefore, if you plan to specifically attend a school that is not part of the LSAC, then congratulations--you may not have to face the LSAT. However, without taking the LSAT, you are giving up the chance to apply to the vast majority of schools that could offer an excellent legal education.

Who Are These LSAC People, Anyway?

The Law School Admission Council (LSAC) is a nonprofit corporation located in the eastern Pennsylvanian town of Newtown, about a half-hour's drive north of Philadelphia. Although best known for composing devilishly tricky questions on the LSAT exam, the LSAC also provides a number of helpful services such as

➤ Organizing law school forums, where prospective applicants can meet with and question admissions counselors and students from the schools they are interested in.

➤ Producing software, videos, and assorted publications to assist in admissions and law school education in general.

➤ Administering the MILE (Minorities Interested in Legal Education) program. The MILE project provides minority students with information about preparation for law school, with the end goal of increasing the numbers of lawyers from underrepresented minority groups in the United States.

➤ Running the Candidate Referral Service (CRS). The CRS is one of the two services that plays directly to the LSAC's main strength—the collection and distribution of law applicant data. If you register with CRS, you have the opportunity to authorize the release of information about yourself to eligible law schools and organizations who may be looking for candidates with a specific ethnic background or range of test scores.

➤ Administering the Law School Data Assembly Service (LSDAS). This is the second of the two LSAC services that specializes in the collection and timely distribution of the Law School Admission Test (LSAT) information and test scores.

On average, about 135,000 prospective law students take the LSAT annually. According to the Law School Admission Council's website, the LSAC administered about 147,600 LSATs in 2004, which is a substantial jump in numbers. Part of the jump is due to the state of the economy (which we'll discuss briefly in Chapter 1). But the uncomfortable fact remains: The overall trend in the number of people applying to law school has been increasing at a faster rate than the number of seats available.

This in turn means that with more applicants, the level of competition is steeper and the need to perform well on the LSAT is correspondingly great, particularly if one wants to get into a brand-name program. If this is your concern, then take a deep breath: You've come to the right book.

How to Use Your *Exam Cram* Book

The main purpose of the *Exam Cram* series is to provide you with tools and information that will help you practice for and attain the best possible score on the LSAT. It's not designed to help you decide which law school is best for you, or even to help you decide if law school is the proper career choice, though the skills taught are applicable. That said, your use of the book may differ slightly depending on your situation.

Entering or in the Middle of College and Seriously Considering Law School

Start by reading this book, which gives you insights and practice for the LSAT, as well as information about the law school admissions process in general. You would also do well to find a pre-law advisor at your school. Most undergraduate institutions offer these services, particularly if you are enrolled in a major that is a "feeder subject" into the legal arena, such as the liberal arts, humanities, and of course, "pre-law."

Consider testing yourself with the exam material found in this book. In fact, if you're a junior or senior, you may not have all that much time left to decide whether this is a field for you. Run through an exam and see whether you're comfortable--not necessarily with the questions, per se. Rather, see whether you're comfortable with exercising the parts of your thought process that you access in order to solve the problem at hand.

A College Graduate and Seriously Considering Law School

You might be interested to know that you have one strong positive and one strong (but correctable) negative off the bat. First off, the good news is that law schools have been and continue to warmly receive returning college graduates. Partly this is because of the schools pledging to continue increasing the diversity of their student body. It is also due to longer-term studies showing that people who go to law school after a few years in the business world (or spending a couple years involved in any activity that provides valuable life experience) tend to have higher retention and bar pass rates.

On the other hand, if you're four years out of college, you're four years further away than the typical college grad from your memories of the SAT. In addition, unless all of the incoming law school applicants went to Party Hearty U., you'll be in competition against people who have been taking multiple-choice scantron tests for the past three to four years. Don't let this put you off--it simply means getting into training, only with the mind instead of the body. Read this book and practice the exams, and pay special attention to the "why" of an answer.

NOTE

According to the LSAC, in Fall 2003, about 25 percent of all law school applicants were 22 years old or younger; about 37 percent were 23 to 25; and about 19 percent were between ages 26 and 29. Applicants who were 30 to 34 years old made up about 10 percent of the applicant pool, while 9 percent were more than 34 years old.

In College and Preparing to Take the LSAT in a Couple Weeks

What are you reading this for? Get started on the practice exams! And when you're done, for last-minute exam jitters, refer to the two-page Cram Sheet in the front of this book for key bits of information that you can use.

About This Book

Each topical *Exam Cram* chapter follows a regular structure, along with graphical cues about important or useful information. Here's the structure of a typical chapter:

➤ Opening Hotlists--Each chapter begins with a list of the terms, tools, and techniques you must learn and understand before you can be fully conversant with that chapter's subject matter. Following the hotlists are one or two introductory paragraphs to set the stage for the rest of the chapter.

➤ Topical coverage--The main text of the chapter follows the opening hotlists. Throughout this section, topics or concerns likely to appear on a test are highlighted in a special Exam Alert layout, like this:

 This is what an Exam Alert looks like. Normally, an Exam Alert stresses concepts, terms, software, or activities that are likely to relate to one or more certification test questions. For that reason, any information found offset in an Exam Alert format is worthy of unusual attentiveness on your part.

Pay close attention to material flagged as an Exam Alert; although all the information in this book pertains to what you need to know to pass the exam, we flag certain items that are really important. You'll find what appears in the meat of each chapter to be worth knowing, too, when preparing for the test.

Because this book's material is very condensed, we recommend that you use this book along with other resources to achieve the maximum possible benefit.

➤ Practice Questions--Although test questions and topics are discussed throughout each chapter, the "Exam Prep Questions" section at the end of each chapter presents a series of mock test questions and explanations of both correct and incorrect answers.

The beginning chapters follow this structure slavishly, but there are a few other elements we'd like to point out.... The bulk of this book is devoted to four full-length practice exams. Each exam is structured in style and difficulty to be as hard as—if not more difficult than--the actual LSAT. Answers follow in a separate chapter after each exam, with complete explanations as to why a given answer was correct or incorrect.

How to Use This CD-ROM

The CD-ROM that comes with this book is an audio version of the text you'll be reading. To play it, you can use the disc with your computer's CD-ROM drive, Walkman, or home stereo. If you're unable to play the disc for any reason, don't panic: There are no Easter Eggs or "extras" that come with the disc the way that DVDs do now.

We've included the CD-ROM with this book for the simple reason that people have different styles of learning. Some retain more material in a simple visual presentation; others prefer a hands-on, or "kinesthetic" approach. Still others prefer to listen to the material in order to concentrate on what is being said.

Even if you're a primarily a visual learner, consider listening to the CD on the car stereo or when you're working on other tasks at hand. You may find that you pick up on different bits of information, or that arguments (which are verbal to begin with) are easier to understand and dissect when listened to and then read. Whichever way promotes the best retention and learning of the proper technique, continue using it for your best LSAT exam result.

Self-Assessment

Education and Experience Requirements for the LSAT

Essentially, there are none.

Surprised?

This is because before you can apply to a graduate legal program, you'll need to graduate from college and have the LSAT completed either during or after you've graduated. However, there are no "pre-law" courses or classes that are required to take the LSAT. Whether your college background was in history, engineering, or the fine arts, you're eligible to take the LSAT.

 Incidentally, if you're thinking of taking the LSAT while you're just starting college, to see whether you're able to perform well on the test—and yes, there are people who wonder whether they should do this—it's probably not a good idea, for two reasons:

1. LSAT scores are only good for five years.
2. Keep in mind that most law schools average multiple test scores, so getting a low score the first time around could come back to haunt you when you decide to take it "for real."

How the LSAT is Structured

The LSAT is a standardized test, meaning that it is a multiple-choice, or "scantron" exam. It is administered over the course of 3.5 hours, or half a day. The test consists of five sections of multiple-choice questions in which you are given 35 minutes per section to complete, and one section called the "writing sample," where you are given 30 minutes to write about a selected topic.

The writing sample is not scored. However, copies of the sample are sent to all law schools to which a candidate applies. This isn't done in order to evaluate the candidate's writing ability so much as to measure consistency in your writing ability between your exam and the written personal statement that you need to submit with most law school applications.

Interestingly enough, only four of the five multiple choice sections contribute to your score. The fifth section, which is also called the "variable" section, does not. This unscored section is used to "try out" or, in LSAT lingo, to "pre-equate" new test forms and questions. The placement and the type of questions in the variable section is varied for each administration of the test, and you will not be told which section is the variable one. For example, in one year, the order of the sections might be as follows:

Section I: Logical Reasoning—35 minutes, scored section

Section II: Analytical Reasoning—35 minutes, scored section

Section III: Logical Reasoning—35 minutes, unscored section

Section IV: Reading Comprehension—35 minutes, scored section

Section V: Logical Reasoning—35 minutes, scored section

Section VI: Writing Sample—30 minutes, never scored

The following year, the LSAT exam might be

Section I: Logical Reasoning—35 minutes, scored section

Section II: Logical Reasoning—35 minutes, scored section

Section III: Analytical Reasoning—35 minutes, scored section

Section IV: Reading Comprehension—35 minutes, scored section

Section V: Analytical Reasoning—35 minutes, unscored section

Section VI: Writing Sample—30 minutes, never scored

This slightly complicates matters in that a person cannot anticipate how to "ration" their energy in order to give their best performance on the scored sessions. For example, some people feel that their concentration is sharpest at the start of an exam; others feel that they have to "warm" to the task at hand and finish strongly.

In that sense, the LSAT combines the best (or worst, depending on your point of view) elements of two contests: the marathon and the sprint. The exam is challenging from a marathoner's point of view in that since you don't know which section won't count, you have to run strongly for the course of the exam. It's also challenging from the sprinting standpoint, because above all else, you'll be feeling a lot of time pressure from the moment the proctor gives you permission to begin the exam.

How the LSAT Is Scored

The LSAT is scored on a scale from 120 to 180, with 180 being the highest possible score. Although the LSAT is a relatively recent innovation to separate out "tiers" of applicants from the crowd, law schools do prefer the current system as opposed to simply selecting applicants by college GPA or undergraduate major.

This is the case even though it's been argued that the LSAT itself is only moderately relevant to understanding the case method of teaching law, the ability to pass the bar exam, or even excel in law school. If this is the case, then why make law school applicants take the LSAT in the first place? There are two answers to that question, and the truth probably is a combination of both.

Why Take the LSAT? The Idealistic Answer: Ensuring a Broad-Based, Useful Mindset

All graduate schools, whether in law, business, or medicine, want to take in students who are able to think critically and write well. They seek out people who have the ability to read and comprehend complex texts with speed and accuracy. Law schools in particular want to screen for people who have a knack for analyzing and evaluating the reasoning and arguments of others, and the LSAT is an excellent way of doing this.

It is also felt that while these abilities can be acquired in any number of college courses, an undergraduate career that is narrowly based or vocationally oriented may not be as suitable for the law classroom.

Why Take the LSAT? The Less Idealistic Answer: Defusing Grade Inflation and Ensuring Retention

There is also the argument that the LSAT helps to defuse the problem of grade inflation at many colleges. Where an extremely rigorous undergraduate institution might produce an environment where a B+ average is a tremendous accomplishment, it is possible for a less rigorous program to routinely produce A- or A averages without exceptional work.

Finally, there is the argument that the LSAT is a good—if imperfect—predictor of law school success. This doesn't mean that if you do well on the LSAT, you are guaranteed a ticket to the biggest law firms and the fattest paychecks. But there does seem to be a positive correlation between high LSAT scores and law student retention—that is, a high LSAT score means that the student is statistically less likely to drop out of law school.

Therefore, the best that can be said about the LSAT is that while it isn't the sole factor law schools use to make admission decisions, it is an equalizer that can fairly measure student ability and likelihood of completing the program. Both of these characteristics are welcomed by law school administrations.

Assessing Law Schools with the LSAT in Mind

The use of the LSAT in the law school selection process is discussed in more detail in Chapter 1. It is true that higher scores mean more potential choices in the types of schools that will likely admit you. However, choosing schools based on how high their LSAT scores are reported to be—or how high you think your score can go—is a foolish and somewhat sterile approach to how one should look at an investment of more than $100,000 and three years of one's life.

Just as you need to assess yourself as to whether your strengths lie in certain areas of the LSAT itself, you need to perform the same process on the types of schools you plan to apply to. When it comes to assessing strengths on the exam, you'll make use of feedback—that is, by practicing with the sample exams in this book to see how well you do on which areas. Similarly, you want to use feedback—generated through research, campus visits, or discussion with a school's admissions counselor—to get a feel for where you think you'll be most comfortable or able to excel.

Therefore, you might start by considering the location, size, and nature of the surrounding community. Some people will thrive in the heart of a big city, with lots of things to do and a high-paced lifestyle. Others may want a quieter, more contemplative environment.

The size, composition, and background of the student body is another factor. Look at not only the total size of the student body, but also the size of the class sections in the first, second, and third year. It's expected that the third-year classes will be the smallest as people focus on specific disciplines, but in the chaotic first year, it's quite different to be in a major section of 15 people versus 50.

You might take into consideration the degree to which clinical experience or classroom learning is emphasized. More clinical experience might be a boon to those who want to become litigators, while classroom learning might be better for those who want to pursue academics or become judges.

Still another area to look at is whether the school has a strong minority recruitment, retention, and mentoring program. Perhaps there is an active student union for students of your particular ethnic background.

One final area to look at is the school's particular faculty strengths or interests, which determine what a school is "known" for. For example, a school might be known locally for producing great judges or prosecutors. Others develop a national reputation for being specialists in environmental or international law.

Take your research results in this last area with a particularly large grain of salt. First off, the lynchpin of the school's reputation in an area might be one nationally known professor—who could easily transfer, retire, or be overbooked in classes so you never get to study with him or her. Second, be wary of deciding your legal specialty three years in advance of when you will get to the job market.

While, say, medical malpractice law may be the hottest item at the present day, over three years a lot can change to cool the market. For example, tort reform or caps on jury awards can do a lot to cool off a sizzling demand for personal injury attorneys.

Pre-Test Assessment

The generalist nature of the LSAT means that you don't have a list of vocabulary items that you'll need to know. You won't need to know specific Latin phrases or mathematical equations, or memorize articles from the Constitution. Instead, you'll want to assess your ability to do two things.

First, you need to honestly evaluate your ability to develop your analytical, creative, and logical reasoning abilities. If it's going to take you more time to raise your score by working these skills out, then allot more time, and allow for the typical disruptions that enter everyone's lives so you don't become stressed out.

Don't' worry too much about strengthening your understanding of "legal-ese" or your debating skills. Once you're admitted, law school will bring these skills up to par very quickly.

Second, honestly evaluate your ability to take the sample tests under simulated LSAT conditions. Consider: Each time you test yourself on a whole exam, you'll have to find a spot that is relatively quiet but that has some outside noise—as when the exam is held in a large auditorium—and you'll have to spend 3.5 hours. You'll also have to train under the exact same time pressures as in the exam. Don't take rest breaks in the middle of sessions. If you need more time to learn how to focus for these lengths of time, plan accordingly.

How to Use the LSAT

✓ Registering for the LSAT

✓ Registering with the LSDAS

✓ Costs to Register

✓ When the LSAT Is Given

✓ When Should You Take the LSAT Exam?

✓ Now that You Mention It, How Many Times Should One Take the LSAT?

✓ How a Good LSAT Score Can Compensate for a Less Impressive GPA

✓ What Is a Good LSAT Score?

✓ LSAT/LSDAS Checklist

✓ Applying to Law School

✓ Recent Law School Admissions Trends

✓ Should You Apply Early?

✓ Your Law School Application Checklist

Registering for the LSAT

If you're still in college, or are located near a college or university, the easiest way to register for the LSAT is to stop by the college's career center. Ask for a copy of the most current LSAT and LSDAS Registration and Information Book. Law school, as one of the four professional graduate programs (the others are business, medicine, and engineering), is a relatively popular choice, so it's highly likely that the information will be available.

If it is not, or you're not located near a college career center, you can also register via through the Law School Admission Council's website at www.lsac.org.

Registering with the LSDAS

Although you may think that you are finished after registering for the LSAT, you're only halfway done. You should also consider registering with the Law School Data Assembly Service (LSDAS). The LSDAS, which is a service provided by the LSAC, is a sort of information clearinghouse that centralizes and standardizes an applicant's undergraduate academic records in a single report. This helps the law school admission process run more efficiently for the schools and with less hassle for the applicants.

LSDAS registrants provide all the required information to the LSAC a single time. This obviates the need to collect transcripts, letters of recommendation, LSAT scores, and other information for multiple law schools.

Of course, it's moot to point out all of the great services that the LSDAS performs for applicants. This is because most American Bar Association–approved law schools require that applicants use this service. The LSDAS then prepares the report for each law school to which you apply. The report contains information that schools use to determine admission, including

➤ Your undergraduate academic summary

➤ Copies of all of your school transcripts: undergraduate, graduate, and law school/professional transcripts

➤ LSAT scores

➤ Copies of your LSAT Writing Sample

➤ Copies of letters of recommendation processed by the LSAC

➤ Access to electronic applications for all ABA-approved law schools

More detail is located in Chapter 2 on supplying this information to the LSDAS so that they can in turn package it for sending to the schools you plan to apply to. Note also that the LSDAS does not fill out your law school application, personal essay, or the letters sent directly to the schools you're applying to.

There is no requirement to register for the LSDAS and the LSAT at the same time. However, given how many schools require you to use the service, it's strongly recommended that you register with the LSDAS as soon as possible before the first law school application deadline.

Once you register, the LSDAS will be able to provide the collected information to any law school for a period of up to five years. If you register for an LSAT exam at any time during your LSDAS period, the LSDAS period will be extended five years from your latest LSAT registration. Therefore, if you initially registered with the LSDAS on July 4, 2001 and then registered for an LSAT on January 1, 2004, your LSDAS records will be available until January 1, 2009.

Costs to Register

As of this writing, the registration fee for the LSAT is $115. Late registrants must pay an additional $58. The later you take the test, the higher the likelihood that the price will have gone up. There is no record of the LSAC reducing the price to register for the LSAT or LSDAS.

As of this writing, the LSDAS registration fee is $106. LSDAS Law School Reports are $12 per school. You may order additional reports at any time for $12 per school, with no limit to the number of schools you wish to apply to.

Therefore, when you're budgeting for your applications, remember that the cost of supplying your LSDAS information to each school is *in addition to* the cost of applying to the school. Therefore, a school that costs $100 to apply to actually costs $112.

When the LSAT Is Given

The LSAT is given four times a year. As of this writing, the dates are

Monday, June 6, 2005

Saturday, October 1, 2005

Saturday, December 3, 2005

Saturday, February 4, 2006

If you observe the Sabbath, as of this writing, special administrations are held

Thursday, September 29, 2005

Monday, December 5, 2005

Monday, February 6, 2006

While these exact dates are only for the 2005–2006 cycle, these times are roughly when the LSAT will be given each year.

When Should You Take the LSAT Exam?

Which LSAT you take depends on your personal timetable to apply to law school and when you feel that you have prepared sufficiently to pass the exam. It is a false belief that taking the LSAT during certain times is any better or worse, or that "fewer people mean a steeper curve" or "more people means worse testing conditions."

In the first place, your score is not judged against the group of 5 or 50 people you took the exam with. Instead, your score is judged against the entire group of applicants to a given law school. Therefore, while it makes no difference if the number of people you take the test with is 100 or 120, it does make a difference if the law school you're applying to receives 1,000 or 1,200 applicants for the year you're trying to gain entrance.

Secondly, the LSAT is a regularly held exam, and the test givers strive to keep conditions adequate no matter the number of exam applicants. Because you have to register for the LSAT before you take the test, the test site knows in advance how many people will attend and will take steps to avoid overcrowding should it happen.

Many people take the early fall test, for reasons ranging from the fact that they're in study-mode at school to the fact that they're already "in the admissions process," filling out applications and researching graduate schools. However, taking the LSAT in June also gives significant advantages if you are sufficiently prepared.

If you have your LSAT score in hand, you'll have more time to realistically gauge your chance of admission into your choice schools. This means you can plan an application strategy more effectively. And finally, you can take the fall test, if you feel it's necessary to take the exam again.

Now that You Mention It, How Many Times Should One Take the LSAT?

Applicants may not take the LSAT more than three times in any two-year period. This policy applies even if you cancel your score. However, you may retake the LSAT if the following conditions are met:

1. The school you are applying to requires a more recent score than any you have on record.

2. The school provides LSAC with written proof of its requirement no later than the last day of registration for the test.

As for how many times to take the test, by all means, you should be shooting for the best score you can get, so you only have to take the test one time. Not only will this save you from having to prepare multiple times, but repeat testers rarely find that they gain significantly higher scores unless the first test was taken during truly atrocious conditions, such as serious illness.

Note also that many schools will average multiple scores. Therefore, a significantly higher score on your second test is needed to raise your overall LSAT score. However, some law schools will use the second score if it is considerably better than the first, and a reason is given for the second testing. Contact the schools you intend to apply to if you need to find this out. If the information isn't in their admission packets, their admissions department will know the answer to this question.

How a Good LSAT Score Can Compensate for a Less Impressive GPA

Simply put, the first hurdle to getting into a competitive law school—to say nothing of a "top ranked" school—is to pass their admissions formula. The formula varies from school to school, but essentially it is a combination of your LSAT score and your GPA. It enables the school admissions officers to begin to get to the bottom of the stack of applications in hand by providing evidence that you have the academic ability and the test-taking skills to survive and thrive in the intense academic environment of law school.

Given that the LSAT is one half of the formula—and depending on the school, they may give it as much if not more weight than GPA—this is an excellent opportunity to maximize your admissions chances. Of course, a stellar LSAT can only go so far in alleviating truly rotten grades, but it is a chance to even the scores in your favor.

Consider: Let's say that over the last 3–4 years, your college GPA has been a solid, if not spectacular 3.3 out of 4.0. Scoring in the top 10% or top 5% of the LSAT field won't help you become competitive with those who got the same score and pulled impressive grades. However, depending on the school you apply to, it will give you an edge—or break even—with those who did not get a sky-high LSAT score but pulled a 3.5 GPA. Therefore, with a great performance on the a critical exam, you can in essence "make up" for some of the classes that you may not have pulled an A in.

Of course, everyone knows of at least one or two people who had mediocre numbers and got into a great school, and another person who had perfect numbers but was inexplicably turned down. This is because the process, while it does rely heavily on the numbers, remains a holistic one. If you have a head-turning life story, have overcome amazing odds, or have given a great deal back to your community, then you've also maximized your potential in the admissions process.

What Is a Good LSAT Score?

The obvious answer: the score that gets you admitted to your number-one choice school!

Beyond that, the term "good" is subjective. However, scoring a 165 out of the LSAT scoring range of 120–180 is considered enough to make you competitive in the top 20 law schools as rated by most sources. In fact, if you do the research on the law schools you're interested in, the "good" score should become extremely apparent: It needs to be in the range of the average person who is admitted into the institution. At present, if you're planning to apply to a school that's in the top 50 or so of the ABA-approved schools, several books and the annual *US News and World Report's Best Graduate Schools* will list the average LSAT score attained by successful admittees.

LSAT/LSDAS Checklist

Finally, consider making a checklist to make sure that you are hitting all of the events that you need in order to complete the application process. We've provided a good checklist to follow:

1. Prepare for the LSAT.

2. Research law schools you're interested in.

3. Create the schedule of application deadlines you'll need to meet. (If a school has rolling admissions or an early decision process, you may want to take advantage of it.)

4. Get the registration material for the LSAT and LSDAS.

5. Register for the LSAT and LSDAS.

6. Obtain your LSAT Admission Ticket and LSDAS Confirmation. This can be requested online or by mail.

7. Check your file status online or receive LSAC Activity Updates each month that activity occurs in your file.

8. Request that an official transcript be sent to the LSAC from the registrar's office of each school you attended.

9. Request that letters of recommendation be written and sent to the LSAC or directly to law schools as appropriate.

10. Take the LSAT.

11. Obtain your LSAT score. You can choose to receive it via email, the LSAC's "Telescore (touch-tone telephone) System," or mail.

12. Obtain your Master Law School Report once all undergraduate transcripts have been summarized.

13. Apply to law schools, making sure to follow the schedule you created in Step 3.

14. Verify that your reports were sent to the law schools to which you applied online or by mail on the Activity Update Report.

Applying to Law School

Now that you're on course to take the LSAT and have your admissions data sent to the schools of your choice, you have a few more actions to take. You'll have to determine the time and place of your application process—specifically, which schools you will apply to, and when you want to actually apply. We've already discussed some of the factors you'll want to consider in choosing a legal program earlier in this book. Therefore, it's now worthwhile to consider the "when" portion of the question.

Recent Admissions Trends

The question "Should I apply now?" is a more complex one than it might at first appear. There are four factors that you should consider.

First, it is true that in some years, admission is more difficult than others. Simply on a statistical basis, the year when applications double is the year when fewer people—and people with higher LSAT/GPA scores—will get in.

An example of the fluctuation in numbers comes from the LSAC:

Years	Number of Applicants
1994–95	78,400
1996–97	66,700
Fall 2004	100,000 (estimated)

Second, demographically it can be argued that the overall trend for admissions standards is creeping up, up, and away. Why? Because although the baby boomers didn't generate as many children as their own parents, the total applicant pool is still larger than it ever was, and continues to get larger as the U.S. population continues to climb. The number of ABA-approved law schools, meanwhile, has not risen as quickly, meaning fewer available seats.

Third, almost all graduate school admissions are counter-cyclical to the economy. In other words, people make rational choices based on what's available to them. If the economy is good, they may stay in the job they have, or they may go directly from college into the workforce while the corporate world is booming. Conversely, if there are a dearth of opportunities, people will often opt to go to graduate school to improve their job skill set, move to another career, or to "sit out" the recession. As of this writing, the recent recessionary years have shown up as a spike in the applicant pool: In 2002, the Law School Admissions Council reported an increase of 17% of applicants over the previous year.

Finally, and most importantly, your decision to go to law school should not come as a result of demographic or statistical factors beyond your control. You should go when you feel you're at the right point in your life to go. This may be right out of college, or it may be that you'll be "ready" when you've put a couple years' work under your belt. Or it may be after you complete a decade's worth of service and decide that a legal career is now right for you. There is no wrong answer, no matter what the demographers or admissions counselors might tell you.

Should You Apply Early?

Overall, earlier is better if you can do so. The main rationale is that applying early allows you to quickly spot—and remedy—any defects you find in your application, such as a school being lax in turning in your transcripts. Additionally, consider the overworked, overtaxed admissions officers who will go through your work. If you were in their shoes, would you be more likely to spot a promising candidate at the top of your "inbox" stack, or at the bottom several weeks or months down the line?

Still another reason to apply early is that more and more schools are using what is called a *rolling admissions process*. Basically, applications are reviewed and accepted—or rejected—as they come in. There are two advantages to applicants who apply early. If they find out their acceptance early, they can save money on applying to other schools if they choose to attend. If they find out their rejection early, they can apply to other schools still in the admissions cycle.

Finally, more schools are offering a financial incentive. For example, Notre Dame Law School offers a $20 discount on its application fees if you apply before a certain date.

 If you qualify, you may be able to waive the application fee to a law school in its entirety. Each school is different as to the criteria that allow you to do this. Be sure to check online or in the hard copy of the school's application form. For example, NYU School of Law will waive the application fee if an applicant submits a photocopy of his or her LSAC-approved LSAT or LSDAS fee waiver form with his or her application. The fee waiver form is part of the LSDAS packet, or can be found online at http://cachewww.lsac.org/pdfs/2005-2006/2005-fee-waiver-form.pdf.

Your Law School Application Checklist

You can find extremely detailed checklists on what you need to do to apply in each law school's information or application packet, or in the registration material from the LSDAS. However, here is a rough guide if you need a quick refresher:

1. Register for the LSAT and with the LSDAS.

2. Give yourself appropriate time to prepare for the LSAT. Best is to practice exams and concepts for two months.

3. Take the LSAT.

4. Submit college transcripts to LSDAS.

5. Line up letters of recommendation for signature and submission to the LSDAS.

6. Determine which law schools you are most likely to apply to depending on your LSAT scores and other criteria.

7. Contact those schools to find out the deadlines for accepting LSAT scores.

8. Apply to the schools you've selected once you have received your LSAT score.

You should begin filing for your financial aid papers well in advance of any school's particular filing deadline. Don't wait until after you receive admission offers to begin this process. The form you want is the Free Application for Federal Student Aid (FAFSA). You can get a copy at your college's financial aid office, from a law school to which you are applying, or at www.fafsa.ed.gov.

Mastering the Reading Comprehension

Terms You'll Need to Understand

✓ Primary Ideas
✓ Author Bias or "Attitude"
✓ Refining Meaning
✓ Furthering Implications or Drawing Conclusions

Techniques and Concepts You'll Need to Master

✓ Anxiety Management
✓ Time Management
✓ Focus
✓ Understanding by Context

The LSAT always contains one Reading Comprehension section. You'll be given 35 minutes to work the section. Typically, the section will contain several reading passages approximately 450 to 500 words in length, most often taken from subjects in social sciences, natural sciences, humanities, or law. Each passage will have 4–6 questions, for a total of 26–28 questions in the entire section.

The one variable in the Reading Comprehension section is that you won't be able to predict where it shows up in the order of the different sections of the exam.

How It Stacks Up
to the Other Sections

Reading Comprehension, like Analytical Reasoning (Logic Games) is a "love it or hate it" kind of section. Some of us who are blessed with photographic memory or simply enjoy pulling information from books or magazine articles view this section as an automatic strength. Others, who may have struggled with dyslexia or dislike reading anything other than the *TV Guide*, will have reactions ranging from antipathy to fright.

The truth as to how well or poorly you do in the Reading Comprehension section probably lies somewhere in the middle. Slower readers will constantly feel "under the gun" when it comes to the ticking of the clock on this section, but as we'll discuss, speed is only part of the equation when it comes to doing well here. Faster readers will be able to dive right into the questions with less of a pause, but they may be lulled into a false sense of confidence and miss key points while they glide through the text.

To its credit, the way the LSAT tests you here relates directly to a core skill for attorneys, which is to quickly and accurately draw conclusions from argument in written text and derive meaning from context. Keep this in mind as you run through these sections on the practice tests.

Unlike the logic games that you'll play in Analytical Reasoning, or the short fact statements in Logical Reasoning, this section probably comes closest to what you will actually face while doing initial research as a law student.

Some other items to keep in mind as you go through this section that separate it from the other two:

➤ Reading Comprehension is one of the portions of the LSAT that will likely subject you to moderate to serious time pressure. Your goal should be to manage your time effectively so as to complete the entire section.

One way to reduce the stress of time management in this section is to take notes next to the paragraphs in each passage. Summarizing the paragraphs in a few words can help you pull out critical points from the passage.

➤ Reading Comprehension is unique in the sections of the LSAT in that you may be asked to take the advocate's role as opposed to simply interpreting the point of view in the question. For example, you may be asked to pick the best title to reinforce the article's point, or to pick an additional fact that would strengthen the argument.

➤ Subtlety is not the byword for Reading Comprehension. Since you'll have access to more of an argument's surrounding context, you may be able to spot "gotchas" that greatly strengthen—or undermine—the point of the article. For example, an argument that praises a point may say "the unassailable truth is" or "there is no doubt that." On the other hand, phrases to undermine an argument will be equally broad, such as "the argument is weakened by the fact that," or "the bald assertion is made."

➤ Unlike in the other sections, Reading Comprehension questions vary in difficulty only in the length of the reading passage and your familiarity with the subject. This is in direct contrast to the Logical Reasoning sections, which tend to be roughly the same difficulty. It's also different from the Analytical Reasoning questions, which tend to be the same length but vary in complexity by the number of people or objects asked about in the question.

Skills People Think They Need

Reading Comprehension exercises different portions of your mind than the other parts of the test. This means there are certain skills that will come in very handy for getting the best score in this section—and they aren't what you think. Most people believe that in order to max out their score in Reading Comprehension, they need

➤ Speed-reading ability

➤ Photographic memory

➤ Vocabulary skills that would put Mr. Webster to shame

Skills You Really Need

Don't get us wrong—these abilities, should you be lucky to possess them, are definitely advantages. However, they're not the core set that you need to do well.

For example, instead of speed-reading, what you need to have is an iron grip on time management. Instead of a photographic memory, you need to be able to focus clearly on what you are reading. Finally, instead of a huge vocabulary, you need to be able to intuit what the meaning of a word is from the passage's surrounding context.

All of these skills are, in turn, based on the ability to manage *anxiety*. The following sections will help you understand and develop the crucial skills you will need to master the Reading Comprehension portion of the LSAT.

Time Management

Time management is simply a way of saying, "don't rush, and don't linger." When you open the Reading Comprehension section, resist the temptation to run through the passage. Similarly, don't read and re-read the passage. Unless the passage contains truly atrocious or dense writing, a single pass will allow you to retain most of the information of note.

You do *not* need to remember the passage in great detail in order to answer questions about it. One trick that the LSAT writers will employ on occasion is to give you a large number of details, or a blizzard of facts that will slow down the unwary and panic the uninitiated.

One question that has no real answer is whether you should you read the questions first, and then go back and read the passage. The reason that there's no real answer is that it depends entirely upon one's learning and reading style. If you're not sure which works for you, try one method on a practice test, then the other on a different test, and see what the results are. Some people report that seeing the questions gives them a good "heads up" as to what to watch for. Others may find that the extra details cause them to lose sight of what the passage means as they read it.

Focus

Focus is a way to manage or eliminate the anxiety of the unknown. For example, say that the passage begins as such:

"The Cassini spacecraft's two close flybys of Saturn's icy moon Enceladus have revealed that the moon has a significant atmosphere. Scientists, using

Cassini's magnetometer instrument for their studies, say the source may be volcanism, geysers, or gases escaping from the surface or the interior."

One of your first thoughts may be, "Oh no, I don't know anything about Saturn, and the rest of this text looks like something out of *Star Trek* to me." Relax. Even if you've never taken a class on astrophysics or astronomy, your familiarity with the field of study is irrelevant—only your ability to pick out the salient facts is being tested. Focusing on the passage as simply a piece of reading to dissect and understand—not as an article on a subject you didn't study for—will remove the anxiety.

Let's take a very quick, very simple look at this example, piece by piece:

"The Cassini spacecraft's two close flybys of Saturn's icy moon Enceladus have revealed that the moon has a significant atmosphere."

You may not have any idea who or what a "Cassini" is, but you can pull out the following points:

1. There is a spacecraft called Cassini.

2. It performed two flybys of a moon of Saturn.

3. This moon is icy, and it's called Enceladus.

4. The spacecraft discovered that the moon has a "significant" atmosphere.

5. Scientists used some kind of instrument called a "magnetometer" to aid their studies.

6. With this instrument, they came up with three candidates for the source of the atmosphere: volcanism, geysers, or gas from the interior.

These are the facts that will make up the basis of any question that the testers care to throw at you. Sometimes they will ask you a question that logically can be deduced from the facts. (What will the climate be like if the moon is "icy"?) Other times, they may ask you to continue the train of thought (what additional evidence would be needed to show that the moon has a "significant" atmosphere?)

Understanding by Context

A final skill that results from controlling your anxiety is understanding a word from its surrounding context. Even when you might be vaguely familiar with the passage's subject matter, you might be put off by the use of a critical word or words that you don't remember coming across in your daily reading. For example, say that the Reading Comprehension question posed made you come back to the word *dimpsy* in the sentence:

"Medieval city dwellers were especially wary once the dimpsy arrived."

Now, if a LSAT taker had no clue what a "dimpsy" is, or why it would bother people in the Middle Ages, there's a good chance that panic would ensue. However, whenever running into unfamiliar material, back off and read the contextual material surrounding the word or phrase. For example, the entire paragraph states:

"Although people became more fearful as the afternoon's sunlight waned, what followed was worse. Medieval city dwellers were especially wary once the dimpsy arrived. Adequate street lighting was hundreds of years in the future, and without the sun's rays, only thieves and wolves roamed the streets."

From the context, you should be able to tell that dimpsy follows the late afternoon, and is dangerous not in and of itself, but because it is a time when there is inadequate light. You can logically conclude that dimpsy is an oddball word for "nighttime" or "evening."

 If you're particularly into writing, your inner editor may call foul on the use of obscure or vaguely inappropriate wording in a passage. Keep two things in mind. First, the testers aren't picking the best writing for you to read, they are picking items that require a second glance and a period of thought. Second, get used to seeing unnecessarily complicated words and writing if you're planning to go to law school. As the old law student joke goes, "Never use a simple word when a more complicated one will ~~do~~ suffice."

Exam Prep Questions

Compared with the Logical or Analytical sections, mastering Reading Comprehension is not really a matter of understanding the component parts of an argument or the spatial relationship of facts. Instead, it involves recognizing certain types of questions, which you can then return to the passage to answer or puzzle out. As a whole, the vast majority of your Reading Comprehension questions will fall into four distinct areas:

➤ Primary ideas

➤ Author bias or "attitude"

➤ Refining meaning

➤ Furthering implications or drawing conclusions

Primary Ideas

Perhaps the most common of all questions on the LSAT's Reading Comprehension section is a variant of "What most accurately summarizes the passage's central idea?" This isn't as straightforward as it may seem at first. For example:

> "Even technologically sophisticated approaches like those employed at MicroGuard are limited in their "scope"; that is, MicroGuard sensors are at the mercy of the winds and the specific release point of a terrorist's cloud of anthrax."

Could the main idea of the passage be that MicroGuard isn't a useful system? Could it be about terrorism in general? Or, could this be part of a larger passage on how climate features such as wind are variable and impossible to predict?

When faced with this type of question, you'll need to keep two things in mind. First, be aware of the context of the entire passage. If this is the opening paragraph of the passage and the next eight paragraphs talk about the development of nuclear and biological weapons, it's unlikely that the main idea of the passage is about the global climate. Second, if you're down to two likely choices for your answer, the correct answer will be the one that captures the passage's ideas with the most accuracy and detail.

This form of question can come in a couple minor variants, such as "What is the passage's main idea?" or "What point is the author most interested in making?" A final version of this question in a slightly disguised form will be the "title" question. The title question that follows a passage containing the paragraph immediately above might read:

> What title would best summarize the passage?
> ❏ A. Limitations on the Scope of Detection Technology
> ❏ B. MicroGuard's Inventions—The Technological Blind Alley
> ❏ C. How Randomness in Nature Can Change World Events
> ❏ D. Terror in a Test Tube: Terrorists and the Dark Side of Biology

Again, the correct answer will depend on the context of the entire passage.

Author Bias or "Attitude"

Questions on an author's viewpoint are rarely if ever literary in nature. You won't be asked whether the author is writing in a witty versus sarcastic manner. Instead, you will be tasked with determining which way the author's biases or attitudes lie by the way they try to persuade you or present information.

While subtlety is not the most common theme in the Reading Comprehension section, determining an author's viewpoint or bias they bring to a passage can occasionally be difficult. This is because although some passages are explicitly written to persuade the reader, many are simply informative—or appear to be purely informative at first glance. For example, consider a passage on a fictitious politician:

> "Surprisingly, Mr. Smith is on track to raise as much money as an independent candidate as he did as the Blue Party candidate. Regardless, the Blue Party is going to run a proper candidate who will earn hardcore industrialist votes. And granted, Mr. Smith is no firebrand (Mr. Smith's strained efforts earned a paltry 3.1% of the vote), but he nonetheless threatens a critical victory for the Blue Party if he stays in the race."

The attitude of the author of the passage toward the independent candidate Mr. Smith can best be described as

- ❑ A. Qualified approval
- ❑ B. Detached and critical
- ❑ C. Enthusiastic and supportive
- ❑ D. Contemplative
- ❑ E. Dismissive and condescending

The column appears to primarily factual. But consider the words and phraseology chosen by the writer: "is no firebrand," "strained efforts," "paltry." It doesn't take a huge stretch of the imagination to come to the conclusion that the writer is either unimpressed with Mr. Smith, or views him quite negatively. While not coming out directly to tell you that "Mr. Smith is a poor political performer who could still act as a spoiler to the Blue Party," a casual reader could infer it from the passage.

This eliminates A, C, and D, which are positive or neutral. Of the remaining options, B is the weakest as it contains an element of neutrality. While appearing factual, note that the passage also contains a certain amount of urgency ("a critical victory") and disapproval for Smith's upstart candidacy ("the Blue Party is going to run a proper candidate"). This is hardly the hallmark of a detached writer and thus E is the most accurate answer.

Refining Meaning

The same skill of inference via context is not only helpful in allowing you to puzzle out odd or rarely used words in a question such as "dimpsy." Rather, it is also helpful in an entire class of questions you'll find in the Reading Comprehension section, which challenge you to refine the meaning of a word or phrase. You may be asked to clarify an ambiguous passage, narrow the meaning of a word, or supply a definition for an expression or local colloquialism.

A good example of this type of question could follow a passage with the following paragraph:

> "When radium was first isolated from pitchblende, this was supposed to be the only source from which radium could be obtained."

> Which one of the following words or phrases, if substituted for the word "pitchblende," would LEAST change the meaning of the passage?
> - ❑ A. sand on the shore
> - ❑ B. the pharmacy
> - ❑ C. raw ore
> - ❑ D. pure radium gas
> - ❑ E. the process of isolating radium

If you don't know what "pitchblende" is, this could be difficult to answer. However, if you were looking at the context that this paragraph appeared in, you'd see that the passage also contained the following text:

> "In order to obtain pure radium, six hundred tons of pitchblende was refined, requiring the labor of 500 men and six months of industrial labor. The process of extracting this radium consumed a deep-core drilling machine, ten thousand tons of distilled water, a thousand tons of coal, and a hundred tons of chemicals."

Given the vast scale of labor needed, it's obvious that one can't get radium by simply stopping by the corner drugstore or sifting sand on a beach. This eliminates A and B. If D were correct, then the radium would have already been concentrated, and no refining would be necessary.

E is simply redundant—we're talking about the process of isolating radium already. C is the only likely answer, as raw ore by definition is the desired substance that needs to be separated from less valuable rock.

Furthering Implications or Drawing Conclusions

The final form of Reading Comprehension question is perhaps the most interesting, because it requires you to move one step beyond a reading of the passage. Instead, you'll be given a selection of facts or arguments that you can choose from to draw a specific point out of the reading passage. These facts or arguments typically are used to do one of two things to the passage: strengthen the main argument, or weaken it.

The examiners will often use other words besides "strengthen" or "weaken" in these kinds of questions. The two giveaway words they use instead are "bolster" to strengthen an argument, or "undermine" to weaken one.

For example, a typical strengthening question, if applied to one of our previous examples, would read:

"Even technologically sophisticated approaches like those employed at MicroGuard are limited in their "scope"; that is, MicroGuard sensors are at the mercy of the winds and the specific release point of a terrorist's cloud of anthrax."

Which one of the following statements, if true, would bolster the presumption that MicroGuard's sensors are limited in their ability to detect a release of anthrax?

❑ A. MicroGuard sensors failed to detect anthrax 9 out of 10 times in an area the size of the Houston Astrodome.

❑ B. Few airports, shopping malls, sports stadiums, and schools have any sensing devices, and it is unlikely that most ever will.

❑ C. MicroGuard sensors are so sophisticated that it is unlikely that operators with less than a dual Ph.D in Physics and Statistics can interpret the results.

❑ D. Anthrax is difficult to detect in quantities of less than 10 spores per cubic meter of air.

❑ E. Terrorists using anthrax will likely use their weapons in areas where there is no wind at all, foiling the use of MicroGuard sensors.

Answers B, C, and D can be dismissed because instead of strengthening the proposition that the sensors are limited, they strengthen other arguments. B discusses the lack of sensor equipment in general, C focuses on the training of the operators, and D talks about the anthrax bacteria itself.

E is a possible answer, but although it does discuss a method of foiling the sensors, the reason is the stratagem used by the terrorists. It also uses the key phrase "will likely," meaning that the reasoning is hypothetical in nature. Only A directly provides a reason for the sensor's limitations and bases it in a demonstration of past performance instead of conjecture.

By contrast, a weakening question as applied to a prior example might read as follows:

"The Cassini spacecraft's two close flybys of Saturn's icy moon Enceladus have revealed that the moon has a significant atmosphere. Scientists, using Cassini's magnetometer instrument for their studies, say the source may be volcanism, geysers, or gases escaping from the surface or the interior."

Which one of the following statements, if true, would undermine the presumption that it is volcanism that gives Enceladus a significant atmosphere?

❑ A. Methane geysers have been photographed by Cassini in the middle of erupting on the moon's surface.

❑ B. The Marhoffer-Whitney Formation, a complex of mountains on the far side of the moon, has been emitting clouds of hot gas since Cassini began its flyby.

❑ C. Satellite photos show that massive lava flows took place throughout Enceladus's past, and that the flows included bubbles of released gas.

❑ D. Geological evidence shows a complete lack of any past or present volcanic activity on the moon.

❑ E. Professor Diane Keppler, NASA's leading authority on Saturn's moons, says that it is highly unlikely that volcanism significantly contributed to the atmosphere on Enceladus.

To begin with, C does the opposite of what you are trying to show—by implying that there was massive volcanic activity that released gas, the argument that volcanism provided Enceladus with a significant atmosphere is strengthened, not weakened.

A and B are not good answers, either. While they talk about alternative ways that the moon could have gotten an atmosphere, neither statement impacts the argument that volcanism was the reason behind it.

E is an answer that falls into the category of "appealing to authority." Professor Keppler is a "leading authority" on the moons of Saturn, and we are instructed to treat every statement as true. Therefore, her argument carries a lot of weight.

However, note that her statement carries with it a little factual "gotcha" that you may not have caught in a speed-reading session. She does not completely rule out volcanism—instead, she says it's "highly unlikely." Thus, while this weakens the argument, it does not weaken it as much as direct evidence showing that volcanism didn't even exist on the moon at all. Answer D is the correct one.

The LSAT examiners leave you with a final proviso in the Reading Comprehension section: the phrase "if true." This means that you need to treat the statements presented as manifestly true. Even if you're certain that the statement presented is illogical in the real world, treat it as if it exists in its own universe. Your job is to determine whether the statement can best support or undermine the reading passage.

Mastering the Analytical Reasoning

Terms You'll Need to Understand

✓ Logic Games
✓ Premise
✓ Conditions
✓ Questions

Techniques and Concepts You'll Need to Master

✓ Practice to increase familiarity with game format
✓ Practice to recognize patterns of question formats
✓ Diagramming
✓ Sequence and Matrix

The LSAT always contains one Analytical Reasoning section. You'll be given 35 minutes to work the section. Typically, the section will contain 23–24 questions. As with Reading Comprehension, the one variable in the Analytical Reasoning section is that you won't be able to predict where it shows up in the order of the different sections of the exam.

How It Stacks Up to the Other Sections

Analytical Reasoning is the definitive "love it or hate it" kind of section. Although the section has no mathematical equations on it per se, it does seem that those who intuitively understand spatial reasoning and variable-laden equations (if set A, not set B) do best here. Those of us who enjoy brain teasers and abstract mental puzzles will enjoy what this section has to offer.

It's important to remember that a lot of the fear people feel when facing this section is not due to the problems being incredibly difficult. Rather, it is unfamiliarity with facing a *logic game* for the first time. A logic game is a particular type of question that you will only find in this section of this exam.

 This section usually contains four or five logic games, each of which commonly includes five to six questions—though seeing an especially complex problem with eight questions isn't unheard of, particularly when the testers are trying to rattle you.

A sample of what a logic game might look like follows:

Charles has to put together a roster for his company's annual softball game against their cross-town rival. He's got eight healthy people that want to bat for the team: Corwin, Dorian, Hal, Joseph, Kamal, Peter, Ralph, and Seth. He's allowed to submit five names for his roster. However, there are some things to take into consideration:

If Ralph plays, Hal must play immediately after Ralph on the roster.

Two of the three managers, Dorian, Kamal, and Ralph, have to be on the team.

Corwin and Seth can't be next to each other on the roster.

If Kamal is on the team, then Joseph can't be picked.

Peter has to play either first or second.

Among the questions that people often have at this point is, "What on earth does this have to do with my ability to become an attorney?" While not as directly applicable as the skills tested for reading and evaluating conclusions from arguments, the Analytical Reasoning does play a vital role in the testing process. Logic games are, at base, designed to measure your ability to quickly understand a system of relationships and to draw conclusions about those relationships.

In this sample logic game, it's arguable that how Charles puts together the roster for his company's annual softball game isn't applicable to legal training. However, what if Charles were your client in a complex tort case involving an industrial accident? Or a murder case where there were multiple gun shots being fired by a half-dozen individuals during a bank robbery? In these cases, being able to untangle a web of facts to draw the right conclusions— and even understanding who sat next to whom as the events unfolded—is a crucial skill.

Mastering the Analytical Reasoning Section

Although it may be frustrating to pre-law students who enrolled in college-level logic classes, those courses provide little solace on this portion of the LSAT. Philosophical argument, and especially the terminology and symbols used in formal logic, is of no practical use in the exam's logic games.

However, not all is lost. There are two points to keep in mind that will allow you to master this section. The first is that your scores will start climbing immediately once you start practicing solving logic games. Because this section of the LSAT bears such little resemblance to any other test question you may have seen, the more you practice, the less the unfamiliarity of the questions will be a factor.

The second key concept to the mastery of this section is your ability to recognize patterns. For example, a great number of logic games will involve spatial awareness. These can be drawn from questions where

➤ You line up objects or people in a sequence.

➤ You divide up an object or set of objects into specific groups.

➤ You arrange subjects in a specific pattern, say on a shelf or around a table.

Other logic games involve applying seemingly random criteria to a category or people or objects to create a specific kind of order:

➤ You draw conclusions as to the sequence of events. (If A, then B happens, creating condition C.)

➤ You select an object that has one or more characteristics.

➤ You assign attributes to each object in a set based on the question's descriptions.

The reason that these two attributes of the Analytical Reasoning section will help you is that logic games, though they look like a tangle of yarn at first glance, are innately limited in how they can be written. With enough practice, it is highly unlikely that the writers of the LSAT will be able to come up with a challenging question that you haven't tried to tackle before.

Some other items to keep in mind to master this section include

➤ Throughout the section, the difficulty of the logic games presented will vary randomly, but there are two general rules. First, the initial game that opens the section will not be the most difficult one. Second, the final one or two questions are typically more complex than the others.

➤ Time is your enemy in this section. You will not be able to rush on any question—there are no "easy questions" that take significantly less time than others. If you can keep a steady place and not allot more than 10 minutes to any one logic game, you will be fine. Of course, the amount of time that you spend on any logic game depends upon how complex or simple it is. A simple game could take you 6–7 minutes, while more complex games might require a solid 10-minute investment of your time.

➤ If you're stuck on one game, it may be best to skip it and return if you can. However, don't skip more than one game. Allocating your entire time to only two of four game results is proof that you need to practice more to pick up your pace. Additionally, trying to skip over no more than one game will reduce the chance that you'll be left with blind guessing over a large number of remaining questions, giving you a better chance for a higher score.

 There is no single question type that is inherently much more difficult or time consuming than other types. You will not benefit if you plan to skip every question of a given type. Remember, the level of difficulty in this section is not raised by changing the type of question (which is already pretty limited by the format). Difficult is only increased by the number of variables (people around a table, colors on a set of objects) in the question.

➤ Diagramming out the question will be useful in this section, so remember that the LSAT includes a couple pages of scratch paper in the back of the test booklet. You can also use the space provided at the bottom of each page of the Analytical Reasoning section.

➤ Unless you think best in your head as opposed to on paper, for most people an effective diagram will help you to think about a question clearly. The key to an effective diagram is to keep it neat. If you misplace people in the wrong set of chairs, it's best to cross out the diagram and redo it; simply scratching out names or writing on top of incorrect answers will likely confuse you at a critical time.

Logic Game Components

Each logic game has three separate components: the premise, the conditions, and the questions. The *premise* establishes the subjects (objects or people) and setting for the game. Part of the difficulty level of the question is established via the number of subjects in a game. This generally ranges from 5 to as many as 10.

In our original example of a logic game, the premise would be

Charles has to put together a roster for his company's annual softball game against their cross-town rival. He's got eight healthy people that want to bat for the team: Corwin, Dorian, Hal, Joseph, Kamal, Peter, Ralph, and Seth.

Conditions follow the premise by imposing series of rules or conditions that determine the relationships among the subjects. Together with the premise, the number of the conditions (usually 4 to 6) is the second variable in determining how difficult the question is. Obviously, the more premises and conditions there are, the higher the level of difficulty you can from expect the question. Continuing with our example, the conditions would include

If Ralph plays, Hal must play immediately after Ralph on the roster.

Two of the three managers, Dorian, Kamal, and Ralph, have to be on the team.

Corwin and Seth can't be next to each other on the roster.

If Kamal is on the team, then Joseph can't be picked.

Peter has to play either first or second.

Questions based on the relationship of the conditions to premises will follow. For this example, one question could be

Which one of these rosters can be submitted?
- ❏ A. Peter, Hal, Corwin, Kamal, Ralph
- ❏ B. Peter, Dorian, Kamal, Corwin, Seth
- ❏ C. Dorian, Ralph, Hal, Peter, Joseph
- ❏ D. Dorian, Peter, Ralph, Hal, Seth
- ❏ E. Peter, Seth, Joseph, Ralph, Hal

Unlike what you may find in the sections on Logical Reasoning or Reading Comprehension, there is usually less hesitation when it comes to picking answers to the question. Rather like mathematical problems, only one—or at most two—answers will be correct—or seem to be correct—based on your deductions. While it is possible to pick the wrong answer if you've misread the question or diagrammed it out incorrectly, you will rarely if ever be in the position where "It could be answer A, B, or C, what does my gut feeling say?"

Don't carry over information provided in any particular question to other questions. Each question exists in its own universe. And just as in the other sections of the LSAT, no matter how odd the answer you come up with may be in real life, it will be correct in the context of that question.

Exam Prep Questions

1. The two most common diagrams that you'll rely on to solve logic games are the sequence and the matrix. Let's start by looking at our initial example question, which can be best solved using the first of these two diagrams.

> Charles has to put together a roster for his company's annual softball game against their cross-town rival. He's got eight healthy people that want to bat for the team: Corwin, Dorian, Hal, Joseph, Kamal, Peter, Ralph, and Seth.
>
> If Ralph plays, Hal must play immediately after Ralph on the roster.
>
> Two of the three managers, Dorian, Kamal, and Ralph, have to be on the team.
>
> Corwin and Seth can't be next to each other on the roster.
>
> If Kamal is on the team, then Joseph can't be picked.
>
> Peter has to play either first or second.

In this game, you can expect the LSAT testers to ask you to solve for two different things. First, you may have to pick five people out of eight, so expect to get three basic questions posed in one form or another:

➤ Who can be in the group?

➤ Who must be in the group?

➤ Who cannot be in the group?

Second, the most likely follow-up question you will encounter in a question when you have positions discussed (for example, Peter has to play first or second) is that you'll have to pick a specific order of the team.

This means you'll have to worry about positions of people in the roster, such as

➤ Who is first/second/third/fourth/last?

➤ Which of these rosters can be submitted?

➤ Which of these rosters is not possible?

 One factor that the LSAT creators always take into account is that they won't add extra levels of difficulty to questions by throwing too many similarly named people at you. For example, it's highly unlikely you'd see a question similar to the example using the names Ralph, Roy, Roark, Ray, Robert, and Rick.

Before you even jump to the questions, it's best to diagram out the conditions so that you can answer whatever the testers plan to throw your way. One simple way to do this here is to represent your answer as a five letter sequence, or roster, from left to right. This would visually signify the order that the people can play in. For example, let's say you choose Corwin, Dorian, Hal, Joseph, and Kamal to play in that specific order. You'd represent it diagrammatically as

C-D-H-J-K

If you're unsure of a certain spot in the roster, just represent it with a question mark (?).

Next, represent the additional conditions cited in the question as "subchains" or pieces of the puzzle to help us determine the final solution.

Rule 1: If R, then R-H.

If Ralph plays, then we know two players on the roster: Ralph, and Hal immediately after him.

Rule 2: From set (D, K, R), exactly two will play.

Basically, out of the set of three people (Dorian, Kamal, Ralph), exactly two will play. Notice that this isn't "can" play, we know that two of these people will be on the roster.

Rule 3: Not (C-S) AND Not (S-C)

Basically, Corwin and Seth cannot be immediately before or after each other, if they are to play on the team.

Rule 4: If K, then not J

If Kamal plays, then Joseph isn't playing. Of course, we can reverse this rule to come up with the corollary:

Rule 4 (reverse): If J, then not K.

If Joseph is on the team, then Kamal can't be on the team, because if he was, it would violate the fourth rule.

Rule 5: P-?-?-?-? or ?-P-?-?-?

We use the roster representation to show that Peter is either on the first or second position on the roster.

Next, apply your newly diagrammed rules to the question that applies to this logic game. Use the rules as tools to go through and eliminate wrong answers, those that break one of the rules given to us, until we're left with one correct answer.

Question:

Which one of these rosters can be submitted?

- ❑ A. Peter, Hal, Corwin, Kamal, Ralph
- ❑ B. Peter, Dorian, Kamal, Corwin, Seth
- ❑ C. Dorian, Ralph, Hal, Peter, Joseph
- ❑ D. Dorian, Peter, Ralph, Hal, Seth
- ❑ E. Peter, Seth, Joseph, Ralph, Hal

2. Our second sample question also pertains to the order of objects in a group (in this case puppies instead of softball players). While this could also conceivably be solved with the sequence diagram, if you need more visual representation of a problem, the "matrix" diagram may be more useful.

The premise and conditions of the logic game are

On the third Thursday of every month, eight Labrador Retriever puppies (Anne, Boris, Cassie, Daisy, Early, Fancy, Gloria, and Harley) from the Guiding Eyes for the Blind visit the veterinarian's office for their monthly checkup. Each puppy is either a black lab or a yellow lab. The puppies each arrive at the office at a different time. The following conditions apply:

➤ Gloria arrives at the vet's office before Fancy but after Anne

➤ Cassie arrives at the vet's office before Gloria

➤ Boris arrives at the vet's office after Anne but before Fancy

➤ Fancy arrives at the vet's office before Daisy.

Again, let's diagram out the conditions so that you can answer whatever the testers plan to throw your way in this game. The first condition tells you the following about the order of arrival of the puppies at the vet's office:

Anne

Gloria

Fancy

The second condition tells you that Cassie arrived before Gloria, but does not tell you whether or not he arrived before Anne. So at this point, either one of the following orders is possible:

Alternative #1	Alternative #2
Cassie	Anne
Anne	Cassie
Gloria	Gloria
Fancy	Fancy

The third condition tells you that Boris arrived after Anne but before Fancy, but does not tell you whether or not he arrived before or after Gloria, or before or after Cassie. So now the following are possibilities:

#1	#2	#3	#4	#5
Cassie	Cassie	Anne	Anne	Anne
Anne	Anne	Cassie	Cassie	Boris
Boris	Gloria	Boris	Gloria	Cassie
Gloria	Boris	Gloria	Boris	Gloria
Fancy	Fancy	Fancy	Fancy	Fancy

The fourth condition tells you that Fancy arrives before Daisy, providing the following alternatives:

#1	#2	#3	#4	#5
Cassie	Cassie	Anne	Anne	Anne
Anne	Anne	Cassie	Cassie	Boris
Boris	Gloria	Boris	Gloria	Cassie
Gloria	Boris	Gloria	Boris	Gloria
Fancy	Fancy	Fancy	Fancy	Fancy
Daisy	Daisy	Daisy	Daisy	Daisy

No information is provided about the relative arrival time of Early or Harley.

If you now provide that Cassie arrives after Boris, but keep all of the other conditions intact, the relative order must be as set forth in Alternative #5:

1. Anne

2. Boris

3. Cassie

4. Gloria

5. Fancy

6. Daisy

Although no information is provided about when Early or Harley arrived, you know that at most the arrival order of all of the others dogs can only shift down one or two spots from the order shown previously.

Finally, apply your newly diagrammed rules to the question and eliminate wrong answers, until we're left with one correct solution. With this information mapped out, you can proceed to answer the following question:

Question:

If Cassie arrives after Boris, which one of the following must not be true?

❑ A. Anne is the second of the puppies to arrive at the vet's office.
❑ B. Boris is the fifth of the puppies to arrive at the vet's office.
❑ C. Cassie is the third of the puppies to arrive at the vet's office.
❑ D. Daisy is the sixth of the puppies to arrive at the vet's office.
❑ E. Fancy is the seventh of the puppies to arrive at the vet's office.

Exam Prep Answers

1. Choice A is incorrect. Rule 1 states that Hal plays after Ralph on the roster. If we go through the list, we see that in answer choice A, Hal plays way before Ralph, so this roster is invalid.

   Choice B is incorrect. Rule 3 states that Corwin and Seth can't be next to each other in the roster. However, we can see that answer choice B has them batting fourth and fifth, which violates this rule.

   Choice C is incorrect. Rule 5 states that Peter must be first or second in the rotation. Going through the two remaining answer choices, we see that he's fourth in answer choice C, which makes this choice an invalid roster.

   Choice E is incorrect. Rule 2 states that of the set Dorian, Kamal, Ralph, exactly two of those three people must be on the team. As we go through the remaining choices, we see that answer choice E only has Ralph and not Dorian or Kamal.

   We're left with one answer choice, **D**, which is the correct answer.

2. Choice A is incorrect. Anne can be anywhere from either the first, second, or third puppy to arrive at the vet's office, so this choice might be true, and therefore is incorrect.

   Choice C is incorrect. Cassie can be the third, fourth, or fifth puppy to arrive at the vet's office, so this answer might be true and therefore is incorrect.

   Choice D is incorrect. Daisy can be the sixth, seventh, or eighth puppy to arrive at the vet's office, so this answer might be true and therefore is incorrect.

   Choice E is incorrect. Fancy can be the fifth, sixth, or seventh puppy to arrive at the vet's office, so this answer might be true and therefore is incorrect.

   By process of elimination, **Choice B** is correct. Boris can be either the second, third, or fourth puppy to arrive at the vet's office. Since he cannot be the fifth to arrive, this choice cannot be true and therefore is the correct answer.

Mastering the Logical Reasoning

Terms You'll Need to Understand

✓ Logical Reasoning
✓ Arguments
✓ Premises
✓ Conclusions
✓ Drawn or Inferred Conclusions
✓ Non sequiturs

Techniques and Concepts You'll Need to Master

✓ Eliminating at least one answer out of the possible choices for a question because the answer does not apply to the situation.
✓ Eliminating at least one answer out of the possible choices for a question because the answer describes a nonexistent issue, an invalid option, or an imaginary state.
✓ Eliminating at least one answer out of the possible choices for a question because of information in the question itself.
✓ After you eliminate all answers that are obviously wrong, applying retained knowledge to eliminate further answers.
✓ Examining the relationships between premises.
✓ Dissecting logical arguments for their innate strengths and weaknesses, determining what conclusion necessarily follows from a set of premises.
✓ In the context of the LSAT, "logical" does not equal "true."

The LSAT always contains two Logical Reasoning sections. You'll be given 35 minutes to work each section. Typically, each section will contain from 22–25 questions. Taken together, the two sections comprise roughly one-half of the questions you'll see on the LSAT.

How Logical Reasoning Stacks Up to the Other Sections

Logical Reasoning fallsinto a sort of middle zone between Reading Comprehension and Logic Games. Deliberate readers chafe at the time constraints in the Reading section, while puzzle-haters loathe the Logic Games as frivolous. But Logical Reasoning, while feared by many test takers, rarely creates as visceral a reaction.

This is probably because Logical Reasoning tests a recognizable core skill for attorneys. Also, the relative weaknesses of many test takers (slow reading, or an aversion to games) are minimized. Logical Reasoning rarely if ever will rely on mental diagrams (If A sits next to B, then who is buried in Grant's tomb?) or ask you to read more text than you would find in a "Factoid" section of *U.S. News and World Report*.

Some other items to keep in mind as you go through this section that separates it from the other two:

➤ Logical Reasoning won't subject you to the same amount of time pressure as the other two sections (no diagramming or heavy reading). Therefore, your goal should be to complete the entire section.

➤ Unlike Reading Comprehension, there are no factual "gotchas" that you will be able to spot. Instead, you should keep your eyes out for "weasel phrases" that subtly over- or underplay a statement.

➤ Unlike the Logic Games, the Reasoning questions rarely vary in difficulty. This is in part because it's relatively difficult to increase the questions' complexity. (By contrast, in logic games, it's easy to add two or three more people for you to place around a table.)

➤ Almost always, at least one answer out of the possible choices for a question can be eliminated immediately because it matches one of these conditions:

  ➤ The answer does not apply to the situation.

  ➤ The answer describes a nonexistent issue, an invalid option, or an imaginary state.

➤ The answer may be eliminated because of information in the question itself.

After you eliminate all answers that are obviously wrong, you can apply your retained knowledge to eliminate further answers. Look for items that sound correct but refer to actions, commands, or features that are not present or not available in the situation that the question describes.

The Components of an Argument

The Logical Reasoning portions of the LSAT are designed to test your ability in two areas. First, you'll be tested on your ability to think logically: in other words, to examine the relationships between premises. Second, you'll be tested on your ability to dissect logical arguments for their innate strengths and weaknesses, determining what—if any—conclusion necessarily follows from a set of premises.

Arguments consist of two basic parts: *premises* and *conclusions*. Premises are the statements that are supposed to—but do not always—lead to a conclusion. They are usually something that is assumed or taken for granted in the course of the argument. Examples of premises might include

Veronica has shown great musical ability from an early age.

Metro City has doubled the length of its commuter rail line.

The witness reported seeing a UFO while strolling home after the party.

Although at first glance this is very simple, Logical Reasoning questions will always give you multiple premises to examine. The key to passing this section is to understand the premises that the LSAT writers create in building their arguments.

They won't give you premises that are completely false. After all, it would be unfair to give you a statement that you can't determine is true or not based on the available evidence. However, that still leaves a lot of room for them to maneuver. Be aware that what the writers give you to read can be left open for interpretation, apparent contradiction, or to draw you towards the wrong conclusion. For example, let's look at some premises that could follow the first set of examples given earlier:

Veronica has shown great musical ability from an early age. Both her mother and father are accomplished pianists who have played at Carnegie Hall before packed audiences.

Metro City has doubled the length of its commuter rail line. The city council, which has laid out in excess of $40 million for the track, doesn't expect the train to run for the next five years. The cost of commuting by automobile continues to rise at more than 15% each year.

The witness reported seeing a UFO while strolling home after the party. He has a strong reputation for truthfully and accurately reporting what he has seen. He has been known to indulge in alcoholic beverages whenever invited to a party.

Premises are offered to support the argument's conclusion. The conclusion can be uncomplicatedly direct, or there can be multiple conclusions that can be drawn or inferred from a given argument. Continuing with our existing examples, they may look as follows:

Veronica has shown great musical ability from an early age. Both her mother and father are accomplished pianists who have played at Carnegie Hall before packed audiences. Therefore, she is also likely to become a great concert pianist.

Before you agree with the conclusion that Veronica will become the next Franz Liszt, consider: Does it logically follow from the premises? If you read carefully, you may note that the premises are very loosely drawn. Veronica's musical ability is never actually defined—she may be a genius at the trumpet, or music composition, and have no interest in following her parent's footsteps to the concert hall.

Metro City has doubled the length of its commuter rail line. The city council, which has laid out in excess of $40 million for the track, doesn't expect the train to run for the next five years. The cost of commuting by automobile continues to rise at more than 15% each year. It is logical to expect that ridership will be higher overall when it opens in five years than if it opened at present.

As for how well the conclusion follows the given premises, note that some premises relate more strongly than others in the statement. For example, the fact that an alternative form of commuting will cost a lot more in five years would make traveling by rail more attractive. The fact that the rail length has doubled is less strong, unless it is also supported by another fact—such as the statement that the line now runs though more commuter areas. And the statement regarding the cost of the track on its face does not relate to the conclusion at all. Only if further information in the multiple choice area makes it relevant will it come in handy.

The witness reported seeing a UFO while strolling home after the party. He has a strong reputation for truthfully and accurately reporting what he has seen. However, the FBI is correct to disregard his reports of UFOs visiting the local community. He has been known to indulge in alcoholic beverages whenever invited to a party.

To begin with, notice that the conclusion in this example doesn't come at the end of the paragraph. Conclusions can be placed anywhere into the text, even at the start.

This example demonstrates how you will have to consider carefully whether or not a premise or series of premises are strong enough to support a given argument, especially in light of the options given to you in the multiple choice format. Although it is strongly implied that the witness is both reliable (by his reputation) *and* unreliable (he is known to drink on occasion), you will have to read the multiple choice options carefully for additional information that will determine the correct answer.

In this example, say that the question posed is "Which one of the following, if true, best supports the FBI's conclusion as described above?"

A. The host of the party saw the witness consume at least four drinks with hard alcohol in the hour before the UFO sighting.

B. The witness has served credibly many times as an expert witness in cases involving strange weather disturbances.

In option A, the FBI's decision—to set aside the witness's report—is strongly supported by the additional information that the witness was probably inebriated. Option B, while not as strong as A because it discusses behavior exhibited over time and not immediately before the sighting, does strengthen the case that the witness is a competent judge of what could be a UFO versus an atmospheric phenomenon. Therefore, it weakens the FBI's conclusion and you should pick answer A over B.

The use of logical analysis is a critical skill you'll use throughout law school and in your legal practice; in fact, many would argue that it is the core skill that a lawyer must have. Unlike the ability to digest large quantities of text (Reading Comprehension) or the ability to hold multiple levels of case detail in your head (Logic Games), the ability to contrast, compare, and analyze Logical Reasoning is not something that is helped with diagrams or slow and careful reading. It is a skill—and it is one that can be developed with practice.

Non Sequiturs

While you won't need to know much, if any Latin when you take the LSAT, the term *non sequitur* is worth knowing. It means a statement that does not follow logically from anything previously said. That is, there is nothing factually incorrect about the statements themselves, but they really don't relate to the argument at hand. If you had a fact pattern such as the one we've been discussing, where a witness reported seeing a UFO while strolling home from a party, non sequiturs given as possible answers could include

> The average party-goer consumes at least three ounces of hard liquor.
>
> Even trained observers are prone to lapses in judgment.
>
> UFOs have been regularly spotted on every continent except Antarctica.

Non sequiturs are not too commonly seen on exams, but they're a good mental category to watch for when you look at logical reasoning questions.

Though it seems counterintuitive at first glance, you should always remember that in the context of the LSAT, "logical" does not equal "true." Once again, a logical argument is a series of statements that must properly follow in order to establish a given proposition. It is not a study of the underlying truth of a given statement.

In fact, it's not unheard of for the LSAT creators to compose arguments that are logical, but manifestly untrue. For example, say that the LSAT examiners create a well-crafted, logical argument that leads to the conclusion that the sun travels around the earth. Now, you of course know from a basic study of astronomy that Copernicus proved otherwise, and that no matter how well put together the argument may be, the earth revolves around the sun, not the other way around.

But the *truth* of the question's conclusion is never up for examination. Remember, even if you're absolutely certain that the statements presented are erroneous, treat them as if they exist in their own universe. Your job is to determine whether the statements properly support and follow each other.

Exam Prep Questions

1. Proven liquid natural gas (LNG) reserves in the country of Monrovia are at the same level as they were a decade ago. Proven reserves are the amount of natural gas considered extractable from known fields. Yet over this same period, no new natural gas fields of any consequence have been discovered, and the annual consumption of domestically produced LNG has actually increased.

   Which one of the following, if true, best reconciles the discrepancy described above?

   - ○ A. Over the past decade the annual consumption of imported LNG has increased more rapidly than that of domestic liquid natural gas in Monrovia.
   - ○ B. Conservation measures have lowered the rate of growth of domestic LNG consumption from what it was a decade ago.
   - ○ C. Liquid natural gas exploration in Monrovia has slowed due to increased concern over the environmental impact of such exploration.
   - ○ D. Due to technological advances over the last decade, much liquid natural gas previously considered unextractable is now considered extractable.
   - ○ E. Consumption of LNG has increased because prices have dropped as more domestically produced LNG has entered the market.

2. Mail and package shipping services suffer when a company combines express mail and freight service. By dividing its attention between its freight and express mail customers, a shipping company serves neither particularly well. Therefore, if a shipping company is going to be a successful business, then it must concentrate exclusively on one of these two areas.

   For the argument to be logically correct, it must make which one of the following assumptions?

   - ❑ A. Express mail and freight service have little in common with each other.
   - ❑ B. The first priority of a shipping company is to be a successful business.
   - ❑ C. Unless a shipping company serves its customers well, it will not be a successful business.
   - ❑ D. If a shipping company concentrates on express mail service, it will be a successful business.
   - ❑ E. Customers who want express mail service rarely want freight service as well.

3. Metro City has doubled the length of its commuter rail line. The city council, which has laid out in excess of $40 million for the track, doesn't expect the train to run for the next five years. The cost of commuting by automobile continues to rise at more than 15% each year. It is logical to expect that ridership will be higher overall when it opens in five years than if it opened at present.

Which one of the following, if true, most seriously weakens the argument?

- ❏ A. The cost of the track should have been only $20 million; because the construction ran over budget, the price of the track doubled.

- ❏ B. The longer rail line will not allow the train company to make more trips per day.

- ❏ C. Given past advances in construction technology, it is likely that the rail line will open in only four years, not five.

- ❏ D. Because the track construction ran over budget, some experts predict that the price of a rail ticket will likely cost double what it would today by the time the train starts to run.

- ❏ E. The Bell Monte canning company, which employs more than 40% of all commuters in Metro City, will relocate its plant in the next three years.

Exam Prep Answers

1. The correct answer is D. If true, the advances in technology would allow more LNG to be pumped from existing sources, thereby increasing supply without increasing the number of discovered reserves.

   A is incorrect because it does not address the core question: Why is the annual consumption of *domestically* produced LNG higher? Consumption levels of *imported* LNG are not relevant to the question.

   B is incorrect, and a very clever trap for those not reading carefully. B talks about lowering the *rate of growth* of LNG consumption. It does not address why the *total* amount of consumption has increased, only how conservation has "decreased the rate of the increase."

   C is incorrect because it answers only part of the question. It answers why no new LNG fields of any consequence have been discovered, but it doesn't explain why consumption has increased.

   E is incorrect because it is a variant of C. Lower prices can help explain why more people are buying natural gas. But if there are no newly discovered reserves of any significance, it doesn't explain how more domestically produced LNG has entered the market in the first place.

2. The correct answer is E. It follows that if companies who concentrate on only one of the two services will succeed, it is because customers don't want the combined services.

   A is incorrect even though it could be true, because it does not necessarily follow. The two services could actually have a lot in common, but commonality or lack thereof is not the argument—only that if a company tries to do both, then they will not succeed.

   B and C are incorrect for the same reason: They are *non sequiturs*. That is, there is nothing factually incorrect about the statements themselves, but they really don't relate to the argument at hand.

   D is incorrect because it only pertains to part of the argument. The case is made that a company can only be successful at concentrating on one area—it does not specify which!

3. The correct answer is E. It follows that if the main source of the commuting workers—the Bell Monte canning company—plans to move before the train's opening, the demand for rail services will be greatly diminished compared to the present.

A is incorrect because it does not necessarily follow that a cost overrun will lead to lower ridership. The cost has to be shown as impacting the consumer of the rail services in a negative way for it to be relevant.

B is incorrect because it misstates the purpose of having a longer rail line. The purpose of the longer line is not to run more trips throughout the day, but to encourage more commuters to use the rail line as it is more conveniently located.

C is a *non sequitur*. That is, there is nothing factually incorrect about the statement but it really doesn't relate to the argument at hand. It is simply a speculative statement that the rail line is likely to open in only four years.

D is actually a fairly good answer and would be correct if not for the stronger answer in E. It does follow that a cost overrun leading to higher ticket prices could lead to lower ridership. However, the answer has two flaws that weaken it compared to E. First, it is speculative in nature. Second, it does not show that the higher ticket prices would be more expensive than the cost of commuting by automobile, especially if the cost of that form of commute is going up by 15% each year.

5

Practice Exam 1

SECTION I—Logical Reasoning

Time—35 minutes

25 Questions

Directions: The questions in this section are based on the reasoning contained in brief statements or passages. For some questions, more than one of the choices could conceivably answer the question. However, you are to choose the best answer; that is, the response that most accurately and completely answers the question. You should not make assumptions that are by common=sense standards implausible, superfluous, or incompatible with the passage. After you have chosen the best answer, blacken the corresponding space on your answer sheet.

1. Old Timers Farm has recently received delivery of a load of new timothy hay. Some of the hay has mold that will make horses ill if they eat it. However, the barn manager tells the grooms to go ahead and feed the horses the hay anyway, since he claims that they will avoid eating hay if they sense something in it that will make them ill.

   Which one of the following assumptions provides the strongest basis for the barn manager's claim?

   ❑ A. The mold that makes horses ill can only be found in timothy hay.

   ❑ B. Only horses become ill from eating moldy timothy hay.

   ❑ C. At least some horses are capable of sensing that hay is moldy before they eat it.

   ❑ D. The mold in the timothy hay cannot be eliminated without destroying the hay.

   ❑ E. The timothy hay also has another type of mold that does not make horses ill if they eat it.

2. At Arches National Park, park rangers have placed a number of signs saying "Don't Bust the Crust" (that is, what looks like normal dirt is really cryptobiotic crust that is holding the desert floor together, and if you walk on it, you may destroy it). Chris points the signs out to his friend, Darrell. Darrell says, "I don't think if just one person walks on it, that it will be destroyed." Chris says, "That's not true. If everyone thought like that, everyone would walk on the crust, and the crust would be destroyed."

   Which one of the following most weakens Chris's argument?

   ❑ A. It attempts to use a statement about the consequence of an action to disprove a statement about the action itself.

   ❑ B. It treats Darrell's statement about the consequences of an action as though it were instead about the consequences of everyone believing the statement.

   ❑ C. It treats Darrell's statement as if it were a statement that everyone believed.

   ❑ D. It fails to recognize that there may be circumstances in which walking on cryptobiotic crust may be justified.

   ❑ E. It attempts to undermine Darrell's statement by calling Darrell's character into question.

3. The Riverstone Fall Classic Horse Show allows amateurs and professionals to compete against one another. Most of the ribbons were won by amateurs.

   Each of the following, if true, could by itself constitute an explanation of this fact, *except*:

    ❑ A. More entries in the horse show were from amateurs than professionals.

    ❑ B. The judge for the horse show was an amateur, and therefore preferred amateurs.

    ❑ C. Amateurs always try their hardest, while professionals do not.

    ❑ D. Professionals are historically not as interested in participating in the Riverstone Fall Classic Horse Show, so relatively few professionals chose to compete against the amateurs.

    ❑ E. 50% more amateurs entered the horse show compared to the previous year.

4. Studies have shown that the average American child between the ages of 10 and 17 accesses the Internet for more than 15 hours per week, and will have viewed more than 500,000 online advertisements by the time he or she graduates from high school. One may conclude, therefore, that online advertisements have influenced the thought patterns of American children.

This conclusion is logical if you assume which one of the following is true?

    ❑ A. A child's thought patterns are largely determined by what a child is exposed to at school.

    ❑ B. A child's thought patterns are influenced by anything to which a child is exposed in great quantity.

    ❑ C. It is impossible to ignore or avoid online advertisements.

    ❑ D. Some children find online advertisements more interesting than the website on which the advertisement is displayed.

    ❑ E. Certain forms of communication to which children are exposed do affect their thought patterns.

5. In a recent survey of superintendents of 150 large city school districts, the majority of superintendents asserted that student safety had the same high priority as standardized test scores. So the common belief that the managers of large city school districts are indifferent to the safety needs of their students is unfounded.

Which one of the following provides the strongest basis for criticism with respect to this conclusion?

    ❑ A. The conclusion fails to define the term "managers."

    ❑ B. The conclusion assumes that one is not indifferent to something that is supposed to be a high priority.

    ❑ C. The conclusion assumes that superintendents' priorities are misplaced.

    ❑ D. The conclusion assumes that superintendents' assertions are truthful and reflected in actual practice.

    ❑ E. The conclusion is based on an unrepresentative sample.

6. College Law School has the following graduation requirements for masters of taxation students (many of whom are part-time or night students). All candidates for a masters of taxation degree who enrolled after 2000 must take a seminar on Internet law, and all candidates for the masters of taxation degree who enrolled after 2004 must take a seminar on ethics.

If a graduate of the masters of taxation program took a seminar on Internet law, but did not take a seminar on ethics, which one of the following must be true?

- ❑ A. The student enrolled after 2000 and prior to 2005.
- ❑ B. The student enrolled prior to 2005.
- ❑ C. If the student was a candidate for the masters of taxation degree, then the student enrolled prior to 2005.
- ❑ D. If the student was a candidate for the masters of taxation degree, then the student enrolled after 2000 and prior to 2005.
- ❑ E. If the student was a candidate for the masters of taxation degree, then the student enrolled prior to 2001.

7. The pence, shilling, and guinea are types of coins minted in England during the reign of George III. If you look at these coins very closely, you will see that each one of them has a very small sceptre (a symbol of the monarchy) engraved on the back of the coin. Kim, a coin collector, believes that any coin that does not have a small sceptre engraved on the back of the coin cannot be an authentic coin minted in England during the reign of George III.

Which one of the following best describes the error in Kim's reasoning?

- ❑ A. It bases a generalization on claims that contradict one another.
- ❑ B. It bases a generalization on examples that are not typical.
- ❑ C. It treats the fact that some members of a category have a certain characteristic as sufficient evidence that possession of that characteristic is necessary for membership in that category.
- ❑ D. It treats the fact that certain specific objects belong to a certain category and that some other objects that belong to that category possess a certain characteristic as sufficient evidence that the former objects also possess that characteristic.
- ❑ E. It treats the fact that some members of a certain category possess certain characteristics as sufficient evidence that other objects that possess that characteristic are also members of that category.

8. An archeologist has unearthed some well-preserved ceremonial weavings. He makes the following statement: The tribe that created these weavings must have used spinning wheels to create thread. Of the three tribes (the Haji, Inosh, and Janix) who inhabited the area around the site where the weavings were found, the Haji could obtain thread, but did not have access to spinning wheels, and the Inosh had no access to thread. Therefore, the Janix is the only tribe who inhabited the area around the site that could have made these ceremonial weavings.

The reasoning in which one of the following statements most closely parallels the reasoning using in the statement above?

❑   A. A mom makes the following statement: One of my three children has left muddy sneaker prints on my freshly cleaned white carpet. Of the three children, Audrey, Darrell, and Noah, Audrey does not yet walk, and Darrell does not have sneakers. Therefore, only Noah could have left the muddy sneaker prints.

❑   B. Anyone who hopes to become a published poetry writer must have a good vocabulary and the ability to rhyme. Of three members of the Poetry club, Mark, Sam, and Emma, only Mark and Sam hope to become published poetry writers, so only Mark and Sam could have a good vocabulary and the ability to rhyme.

❑   C. A forensic psychologist makes the following statement: The person who committed the crime must have been left-handed. Of three suspects, Ames, Barnes, and Cheeves, Ames and Cheeves are right-handed. Therefore, Barnes is the only person who could have committed the crime.

❑   D. An instructor makes the following statement: Anyone wishing to sign up for my new seminar must first obtain my signature on the registration form and then deliver the form to the registrar's office. Of Caroline, Ann, and Elizabeth, Caroline and Elizabeth each obtained the instructor's signature and delivered the form to the registrar's office, so Caroline and Elizabeth can each sign up for the instructor's new seminar.

❑   E. The person who left a message on my voice mail said his name was Arnold. Because I do not know anyone whose name is Arnold, the person who left the message on my voice mail could only be someone who I do not know.

9. All of the children born in the country of Moravia have either blue eyes or green eyes. A recent survey of Moravian eye color found that 5 percent of 75-year-old Moravians have green eyes, compared to 20 percent of 50-year-old Moravians and 40 percent of 25-year-old Moravians. Yet over the past 75 years, the proportion of Moravians born with green eyes has not increased, nor have Moravian attitudes toward green eyes changed.

Which one of the following, if true, most helps to explain the survey results?

❑   A. In Moravia, people with green eyes are no more likely than people with blue eyes to be involved in car accidents.

❑   B. In Moravia, green eyes are considered to be very beautiful.

❑   C. In Moravia, where women have a shorter average life expectancy than do men, green eyes are less common in men than they are in women.

❑   D. Green-eyed Moravians have never accounted for more than 50% of the population in Moravia.

❑   E. The population in Moravia has been stable over the past 75 years.

10. Pizza maker: The ingredients required to make this pizza are very expensive. We should switch to a less expensive brand of mozzarella cheese.

    Sales Manager: The pizza sells so well because it tastes so good. No other brand of mozzarella cheese tastes as good. We should keep using the same brand of cheese because we know people like it.

    About which one of the following issues do the pizza maker and the sales manager disagree?

    ❑ A. Whether the brand of mozzarella cheese used for the pizza is more expensive than other brands.

    ❑ B. Whether the pizza store should make the pizza with a different brand of mozzarella cheese.

    ❑ C. Whether customer preferences should be taken in account in deciding what ingredients should be used in a pizza.

    ❑ D. Whether other brands of mozzarella cheese taste as good as the brand currently used.

    ❑ E. Whether the pizza store is selling as much pizza as expected.

11. CEO: Thomas would not be a good manager. He is too friendly to yell at employees with low ratings, and too negative to reward employees with high ratings.

    Which one of the following assumptions is central to this argument?

    ❑ A. In order to yell at employees with low ratings and reward employees with high ratings, one must be a good manager.

    ❑ B. To be a good manager, one must be capable of yelling at employees with low ratings and rewarding those with high ratings.

    ❑ C. If Thomas were less friendly, he would yell at employees with low ratings.

    ❑ D. It is not possible to yell at an employee with a low rating and then later reward that employee when she has a high rating.

    ❑ E. If Thomas were less negative, he would reward employees with high ratings.

12. Over the past five years, the cost of a ticket to a Broadway show has increased, resulting in a decrease in the number of people attending Broadway shows. Broadway show revenues, however, have progressively increased in each of the years during this period, and analysts predict further increases in the years to come.

    Which one of the following, if true, offers the best explanation for this situation?

   ❑ A. Attendance at movie theaters exceeds attendance at Broadway shows.

   ❑ B. Most Broadway shows producers increase ticket rates approximately once every year.

   ❑ C. The increase in ticket rates at Broadway theaters has influenced prospective show-goers to seek alternative forms of entertainment.

   ❑ D. Broadway shows gain a larger percentage of their revenue from group sales than do movie theaters.

   ❑ E. The decrease in the number of people attending Broadway shows has been more than offset by the increases in ticket prices.

13. Christopher's mother suggests that he purchase a stamp album that contains special display pages that will allow him to organize and display the most valuable stamps in his stamp collection. Christopher uses the Internet to investigate the different albums available, but concludes that his mother's suggestion will not help him organize his collection because none of the stamp albums with special display pages are big enough to hold all of his stamps.

On which one of the following assumptions is Christopher's conclusion based?

   ❑ A. A stamp album without special display pages is not as effective for organizing a stamp collection as is a stamp album with such pages.

   ❑ B. His stamp collection is disorganized because he has more stamps in his collection this year than last year.

   ❑ C. His stamp collection would not be more organized if displayed in several stamp albums with special display pages.

   ❑ D. A stamp album large enough to hold all of his stamps would include enough special display pages to display all him most valuable stamps.

   ❑ E. Stamp albums with special display pages that are big enough to hold all of his stamps were available last year.

14. William received the following letter from a magazine to which he has submitted a short story:

We regret to inform you that we will not be able to publish your short story in our magazine. We have been forced to reject many well-written short stories because due to size considerations, we must restrict the number of short stories that we publish in any issue of the magazine to no more than five stories.

Which one of the following can be logically inferred from the information in the letter?

   ❑ A. Only very well-written stories are published by the magazine.

   ❑ B. The magazine had already accepted its maximum number of short stories.

   ❑ C. Most of the short stories submitted were very well-written.

   ❑ D. The quality of a short story is not the only factor affecting the magazine's decision whether to publish it or not.

   ❑ E. The writer's short story was considered to be very well-written.

15. Linda: Being happy and sad are mutually exclusive. Therefore, it is impossible for a person to both laugh and cry simultaneously.

Paul: That's not true. Many people laugh so hard that they cry, or cry when they are happy.

Paul has weakened Linda's argument by doing which one of the following?

- ❑ A. By showing that Linda's argument is circular.
- ❑ B. By providing evidence that challenges her conclusion.
- ❑ C. By challenging Linda's understanding of the emotions at issue.
- ❑ D. By attacking Linda's character.
- ❑ E. By presenting an analogy showing that her argument doesn't make sense.

16. At current levels, a new $1.50 per car toll to cross the Tappan Zee Bridge would raise $1 billion in additional funding. This would be a good way to pay for much needed road repairs caused by the incessant traffic in the Tappan Zee/Interstate 287 corridor. Not only that, but the increased toll might reduce the need for future road repairs, by encouraging commuters to use alternative means of transportation, and in the future, the money collected from the toll could support other programs, such as the new Greenbelt program.

Which one of the following most clearly identifies the flaw in the author's reasoning?

- ❑ A. The author generalizes based on insufficient data.
- ❑ B. The author fails to consider other possible ways to accomplish the same goals.
- ❑ C. The author mistakes cause for effect.
- ❑ D. The author's logic is circular.
- ❑ E. The author fails to consider that if commuters end up using alternative means of transportation, fewer auto commuters means less income collected.

17. Economics student: The key factors in a strong economy are a strong dollar and high job growth. Because there cannot be job growth without a strong dollar, it can be concluded that when the dollar is strong there is job growth.

Which one of the following, if true, would most weaken this argument?

- ❑ A. Many strong economies with weak currencies have little job growth.
- ❑ B. Weak economies with weak currencies have little job growth.
- ❑ C. Weak economies with strong currencies have little job growth.
- ❑ D. High job growth guarantees a strong dollar.
- ❑ E. Some weak economies have weak currencies.

18. Ounce for ounce, Brand X beer costs less than Brand Y beer and tastes better. Yet a six-pack of Brand X beer costs more than a six-pack of Brand Y beer.

Which one of the following statements, if true, best explains this situation?

❑ A. Both Brand X and Brand Y are manufactured by the same company.

❑ B. A six-pack of Brand X beer tastes better than a six-pack of Brand Y beer.

❑ C. A six-pack of Brand Y beer tastes better than a six-pack of Brand X beer.

❑ D. The cost of a six-pack of Brand X beer has risen every year for the past five years.

❑ E. A six-pack of Brand X beer has more ounces than a six-pack of Brand Y beer.

19. A low-carbohydrate diet is essential to good health because it lowers cholesterol and helps people lose weight. If you want remain healthy, you must maintain a low-carbohydrate diet.

Which one of the following conclusions can most logically be drawn from this statement?

❑ A. Only if you lose weight, you will be healthy.

❑ B. Only a low-carbohydrate diet will lower cholesterol and lead to weight loss.

❑ C. A healthy person has low cholesterol.

❑ D. You will not remain healthy if you do not maintain a low-carbohydrate diet.

❑ E. A person who is not healthy must not lose weight.

20. Ken: I make financial decisions based on what my head tells me. I make political decisions based either on what my head tells me or what my heart tells me. I never make decisions about relationships based on what my head tells me.

Which one of the following can be logically inferred from this statement?

❑ A. If Ken is relying on what his head tells him, he may be making a decision about a relationship.

❑ B. If Ken is relying on what his head tells him, he is not making a decision about a financial issue.

❑ C. If Ken is not making a decision based on what his head tells him, he is making a political decision.

❑ D. If Ken is not making a decision based on what his head tells him, he must be making a financial decision.

❑ E. If Ken is making a decision based on what his head tells him, he might be making a political decision.

21. Hannah and Jake are security guards stationed at the entrance to the county courthouse. They are required to remain at their posts until the next shift arrives. However, if someone attempts to enter the courthouse without passing through the security scanner at the entrance, they no longer have to remain at their post but instead are required to immediately pursue that person. On September 2, at 5 p.m., when Hannah and Jake finished their six-hour shift and the next shift arrived, it was discovered that Hannah had violated these rules, but that Jake had not.

If the statements above are true, each of the following statements could be true *except*:

❑ A. Hannah and Jake were at their respective posts at 5 p.m.
❑ B. Jake left his post before 5 p.m. but Hannah did not.
❑ C. Hannah left her post before 5 p.m. but Jake did not.
❑ D. Someone attempted to enter the courthouse without passing through the security scanner at 3 p.m. and neither Hannah nor Jake left his or her respective post before 5 p.m.
❑ E. Someone attempted to enter the courthouse without passing through the security scanner at 3 p.m. and both Hannah and Jake left their respective posts before 5 p.m.

22. Jean: For five years, doctors have prescribed naxopraxen for my arthritis pain. Recent studies, however, have shown that when given to guinea pigs, naxopraxen can cause sudden unexpected strokes. Thirty percent of the female guinea pigs in the study had a stroke, but the male guinea pigs were not affected. Even though I am healthy now, I should stop taking naxopraxen; only then will I be sure not to have a stroke.

Which one of the following provides the strongest base for criticizing Jean's reasoning?

❑ A. Jean does not consider how guinea pigs differ from people.
❑ B. Jean does not consider whether naxopraxen causes other diseases.
❑ C. Jean does not focus on the positive effects that naxopraxen provides.
❑ D. Jean does not consider the possibility of other causes of stroke.
❑ E. Jean is healthy even though she has been taking naxopraxen for five years.

23. Chuck: We need to change our tax policy, so why not get it over with once and for all? If you need to remove an aching tooth, it's much quicker to give it a hard yank than to wiggle it back and forth.

Allison: I agree we need to change our tax policy, but it will cause a lot of disruption if we change most or all of the tax policies at the same time. We should phase in changes slowly, even if it's more painful over time.

Chuck and Alison disagree over whether:

- ❑ A. A change in tax policy is needed.
- ❑ B. Revising tax policy incrementally is like wiggling an aching tooth.
- ❑ C. The faster tax policies are revised, the less painful it will be.
- ❑ D. Changes to tax policies should all be made at the same time.
- ❑ E. The current tax policy situation is unacceptable.

24. City Manager: Recently, the number of trucks carrying radioactive waste through the city has grown dangerously high. We need to limit the number of such trucks allowed on our city streets.

Nuclear Waste Manager: There is no need to impose such a limit. Trucks have been carrying radioactive waste through the city for 30 years without a problem.

The reasoning expressed in the Nuclear Waste Manager's rebuttal to the City Manager is flawed because it

- ❑ A. Does not explain why the number of trucks carrying radioactive waste has increased.
- ❑ B. Does not focus specifically on the issue of radioactive waste.
- ❑ C. Ignores the possibility that the radioactive waste itself may have become more dangerous.
- ❑ D. Does not defend the need for transporting radioactive waste through the city.
- ❑ E. Does not address the increased potential for harm due to the recent increase in the number of trucks carrying radioactive waste through the city.

25. Doctor Simon recommends that patients have a piece of chocolate every day with breakfast, based on a study that found that doing so can lower high blood pressure. However, subsequent research found that many patients who followed this recommendation continued to have high blood pressure.

Which one of the following, if true, would explain this apparent contradiction?

- ❑ A. The cost of chocolate is so high that patients could only afford to have one piece each day.
- ❑ B. Chocolate has not been found to prevent heart disease.
- ❑ C. Many patients failed to have chocolate every day with breakfast.
- ❑ D. Eating more than several pieces of chocolate a day can raise blood pressure.
- ❑ E. The worldwide consumption of chocolate has increased each year, in part as a result of the study.

SECTION II—Analytical Reasoning

Time—35 minutes

24 Questions

Directions: Each group of questions in this section is based on a set of conditions. In answering some of the questions, it may be useful to draw a rough diagram. Choose the response that most accurately and completely answers each question and blacken the corresponding space on your answer sheet.

QUESTIONS 1–6 RELATE TO THE FOLLOWING LOGIC GAME:

A university research study is selecting a control group of people for a medical experiment. There are exactly five married couples that qualify for this study: the Harrisons, Lesters, Murrays, Olsons, and Petersons. The following restrictions apply:

If neither of the Petersons are picked, then Mr. and Mrs. Olson must be picked.

Mr. Peterson cannot be in the group unless Mrs. Lester is also selected.

If Mr. Murray is selected, then neither Mrs. Olson nor Mrs. Peterson can be picked.

At least one of the Harrisons must be in the group.

1. Which one of the following is an acceptable control group for the study?
   - ❑ A. Mrs. Harrison, Mr. Murray, Mrs. Murray, Mr. Olson, Mr. Peterson
   - ❑ B. Mrs. Harrison, Mr. Lester, Mrs. Murray, Mr. Olson, Mrs. Olson
   - ❑ C. Mr. Harrison, Mr. Lester, Mrs. Lester, Mrs. Murray, Mrs. Olson
   - ❑ D. Mr. Harrison, Mrs. Lester, Mr. Murray, Mr. Peterson, Mrs. Peterson
   - ❑ E. Mr. Lester, Mrs. Lester, Mr. Murray, Mrs. Olson, Mr. Peterson

2. Which one of the following must be false?
   - ❑ A. Both Mrs. Harrison and Mr. Peterson are selected.
   - ❑ B. Both Mr. Murray and Mrs. Lester are selected.
   - ❑ C. Both Mrs. Olson and Mr. Harrison are selected.
   - ❑ D. All the women are selected.
   - ❑ E. All the men are selected.

3. If Mr. Murray is part of the group, who else MUST be selected?

- ❑ A. Mrs. Harrison
- ❑ B. Mr. Harrison
- ❑ C. Mrs. Lester
- ❑ D. Mrs. Murray
- ❑ E. Mr. Olson

4. If the smallest number of people are picked for this control group, which person must be selected?

- ❑ A. Mr. Harrison
- ❑ B. Mrs. Lester
- ❑ C. Mr. Murray
- ❑ D. Mrs. Peterson
- ❑ E. Mr. Peterson

5. All of the following could be true *except*:

- ❑ A. Mrs. Lester is the only woman selected.
- ❑ B. Mrs. Murray is the only woman selected.
- ❑ C. Mrs. Olson is the only woman selected.
- ❑ D. Mr. Olson is the only man selected.
- ❑ E. Mr. Peterson is the only man selected.

6. If Mrs. Lester is not picked, then which of the following pairs of people contain someone that must be selected?

- ❑ A. Mrs. Harrison, Mrs. Murray
- ❑ B. Mr. Harrison, Mr. Lester
- ❑ C. Mrs. Olson, Mr. Olson
- ❑ D. Mr. Olson, Mrs. Peterson
- ❑ E. Mrs. Peterson, Mr. Peterson

QUESTIONS 7–11 RELATE TO THE FOLLOWING LOGIC GAME:

Each of seven students—Andrew, Brian, Eddie, Joel, Michael, Traci, and Yana—will be assigned to exactly one of nine bus seats. The seats are numbered from 1 through 9 and arranged in rows as follows:

Front row: 1 2 3

Middle row: 4 5 6

Last row: 7 8 9

Only seats in the same row as each other are immediately beside each other. Seat assignments must meet the following conditions:

Brian's seat is in the last row.

Eddie's seat is immediately beside Joel's seat and also immediately beside an unassigned seat.

Joel's seat is in the row immediately behind the row in which Andrew's seat is located.

Neither Michael nor Yana is seated immediately beside Andrew.

7. Which one of the following is a pair of travelers who could be assigned to seats 2 and 8, respectively?
   - ❏ A. Andrew, Michael
   - ❏ B. Brian, Yana
   - ❏ C. Eddie, Brian
   - ❏ D. Joel, Michael
   - ❏ E. Yana, Traci

8. If Michael and Yana are not assigned to seats in the same row as each other, which one of the following must be false?
   - ❏ A. Andrew is assigned to seat 2.
   - ❏ B. Eddie is assigned to seat 5.
   - ❏ C. Joel is assigned to seat 4.
   - ❏ D. Traci is assigned to seat 2.
   - ❏ E. Yana is assigned to seat 1.

9. If Michael is assigned to a seat in the same row as Yana, which one of the following travelers could be assigned to a seat immediately beside one of the unassigned seats?
   - ❏ A. Brian
   - ❏ B. Joel
   - ❏ C. Michael
   - ❏ D. Traci
   - ❏ E. Yana

10. If the seat to which Traci is assigned is immediately beside a seat assigned to another traveler and also immediately beside one of the unassigned seats, which one of the following must be true?
    - ❏ A. Traci is assigned to a seat in the front row.
    - ❏ B. Traci is assigned to a seat in the last row.
    - ❏ C. Brian is assigned to a seat immediately beside Michael.
    - ❏ D. Brian is assigned to a seat immediately beside Traci.
    - ❏ E. Michael is assigned to a seat immediately beside Yana.

11. If Brian is assigned to a seat immediately beside one of the unassigned seats, which one of the following must be true?
    - ❏ A. Brian is assigned to seat 8.
    - ❏ B. Traci is assigned to seat 2.
    - ❏ C. Yana is assigned to seat 1.
    - ❏ D. Seat 4 is unassigned.
    - ❏ E. Seat 9 is unassigned.

QUESTIONS 12–18 RELATE TO THE FOLLOWING LOGIC GAME:

A high school principal must make exactly five budget cuts from eight subject areas—Gym, Library, Math, Nutrition, Physics, Reading, Science, and Writing—in accordance with the following conditions:

If both Gym and Science get budget cuts, Writing is also cut.

If Nutrition is cut, neither Reading nor Science is cut.

If Physics is cut, Library is not cut.

Of the three areas Library, Math, and Reading, exactly two can be cut.

12. Which one of the following could be a complete and accurate list of the budget cuts by the principal?
   - ❑ A. Gym, Library, Math, Nutrition, Writing
   - ❑ B. Gym, Library, Math, Physics, Writing
   - ❑ C. Gym, Math, Nutrition, Reading, Writing
   - ❑ D. Gym, Math, Physics, Reading, Science
   - ❑ E. Library, Math, Reading, Science, Writing

13. If Writing is cut, which one of the following could be a complete and accurate list of the four other areas of expenditure that would be cut?
   - ❑ A. Gym, Math, Physics, Science
   - ❑ B. Library, Math, Nutrition, Reading
   - ❑ C. Library, Math, Physics, Science
   - ❑ D. Math, Nutrition, Physics, Science
   - ❑ E. Math, Physics, Reading, Science

14. If Physics is cut, which one of the following is a pair of areas of expenditure, both of which must be cut?
   - ❑ A. Gym, Math
   - ❑ B. Math, Reading
   - ❑ C. Nutrition, Reading
   - ❑ D. Reading, Science
   - ❑ E. Science, Writing

15. If both Library and Science are cut, which one of the following could be a pair of areas of expenditure both of which are cut?
   - ❑ A. Gym, Math
   - ❑ B. Gym, Physics
   - ❑ C. Nutrition, Reading
   - ❑ D. Nutrition, Writing
   - ❑ E. Physics, Science

16. If Reading is not cut, which one of the following must be true?

  ❏ A. Gym is cut.

  ❏ B. Nutrition is not cut.

  ❏ C. Physics is cut.

  ❏ D. Science is cut.

  ❏ E. Writing is not cut.

17. If both Math and Reading are cut, which one of the following is a pair of areas that could not be cut?

  ❏ A. Gym, Library

  ❏ B. Gym, Nutrition

  ❏ C. Library, Nutrition

  ❏ D. Library, Physics

  ❏ E. Physics, Science

18. Which one of the following areas must be reduced?

  ❏ A. Gym

  ❏ B. Library

  ❏ C. Nutrition

  ❏ D. Physics

  ❏ E. Writing

QUESTIONS 19–24 RELATE TO THE FOLLOWING LOGIC GAME:

At a karaoke bar, three friends—Phil, Renae, and Scott—decide to sing a total of six songs marked F, G, H, I, J, and K on the machine. The songs will be sung consecutively as solos, and each song will be performed exactly once. The following constraints govern the order of the songs:

    J must be performed earlier than H and earlier than F.

    G must be performed earlier than K and later than F.

    Phil will only sing I, J, or K.

    Renae will only sing G, H, or I.

    Scott will only sing F, G, or I.

    Whoever sings the first song cannot sing the last song.

19. Which one of the following is an acceptable schedule for the performance of the songs, in order from the first to last song performed?

  ❏ A. I, H, J, F, G, K

  ❏ B. I, K, J, H, F, G

  ❏ C. J, F, G, I, H, K

  ❏ D. J, G, F, K, H, I

  ❏ E. J, I, F, G, K, H

20. Which one of the following must be true about the program?

    ❑ A. Phil performs I.

    ❑ B. Renae performs F.

    ❑ C. Renae performs H.

    ❑ D. Scott performs G.

    ❑ E. Scott performs I.

21. Which one of the following is a complete and accurate list of the possible songs to be sung last at the bar?

    ❑ A. F, G, K

    ❑ B. F, H, K

    ❑ C. H, G, K

    ❑ D. H, I, K

    ❑ E. I, G, K

22. If I is performed first, which one of the following must be true?

    ❑ A. I is performed by Phil.

    ❑ B. I is performed by Renae.

    ❑ C. G is the fourth song performed.

    ❑ D. J is the second song performed.

    ❑ E. J is the third song performed.

23. Each of the following is an acceptable playlist of the songs performed, from first to last, *except*:

    ❑ A. J, F, G, H, K, I

    ❑ B. J, H, F, G, K, I

    ❑ C. J, I, F, G, K, H

    ❑ D. I, J, F, G, K, H

    ❑ E. I, J, F, H, G, K

24. If J is performed first, the songs performed second, third, and fourth, respectively, could be

    ❑ A. H, I, and F

    ❑ B. H, K, and F

    ❑ C. I, F, and G

    ❑ D. I, G and K

    ❑ E. I, H, and F

THIS IS THE END OF THE SECTION.

SECTION III—Reading Comprehension

Time—35 minutes

26 Questions

Directions: Each passage in this section is followed by a group of questions to be answered on the basis of what is stated or implied in the passage. For some of the questions, more than one of the choices could conceivably answer the question. However, you are to choose the best answer; that is, the response that most accurately and completely answers the question, and blacken the corresponding space on your answer sheet.

Across this wilderness, which is now the great plain of Europe, wandered a various fauna. At first there were hippopotami, rhinoceroses, mammoths, and elephants. The saber-toothed tiger was diminishing toward extinction. Then, as the air chilled, the

5   hippopotamus, and then other warmth-loving creatures, ceased to come so far north, and the saber-toothed tiger disappeared altogether. The woolly mammoth, the woolly rhinoceros, the musk ox, the bison, the aurochs, and the reindeer became prevalent, and the temperate vegetation gave place to plants of a more arctic type. The glaciers,

10   spread southward to the maximum of the Fourth Glacial Age (about 50,000 years ago), and then receded again. In the earlier phase, the Third Interglacial period, a certain number of small family groups of men (Homo Neanderthalensis) and probably of sub-men (Eoanthropus) wandered over the land, leaving nothing but their flint

15   implements to witness to their presence.

They probably used a multitude and variety of wooden implements also; they had probably learned much about the shapes of objects and the use of different shapes from wood, knowledge that they afterward applied to stone. But none of this wooden material has

20   survived; we can only speculate about its forms and uses. As the weather hardened to its maximum of severity, the Neanderthal men, already it would seem acquainted with the use of fire, began to seek shelter under rock ledges and in caves and so leave remains behind them.

25   This period also had a cave lion, a cave bear, and a cave hyena. These creatures had to be driven out of the caves and kept out of the caves

in which these early men wanted to squat and hide, and no doubt, fire
was an effective method of eviction and protection. Probably early men
did not go deeply into the caves, because they had no means of
30   lighting their recesses. They got in far enough to be out of the
weather, and stored wood and food in odd corners. Perhaps they
barricaded the cave mouths. Their only available light for going deeply
into the caverns would be torches.

What did these Neanderthal men hunt? Their only possible weapons for
35   killing such giant creatures as the mammoth or the cave bear, or even
the reindeer, were spears of wood, wooden clubs, and those big pieces
of flint they left behind them, the Chellean and Mousterian implements,
and probably their usual quarry was smaller game. But they did
certainly eat the flesh of the big beasts when they had a chance, and
40   perhaps they followed them when sick or when wounded by combats,
or took advantage of them when they were bogged or in trouble with
ice or water. (The Labrador Indians still kill the caribou with spears at
awkward river crossings.) At Dewlish, in Dorset, an artificial trench has
been found that is supposed to have been a Palaeolithic trap for
45   elephants.

We know that the Neanderthals partly ate their kill where it fell, but
they brought back the big narrow bones to the cave to crack and eat
at leisure, because few ribs and vertebrae are found in the caves, but
great quantities of cracked and split long bones. They used skins to
50   wrap about them, and the women probably dressed the skins.

We know also that they were right-handed like modern men, because
the left side of the brain (which serves the right side of the body) is
bigger than the right. But while the back parts of the brain—which
deal with sight and touch and the energy of the body—are well
55   developed, the front parts, which are connected with thought and
speech, are comparatively small. It was as big a brain as ours, but
different. This species of Homo had certainly a very different mentality
from ours. Its individuals were not merely simpler and lower than we
are; they were on another line. It may be they did not speak at all, or
60   very sparingly. They had nothing that we should call a language.

Source: Excerpt from *The Outline of History* by H.G. Wells, 1920
http://www.ibiblio.org/pub/docs/books/sherwood/Wells-Outline/Text/Part-I.htm

1. Which of the following would be a good title for this passage?
- ❑ A. Man versus Animal
- ❑ B. The Extinction of the Saber-Toothed Tiger
- ❑ C. The Life and Times of a Neanderthal
- ❑ D. The Spread of Fauna across Ancient Europe
- ❑ E. The Attack Patterns of Neanderthal Tribes

2. The author refers to the possibility of Neanderthals using wooden implements in order to

- ❏ A. Illustrate how they hunted their prey
- ❏ B. Suggest how they developed their stone weapons
- ❏ C. Debate the possibility of the Neanderthals having hunting patterns
- ❏ D. Show that previous studies proved the Neanderthals used them
- ❏ E. Demonstrate the sophistication of their craftsmanship

3. According to the passage, which of the following was NOT present in the Third Interglacial period?

- ❏ A. Saber-toothed tiger
- ❏ B. Cave bear
- ❏ C. Woolly mammoth
- ❏ D. Cave lion
- ❏ E. Reindeer

4. The passage specifies "implements" in line 16 in order to represent

- ❏ A. Bones
- ❏ B. Weapons
- ❏ C. Skins
- ❏ D. Torches
- ❏ E. Game

5. The passage suggests that Neanderthals were able to kill their prey by

- ❏ A. Hunting in large groups to bring down a large animal
- ❏ B. Using sophisticated weaponry
- ❏ C. Taking advantage of a prey's weakness
- ❏ D. Leaving traps for their prey
- ❏ E. Using fire as an offensive weapon

6. Which of the following would undermine the argument that Neanderthals did not have a language of their own?

- ❏ A. The presence of sophisticated hieroglyphics on the cave walls that translated into stories and events
- ❏ B. Organized storerooms of weapons, food, and skins found within the caves
- ❏ C. Studies that proved language came about due to specific relationships in the front part of the brain.
- ❏ D. Fossilized remains that prve Neanderthals congregated as a tribe
- ❏ E. Research from a leading authority that states language could be possible with a Neanderthals' brain configuration

FABRIZIO: I say thusly, that in many places in our histories you will find the Roman infantry to have defeated numberless cavalry, but you will never find them to have been defeated by men on foot because of some defect they may have had in their arms or because of

5   advantage the enemy had in his.

For if their manner of arming had been defective, it was necessary for them to follow one of two courses: either when they found one who was better armed than they, not to go on further with the conquest, or that they take up the manner of the foreigner, and leave off theirs.

10   And since neither ensued, there follows, what can be easily conjectured, that this method of arming was better than that of anyone else.

This has not yet occurred with the German infantry; for it has been seen that anytime they have had to combat with men on foot

15   organized and as obstinate as they, they have made a bad showing; which results from the disadvantage they have in trying themselves against the arms of the enemy.

When Filippo Visconti, Duke of Milan, was assaulted by eighteen thousand Swiss, he sent against them Count Carmingnuola, who was

20   his Captain at that time. This man with six thousand cavalry and a few infantry went to encounter them, and, coming hand to hand with them, was repulsed with very great damage.

Whence Carmingnuola as a prudent man quickly recognized the power of the enemy arms, and how much they prevailed against cavalry, and

25   the weakness of cavalry against those on foot so organized; and regrouping his forces, again went to meet the Swiss, and as they came near he made his men-at-arms descend from their horses, and in that manner fought with them, and killed all but three thousand, who, seeing themselves consumed without having any remedy, threw their

30   arms on the ground and surrendered.

COSIMO: Whence arises such a disadvantage?

FABRIZIO: I have told you a little while ago, but since you have not understood it, I will repeat it to you. The German infantry…has almost no armor in defending itself, and use pikes and swords for

35   offense.

They come with these arms and order of battle to meet the enemy, who (if he is well equipped with armor to defend himself, as were the men-at-arms of Carmingnuola who made them descend to their feet) comes with his sword and order of battle to meet him, and he has no

40   other difficulty than to come near the Swiss until he makes contact with them with the sword; for as soon as he makes contact with them, he combats them safely, for the German cannot use the pike against the enemy who is next to him because of the length of the staff, so he must use the sword, which is useless to him, as he has no armor and

45   has to meet an enemy that is (protected) fully by armor.

Whence, whoever considers the advantages and disadvantages of one and the other, will see that the one without armor has no remedy, but the one well armored will have no difficulty in overcoming the first blow and the first passes of the pike.

50   COSIMO: I see that those with Carmingnuola were men-at-arms, who, although they were on foot, were all covered with iron (armor), and, therefore, could make the attempt that they made; so that I think it would be necessary to arm the infantry in the same way if they want to make a similar attempt.

55   FABRIZIO: If you had remembered how I said the Romans were armed, you would not think this way. For an infantryman who has his head covered with iron, his breast protected by a cuirass and a shield, his arms and legs with armor, is much more apt to defend himself from pikes, and enter among them, than is a man-at-arms (cavalryman) on
60   foot.

Source: Excerpt from *The Seven Books on The Art of War* by Niccolo Machiavelli, Citizen and Secretary of Florence, 1520.
http://www.constitution.org/mac/artofwar.htm

7. What kind of combat were the Germans unprepared to handle?
   - ❑ A. Long-range battles
   - ❑ B. Close-quarter combat
   - ❑ C. Horseback combat
   - ❑ D. Fighting in the trenches
   - ❑ E. Being outnumbered

8. Who used his tactical smarts in this story?
   - ❑ A. Fabricio
   - ❑ B. Cosimo
   - ❑ C. Viscotti
   - ❑ D. Carmingnuola
   - ❑ E. Duke of Milan

9. The Germans used all of the following in combat *except*:
   - ❑ A. Horses
   - ❑ B. Armor
   - ❑ C. Pikes
   - ❑ D. Swords
   - ❑ E. Armies

10. The passage uses the word "arms" in line 24 to mean:
   - ❑ A. Limbs
   - ❑ B. Armor
   - ❑ C. Pikes
   - ❑ D. Shields
   - ❑ E. Cavalry

11. What was the key to the Romans beating their opponents?
    - ❏ A. Adopting their opponent's methods
    - ❏ B. Outnumbering their opponents
    - ❏ C. Attacking their opponents first
    - ❏ D. Stealth combat with their opponents
    - ❏ E. Riding on horseback

12. What trait does the Roman soldier appear to have, according to Fabricio?
    - ❏ A. Stubbornness
    - ❏ B. Obedience
    - ❏ C. Brutality
    - ❏ D. Cowardliness
    - ❏ E. Observation

Very early in the history of civilization, man must have felt the need of a means of measuring time. In the far-distant Stone Age he must have soon noted that the shadows cast by familiar objects moved in a regular manner, according to the hour, and no doubt made use of this

5   knowledge to arrange meeting places near to such objects when the shadows should have reached a given mark.

In the heavens above he observed the godlike progress of the sun, so regular in its movements, and his own habits of waking and working and sleeping must, willy-nilly, depend upon it. Later on, as he learned

10   to know and recognize the ordered procession of the stars, he had a clock by night as well as by day, and as the ages moved on and existence became more complicated he divided periods of time into "moons" and then into years, all by means of the heavenly bodies.

But this came slowly, and much more slowly came a measuring

15   instrument. We do not hear of the sundial until some twenty-seven centuries ago, which is quite a brief span in the many millions of years that have passed since man first realized that "time flies." The sundial, however, was invented long before these known records and, after all, was only a step onward from the cave man's habit of using fixed

20   objects and their shadows to mark the flight of time.

But as the sundial depended upon the beams of a sun that did not always shine during the day and never during the night, it could not entirely satisfy, and so man's inventive mind produced the clepsydra, or water clock. This was but a simple contrivance, but nevertheless it

25   was the first time machine and from it evolved all the complicated mechanisms of the modern clock. At first it was merely a jar of water with a small hole at the bottom, which permitted the contents to drip out at a steady uniform rate. As the level of the water in the jar sank, the hours that had passed since the vessel was last filled were

30   indicated.

The first water clock was, however, but a rough-and-ready machine, and the next onward step was the addition of a smaller jar above, from which the water dripped into the larger one. As the level rose in the latter it carried up with it a float, which marked the hours against an indicator upon the side of the jar.

Source: Excerpt from Chapter 5 of *The Young Folk's Book of Invention* by T.C. Bridges, 1925.
http://www.usgennet.org/usa/topic/preservation/science/inventions/chpt5.htm

13. What was the point of this passage?
   - ❑ A. Shadow patterns during the day
   - ❑ B. Sun- and star-watching by man
   - ❑ C. How the sundial was created
   - ❑ D. The origin and development of time keeping devices
   - ❑ E. Water vessels

14. Which one of these devices was invented first?
   - ❑ A. The modern clock
   - ❑ B. The two-jar water clock
   - ❑ C. The sundial
   - ❑ D. The clepsydra
   - ❑ E. The wristwatch

15. Which one of these things was NOT used by early man to tell time?
   - ❑ A. The dripping of water
   - ❑ B. Shadows on objects
   - ❑ C. The arrangement of stars
   - ❑ D. The level of water in a jar
   - ❑ E. The brightness of moonlight

16. The word "contrivance" is used in line 24 to signify:
   - ❑ A. A machine
   - ❑ B. A thought
   - ❑ C. A shadow
   - ❑ D. A sundial
   - ❑ E. A unit of time

17. What piece of information is critical for the invention of the clepsydra?
   - ❑ A. The length of a shadow
   - ❑ B. The position of the stars
   - ❑ C. The position of the sun
   - ❑ D. The volume of a water drop
   - ❑ E. The size of a sundial

18. If the author were to add another paragraph to this passage, what would be a logical topic for that paragraph?

❑   A.   How the sundial helped shape organizational behavior in man

❑   B.   The precise workings of a modern clock

❑   C.   How the constellations were defined and cataloged

❑   D.   How man improved on the two-jar clepsydra

❑   E.   What the markings on the float looked like and signified

So great had been the incline of the schooner that the end of the yard of the mainsail was plunged three or four feet into the crest of a wave. When it emerged, Martin Holt, who had been astride on it, had disappeared. A cry was heard, uttered by the sailing-master, whose

5   arm could be seen wildly waving amid the whiteness of the foam. The sailors rushed to the side and flung out one a rope, another a cask, a third a spar—in short, any object of which Martin Holt might lay hold. At the moment when I struggled up to my feet, I caught sight of a massive substance, which cleft the air and vanished in the whirl of

10   the waves.

Was this a second accident? No! It was a voluntary action, a deed of self-sacrifice. Having finished his task, Hunt had thrown himself into the sea, that he might save Martin Holt.

"Two men overboard!"

15   Yes, two—one to save the other. And were they not about to perish together?

The two heads rose to the foaming surface of the water.

Hunt was swimming vigorously, cutting through the waves, and was nearing Martin Holt.

20   "They are lost! Both lost!" exclaimed the captain. "The boat, West, the boat!"

"If you give the order to lower it," answered West, "I will be the first to get into it, although at the risk of my life. But I must have the order."

In unspeakable suspense the ship's crew and myself had witnessed this scene. None thought of the position of the Halbrane, which was

25   sufficiently dangerous; all eyes were fixed upon the terrible waves. Now fresh cries, the frantic cheers of the crew, rose above the roar of the elements. Hunt had reached the drowning man just as he sank out of sight, had seized hold of him, and was supporting him with his left arm, while Holt, incapable of movement, swayed helplessly about like

30   a weed. With the other arm Hunt was swimming bravely and making way towards the schooner.

A minute, which seemed endless, passed. The two men, the one dragging the other, were hardly to be distinguished in the midst of the surging waves.

35   At last Hunt reached the schooner, and caught one of the lines hanging over the side.

In a minute Hunt and Martin Holt were hoisted on board; the latter was laid down at the foot of the foremast, and the former was quite

40 ready to go to his work. Holt was speedily restored by the aid of
vigorous rubbing; his senses came back, and he opened his eyes.

"Martin Holt," said Captain Len Guy, who was leaning over him, "you
have been brought back from very far…"

"Yes, yes, captain," answered Holt, as he looked about him with a
searching gaze, "but who saved me?"

45 "Hunt," cried the boatswain, "Hunt risked his life for you."

As the latter was hanging back, Hurliguerly pushed him toward Martin
Holt, whose eyes expressed the liveliest gratitude.

"Hunt," said he, "you have saved me. But for you I should have been lost. I
thank you."

50 Hunt made no reply.

"Hunt," resumed Captain Len Guy. "don't you hear?"

The man seemed not to have heard.

"Hunt," said Martin Holt again, "come near to me. I thank you. I want
to shake hands with you."

55 And he held out his right hand. Hunt stepped back a few paces, shaking his
head with the air of a man who did not want so many compliments for a thing
so simple, and quietly walked forward to join his shipmates, who were working
vigorously under the orders of West.

Source: Excerpt from *An Antarctic Mystery*, by Jules Verne, 1865
http://www.literature.org/authors/verne-jules/an-antartic-mystery/index.html

19. What was the author's main intention of capturing with this passage?
   - ❑ A. A day onboard the Halbrane
   - ❑ B. The leadership style of Capt. Len Guy
   - ❑ C. The rescue of Martin Holt by seaman Hunt
   - ❑ D. A sailor's swimming ability
   - ❑ E. Navigating through rough weather

20. Who is the "he" referred to in line 48 of the passage?
   - ❑ A. Hunt
   - ❑ B. Hurliguerly
   - ❑ C. Len Guy
   - ❑ D. Martin Holt
   - ❑ E. West

21. What personal trait does the author imply that sailor West has in this story?
   - ❑ A. Heroism
   - ❑ B. Determination
   - ❑ C. Foolishness
   - ❑ D. Responsibility
   - ❑ E. Shyness

22. What is the "massive substance" referred to by the author in line 9?
  ❏ A. The waves
  ❏ B. Martin Holt
  ❏ C. The Halbrane
  ❏ D. The mainsail
  ❏ E. Sailor Hunt

23. If Captain Guy were to bestow an award onto sailor Hunt for his actions, what would the award be for?
  ❏ A. Valor
  ❏ B. Stamina
  ❏ C. Swimming
  ❏ D. Navigation
  ❏ E. Loyalty

24. Assuming this story is set in modern times, which one of these devices would NOT have been helpful to the entire crew after Martin Holt was swept offboard?
  ❏ A. Floating life preserver
  ❏ B. Inflatable life jacket
  ❏ C. Battery-powered searchlights
  ❏ D. Real-time weather reports
  ❏ E. On-board radar system

25. Which of the following best expresses the meaning of "liveliest" as that word is used in line 47 of the passage?
  ❏ A. Equivocating
  ❏ B. Most vivacious
  ❏ C. Most sincere
  ❏ D. Most combative
  ❏ E. Ambivalent

26. Which of the following can you deduce about the end of the yard of the mainsail as described in line 2 of the passage?
  ❏ A. It is the most dangerous place on the ship.
  ❏ B. It is normally close to the waterline.
  ❏ C. It is not normally a place Martin Holt sits.
  ❏ D. It is not normally close to the waterline.
  ❏ E. It is normally a place Martin Holt sits.

THIS IS THE END OF THE SECTION.

SECTION IV—Logical Reasoning

Time—35 minutes

24 Questions

Directions: The questions in this section are based on the reasoning contained in brief statements or passages. For some questions, more than one of the choices could conceivably answer the question. However, you are to choose the best answer; that is, the response that most accurately and completely answers the question. You should not make assumptions that are by commonsense standards implausible, superfluous, or incompatible with the passage. After you have chosen the best answer, blacken the corresponding space on your answer sheet.

1. A study of grizzly bears and brown bears is being conducted by biologists in Montana. The study analyzes the chemical content of hair plucked from the bellies of tranquilized bears. The hair of grizzly bears contained a higher ratio of [X] to [Y] than the hair of the brown bears. The higher the ratio of [X] to [Y] in the bear hair, the more blueberries the bear had in its diet. Biologists have observed brown bears eating blueberries.

   The statements above, if true, most strongly support which one of the following conclusions:

   ❏ A. The diet of the grizzly bears included at least some blueberries.

   ❏ B. The blueberries in the diet of the brown bears were higher in [X] than was the blueberries in the diets of other types of bears.

   ❏ C. The diet of brown bears is richer in [Y] than the diet of grizzly bears.

   ❏ D. The diets of grizzly bears and brown bears both contained less [X] than [Y].

   ❏ E. The process of collecting the hairs from the bears altered the ratio of [X] to [Y] in the hairs of both the grizzly bears and the brown bears.

2. As the war dragged on into the 1990s, the chief of staff gave the order for the army to be vaccinated against orthopox. It was a grim but necessary calculation because the mortality rate from vaccination is approximately 1 in 100. However, the death rate of troops exposed to orthopox with no prior protection was closer to 1 in 5. The army's cohesion as a fighting force could be preserved with a casualty rate caused by vaccination.

Each of the following is an assumption required by the writer's argument *except*:

- ❏ A. Orthopox is an extremely lethal disease if caught by an unvaccinated person but a mild one otherwise.
- ❏ B. A casualty rate of greater than 20 percent is unacceptable in modern warfare.
- ❏ C. An army can lose one percent of its manpower and still remain an effective, cohesive fighting force.
- ❏ D. Measures to prevent soldiers from becoming infected with orthopox if they are not vaccinated are ineffective and difficult to implement under battlefield conditions.
- ❏ E. To expose the army to orthopox without vaccinations would have weakened the general's army so much that it could have been rendered ineffective.

3. Peshawan's climate is typically warm and humid during the annual monsoon season. But during monsoon periods when the average daily temperature and humidity throughout the region were slightly lower than their normal levels, the country's yield of rice crops more than doubled. Due to expected global warming, the region's average humidity and temperature will remain at these modestly depressed levels for the upcoming centuries. However, it is predicted that the local rice crop will not increase as a result.

Which of the following statements, if true, most helps to resolve the apparent paradox in the information above?

- ❏ A. The decreased temperature and humidity in the upcoming seasons will increase the yield of all the cash crops that Peshawan grows, not just rice.
- ❏ B. Increased rice production will lead to a higher population in the country of Peshawan.
- ❏ C. Agricultural studies have shown that rice plants flourish under daily temperature and humidity conditions that are slightly cooler than Peshawan's climate in the last decade.
- ❏ D. The recent climate shift has been too recent for populations of rice-eating insect pests to become re-established.
- ❏ E. The monsoon cycle is not perfectly predictable. Next year, if the monsoon is late, the average daily temperature and humidity will not be slightly lower, preventing the rice crop from sustaining its higher yield.

QUESTIONS 4–5

A powerful, convincing presentation to Congress by the veteran head of the AARG (American Automotive Research Group) conclusively demonstrated that mandating car manufacturers to install side-impact airbags in cars driven by teenagers has resulted in fewer teen fatalities over the past decade. Compared to the prior decade when the installation of airbags was not mandated, teen fatalities in automobile crashes have declined by over half.

4. Which one of the following, if true, most substantially strengthens the preceding argument?

   ❑ A. Over the past decade, the number of teenagers driving SUVs has doubled compared to the prior one.

   ❑ B. Automobile accidents involving teenagers have decreased sharply over the past ten years.

   ❑ C. The number of teenage drivers on the nation's highways has decreased by half over the past decade.

   ❑ D. Over the past twenty years, the types of vehicles that teenagers drive have shifted back and forth between light, sporty cars to heavy pickup trucks, and back to cars.

   ❑ E. The number of serious automobile accidents involving teenagers has remained steady over the past five years.

5. Which one of the following most accurately describes the method of reasoning the writer uses to reach the conclusion of the argument?

   ❑ A. Accepting a claim on the basis of authority

   ❑ B. Accepting a claim on the basis of public opinion

   ❑ C. Basing a generalized conclusion on representative groups of data

   ❑ D. Demonstrating that a measure claimed to be effective in achieving a certain effect would actually make achieving the effect more difficult

   ❑ E. Finding a claim to be false on the grounds that it would actually have negative consequences if true

6. Local high schools came under a barrage of heavy criticism when a recent report came out showing that Metropolis was among the top ten cities in the nation with the highest illiteracy rates in high-school graduates. Data for the report was generated by conducting a telephone marketing survey that asked all Metropolis residents over the age of 18 whether they were high school graduates and whether or not they read the local newspaper. A Metropolis high-school principal objected that the conclusion arrived at by the report was inaccurate and misleading.

The high-school principal can most properly criticize the reasoning by which the report reached its conclusion for not taking into account:

   ❑ A. The fact that some people taking the phone survey might not tell the truth about their level of education or their reading habits

   ❑ B. The fact that the residents might not have completed their high school reading through remedial education programs

   ❑ C. How the data received might have been skewed because the survey was done on Monday afternoon, when most high-school graduates may have been at work

   ❑ D. How the data received might have been skewed because the survey was done on Saturday morning, when most high-school graduates may have been at home

   ❑ E. The fact that whether or not a resident read the local newspaper was inconclusive in proving that a survey respondent was illiterate

7. Ringed planets—heavenly bodies that are accompanied by a mass of rocky particles that orbit in a tight equatorial plane—are very similar in appearance to Oort asteroids, which are circled by icy ringlets. The ring material surrounding most asteroids contains at least 51% hydrogen. All planets but the ones farthest from the sun radiate enough heat to dissipate hydrogen. Accordingly, any loose ring material examined by astronomers that contains little or no hydrogen can be said to have come from a ringed planet.

The argument depends on assuming which one of the following statements?

   ❑ A. None of the Oort asteroids has ever been hot enough to dissipate the hydrogen found in its ring particles.

   ❑ B. No asteroids are more similar in appearance to ringed planets than Oort asteroids.

   ❑ C. Most ring particles, when first formed, contain roughly the same percentage of hydrogen.

   ❑ D. Asteroids are too cool to substantially dissipate their hydrogen.

   ❑ E. Ringed planets that are not hot enough to dissipate hydrogen are hot enough to dissipate helium.

8. Alan: All college graduates are superb debaters.

Timothy: I strongly disagree—I've met amazing debaters who were plumbers or mailmen.

Timothy's reply to Alan demonstrates that he has taken Alan's remark to mean which of the following?

   ❑ A. College graduates are likely to be better debaters than plumbers or mailmen.

   ❑ B. Every superb debater is a college graduate.

   ❑ C. Plumbers and mailmen can be just as good at debating as college graduates.

   ❑ D. There is a correlation between attending college and learning to debate superbly.

   ❑ E. Plumbers and mailmen don't attend college.

9. Backbeat Music has been involved in a major lawsuit with its leading artist over involving copyright law, and its stock value tumbled. According to the leading business magazines, whenever an entertainment company loses a lawsuit, its stock is sure to plummet. It's safe to conclude that Backbeat Music lost its suit with its leading artist.

Which one of the following contains flawed reasoning that most closely parallels that in the argument above?

☐   A. Whenever a business school graduate is hired by Cowtop Consulting, he or she receives a $5,000 signing bonus. Therefore, Mr. Elad, the most recent business school graduate, must have been hired by Cowtop Consulting, because he just received $5,000.

☐   B. Subway systems that don't want funding cuts made to their budget need high ridership. If riders are treated rudely, they won't ride in great numbers. Therefore, subway systems will always treat riders with great courtesy.

☐   C. Whenever the prime minister shows a lack of leadership on arms control, respect for her country's international stature begins to decline. Therefore, to avoid diminishing international stature, the prime minister should show leadership on arms control.

☐   D. If Zap Comics advertises its graphic novels effectively, their sales volume will increase. Zap Comic's sales have increased; therefore, it is likely that the company did not advertise its products effectively.

☐   E. Whenever WidgetCo wants to increase sales of their widgets, they will start selling lots of widgets on the Internet auction site, eBay. WidgetCo wants to increase the sales of their widgets, so they will immediately move to selling on eBay.

10. Thomas Hobbes would have viewed a totalitarian government as a blessing. According to his very words in his book *Leviathan*, he felt that without strong government, the life of the average person would be "solitary, poor, nasty, brutish, and short," and you cannot help but agree with him.

Which one of the following is the strongest criticism of the statement above?

☐   A. The author never actually met Thomas Hobbes.

☐   B. *Leviathan* is considered to be an outdated book of political philosophy by many scholars.

☐   C. The author does not offer a biographical sketch of Thomas Hobbes.

☐   D. The author does not offer any stronger argument then the presentation of the quote.

☐   E. The author does not elucidate what a "strong government" would actually do to remedy the life of the average person.

QUESTIONS 11–12

Cayuga City has doubled the length of its commuter rail line. The city council, which has laid out in excess of $40 million for the track, doesn't expect the train to run for the next five years. The cost of commuting by automobile continues to rise at more than 15% each year. It is logical to expect that ridership will be higher overall when it opens in five years than if it opened at present.

11. If the preceding statements are true, which one of the following is most likely to be true on the basis of them?

    ❏ A. The average cost of rail projects in states surrounding Cayuga City is $40 million.

    ❏ B. The city council was unclear on how much the cost of the rail line would really be, so their "best guess" estimate came in at the proposed $40 million.

    ❏ C. Due to a worldwide shortage of durable Rearden metal, the city council will have to increase the price of rail tickets in order to cover the cost of installing the track.

    ❏ D. Over the last nine years, the total cost of commuting by car has risen by 200%.

    ❏ E. Over the last nine years, the price of gas at the local service station pumps has risen by 200%.

12. Which one of the following, if true, most seriously weakens the argument?

    ❏ A. The cost of the track should have been only $20 million; because the construction ran over budget, the price of the track doubled.

    ❏ B. The longer rail line will not allow the train company to make more trips per day.

    ❏ C. Given past advances in construction technology, it is likely that the rail line will open in only four years, not five.

    ❏ D. Because the track construction ran over budget, some experts predict that the price of a rail ticket will likely cost double what it would today by the time the train starts to run.

    ❏ E. The Bell Monte canning company, which employs more than 40% of all commuters in Cayuga City, will relocate its plant in the next three years.

13. Sally: I hope that my mom isn't making broccoli again for dinner tonight, because I hate eating it.

    Bob: You should count yourself lucky. If you liked broccoli you'd eat it more often, and you would just hate it.

Which one of the following is the strongest criticism of Bob's statement?

☐ A. Bob incorrectly assumes that the more someone likes a given food, the more they will eat it.

☐ B. Bob's logic is circular.

☐ C. Bob is not aware that Sally's dislike of broccoli stems from the fact that it upsets her stomach.

☐ D. Bob's logic is premised on the fact that Sally is being truthful in her dislike of broccoli.

☐ E. Broccoli has such healthy qualities that she should overcome any objections to eating it.

14. Someone who develops an allergic reaction to smoking a cigarette will often develop a strong distaste for brands of tobacco that have the most distinctive flavor, whether or not that brand caused the reaction. This phenomenon explains why some smokers are especially likely to develop strong loyalty to some brands and aversions to others.

Which one of the following, if true, provides the strongest support for the explanation?

☐ A. People who develop reactions to food such as shellfish and honey also develop a strong distaste for certain kinds of food.

☐ B. According to the American Medical Association, smokers are less likely than the general public to see a connection between their health and the cigarettes they smoke.

☐ C. Smokers tend to have more acute taste in cigarettes than nonsmokers and can easily pick out tobacco with a strong flavor.

☐ D. Market research shows that smokers are more likely than nonsmokers to be adventurous when trying new things.

☐ E. Smokers typically recover more slowly than other people do from allergic reactions.

15. Thousands of Chinook salmon return to spawn in the Sacramento and American rivers every spring. Although the salmon leave their individual creeks at the headwaters of these rivers as fry and spend much of their life in the Pacific, they always return to the exact same spot they were hatched to spawn the next generation. Salmon have extremely poor vision and do not navigate by landmarks or the magnetic pole. Therefore, it is clear that they use their sense of smell to detect the exact mineral composition and flow of the water in a stream, allowing them to follow it back to their place of birth.

This argument seeks to do which one of the following?

❑ A. Derive a general conclusion about all members of a group from facts known about representative members of that group

❑ B. Establish the validity of one explanation for a phenomenon by excluding alternative explanations

❑ C. Support, by describing a suitable mechanism, how a certain phenomenon can occur

❑ D. Conclude that members of two groups are likely to share a certain ability because of other characteristics they share

❑ E. Demonstrate that a specific rule applies to all species of Pacific salmon

16. By refusing to ban timber mills in our country's endangered rain forests, the government has put the financial well-being of paper and pulp barons above the health of our planet. No doubt the government would support the remaining industrial giants if they decided to donate the forest's devastated animals to the fur trade or use the remaining tree stumps to store nuclear waste. After all, these actions would be no more dangerous to the health of our environment.

The author of this paragraph makes her case

❑ A. From direct observation of the fur trade and nuclear industry.

❑ B. From experience with the paper and pulp industries.

❑ C. By citing authority.

❑ D. By drawing from analogy.

❑ E. Appealing to common sense.

17. Mr. Lynch reported seeing a UFO buzzing the local community while strolling home after an evening party. He has a strong reputation in the local community for truthfully and accurately reporting what he has seen. However, the FBI is correct to disregard his report of seeing a UFO that evening.

Which one of the following, if true, best resolves the discrepancy between the witness's reputed truthfulness and the FBI's conclusion to disregard his testimony?

❑ A. Witnesses report that Mr. Lynch has been known to indulge in alcoholic beverages whenever invited to a party.

❑ B. Mr. Lynch has served credibly many times as an expert witness in cases involving weather disturbances.

❑ C. Multiple people have testified that Mr. Lynch did not drink alcohol at that evening's party because he expected to be the designated driver for a group of his friends.

❑ D. An F-14 fighter jet reported seeing a saucer-shaped object flying over the community on the evening in question.

❑ E. Atmospheric phenomena such as ball lightning can be mistaken by even truthful people as UFOs.

QUESTIONS 18–19

By passing more and more regulations allegedly to protect the beaches, the state government here in Ecotopia is driving the manufacturing industry away. And when the manufacturing industry leaves, the workers will either have to go on welfare or leave the state for better paying jobs. The number of environmental measures passed has doubled each year for the past four years. The local fertilizer and smelting industries have been repeatedly fined for fouling the state beaches with crude oil, even though they have nothing to do with the pollution.

18. The author's argument that regulations designed to protect the beach will cause workers to leave or go on welfare is most weakened if the following statement is true:

❑ A. Ecotopia's neighboring states also have strict laws to protect their beaches, and the manufacturing industry is thriving and has no plans to move.

❑ B. Four years ago, only one environmental measure was passed.

❑ C. The majority of the workers who leave Ecotopia are not employed with the fertilizer or smelting industries.

❑ D. So far, the number of manufacturers who have left the state is small.

❑ E. The unemployment rate has doubled with the passing of each new environmental measure.

19. For the argument to be logically correct, it must make which one of the following assumptions?

❑ A. Fertilizer plants and smelting factories use oil in their industrial processes, so therefore they were justly fined for their polluting of the state beach.

❑ B. States that border Ecotopia offer special tax breaks and incentives to get businesses to move.

❑ C. A state that borders Ecotopia managed to get Avalon Industries to leave, displacing 100 workers and putting 75 on state welfare.

❑ D. Strictly enforced measures to protect beaches are enough of a burden to cause industries to move to a different state.

❑ E. Strictly enforced measures to protect beaches are enough of a burden to cause the fertilizer and smelting industries to move to a different state.

20. Dr. Goldberg's economics department teaches a maximum of two introductory-level classes in any one academic quarter. After the first quarter, only upper-division economics classes are taught for the remainder of the year. Therefore, it is false to say that Dr. Goldberg will be teaching more than two introductory-level classes in economics this year.

This style of reasoning most closely parallels which one of the following arguments?

   ❑ A. Businesses in the financial district will be reassessed for tax purposes by the end of the year and ABC Company's headquarters is in that district, so ABC's tax burden will be higher next year.

   ❑ B. Extremely hazardous activities utilizing explosives and excavation equipment are charged a special "hazard fee" by the city. Because the Orion mining company utilizes high explosives and excavation equipment in its work, it will be charged the city's special hazard fee.

   ❑ C. Newly built condominiums are exempt from property taxes for three years, and the newly built condos in the city's downtown district were only completed last year, so these condos will not be subject to property taxes next year.

   ❑ D. The updated nuisance laws do not apply to open lots purchased before 1896. Furthermore, only the first section of the law applies to open lots purchased between 1850 and 1880. Therefore, the updated nuisance law applies to the Brown family lot, because it was purchased in the 1898.

   ❑ E. The United Growers' farm co-operative will be fully planted by April. Because fully planted farms are charged water at new rates by the local treatment plant, come April the farm co-operative will be taxed according to these new rates.

21. Mail and package shipping services suffer when a company combines express mail and freight service. By dividing its attention between its freight and express mail customers, a shipping company serves neither particularly well. Therefore, if a shipping company is going to be a successful business, then it must concentrate exclusively on one of these two areas.

For the argument to be logically correct, it must make which one of the following assumptions?

   ❑ A. Express mail and freight service have little in common with each other.

   ❑ B. The first priority of a shipping company is to be financially successful.

   ❑ C. Unless a shipping company serves its customers well, it will not be considered "customer friendly."

   ❑ D. If a shipping company concentrates on express mail service, it will be a successful business.

   ❑ E. Customers who want express mail service rarely want freight service as well.

22. Doctors in medical school are rarely exposed to the way the public health system operates. It's unlikely that they've even taken a course that delves into public health as a critical component in our modern medical system. Far more time is devoted to obscure anatomical discussions than to discussions about how to keep the public healthy and protected against disease. For the most part, doctors only learn about public health if they decide to pursue a position in the field as part of their post-graduate training.

For the argument to be logically correct, which one of the following conditions must not be true?

❑ A. How the public health system works can be learned at most medical schools, where it can be offered as an optional course if the students request it.

❑ B. Nine out of ten doctors finish their year of residency in public health clinics, where they serve the public as general practitioners.

❑ C. The role of protecting the health of the average citizen against disease is primarily shouldered by small city clinics run by registered nurses, not doctors.

❑ D. Discussions of anatomical irregularities, no matter how rare or obscure, have the potential to impact public health.

❑ E. The topic of public health is covered in the course textbook for "General Surgical Practice."

23. Isn't it wrong for politicians to lie when they make campaign promises? Aren't politicians similar to other professions in that we bring them in to fix problems? Surely, we would not tolerate being lied to about the time it would take to paint our house from the painter, or the cost of trimming the lawn from a gardening service. Politicians who lie to get into office violate our good faith contract as well, which is an abuse of our trust.

The conclusion of the argument is best expressed by which of the following?

❑ A. The vast majority of politicians often lie just to get into office.

❑ B. Politicians who lie to get into office abuse our trust in the same way a gardener or painter would if they lied to us on the time or cost of a project.

❑ C. We should hold politicians to the same standard of truth as we do gardeners and painters.

❑ D. Politicians who lie to voters violate their good faith contracts with their constituents.

❑ E. It is wrong for politicians to lie in their campaign promises.

24. Jeannie: We should not go to that restaurant. It's too crowded.

Amy: Yes we should. Restaurants that are empty usually have bad food.

Which one of the following most closely parallels the questionable reasoning used by Amy in the interchange above?

❑ A. Jeannie: Kendall shouldn't be a manager. He's too nice.
Amy: Yes he should. People will work harder if their manager is nice.

❑ B. Jeannie: We shouldn't go to see that movie. I heard that it was very scary.
Amy: Yes we should. I like scary movies.

❑ C. Jeannie: We should rent this office. It's in a great location.
Amy: No we shouldn't. Great locations are usually too expensive.

❑ D. Jeannie: We shouldn't purchase a light-colored carpet for the living room. It will show too much dirt.
Amy: Yes we should. A light-colored carpet will make the room look bigger.

❑ E. Jeannie: Brian should not eat that soup. It's too salty.
Amy: Yes he should. Soup that is too sweet doesn't taste good.

Answer Key for Practice Exam 1

SECTION I—Logical Reasoning

1. C	10. B	19. D
2. B	11. B	20. E
3. E	12. E	21. D
4. B	13. C	22. D
5. D	14. D	23. D
6. C	15. B	24. E
7. C	16. E	25. A
8. A	17. C	
9. C	18. E	

1. The claim that you must examine in this question is "horses will avoid eating hay if they sense something in it that will make them ill." You must examine each of the choices to see which of them provides the strongest basis for this claim.

   Choice C is correct. The claim that horses avoid eating hay if they sense something in it that will make them ill requires the assumption that at least some horses are capable of sensing that hay is moldy before they eat it. Choice A is incorrect. The claim states that timothy hay is the only kind of hay in the new load, and that some of this hay has mold that will make horses ill if they eat it. Whether or not the mold that makes horses ill can be found in other types of hay besides timothy is irrelevant to the claim. Choice B is incorrect. The only animals at issue are horses. Whether or not the mold that makes horses ill can make other animals ill as well is irrelevant to the claim. Choice D is incorrect. While the assumption that the mold in the timothy hay cannot be eliminated without destroying the hay may provide a rationale for feeding the hay to the horses despite the presence of mold, it is irrelevant to the claim that horses will avoid eating hay if they sense something in it that will make them ill. Choice E is incorrect. The claim focuses solely on the mold in the timothy hay that will make horses ill if they eat it. The fact that the timothy hay contains another type of mold that will not make horses ill if they eat it is irrelevant to the claim.

2. The argument that you must examine in this question is "If everyone thought like that, everyone would walk on the crust, and the crust would be destroyed." You must examine each of the choices to determine which of them most weakens this argument.

   Choice B is correct. Chris treats Darrell's statement about the consequences of an action (if just one person walks on the crust, it won't be destroyed) as though instead it were about the consequences of everyone believing the statement ("if everyone thought like that..."). This weakens Chris's argument, because the statement he is disproving is different than the one he is arguing against. Choice A is incorrect. Darrell's statement is about the consequence of an action, not a statement about an action itself. Choice C is incorrect. Chris's argument focuses on the consequences of everyone believing the statement that one person stepping on the crust wouldn't destroy it. That is not the same as treating the statement as if it were a statement that everyone believed (without any consideration of the consequences of that belief). As a result, Choice B is a better choice. Choice D is incorrect. Chris's argument does not address whether there are circumstances in which stepping on crytobiotic crust may be justified. Choice E is incorrect. Chris's argument does not attempt to undermine Darrell's statement by calling Darrell's character into question.

3. **Choice E** is correct. This statement on its own cannot explain why more amateurs than professionals won ribbons at this particular show. Choices A and D are incorrect. If either A or D is true, then statistically this could explain why more amateurs than professionals won ribbons. Choice B is incorrect. If this is true, this provides a reasonable explanation as to why more amateurs than professionals won ribbons. Choice C is incorrect. If this is true, then it provides a reasonable explanation as to why more amateurs than professionals won ribbons. Although one might normally assume that a professional has more skill than an amateur, an amateur trying his or her hardest when a professional is not may be more successful than the professional.

4. The conclusion that you must examine in this question is that "online advertisements have influenced the thought patterns of American children." You just examine each of the choices to determine which one, if true, makes this conclusion logical.

    Choice B is correct. Viewing more than 500,000 online advertisements qualifies as being exposed to them in great quantity. So if this assumption, that anything to which a child is exposed in great quantity influences the child's thought patterns, is true, then it logically follows that online advertisements have influenced the thought patterns of American children. Choice A is incorrect. If the statement noted that children predominantly used the Internet at school rather than at home, this might be the correct choice. However, at it stands, there is nothing in the statement about use of the Internet in school and therefore this choice cannot be correct. Choice C is incorrect. While the inability to ignore or avoid online advertisements might be a reason why children view so many of them, this assumption says nothing about the impact of such advertisements on a child's thought patterns. Choice D is incorrect. The assumption that some children find online advertisements more interesting than the website on which the advertisement is displayed, if true, may explain why children view so many of them, but it says nothing about the impact of such advertisements on a child's thought patterns. Choice E is incorrect. This assumption states only that "certain forms of communication" affect a child's thought patterns. Because it does not specify online advertisements as one of these "certain forms of communications," this assumption is not sufficient to make the earlier conclusion follow as a logical matter.

5. The conclusion that you must examine in this question is "the common belief that the managers of large city school districts are indifferent to the safety needs of their students is unfounded." You must examine each of the choices to determine which provides the strongest basis for criticism with respect to this conclusion.

Choice D is correct. The conclusion assumes that superintendents are in fact not indifferent to their students' safety needs based on superintendents' assertion in a survey that student safety has the same high priority as standardized test scores. However, the statement does not provide any evidence that the superintendents' assertions are truthful or reflected in actual practice. This choice provides the strongest basis for criticism with respect to the conclusion. Choice A is incorrect. While it is true that the conclusion fails to define the term "managers," it is clear from the context of the statement that this term refers to the superintendents. Further, defining "managers" as superintendents has no effect, one way or the other, on the strength of the conclusion, and therefore this choice does not provide a strong basis for criticism with respect to the conclusion. Choice B is incorrect. It is fair to assume that if someone characterizes something as a "high priority," that the person is not indifferent to the thing so characterized. Therefore, this choice does not provide a strong basis for criticism with respect to the conclusion. Choice C is incorrect. Whether the superintendents' priorities are misplaced or not does not provide a basis of criticism with respect to the conclusion, as they are irrelevant to the conclusion. Choice E is incorrect. There is no reason to believe that a sample size of 150 is unrepresentative.

6. Choice C is correct. If the student was a candidate for the masters of taxation degree, since the student took a seminar on Internet law, but not a seminar on ethics, then the student must have enrolled prior to 2005, because under the College Law School graduation requirements, all candidates for the masters of taxation degree who enroll after 2004 (that is, in 2005 or later) must take a seminar on ethics. Choice A is incorrect. The information provided in the question addresses only students who are candidates for the masters of taxation degree. Because this choice is not limited to such students, it need not be true given the information provided in the question, and is therefore incorrect. Choice B is incorrect. The information provided in the question addresses only students who are candidates for the masters of taxation degree. Because this choice is not limited to such students, it need not be true given the information provided in the question, and is therefore incorrect. Choice D is incorrect. Although we know that the student must have enrolled prior to 2005, there is no information in the statement that requires that the student to have enrolled after 2000 but before 2005. Choice E is incorrect. Although we know that the student must have enrolled prior to 2005, there is no information in the statement that requires that the student to have enrolled before 2001.

7. This question asks you to examine the conclusion that "any coin that does not have a small sceptre engraved on the back of the coin cannot be an authentic coin minted in England during the reign of George III."

   Choice C is correct. The statement deals with a category (authentic coins minted in England during the reign of King George III), and the fact that some members of this category (pence, shillings, and guineas) possess a certain characteristic (a small sceptre engraved on the back of the coin). Kim concludes from this that for a coin to be an authentic coin minted in England during the reign of King George III, it must have this characteristic. This is an error in reasoning because it is possible that there are other types of authentic coins minted in England during the reign of King George III that do not have a small sceptre engraved on the back of the coin. Choice A is incorrect. The statement does not present any claims that contradict one another. Choice B is incorrect. There is no information in the statement to indicate whether the examples given are atypical or not. Choice D is incorrect. This choice does not accurately reflect the reasoning on which the conclusion is based. A conclusion based on the reasoning given in this choice would be as follows: "X, Y, and Z are authentic coins minted in England during the reign of King George III. Pence, shillings, and guineas that have a small sceptre engraved on the back of the coin are also authentic coins minted in England during the reign of King George III. Therefore, X, Y, and Z must also have small sceptres engraved on their backs." Choice E is incorrect. This choice does not accurately reflect the reasoning on which the conclusion is based. A conclusion based on the reasoning given in this choice would be as follows: Pence, shillings, and guineas that have a small sceptre engraved on the back of the coin are authentic coins minted in England during the reign of King George III. X, Y, and Z are coins that have a small sceptre engraved on their backs, and so they, too, must be authentic coins minted in England during the reign of King George III.

8. Note that in assessing the choices for this question, you do not need to focus on the quality of the reasoning in either the statement or the choices. You need only find the choice that most closely parallels the reasoning expressed in the statement in the question.

Choice A is correct. The reasoning expressed in this choice most closely parallels the reasoning expressed in the statement in the question. Both set up a "closed" group of three possible candidates (that is, there are no other possible candidates), eliminate two from consideration based on a set of facts, and then conclude that only the possible candidate is the third of the group. Choice B is incorrect. The reasoning expressed in this choice does not parallel the reasoning expressed in the statement in the question. Instead, the reasoning in this choice expresses the following logic: Anyone who wishes to do "X" must meet both of two criteria. Of a group of three, two wish to do "X", and therefore they must be the only two that could meet both of the two criteria. Choice C is incorrect. The reasoning expressed in this choice, while close, does not exactly parallel the reasoning expressed in the statement in the question. Instead, the reasoning in this choice expresses the following logic: A certain fact (quality "X") identifies an individual who committed some action. Of three members of a group, two did not have quality "X" and therefore the third must have been the individual who committed the action. Note that in C, there is only one fact used as the determinant, while in the statement in the question (and in Choice A), there are two (in the statement, spinning wheels and thread, and in Choice A, the ability to walk and sneakers). Also note that in C, the group of three is not a closed group (there are three suspects, but there could also be others who committed the crime who are not yet suspects), while in both the statement in the question and in Choice A, the group of three is closed (only three tribes who inhabited the area in the question and only three children in Choice A). Choice D is incorrect. The reasoning expressed in this choice does not parallel the reasoning expressed in the statement in the question. Instead, the reasoning in this choice expresses the following logic: Anyone who wishes to do "X" must first do two things. Of a group of three persons, two out of the three do those two things, and therefore can do "X." Choice E is incorrect. The reasoning expressed in this choice does not parallel the reasoning expressed in the statement in the question.

9. **Choice C** is correct. If Moravian women have a shorter average life expectancy than Moravian men, then this means that as the population ages, there are likely to be less women than men. Coupled with the fact that green eyes are more common in Moravian women than they are in men, this helps to explain the survey results (why there is a much smaller percentage of 75-year-old, green-eyed Moravians): Many of the green-eyed Moravian women are no longer alive at that age. Choice A is not correct. If this choice said that people with green eyes were *more*

likely to become involved in car accidents than people with blue eyes, that might help explain the decrease in the number of green-eyed Moravians as the population age. However, this choice says that there is no difference in the incidence of car accidents for green-eyed Moravians versus blue-eyed Moravians, and therefore this fact does not help to explain the survey results. Choice B is not correct. Even if green eyes are considered to be very beautiful in Moravia, this fact does not does not help to explain the survey results. Choice D is not correct. The fact that green-eyed Moravians have never accounted for more than 50% of the population in Moravia does not help to explain the survey results. Choice E is not correct. The fact that the Moravian population has remained stable over the past 75 years does not help to explain the survey results.

10. To answer this question, you must determine a point in the argument that both speakers address, because in order for two people to disagree about something, they both must discuss it.

   Choice B is correct. The pizza maker wants to switch to a different brand of mozzarella cheese, while the Sales Manager wants to keep using the same brand of mozzarella cheese. Choice A is incorrect. The Sales Manager never addresses the cost of the mozzarella cheese in his argument. Choice C is incorrect. While the Sales Manager indicates that he thinks customer preferences should be taken into account ("we should keep using the same brand of cheese because we know people like it"), the pizza maker never addresses this point. Choice D is incorrect. While this point is addressed by the Sales Manager ("no other brand of mozzarella cheese tastes as good"), it is never discussed by the pizza maker. Choice E is incorrect. Neither the pizza maker nor the Sales Manager ever address whether or not the pizza store is selling as much pizza as expected.

11. **Choice B** is correct. The CEO is assuming that one must be able to yell at employees with low ratings and reward employees with high ratings in order to be a good manager. Choice A is incorrect. This assumption reverses the cause and effect of the argument. Choice C is incorrect. This assumption deals with whether friendliness is related to the inability to yell at employees with low ratings, not its relation to being a good manager. Choice D is incorrect. As with Choice C, this assumption does not relate to what it takes to be a good manager. Choice E is incorrect. This assumption deals with whether negativity is related to the inability to reward employees with high rankings, not its relation to being a good manager.

12. The finding that you are seeking to explain is the fact that while the number of people attending Broadway shows has decreased, Broadway ticket show revenues have increased.

    Choice E is correct. This statement, if true, best explains how Broadway show revenues could increase while the number of people attending the shows has decreased. Choice A is incorrect. Although the fact that attendance at movie theaters exceeds attendance at Broadway shows may explain where all the audience members have gone, it is not relevant to the finding that you are seeking to explain. Choice B is incorrect. The frequency with which Broadway shows increase ticket rates is irrelevant to the finding that you are seeking to explain. Choice C is incorrect. As with choices A and B, the information offered by this choice is not relevant to the finding that you are seeking to explain. Choice D is incorrect. As with choices A, B, and C, this information is not relevant to the finding that you are seeking to explain.

13. Christopher's conclusion is that because none of the stamp albums with special display pages are big enough to hold all of his stamps, he cannot organize his stamp collection.

    Choice C is correct. Christopher's conclusion is based on the assumption that his stamp collection would not be more organized if displayed in several stamp albums with special display pages. Choice A is incorrect. This assumption relates primarily to stamp albums without special display pages, which is not the type of album addressed by Christopher's conclusion. Choice B is incorrect. While this assumption may explain why his stamp collection is disorganized, it does not provide a basis for Christopher's conclusion. Choice D is incorrect. The focus of this assumption is whether a stamp album has enough special display pages, but Christopher's conclusion is more concerned with whether his stamp collection can be considered organized if his stamps are not in a stamp album large enough to hold his entire collection. Therefore, this assumption is not relevant to Christopher's conclusion. Choice E is incorrect. The fact that such an album was available last year is irrelevant to Christopher's conclusion.

14. **Choice D is correct.** The letter specifically states that in addition to the quality of the story, size considerations (the number of short stories that can be published in the magazine is restricted to 5) are also a factor. Choice A is incorrect. This statement does not necessarily follow from the information in the letter. The information in the letter says only that the magazine has been forced to reject many well-written

stories; it does not say anything about the quality of the stories that were accepted. Choice B is incorrect. This statement is not necessarily true based on the information in the letter. The letter does not say anything about the number of short stories already accepted at the time the letter was written. Choice C is incorrect. This statement is not necessarily true based on the information in the letter. The information in the letter says only that the magazine has been forced to reject many well-written stories; it does not say anything about the proportion of well-written stories to all stories submitted. Choice E is incorrect. This statement does not necessarily follow from the information in the letter. The letter does not say anything about the quality of the story submitted by the writer.

15. **Choice B** is correct. Paul has weakened Linda's argument by giving two examples that contradict her conclusion. Choice A is incorrect. Linda's argument is not circular, nor does Paul attempt to characterize it as circular. Choice C is incorrect. Paul has not challenged Linda's understanding of the emotions at issue. Choice D is incorrect. Paul has not attacked Linda's character. Choice E is incorrect. Paul does not present an analogy to Linda's argument.

16. **Choice E** is correct. The author fails to consider that the result of the plan offered may be to encourage commuters to take alternative methods of transportation, and that therefore, toll fees may be so reduced such that there will not be any additional to fund other programs. Choice A is incorrect. The author does not generalize, but rather writes about a specific plan. Choice B is incorrect. Although it is true that the author fails to consider other possible ways to accomplish the same goals, in this case, this cannot be considered a flaw since the plan set forth appears to be a useful one. Choice C is incorrect. The author does not mistake cause for effect. Choice D is incorrect. The author does not use circular logic.

17. **Choice C** is correct. If this statement is true, then it contradicts the conclusion that strong currencies produce job growth. Choice A is incorrect. This statement strengthens the argument. Choice B is incorrect. This statement strengthens the argument. Choice D is incorrect. This statement does not weaken the argument; it just offers a reversal of cause and effect. Choice E is incorrect. This statement does not weaken the argument because it does not address job growth.

18. The issue here is how Brand X could cost less on a per-ounce basis than Brand Y, while a six-pack of Brand X costs more than a six-pack of Brand Y.

Choice E is correct. This statement, if true, explains why a six-pack of Brand X costs more than a six-pack of Brand Y, even though Brand X costs less than Brand Y on a per-ounce basis. If there are more ounces in the Brand X six-pack than the Brand Y six-pack, it could be more expensive. Choice A is incorrect. Even if this is true, it does not explain how Brand X costs less on a per-ounce basis than Brand Y, while a six-pack of Brand X costs more than a six-pack of Brand Y. Choice B is incorrect. This factor has nothing to do with the issue at hand, namely the cost of the two respective brands of beer. Choice C is incorrect. This factor has nothing to do with the issue at hand, namely the cost of the two respective brands of beer. Choice D is incorrect. This statement does not help explain the situation.

19. **Choice D** is correct. This is the reverse of the last sentence in the argument and thus can be most logically drawn. Choice A is incorrect. This does not necessarily have to be true, given that it could logically be implied that one also needs a low cholesterol level to be healthy. Choice B is incorrect because it is too restrictive. Nothing in the statement indicates that this must necessarily be true. Different diets could also lead to lower cholesterol and weight loss. Choice C is incorrect. It is implied in the passage that both low cholesterol and losing weight are necessary for good health, not low cholesterol alone. Choice E is incorrect. Nothing in the statement relates to the truth or falsity of this conclusion.

20. **Choice E** is correct. Because Ken specifically states that he makes political decisions based on either what his heart tells him or his head tells him, if he is relying on what his head tells him, he might be making a political decision. Choice A is incorrect. Ken specifically states that he never makes decisions about relationships based on what his head tells him. Choice B is incorrect. Ken specifically states that he makes financial decisions based on what his head tells him. Choice C is incorrect. He could also be making a decision about a relationship. Choice D is incorrect. Ken specifically states that he relies on what his head tells him for financial decisions.

21. **Choice D** is correct. If someone attempted to enter the courthouse without passing through the security scanner at 3 p.m. and neither Hannah nor Jake left his or her respective posts before 5 p.m., then both of them must have broken the rules. But the statement above says that only Hannah broke the rules. Therefore this statement cannot be true. Choice A is incorrect. This statement could be true. Hannah may have violated some rule unrelated to her being at her post when her shift ended. Choice B is incorrect. This statement could be true. Jake

may have left his post before 5 p.m. without violating any rules if he was pursuing someone trying to enter the courthouse without passing through the security scanner, while Hannah may have violated this rule by not pursuing someone who was trying to enter the courthouse. Choice C is incorrect. This statement could be true. Hannah may have violated a rule by leaving her post before 5 p.m., while Jake did not violate any rules by not leaving. Choice E is incorrect. This statement could be true. If someone attempted to enter the courthouse without passing through the security scanner at 3 p.m., and both Hannah and Jake left their respective posts to pursue this person, neither would have been in violation for this, but Hannah may have broken some other rule.

22. This question asks you to determine the strongest basis for criticizing Jean's conclusion that she should stop taking naxopraxen to ensure that she does not have a stroke.

    Choice D is correct. The fact that Jean does not consider the possibility of other causes of stroke is a strong basis for criticizing her reasoning. Even if she stops taking naxopraxen, this will not ensure that she does not have a stroke due to other causes. Choice A is incorrect. Although guinea pigs undoubtedly differ from people, and could be used as a basis for criticizing the conclusion that naxopraxen causes strokes in people, it does not provide the strongest basis among the choices offered for criticizing Jean's reasoning that if she stops taking naxopraxen she will not have a stroke. Choice B is incorrect. Whether naxopraxen causes other diseases is irrelevant to the validity of Jean's reasoning. Choice C is incorrect. The fact that naxopraxen may have positive effects is irrelevant to Jean's reasoning. Choice E is incorrect. The fact that Jean is healthy even though she has been taking naxopraxen for 5 years could be used as a basis for criticizing her reasoning on the grounds that this is a factor she should have considered. However, given that the guinea pig study found a relatively high incidence of sudden unexpected strokes in female guinea pigs, Jean cannot be unduly faulted for not wanting to ignore the study's findings despite the fact that she herself was still healthy after taking naxopraxen for 5 years. Her current healthiness does not preclude her from being subject to a sudden unexpected stroke due to naxopraxen at some time in the future.

23. **Choice D** is correct. From the statements made and metaphors used by Chuck and Alison, one can see that the main disagreement between them is whether changes to tax policies should be all made at the same time (yank the rotten tooth, don't just wiggle it versus you have to

teach the ABCs first before you can learn to read). Choice A is incorrect. Alison explicitly states that she agrees with Chuck that a change in tax policy is needed. Choice B is incorrect. Chuck uses this as a metaphor to describe his position about the speed at which he thinks changes to tax policy should be made. Alison does not directly address whether she thinks the metaphor is an apt one. Choice C is incorrect. While, based on his metaphor, Chuck appears to be stating that he thinks that the faster tax policies are revised, the less painful it will be, Alison counters with her own metaphor, which though it tangentially addresses the speed issue, does not address the pain issue. Choice E is incorrect. Chuck and Alison both agree that the tax policy should be changed and therefore one may infer that they both think the current tax policy is unacceptable.

24. **Choice E** is correct. The Nuclear Waste Manager's rebuttal, which focuses on past history as evidence that no change is needed, is flawed because it does not address the increased potential for harm due to the recent increase in the number of trucks carrying radioactive waste through the city. Choice A is incorrect. The reason why the number of trucks carrying radioactive waste has increased is not relevant to the validity of the reasoning expressed in the Nuclear Waste Manager's rebuttal. Choice B is incorrect. The Nuclear Waste Manager specially addresses the issue of radioactive waste. Choice C is incorrect. Because the City Manager never suggests that the radioactive waste being carried by the trucks may itself have become more dangerous, the Nuclear Waste Manager cannot be faulted for not addressing this in his rebuttal. Choice D is incorrect. Because the City Manager does not want to eliminate all trucks carrying nuclear waste through the city, but just limit them, he apparently recognizes the need for such transport. Therefore the Nuclear Waste Manager cannot be faulted for not defending the need for such transport in his rebuttal, because it is not being challenged.

25. **Choice D** is correct. If patients followed the recommendation, but then eat more chocolate during the day, this could explain the results. Choice A is incorrect. The study found that one piece of chocolate was all that was required. Choice B is incorrect. Chocolate's failure to prevent heart disease is not at issue. Choice C is incorrect. The statement specifically says that patients followed the recommendation. Choice E is incorrect. It is a non sequitur that does not relate directly to the question.

SECTION II—Analytical Reasoning

1. B	**9.** D	**17.** C
2. E	**10.** A	**18.** E
3. C	**11.** B	**19.** E
4. D	**12.** A	**20.** C
5. B	**13.** E	**21.** D
6. D	**14.** B	**22.** D
7. A	**15.** A	**23.** D
8. A	**16.** A	**24.** C

QUESTIONS 1–6 RELATE TO THE FOLLOWING LOGIC GAME:

A university research study is selecting a control group of people for a medical experiment. There are exactly five married couples that qualify for this study: the Harrisons, Lesters, Murrays, Olsons, and Petersons. The following restrictions apply:

> If neither of the Petersons are picked, then Mr. and Mrs. Olson must be picked.
>
> Mr. Peterson cannot be in the group unless Mrs. Lester is also selected.
>
> If Mr. Murray is selected, then neither Mrs. Olson nor Mrs. Peterson can be picked.
>
> At least one of the Harrisons must be in the group.

ACTION:

We see from the first sentence of this logic game that the action of this game is to pick a group of people, from a pool of candidates, to be used for a study. Therefore, the issue you're going to face when having to pick a group will usually come down to three questions:

> Who *can* be in the group?
>
> Who must be in the group?
>
> Who cannot be in the group?

Usually, one of the elements of picking a group involves the size of the group, whether it's a fixed size, has a minimum size, or a maximum size. This element is not addressed in the setup, so we do not worry about it here. Note that it can (and does) come up as an additional piece of information for one or more of the individual questions.

SETUP:

This kind of game has no fixed diagram to map out. Instead, you simply need to have a list of the potential people so you can circle potential group members and X out people who don't qualify. In this case, we have a total of 10 people from 5 couples. You can list them out by this abbreviation:

Mr. H, Mrs. H, Mr. L, Mrs. L, Mr. M, Mrs. M, Mr. O, Mrs. O, Mr. P, Mrs. P

To simplify matters, you can represent the men by m and the women by w, and list out the participants this way:

mH, wH, mL, wL, mM, wM, mO, wO, mP, wP

RULES:

Using the second set of abbreviations, let's now map out the rules presented and see whether we can use these rules to deduce other rules we can use to solve the questions:

Rule 1: If no P, then mO and wO.

Of course, we can work through the reverse of this situation. If neither Mr. nor Mrs. Olson is picked, then we must pick one of the Petersons or we violate this rule. Therefore, we can also deduce

Rule 1 (Reverse): If not (mO and wO), then mP or wP.

Rule 2: If mP, then wL.

When working through the reverse of this rule, however, it is not true that if Mrs. Lester is included, we must pick Mr. Peterson. However, we can conclude that, if Mrs. Lester is NOT picked, then Mr. Peterson cannot be picked either.

Rule 2R: If not wL, then not mP.

Working through the last two rules, we can devise the following rules:

Rule 3: If mM, then not (wO or wP).
Rule 3R: If wO or wP, then not mM (reverse of rule 3).
Rule 4: mH or wH.

DEDUCING NEW RULES

If we look at the existing rules, we can use logic to create additional rules we can use to help answer the questions. Let's first look at Rules 3 and 1. If we pick Mr. Murray, we cannot pick Mrs. Olsen or Mrs. Peterson. However, when we reversed Rule 1, we deduced that if Mrs. Olsen is not picked, then either Mr. or Mrs. Peterson must be picked. However, Rule 3 states that we can't pick Mrs. Peterson as well, so we can conclude that, if we pick Mr. Murray, we have to pick Mr. Peterson. Furthermore, Rule 2 states that if you pick Mr. Peterson, you must pick Mrs. Lester as well. Combined, we can create a new rule:

New Rule: If mM, then mP and wL.

Performing deductions like this in advance is very beneficial to solving the questions and getting to the heart of the answers of this game. We revisit this deduction in Question 3 because this rule instantly solves the question.

1. **Answer: B.** Typically, the first question in a group for a logic game like this can be solved simply by process of elimination from the rules given. So, you can either go through each answer and look through the rules to find a violation in each answer, eliminating that choice, until you find the correct answer. Or, you can go through each rule, look through all the answers to see whether any answer violates that rule, and eliminate choices that way. This is the method we'll use. The first rule states that either Mr. or Mrs. Peterson is selected, and if not, then both the Olsons must be selected. Looking through the answers, there are two options that do not include one of the Petersons: B and C. Looking at B, both Olsons are included, so that answer is safe so far. Answer C only includes Mrs. Olson, so this answer cannot be valid. C is incorrect. The next rule states that, if Mr. Peterson is selected, Mrs. Lester must also be in the group. We look at the answers and find that A, D, and E have Mr. Peterson in the group. However, while D and E include Mrs. Lester, A does not. Therefore, A is not a valid answer. A is incorrect. The third rule states that if Mr. Murray is part of the group, neither Mrs. Olson nor Mrs. Peterson can be part of the same group. We see that three choices contain Mr. Murray in the group: A, D, and E. We've already eliminated A, so let's examine D and E. We can see that D includes Mrs. Peterson, while E includes Mrs. Olson. Therefore, both of these answers are invalid. D and E are incorrect. By process of elimination, we find that B is the only valid answer left, and therefore, B is the correct answer. Side note: If we had gotten to the fourth rule, which stipulated that at least one of the Harrisons be included, that would also have eliminated answer choice E.

2. **Answer: E.** At this point, we have to start combining the rules to form deductions, and apply each of the answer choices to see which ones follow the rules and which ones break the rules. Remember, look at the question: We're looking for something that must be false, and there's only going to be one answer, so the moment you find something you can prove not to be possible, you're done. So, let's look at each answer choice and the rules that apply to it: A says that both Mrs. Harrison and Mr. Peterson are selected. Well, we know from the fourth rule that one of the Harrisons has to be picked, so that's good. If Mr. Peterson is picked, then we just have to include Mrs. Lester in the group to be valid. This choice is possible, so A cannot be our answer. B states that Mr. Murray and Mrs. Lester are selected. The only rule we have here is the third rule: If Mr. Murray is selected, we don't pick Mrs. Olson or Mrs. Peterson. Answer choice B is possible, so B cannot be our answer. C states that Mrs. Olson and Mr. Harrison are selected. Once again, we know that one of the Harrisons must be picked, and as long as Mr. Murray isn't in the group, we can have Mrs. Olson (so says the third rule). Therefore, C is possible, so C cannot be our answer. D states that all the women are selected. Let's go through the rules again: If we pick Mrs. Harrison, that satisfies the fourth rule. As long as we pick Mrs. Peterson, we don't *have* to take Mr. and Mrs. Olson, so we satisfy the first rule. Rule 2 doesn't apply here because we can have Mrs. Lester without Mr. Peterson, but we can't have Mr. Peterson without Mrs. Lester. As for the third rule, as long as we don't pick Mr. Murray, we're fine, and an all-female group would preclude us from picking Mr. Murray. Therefore, the control group can be all female, so D is possible, and D cannot be our answer. Once again, by process of elimination, we find that E is left, and must be the answer we choose. However, let's assume that you couldn't eliminate all of the other choices, so let's prove that E must be false:

> If we look at the first rule, we must take both the Olsons unless one of the Petersons is included. Therefore, we'd have to take Mr. Peterson.
>
> However, if we take Mr. Peterson, Rule 2 states that we must pick Mrs. Lester as well.
>
> Therefore, we need to have either Mrs. Olson or Mrs. Lester in the group. Because of this, we cannot pick an all-male group, and E has to be false.

3. **Answer: C.** Once again, let's look at the rules and interpolate who else must be in the group and who is prohibited from being in the group.

Let's start by revisiting a rule we could have deducted from the initial setup. Rule 3 states that if Mr. Murray is selected, then we cannot have Mrs. Olsen or Mrs. Peterson. Now, if we look at Rule 1, Mrs. Olson must be selected if neither Mr. nor Mrs. Peterson is selected. Therefore, by combining these two rules, we can deduce the following:

> If Mr. Murray is selected, than either Mr. or Mrs. Peterson must be selected, too.

However, we need to refine this new rule. Going back to Rule 3, we cannot have Mr. Murray and Mrs. Peterson in the same group. Therefore, our new rule reads as follows:

> If Mr. Murray is selected, then Mr. Peterson must be selected, too.

Now, we combine this rule with Rule 2, which states that, if Mr. Peterson is selected, Mrs. Lester must be picked, too. Therefore, by deduction, if Mr. Murray is selected, Mr. Peterson and Mrs. Lester must be selected. Answer C is correct.

4. **Answer: D.** By this point, the questions usually add another element to include in your conclusions that can change your mode of thinking. If you've noticed, we've never discussed the size of the group before; we just made sure that the membership of the group didn't violate the four rules set out before us. Now, we have to build a possible answer without violating any of the rules and we want to minimize the people we have to include. Let's look at Rule 4 first. We have to pick one of the Harrisons, so the group size must be at least one. Next, let's look at Rule 1: If we pick neither of the Petersons, then we must pick both the Olsons. Let's look at it another way. The group must have one of the following three options:

> Mr. Peterson
>
> Mrs. Peterson
>
> Mr. and Mrs. Olson

Because we're trying to minimize the group size, we would rule out the third option, Mr. and Mrs. Olson. Now, our minimum group size is two: one of the Harrisons, and one of the Petersons. Ah, but the option of Mr. Peterson brings up the second rule: If we pick Mr. Peterson, we must also include Mrs. Lester. This increases the group size to three. Therefore, our minimum group is as follows: Mrs. Peterson and one of the Harrisons. Looking at the answer choices, answer choice D is what we want. Answer choice A is incorrect because we could choose Mrs. Harrison with Mrs. Peterson. One last note: Because Mr. Murray is not in the minimum group, we are not violating Rule 3, so we don't violate any of the rules.

5. **Answer: B.** This situation involves going through what is required for the control group and seeing which answer cannot be true. Once we find an answer that we know cannot be true, we have found our answer to this question. Let's look at answer choice A: If Mrs. Lester is the only woman selected, then looking at Rule 1, we must pick Mr. Peterson as well. Because we're picking Mr. Peterson, we'd *have* to pick Mrs. Lester anyway. If we pick Mr. Harrison, we can satisfy Rule 4 while keeping Mrs. Lester as the only woman selected. Therefore, answer choice A could be true, so we can rule out A. Next, let's look at answer choice B: We know from Rule 1 that either Mr. Peterson, Mrs. Peterson, or Mr. and Mrs. Olson must be in the group. By deduction, if we pick Mr. Peterson, we must also pick Mrs. Lester to be in the group. Therefore, Mrs. Murray cannot be the only woman in the group, so answer choice B cannot be true, and the answer to this question is B. However, let's look at the other options. If we pick Mr. and Mrs. Olson, we satisfy Rule 1. We can then pick Mr. Harrison to satisfy Rule 4. We don't have to pick Mr. Peterson, so Rule 2 does not apply, and because we don't have to pick Mr. Murray, Rule 3 doesn't apply. Therefore, answer choice C can be true, so we can rule out C. If we look at answer choice D, we can pick Mr. and Mrs. Olson to satisfy Rule 1, then we can pick Mrs. Harrison to satisfy Rule 4. If we don't pick Mr. Peterson, we don't have to take Mrs. Lester, so we don't violate Rule 2. Whether we pick Mr. Murray or not, Rule 3 states that we can't pick two women. Therefore, Mr. Olson could be the only man selected, so answer choice D could be true, so we can rule out D. Finally, answer choice E states that Mr. Peterson is the only man selected. If we look at Rule 1, Mr. Peterson is a valid choice for the group to satisfy that rule. Rule 2 says that we must pick Mrs. Lester as well, and we can pick Mrs. Harrison to satisfy Rule 4. If we don't pick Mr. Murray, Rule 3 doesn't apply. Therefore, Mr. Peterson could be the only man selected, so answer choice E could be true, so we can rule out E.

6. **Answer: D.** Because of the rules presented, there are many options as to who can serve in a group. We solve this question by determining a couple of people where at least one person within that couple must be selected. From the question, we can see that Rule 2 must come into play. If Mrs. Lester is not picked, then by reversing that rule, we see that Mr. Peterson cannot be picked either. We can immediately rule

out answer choice E because Mr. Peterson is in that list. Now, let's take that conclusion and apply it to Rule 1. We can either pick Mr. or Mrs. Peterson, or we have to pick both the Olsons. Because we can't pick Mr. Peterson, we must pick either Mrs. Peterson or Mr. and Mrs. Olson. Looking at the answer choices, answer choice D satisfies the question. Either you pick Mr. Olson (and get Mrs. Olson as well) or you pick Mrs. Peterson.

QUESTIONS 7–11 RELATE TO THE FOLLOWING LOGIC GAME:

Each of seven students—Andrew, Brian, Eddie, Joel, Michael, Traci, and Yana—will be assigned to exactly one of nine bus seats. The seats are numbered from 1 through 9 and arranged in rows as follows:

Front row: 1 2 3

Middle row: 4 5 6

Last row: 7 8 9

Only seats in the same row as each other are immediately beside each other. Seat assignments must meet the following conditions:

Brian's seat is in the last row.

Eddie's seat is immediately beside Joel's seat and also immediately beside an unassigned seat.

Joel's seat is in the row immediately behind the row in which Andrew's seat is located.

Neither Michael nor Yana is seated immediately beside Andrew.

ACTION:

We have to assign seven people to a specific spot in a diagram and, by default, leave two of the nine designated spots empty. This involves specific positions in a picture, but we are given certain leeway when using the rules to determine seats. When it comes to interpreting the words "besides someone," we do not have to worry about forward or backward proximity (or the Y axis if this was a graph), but rather the left-to-right or X axis of the diagram.

The obvious set of questions will be as follows:

Which person is sitting in specific seat X?

Which person (or persons) could *not* sit in specific seat X?

Which set of people can (or must) sit in specific row Y? (Front, Middle, Last)

You could also expect to be asked about certain scenarios or which seats can or must be empty.

SETUP:

You could represent this game as the specific nine-point representation above, or as three arrays to represent rows, but not specific seats within the row, such as follows:

Front:	(A, B, C)
Middle:	(D, E, F)
Last:	(G, H, I)

For some questions, the row assignment will be enough to answer the question, while in others, you'll have to be very specific, such as this:

Front:	A B E
Middle:	J M T
Last:	Y x x (where x is an empty seat)

RULES:

The first rule could be represented as

Rule 1: Last: (Eddie, ?, ?)

Rule 2 states that Eddie and Joel sit next to each other, and Eddie sits next to an empty chair as well. Because we know that there are exactly three seats in a row, we know that one of the rows of our diagram must be:

Specific Order:	Row: (Joel, Eddie, empty) or Row: (empty, Eddie, Joel)
Non-specific Order:	Row: (Eddie, Joel, empty)

Rule 3 states that Joel sits in the row directly behind Andrew. From this rule, we get several pieces of information. Joel cannot sit in the first row, because Andrew would not be in the row ahead of Joel. That means Joel must sit in either the middle or last row, which means Andrew must sit in either the front or middle row:

Scenario 1:	Scenario 2:
Front: (Andrew, ?, ?)	Front: (?, ?, ?)
Middle: (Joel, ?, ?)	Middle: (Andrew, ?, ?)
Last: (?, ?, ?)	Last: (Joel, ?, ?)

Rule 4 is the hardest to represent in the diagram. When you put Andrew in one of the three arrays of rows, you cannot put both Michael and Yana in the same row. With each row only three seats wide, Andrew would have to sit next to one of the two, if both Michael and Yana were assigned to the same row. One person could sit on one end of the row, and Andrew could sit on the other side.

DEDUCING NEW RULES:

If we look at the two scenarios that come out of Rule 3, we can combine it with Rules 1 and 2 and actually come up with one potential scenario to help us answer all our questions.

If we look at Scenario 2, Joel is in the last row. But Rule 1 tells us that Brian is in the last row. However, Rule 2 says that Joel's row is made up of Joel, Eddie, and an empty seat. There is no room for Brian in Joel's row!

Therefore, Joel cannot sit in the last row, and Scenario 2 is invalid.

Our one and only scenario, represented without specific order, is now as follows:

Front:	(Andrew, ?, ?) not Michael and Yana
Middle:	(Eddie, Joel, empty)
Last:	(Brian, ?, ?)

7. **Answer: A.** Because this is the first question, let's use the rules to rule out possibilities until we are left with one possibility, which will be the correct answer. The first rule states that Brian is in the last row, so he either has seat 7, 8, or 9. Therefore, he cannot be in seat 2, so we can rule out answer Choice B. The third rule states that Joel's seat is behind the row where Andrew is seated. Therefore, Joel cannot sit in the first row; he must be in either the second or third row. Therefore, we can rule out answer choice D. The second rule states that Eddie's seat is immediately beside Joel's seat, meaning they're both in the same row. We've deduced from Rule 3 that Joel cannot be in the first row. Therefore, combining these two elements, we can deduce that Eddie cannot be in the first row. We can now rule out answer choice C. Let's look at Rules 2 and 3 in another light. We know that Joel cannot be in the first row because he has to sit behind Andrew. However, we also know that Joel sits next to Eddie and an empty seat. Now, Rule 1 states that Brian must be in the last row. So, if Joel were to sit in the last row, there's no room for Brian. We can deduce that Joel must sit in the second row, and Andrew must sit in the first row, as deduced previously.

Now, if Andrew must sit in the first row, Rule 4 states that Yana does not sit immediately beside Andrew, meaning Yana cannot sit in seat 2. Therefore, we can rule out answer choice E. We've eliminated everything but A, so that is the correct answer.

8. **Answer: A.** Let's start this question by going back to the scenario we came up with after diagramming all the rules, without assigning particular seats:

First row: (Andrew, ?, ?)

Middle row: (Eddie, Joel, empty)

Last row: (Brian, ?, ?)

Now, if Michael and Yana are assigned to separate rows, that means that one of them is assigned to the first row, and the other person is assigned to the third row. Next, because Rule 4 states that Andrew does not sit immediately besides Michael or Yana, we know that Andrew is either in seat 1 and Michael/Yana is in seat 3, or vice versa; Andrew is in seat 3 and Michael or Yana is in seat 1. Worded another way, Andrew cannot sit in seat 2. If we look at answer choice A, we see that that statement has to be false, so we choose answer choice A.

9. **Answer: D.** Given this new piece of information, we can now map out the general seating of the bus to rule out answer choices. We know from Rule 4 that neither Michael nor Yana can sit next to Andrew, and we've deduced that Andrew must be in the first row. Therefore, if Michael and Yana are in the same row, they can't be in the first row. Next, we've deduced that Joel and Eddie are in the second row, so Michael and Yana cannot be in the second row. That means that Michael and Yana are assigned to the third row. We also know from Rule 1 that Brian must sit in the third row. Therefore, this row is full, and neither Brian, Michael, nor Yana can sit immediately beside an unassigned seat, so we can rule out answer choices A, C, and E. Now, let's carefully interpret Rule 2: Eddie's seat is immediately beside Joel's seat and Eddie's seat is immediately beside an unassigned seat. For this to be true, Eddie must be assigned to seat 5, which means that Joel cannot be assigned a seat immediately beside an unassigned seat. Therefore, we can rule out answer choice B. This means that Traci, answer choice D, is the correct answer, and could be assigned a seat (in the first row) next to an unassigned seat.

10. **Answer: A.** We get quite a bit of information from this question to help us nail down exactly where people are sitting. First, by dissecting the first part of the question, we know exactly where Traci could be

sitting. If Traci is sitting beside another student and Traci is sitting beside an unassigned seat, that means Traci is in the middle seat of the row. We know that she cannot sit in the second row, so she's either in the first or third row, in seat 2 or 8. However, let's assume Traci is in the third row. We know from Rule 1 that Brian must sit in the third row. Therefore, the third row would have Brian, Traci, and an empty seat. That means the first row would have to have Andrew, Michael, and Yana. Rule 4 states that Andrew does not sit besides either Michael or Yana, so this scenario is *not* possible. This leaves us with one possible scenario: Traci is sitting in the first row, next to Andrew and next to an unassigned seat. Looking through the answer choices, we see that it must be answer choice A. We've ruled out answer choice B, because Traci can't sit in the last row. Also because of that, she can't be assigned a seat next to Brian, so that rules out answer choice D. We know that Brian, Michael, and Yana sit in the third row, but we don't know exactly which seats they have in the third row, so we can rule out answer choices C and E.

11. **Answer: B.** One way to look at this question is to first figure out where the unassigned seats are going. We know from the onset that there are seven students and nine seats, so there are exactly two unassigned seats. One of those seats is next to Eddie in the second row. We know now from this question that the other unassigned seat is next to Brian, who from Rule 1 is assigned to the third row. This means that the first row has three students, one of which must be Andrew's seat. Now, we know from Rule 4 that neither Michael nor Yana is sitting next to Andrew, which means that only one of them (Michael or Yana) can sit in the first row, and the other person must sit in the third row next to Brian. This leaves exactly one person: Traci. She can't sit in the second row; that's for Eddie and Joel. She can't sit in the third row; that's for Brian, Michael/Yana, and an unassigned seat. So, she must sit in the first row, and because Andrew can't sit next to Michael/Yana, Traci must sit in seat 2. If we look at the answer choices, we see that answer choice B is correct.

QUESTIONS 12–18 RELATE TO THE FOLLOWING LOGIC GAME:

A high school principal must make exactly five budget cuts from eight subject areas—Gym, Library, Math, Nutrition, Physics, Reading, Science, and Writing—in accordance with the following conditions:

If both Gym and Science get budget cuts, Writing is also cut. If Nutrition is cut, neither Reading nor Science is cut.

If Physics is cut, Library is not cut.

Of the three areas Library, Math, and Reading, exactly two can be cut.

ACTION:

Like the first logic game, we must choose a subgroup from a larger group of potential candidates. Therefore, we can expect that many of our questions will revolve around these three questions:

What *can* be in the group?

What must be in the group?

What cannot be in the group?

Unlike the first game, however, we have a definite size of this subgroup, which allows us to make certain deductions and rules to help us determine who is in the group and who is not in the group.

NOTE: For purposes of this game discussion, if a subject area is *not* to be cut, we will say that we are "saving" that area from budget cuts.

SETUP:

We have a list of eight potential subject areas that we can abbreviate as follows:

G, L, M, N, P, R, S, W

We know that we're going to have Group C (for Cut) of exactly *five* areas. Conversely, we're also going to have Group S (for Save) of exactly *three* areas. So, we can have three lists:

GROUPS	CUT	SAVE
G	1	1
L	2	2
M	3	3
N	4	
P	5	
R		
S		
W		

As we make decisions, we can move letters from the Groups category into either the Cut or Save list.

RULES

So, let's look map out our rules and boil them down into specific scenarios:

Rule 1: If G and S, then W.

Rule 1 (Reverse): If not W, then either (Not G) or (Not S)

This means that, if Writing is *not* to be cut, then either G or S would not be cut, because if G and S were both cut, W would *have* to be cut. Note, however, that we can cut W and either G or S; we don't *have* to cut both G and S in order to cut W.

Rule 2: If N, then (Not R) and (Not S)

Rule 2(Reverse): If R or S, then (Not N)

This means that if we have to cut Reading or Science, we couldn't cut Nutrition, because doing so would violate Rule 2.

Rule 3: If P, then (Not L)

Rule 3 (Reverse): If L, then (Not P)

Quite simply, if we do have to cut Library, we couldn't cut Physics, because doing so would violate Rule 3.

Rule 4: This one isn't as easy to specifically quantify. We can simply draw out the three possible scenarios this rule tells us:

L and M

L and R

M and R

However, the language states that this scenario is possible, (exactly two *can* be cut), which means that, for right now, to fully state the rule means saying:

(L and M) or (L and R) or (M and R) or (Not [L and M and R])

The fourth option simply states that you can't cut all three. You either cut exactly two of the three, or you don't cut at all.

REVISING RULES THROUGH DEDUCTION

However, looking at our statement for Rule 4. Is that last scenario really possible? Let's break it out. If you don't cut Library, Math, or Reading, you're left with these two groups:

Cut: Gym, Nutrition, Physics, Science, Writing

Save: Library, Math, Reading.

However, Rule 2 states that if you cut Nutrition, you cannot cut Science. Therefore, this scenario is not possible. Because you cannot spare all three areas of Library, Math, and Reading, you must cut exactly two of those areas. The rule is simply

Rule 4: (L and M) or (L and R) or (M and R)

However, we will discuss this aspect again during the questions, in case this deduction wasn't made initially before solving the questions.

12. **Answer: A.** Like before, let's look through the rules to eliminate possibilities until we're left with the one and correct answer. In this case, we're looking for groups that cannot be the complete list because they violate at least one rule. Starting with the first rule, we need to look for groups that contain both Gym and Science, but do *not* contain writing. Going through the answers, we see that D contains both, but not writing. Therefore, answer D is incorrect. Going onto the next rule, we should look for answers that contain Nutrition, and if that answer contains Reading or Science, you can rule it out. Answer C contains both Nutrition and Reading, so that answer cannot be valid. Answer C is incorrect. The third rule involves Physics and Library. Therefore, if we find a group that contains Physics and Library on the list of budget cuts, we know that this violates the third rule and cannot be a valid answer. Answer B has both, so that means answer B is incorrect. The last rule is a little harder to quantify but easy to check. Out of the three areas Library, Math, and Reading, exactly two can be cut. Note that this rule says that the areas *can* be cut, not "must be cut." If that was the case, we could rule out answer choices that didn't have these three areas. In our case however, we simply need to look for answer choices that have *all three* areas, and eliminate that possibility, because that would clearly violate the rule. Answer choice E has all three areas right up front, so we can rule that out. Answer choice E is incorrect. We have now eliminated four of the five choices, so we know that answer A *is right*.

13. **Answer: E.** We first look at all rules that involve this new piece of information—mainly, the first rule that states that *if* Gym and Science are both cut, then Writing must be cut as well. Note, however, that the reverse is *not* necessarily true: Cutting Writing does not automatically add Gym and Science to the list. Therefore, noting the language "could be a complete and accurate list," we can use the same technique as the previous question, and rule out answers that could *not* be a

complete and accurate list. The fourth rule states that only two of these three areas (Library, Math, and Reading) can be cut, but we see that answer choice B contains all three, so Answer B is incorrect. The third rule states that you can't cut Physics and Library, but we can see that answer choice C contains both areas, so we know that answer C is incorrect. The second rule states that you can't cut Reading or Science if you've cut Nutrition. However, going through the answer choices that are left, we see that answer choice D contains Nutrition and Science, so we know that answer D is incorrect. If we re-examine the fourth rule, we see that it states "exactly" two can be cut. Answer choice A only cuts one area, Math, while Answer choice E cuts exactly two areas: Math and Reading. We can therefore rule out answer choice A and conclude that answer E is correct.

14. **Answer: B.** At this point, we can take the new piece of information, and apply the existing rules to come up with budget areas that must be cut. Specifically, let's start with Rule 3, which is the only stated rule that applies to Physics. We know that, if you cut Physics, you cannot cut Library. We scan the answers to see whether Library is on the list, so we can eliminate that answer. However, none of the answers contain Library, so there's nothing to eliminate. However, this influences Rule 4, as we deduced in the beginning. We know that we can only cut two of the three areas (Library, Math, and Reading) and we now know that we cannot cut Library. Therefore, combining these two rules, we know that we can cut Math and Reading. Note the language, however. We're looking for two areas that must be cut. So, let's back up and look at the entire problem another way. We have eight areas and five have to be on the list. Therefore, if we find scenarios where we rule out three areas, we know the five left are our group. We know that Library is one of the three areas that cannot be cut, so let's find out what two other areas cannot be cut. If we don't cut Math and Reading as well, we don't violate the fourth rule. That means that we would cut Gym, Nutrition, Physics, Science, and Writing. Let's check to see if this option doesn't violate any of the other rules:

> Rule 1: We see that we're cutting Gym, Science, and Writing, so this passes Rule 1.

> Rule 2: We're cutting Nutrition, so we're not allowed to cut Reading and Science. However, Science is on this list, so this scenario fails.

Because this scenario fails, we know now that we must cut Math and Reading, so B is correct.

15. Answer: A. Always look at the exact wording of the question before you start to answer it. In this case, we are looking for two areas that *can* be cut, not must be cut. Like before, let's take the existing rules and eliminate possibilities:

> If we reverse the third rule, we know that if we cut Library, we cannot cut Physics, because both areas cannot be cut. If we look at the answer choices, we see that answers B and E contain Physics. These answers cannot be possible, so B and E are incorrect.

> Now, if we reverse the second rule, we know that if either Reading or Science are cut, then Nutrition cannot be cut. (If Nutrition was also cut, it would fail the second rule.) By looking at the answer choices we see that Answers C and D contain Nutrition, which cannot be possible. Therefore, C and D are incorrect.

> This quickly brings us to our correct answer—A. By scanning the four rules, we can see that Gym and Math are not explicitly eliminated, so we know for sure that this answer is correct.

16. Answer: A. We see that Reading is involved in two of our four rules, so let's take our new piece of information (Reading is not cut) and see what deductions we can make. Rule 2 states that if Nutrition is cut, Reading and Science cannot be cut. Because we're not given any specific information about Science, we can't say for sure that Nutrition will be cut. Besides, that isn't even an option, so we don't have to worry about it…yet. Now, by looking at the fourth rule, and the fact that Reading is *not* going to be cut, we know that Library and Math can be cut. However, neither subject matter is an answer choice, so no obvious answer either. However, let's take this new deduction further. If we can cut Library and Math, we know from the third rule that we cannot cut Physics. We now have two areas that aren't going to be cut, so all we need is one more area to avoid getting cut out of the six remaining: Gym, Library, Math, Nutrition, Science, and Writing. Let's pull out two areas in specific and play out scenarios: Nutrition and Science. If we cut Nutrition, Rule 2 states that we cannot cut Reading and Science. If we cut Science, the reverse of Rule 2 states that we cannot cut Nutrition. This means that either Nutrition or Science cannot be cut. That means the other four areas: Gym, Library, Math, and Writing must be cut. Answer choice A is valid, so that's the one we pick.

17. Answer: C. Based on this new piece of information, we can quickly deduce one of the pair of areas that could not be cut. We know from the fourth rule that exactly two of these three areas (Library, Math, and

Reading) can be cut. We've been told these are Math and Reading, so we know that Library could not be cut. This rules out answer choices B and E, so we know it's either A, C, or D. Look at the second rule: If Nutrition was cut, we couldn't cut Reading. We know from this question that Reading is being cut, so the reverse holds true—Nutrition could not be cut. Answer choice C is our logical conclusion.

18. **Answer: E.** After working through all these questions, it's easy to attempt to solve this problem using information from the previous questions. Remember, though, that *none* of the additional rules from the actual questions comes into play. All we have to work with is the original setup and the four rules presented in the game description. Don't fall into the trap of thinking you can automatically cut or "save" one particular area. Let's use the rules and action in reverse to narrow our options. We know we have to cut five of the eight areas. That means we have to save exactly three of the eight areas as well. So, let's break down the data set:

> Set A: Two of the following three must be cut: Library, Math, Reading

> Set B: Three of the following five must be cut: Gym, Nutrition, Physics, Science, Writing

Rule 1 gives us at least one clear possibility for Set B: If we cut Gym and Science, we must also cut Writing. That tells us that, because we're cutting Science, we're not cutting Nutrition. Because we're not cutting Physics, we could cut Library. This is a valid scenario. But what if Nutrition was cut? We couldn't cut Reading or Science. That means we'd have to cut Library and Math from Set A. Because we're cutting Library, we couldn't cut Physics from Set B. That means we'd have to cut Gym, Nutrition, and Writing from Set B. If we look at both sets, we see from these scenarios that Gym and Writing show up in both cases as being cut. We're getting closer. What if you don't cut Writing? That means either Gym or Science doesn't get cut, because, after all, if both Gym and Science get cut, Writing is an automatic cut. So, let's say we save Writing and Gym. Can we cut Nutrition, Physics, and Science? *Nope*, that violates Rule 2: You can't cut Nutrition and Science. So, let's say you save Writing and Science. Can we cut Gym, Nutrition, and Physics? Rule 1 is fine, Rule 2 appears fine, and Rule 3 says that, because we're cutting Physics, we can't cut Library. That means we must cut Math and Reading from Set A. However, Rule 2 says that, because we're cutting Nutrition, we can't cut Reading. That fails as well. Given that we can't find a scenario to save Writing, it appears we must cut Writing and we choose answer choice E.

QUESTIONS 19–24 RELATE TO THE FOLLOWING LOGIC GAME:

At a karaoke bar, three friends—Phil, Renae, and Scott—decide to sing a total of six songs marked F, G, H, I, J, and K on the machine. The songs will be sung consecutively as solos, and each song will be performed exactly once. The following constraints govern the order of the songs:

J must be performed earlier than H and earlier than F.

G must be performed earlier than K and later than F.

Phil will only sing I, J, or K.

Renae will only sing G, H, or I.

Scott will only sing F, G, or I.

Whoever sings the first song cannot sing the last song.

ACTION:

In this game, the main objective is to come up with a valid order of six songs, in a sequential fashion, to form a "chain" of songs. This chain contains only one instance of each song, and each person must sing two, on average.

Therefore, we're going to expect two sets of types of questions. The first relates to the specific order of the songs in the playlist:

Which song goes first/second/third/fourth/fifth/last?

What's a possible/legal/illegal playlist of all songs?

What is a list of all songs that can be played first/second/third/fourth/fifth/last?

The other set of questions will pertain to who sings which song, such as "Who is singing song X?" And then, these could be combined to form questions such as

Who could sing first/second/third/fourth/fifth/last?

Which singers could sing a particular song?

Which singer must sing a particular song?

SETUP:

The main diagram to worry about is the playlist of potential songs, with their order represented by the left-to-right notation of the playlist. For example, if we played F first, G second, and so on with K being the last song, our diagram would look as follows:

F-G-H-I-J-K

We could represent a second letter next to each song to represent the singer, but let's put that off until we interpret all the rules of the game.

RULES:

The first two rules deal exclusively with the order of songs, so we can represent them as subchains of songs, as so:

Rule 1: J-?-F-? and J-?-H-?

Notice that we don't say, J-F-H or J-H-F, because that would imply a relationship or rule regarding F and H. As long as J comes before F and J comes before H, we don't violate the rule, and F and H are independent.

Rule 2: F-?-G-?-K

In this case, we can make a specific subchain of F-G-K, because F has to come before G (the same as G coming after F), and G has to come before K.

Rule 3: Phil sings two of (I,J,K)

Rule 4: Renae sings two of (G,H,I)

Rule 5: Scott sings two of (F,G,I)

Rule 6: S1 <> S6, where S1 is the singer of the first song, and S6 is the singer of the sixth, or last song.

DEDUCING NEW RULES:

By looking at Rule 1 and 2, we can come up with a longer subchain of a song playlist:

J-F and F-G-K = J-F-G-K

We know that J has to come before F, which comes before G, which comes before K. Now the only question is where to stick I and H into the equation.

By looking at Rules 3–5, knowing that each song is played exactly once, and each person sings two songs, we can conclude the following:

Phil is the only singer of the three who will sing J and K.

Renae is the only singer of the three who will sing H.

Scott is the only singer of the three who will sing F.

This means Renae sings H and (G or I) and Scott sings F and (I or G).

Lastly, because we know for sure that Phil will sing J and K, we know that the complete playlist cannot begin with J and end with K, thanks to the last rule.

19. **Answer: E.** Because we're on the first question, let's go through the rules and eliminate obvious *wrong* answers to get at the correct answer. The first rule says that J comes before H, and J comes before F. There's no specific chain of J-H-F, so remember H does *not* have to come before F, as long as J comes before both of them. Scanning through the answers, we can rule out answer choice A. Answer A is incorrect. The second rule states that G comes before K, and G comes after F. That means we can set a specific chain of F-G-K, though other songs can come between them. Answer B shows G *after* K, and Answer D shows F *after* G. Answers B and D are incorrect. That leaves us with answer choices C and E. You can note that both choices indicate that J is the first song sung. We know from the rules that only Phil can sing J, which means, thanks to the last rule, that Phil cannot sing the last song. Because only Phil can sing K, we can deduce that Phil will sing J and K, and answer choice C violates the last rule, because picking that answer means that Phil sings the first and last song. Answer C is incorrect. We are left with answer choice E as the correct answer.

20. **Answer: C.** Let's just go through and make the obvious conclusions, as we did in the Rules section:

    Of the three singers, only Phil can sing J and K. That means Phil is singing J and K.

    Of the three singers, only Renae can sing H. Her other song is either G or I.

    Of the three singers, only Scott can sing F. His other song is either G or I.

    Looking through the answer choices, it's clear that answer choice C must be true, and that's our answer. A is incorrect, as our analysis showed, and B wasn't even a valid option.

21. **Answer: D.** Sometimes, the answer choices themselves give us more information on how to solve the question than intended. Because it's clear that K is a possible last song, because it's in all the answer choices, we don't have to worry about it. Because J is in none of the answer choices, we don't have to worry about that particular song. But in order to get the list of all the possible answers, let's rule out the answers that can't be right. Rule 1 tells us that song J has to be played before F or H, so it can't be last. However, since J isn't an option, we don't have to worry about it. Rule 2, however, says that G must come before K. That means that G cannot be the last song. This eliminates

answer choices A, C, and E right away. Rule 2 also states that G must come after F. That means F cannot be a potential last song, so that rules out answer choices A and B. Add all this up, and D is the only potential correct answer.

22. We know from before that one subchain of the song playlist reads J-F-G-K. If I is the first song played, we know that we're left with I-J-F-G-K, with H inserted somewhere in the mix, *after* J: (thanks to Rule 1)

    I-J-H-F-G-K

    I-J-F-H-G-K

    I-J-F-G-H-K

    I-J-F-G-K-H

    In all these scenarios, we see one of the answer choices is always true: J is the second song performed. Therefore, we choose answer Choice D. As a side note, answer choice A is impossible anyway, because Phil has to sing J and K and can *only* sing a total of two songs. Answer choice B is unable to be confirmed based on the information we have at present plus the question itself.

23. The question tells us that four of the five answer choices are acceptable possibilities, and one (and *only* one) is not acceptable. Therefore, we look for a playlist that breaks one of the rules, and we have our answer. First, we know that the subchain J-F-G-K has to be present for the playlist to be acceptable. Scanning through the choices, we see that all five answers have that subchain, so we cannot rule out any answer choices. Next, we look for the rule of J playing before H (the second part of Rule 1). In all five instances, J comes before H, so we cannot rule out any answer choices. Because we do not have any additional information on who is singing which songs, we can assume that we need an acceptable playlist *regardless* of who sings which songs. From our analysis, the only doubt we have is whether Scott or Renae sings G or I. Therefore, we should look for an answer that is unacceptable in either scenario and see whether the last rule is broken and one person sings the first and last song.

    Scenario 1: ji, ji, jh, ih, ik

    Phil sings JK

    Renae sings HG

    Scott sings FI

If we go through our answer choices, we see that the (First, Last) singers are

A. Phil, Scott

B. Phil, Scott

C. Phil, Renae

D. Scott, Renae

E. Scott, Phil

Scenario 2:

Phil sings JK.

Renae sings HI.

Scott sings FG.

If we go through our answer choices, we see that the (First, Last) singers are

A. Phil, Renae

B. Phil, Renae

C. Phil, Renae

D. Renae, Renae

E. Renae, Phil

Now it is clear that answer choice D is *not* an acceptable playlist if Renae is singing songs H and I, which is a legal possibility given the rules of the game. Our answer is D.

24. **Answer: C.** Because J is going first, we know that Rule 1 will be satisfied no matter what: J will be performed before F and before H. So let's look at Rule 2. We know that F has to be played before G, and G has to be played before K. In answer choice B, K is played before F, which violates the rule. In answer choice D, G is played before F. Answers B and D are incorrect. Now, let's look at what is *not* mentioned. If J is played first, we can figure out what the fifth and sixth song would be for our remaining choices. Because we also know that G has to come before K (as stated in Rule 2), we get the following:

A: J-H-I-F-G-K

C: J-I-F-G-K-H or J-I-F-G-H-K

E: J-I-H-F-G-K

Now, going back to the last rule, we know that the person who sings the first song cannot sing the last song. We know from the initial rules and our deduction that Phil sings J and K. We know from the question that J is sung first, which means Phil sings first, and that Phil will sing K later. In answer choices A and E, however, K is the *last* song played, which means Phil would have to sing the first and last song, which violates the last rule. Therefore, A and E are invalid options, and the playlist would *have* to be J-I-F-G-K-H, which makes answer choice C the correct one.

SECTION III—Reading Comprehension

1. C	**10.** C	**19.** C
2. B	**11.** A	**20.** D
3. A	**12.** E	**21.** D
4. B	**13.** D	**22.** E
5. C	**14.** C	**23.** A
6. A	**15.** E	**24.** D
7. B	**16.** A	**25.** C
8. D	**17.** D	**26.** D
9. B	**18.** D	

1. **Answer: C.** As mentioned before, hopefully you are reading the questions first and then going through and reading the passage, looking for answers as you go. This first question asks you to ascertain the basic point of the entire passage and pick the title that best describes the *entire* passage. While the passage begins with a mini-history of development in the land mass we know as Europe, the end of the first paragraph gets to our main topic—the Neanderthal. Answer D is a typical trap for people who assume that the first sentence will naturally reflect the content of the entire passage. We can rule out Answer D. Likewise, answer choice B is something discussed in the first paragraph, but not discussed later in the passage, so this title is not appropriate. We can rule out Answer B. So, now, we're left with answer choices A, C, and E, all dealing in some form with the Neanderthal. However, looking at

answer choice A, it's a little too general. More importantly, while sections of the passage do discuss how the Neanderthal engages his animals in combat and how he eats the animal, there are other discussions of the Neanderthal that would not be reflected in this title. We can rule out Answer A. If we look at Answer E, we see that it discusses one aspect of the passage—how Neanderthals attacked their prey—but doesn't accurately convey the point of the entire passage. We can rule out Answer E. We're left with Answer C, which accurately conveys the general sense of the passage and doesn't necessarily exclude anything.

2. **Answer: B.** In a reading comprehension passage, when you're asked to infer what the author meant regarding a specific word or phrase, it's best to isolate the part where it's mentioned, and draw out the context in order to determine which answer choice best fits as the right answer. In this case, let's look at the second paragraph:

> They probably used a multitude and variety of wooden implements also; they had probably learned much about the shapes of objects and the use of different shapes from wood, knowledge which they afterward applied to stone. But none of this wooden material has survived; we can only speculate about its forms and uses.

It appears the author is trying to imply that the Neanderthals must have had wooden implements first, and used those as a template when they created their flint equivalents. Because there's no proof of the wooden implements for the historians to find, this is a theory. It's clear that this paragraph doesn't illustrate how the Neanderthals hunted, so you can eliminate A. Their hunting patterns aren't yet discussed, so you can rule out C. No previous studies are mentioned, so D is irrelevant and you can rule it out. While there is discussion about the workmanship, the answer you are looking for here is B, and it's the best fit for this situation.

3. **Answer: A.** Just like in question 2, we're looking for the one and only one correct answer to this question. In this case, we're looking for one animal that was *not* present in this time period and not the four animals that were present in the Third Interglacial period. Scanning the passage for references to this exact period, we find this section starting around line 11:

> "In the earlier phase, the Third Interglacial period, a certain number of small family groups of men (Homo Neanderthalensis) and probably of sub-men…"

Therefore, we know that this period is the one that's being discussed at length in this passage, namely the Neanderthal period. So, let's look for mentions of animals during this period:

> Line 25: "This period also had a cave lion, a cave bear, and a cave hyena."

We can rule out answers B and D.

> Lines 34–36: "Their only possible weapons for killing such giant creatures as the mammoth or the cave bear, or even the reindeer, were…"

We can rule out answers C and E.

We also see in lines 3–4 that

> "The saber toothed tiger was diminishing toward extinction."

This line mentions a period before the Third Interglacial period, so we know it's our answer.

4. **Answer: B.** When we're asked for the meaning of a specific word or phrase, given a placement, it's best to evaluate that phrase in the entire sentence where it's contained, define its meaning, and if necessary, use supporting text near that sentence to come to a definite conclusion. In this case, the sentence in question reads as follows:

> "In the earlier phase, the Third Interglacial period, a certain number of small family groups of men (Homo Neanderthalensis) and probably of sub-men (Eoanthropus) wandered over the land, leaving nothing but their flint implements to witness to their presence."

We can gather from this sentence that the implement was something the Neanderthal owned, which probably rules out torches and game. To be sure, let's look for another instance of implement or flint. While they talk about wooden implements in the next paragraph, no definite clues are left. However, in the fourth paragraph, we find the critical sentence:

> "Their only possible weapons for killing such giant creatures as the mammoth or the cave bear, or even the reindeer, were spears of wood, wooden clubs, and those big pieces of flint they left behind them, the Chellean and Mousterian implements."

This clearly compares implements to weapons, which is answer B.

5. **Answer: C.** We look at the fourth paragraph, which begins with this line:

   What did these Neanderthal men hunt?

   As we read this paragraph, we see that the author assumes that the Neanderthals waited for prime opportunities, or used specific circumstances, such as "perhaps they followed them when sick or when wounded by combats, or took advantage of them when they were bogged or in trouble with ice or water" in order to hunt their prey. There is no mention of large hunting groups, so we can eliminate A. While there was one mention of another era using trenches as a trap, this is not a direct correlation to the Neanderthal, so we should eliminate D. The previous paragraph clearly discusses how fire was used as a *defensive* mechanism to clear caves of animal dwellers, so E is not correct. While their weaponry was discussed and could be advanced for their time, it is not described as sophisticated and the reason they were able to succeed. Rather, the theory is that the Neanderthal sensed a weakness in the prey and used that opportunity to strike for the kill. Our choice is answer C.

6. **Answer: A.** Remember, when we're looking to undermine a statement, we want something that absolutely proves the statement false. In this case, we want something that would really prove that Neanderthals did have a language. Answer choice C is actually the opposite of what we want; this would prove that language would depend on the brain's makeup, which the last paragraph of the study clearly stated is impossible for a Neanderthal because the front part of their brain is completely different from modern man. Answer choice B, organized storerooms of remains, only proves that Neanderthals were good with accounting, but it says nothing for language. Same with answer choice D. Just because Neanderthals hung out in tribes doesn't mean they had a language. While answer choice C does weaken the argument of a Neanderthal language, answer choice A completely undermines it because it gives written proof of a language. Therefore, we'd choose answer A.

7. **Answer: B.** This is a typical question within a reading comprehension section, where you have to sift through the clues left in the passage, and either eliminate impossible or incorrect answers to get the one right answer, or find the right citation that answers the question. In this case, we're looking for the crux of the story: How the Romans won and the Germans lost. For that, what hopefully catches your eye is

Cosimo's comment around line 31: "Whence arises such a disadvantage?" Let's look at the next two paragraphs. First, Fabricio comments that

"The German infantry...has almost no armor in defending itself, and use pikes and swords for offense."

Then, he remarks in the next paragraph:

"[T]he German cannot use the pike against the enemy who is next to him because of the length of the staff."

In other words, the Romans learned that they needed to get "up close and personal" with the Germans, and when the Romans were close, the Germans' pikes were useless against them. Therefore, the Germans couldn't handle close-quarter battle, and B is the correct answer.

8. **Answer: D.** In a conversation passage, it's important to assign the right role to the right person. In this case, the two people who are talking are Fabricio and Cosimo, which is indicated by their names being next to their respective dialog. Because they're talking, and they don't mention actually being in the story themselves, you can't really assume that either of them actually "used any smarts" because they are solely recounting the events. Therefore, we've ruled out A and B. By going through the story, we see that Viscotti is actually the Duke of Milan, so C and E are the same person. Because there can only be *one* correct answer, we can probably rule out these two choices as well. Just to be safe, as you go through the passage, you can note around line 23 where you hear about Carmingnuola's decision on the battlefield:

Whence Carmingnuola as a prudent man quickly recognized the power of the enemy arms, and how much they prevailed against cavalry, and the weakness of cavalry against those on foot so organized; and regrouping his forces, again went to meet the Swiss, and as they came near he made his men-at-arms descend from their horses, and in that manner fought with them, and killed all but three thousand, who, seeing themselves consumed without having any remedy, threw their arms on the ground and surrendered.

This passage simply confirms that the correct answer is D.

9. **Answer: B.** Whenever we're given a question that has the keyword "EXCEPT" in it, our goal is to find the one answer that makes the question *wrong*. So, in short, four of the five options are correct to the question, and the one incorrect option is what we need to put down on

the answer sheet. So, let's look for references to when the Germans are in combat. Line 13:

"This has not yet occurred with the German infantry;"

This implies that the Germans fought in armies (or "infantries") so we can rule out E. Lines 33–35 has this mention:

"The German infantry…has almost no armor in defending itself, and use pikes and swords for offense."

It clearly states that the Germans used pikes and swords for offense, so we can rule out C and D. More importantly, however, it states that they hardly used armor, which is answer choice B. We can confirm that answer choice B is the correct one by looking at line 42:

"*[F]or the German* cannot use the pike against the enemy who is next to him because of the length of the staff, so he must use the sword, which is useless to him, *as he has no armor…*"

This confirms that the Germans have no armor. While the passage mentions that the Romans got off their horses to fight the Germans, there is no mention of horses for the Germans. However, with armor so clearly defined, it's a better answer than horses and the one you should choose.

10. **Answer: C.** In order to interpret the meaning of a particular word or phrase, it's important to gather the specific context from the paragraph it's in, and look for clues in other parts of the passage to gain its true meaning. In this case, let's look at the specific mention of "arms" in line 23:

Whence Carmingnuola as a prudent man quickly recognized the power of the enemy arms, and how much they prevailed against cavalry, and the weakness of cavalry against those on foot so organized; and regrouping his forces, again went to meet the Swiss, and as they came near he made his men-at-arms descend from their horses, and in that manner fought with them, and killed all but three thousand, who, seeing themselves consumed without having any remedy, threw their arms on the ground and surrendered.

It's clear that the arms here are something the Germans held that were used against the Romans. Later on in the paragraph, we see that the enemy "threw their arms on the ground and surrendered." This helps us eliminate some choices. Because you can't physically detach your own limb and throw it on the ground, we can rule out A (limbs). Also, you can't throw your cavalry on the ground, so we can rule out E as well. Let's look at another mention of arms, down around line 33:

> "The German infantry…has almost no armor in defending itself, and use pikes and swords for offense.

> "They come with these arms and order of battle to meet the enemy…"

It specifically refers to the Germans' pikes and swords, and in the next sentence says that they come with "these" arms, which leads us to believe that the arms in question are in fact the pikes and swords. Looking through the remaining answers, we see that answer choice C is valid and that's the answer you should choose.

11. **Answer: A.** Your first instinct in reading this question is to look at question 1 and go, "Hey, I know, it's because the Romans fought the Germans up close and were able to disarm them because, etc. etc. etc." And you'd be correct…if the question was "What was the key to the Romans beating *the Germans*?" But now, we're dealing with a more abstract question, and thankfully, one that is addressed correctly in the passage. In a sense, this is the "overview" question that you normally get with each reading comprehension set of questions. Fabricio's whole point in why the Romans succeed in battle was the point of this reading, with the story about the Germans just to illustrate his point. Let's look over the first two paragraphs again:

> "I say thusly, that in many places in our histories you will find the Roman infantry to have defeated numberless cavalry, but you will never find them to have been defeated by men on foot because of some defect they may have had in their arms or because of some advantage the enemy had in his.

> "For if their manner of arming had been defective, it was necessary for them to follow one of two courses: either when they found one who was better armed than they, not to go on further with the conquest, or that they take up the manner of the foreigner, and leave off theirs. And since neither ensued, there follows, what can be easily conjectured, that this method of arming was better than that of anyone else."

The first paragraph basically says that you'd never see the Romans defeated because they had defective weapons or their opponents had great weapons. The second paragraph brings it home. The Romans, when faced with a losing situation, did one of two things: give up (or "not to go on further with the conquest") or pick up the opponent's methods instead of their previous methods. He concludes the paragraph by saying that, because the Romans never appeared to have a problem, that this method of combat was better than anyone else's. In other words, they either ran or learned from their opponents and used their own methods against them. They adopted their methods, so we would choose answer choice A.

12. **Answer: E.** This question asks us to interpret the passage and make our conclusion based on the facts we read from the selection. In this case, we're looking for evidence of how the Romans fought, which Fabricio covers in some detail. From the previous question, we know that the Romans would adopt the methods of their opponents in order to succeed. There's no mention of any specific viciousness, so we can rule out brutality, answer C. Because the Romans were willing to learn other methods and not just stick to one way of doing battle, we can rule out stubbornness, answer A. While one of the methods the Romans "could" have adopted was to run from an enemy they couldn't beat, you don't see any mention of the Romans running in the story; you see a mention of the Romans beating the Germans by rendering the German's weapons useless. This makes it seem that Fabricio doesn't see the Roman solder as cowardly, so you can probably rule out answer D. In fact, in order for this technique to work, the Roman soldier needs to be observant. In fact, Fabricio's story tells of Captain Carmingnuola and how he saw the power of the German's pikes and how to overcome this obstacle. This leads us to believe that the correct answer should be E, observant.

13. **Answer: D.** One of the basic questions to expect when reading a passage is to come up with the main point or intended message of the entire passage. When going through this particular reading, we see that the discussion starts with early man noticing the shadows as the sun moves through the sky. It then advances to the invention of the sundial, and the refinement of time-keeping devices with things such as the one- and two-jar water clocks. Answer A is the quick answer for people who think that the first paragraph contains the point of the entire passage, and it's a red herring. Don't fall for it. Answer C goes further into the passage. While the biggest paragraph details the invention of the sundial, the passage talks about other inventions, such as the water clock, which is not directly related to the sundial. Therefore, answer C is limited in scope and should be eliminated. Likewise, answer E talks about one specific invention in the passage, this time at the very end of the passage, and it's meant to trap people who just skim the end of the reading to get the answer. We're left with B and D.

While B has some merit, because sun and star watching enables man to tell time, answer D is the proper answer that best conveys the point of the entire passage, not just pieces of it.

14. **Answer: C.** This question requires you to pick out key pieces of information from the passage, and go one step further by creating a timeline and picking the first item in that timeline. Answer E may trip up a few people, because it actually relies on your current knowledge and not specific information in the passage. There is no mention of the wristwatch in the passage, but the test assumes that you know that a wristwatch is a modern invention that comes much later than anything else on this list. Ignore it immediately and move on. As the passage progresses, we see mentions of the sundial and the clepsydra, or the one-jug water clock. We also see in line 25–26 that the sundial "was the first time machine and from it was evolved all the complicated mechanism of the modern clock." This clearly puts the sundial ahead of answer A, the modern clock, so we can rule out A. As the rest of the passage will reveal, the sundial was invented first, followed by the clepsydra, followed by the two-jug water clock. Therefore, our answer is C.

15. **Answer: E.** Once again, your job with this question is to go through and either find the one instance that cannot be true, or find the four instances that are true and reach the answer by process of elimination. We can rule out:

Answer B, shadows on objects, in lines 3–6:

> "[T]he shadows cast by familiar objects moved in a regular manner, according to the hour, and no doubt made use of this knowledge to arrange meeting places near to such objects when the shadows should have reached a given mark."

Answer C, arrangement of stars, in lines 9–11:

> "[A]s he learned to know and recognize the ordered procession of the stars, he had a clock by night."

Answer A, dripping of water, in lines 26–28:

> "At first it was merely a jar of water with a small hole at the bottom, which permitted the contents to drip out at a steady uniform rate."

Answer D, level of water in a jar, in lines 28–30:

> "As the level of the water in the jar sank, the hours that had passed since the vessel was last filled were indicated."

While the moon is mentioned as a period of time in line 13, there is *no* mention of moonlight in the passage. For this reason, and by the process of elimination, you should choose answer E.

16. **Answer: A.** The key here is to pick out the section of the passage where this exact word lies, and define the meaning of this word based on context and other uses of the same word within the passage. Pulling out, let's look at the context of "contrivance" in line 24:

> "But as the sundial depended upon the beams of a sun which did not always shine during the day and never during the night, it could not entirely satisfy, and so man's inventive mind produced the clepsydra, or water clock. This was but a simple **contrivance**, but nevertheless it was the first time machine and from it was evolved all the complicated mechanism of the modern clock."

Thankfully, all the information we need is present in this one section. As we can see from the previous sentence, the contrivance is referring to the clepsydra, or the water clock. In addition, the rest of the sentence (where *contrivance* is located) confirms that it is a "time machine" and the basis of the modern clock. While the actual answer, clepsydra, or water clock, is *not* one of the five choices offered to us, we can use the closest meaning, answer A (a machine), and pick that as our answer. We see that answers B, C, and E are either abstract concepts or intangible items, and answer D is too specific and therefore an incorrect answer as well.

17. **Answer: D.** This question requires you to understand exactly how the clepsydra works, and use that information to figure out which answer choice is relevant to that process. While you don't have to be a civil engineer to get this question right, you do have to be able to visualize this concept and use the reading to get an idea of how it functions. The clepsydra, or water clock, works by filling a jug, and having a small droplet of water exit the jug through a hole. Because the water exits at a uniform rate, they can know when an hour, two hours, six hours, and so on have passed, by looking at how much water is left in the jug, through markings on the side of the jug. Therefore, the main concept here is the volume of water in the jug versus how much has left the jug. Stretching this concept further, the concept of gravity explains how the droplets leave the jug, but there is no mention of gravity here. Instead, there is *one* and only one mention of anything water-related in our five answer choices, which makes D the logical answer. The other answers have to do with other concepts discussed in

the passage, concepts of telling time, but *not* in the specific function of the specific device mentioned here.

18. **Answer: D.** Whenever you're asked to add something to the passage, it's not just the main point of the passage that is critical. You have to understand the flow of information and facts and where the passage is leading, so you can figure out the next move. In this case, we start with man's observance of the shadows made by the sun against objects on Earth, how those shadows move throughout the day in a regular fashion, and ultimately, how those shadows mark the passage of time. From there, we move on to man observing stars in the sky at night in order to tell time, too. From this we get the invention of the sundial, then the one-jug water clock, and finally the two-jug water clock. More importantly, if we look at the key points in order:

1. Man notices the existence of time, uses shadows to keep track.

2. With no shadows at night, man improves time-telling by using stars as well.

3. Man improves preciseness of time-telling by inventing sundial to interpret shadows.

4. Man improves sundial by using water clock, to eliminate problems such as cloudy days and nights.

5. Man improves water clock by adding second jug.

The progression of the passage seems to indicate man's ability to improve his skill at telling time throughout the ages. Therefore, the logical next topic is to stay on that track and talk about how they would improve the two-jug water clock. So, our answer is D. Answers A and C wouldn't make sense as the next paragraph because they interrupt the flow of the passage completely. The topics there were presented much earlier in the reading and have no direct bearing on the last paragraph or the logical topic to follow. Answer E would be a great answer…if the question was to create the next sentence, not the next paragraph. It's too limited of a topic to devote an entire paragraph to, and for that reason, we should eliminate it. Answer B jumps ahead somewhat radically to the modern day and is not like the flow of the entire passage. We've seen an incremental improvement throughout this reading, and to jump ahead to modern day wouldn't be the logical choice. Having said that, however, if all four other answers were completely off-base, this would be a possibility. After all, the point of this is the refinement of time-telling devices. The modern clock fits into that timeline, albeit at the end of that chain.

19. Answer: C. The key to the first question of a set of reading comprehension questions is to read and digest the entire passage, and come up with the main point or message. In this case, the author sets up the situation: A stormy day at sea, Martin Holt goes overboard, Hunt jumps in after him, the crew rally around and figure out how to save Holt. They watch Hunt get closer, grab Martin Holt, and bring him back to the ship. Onboard, Holt thanks Hunt for his heroism, and Hunt just chalks it up to business as usual, expected behavior. While all of the answers have something to do with an element of this passage, most are too specific or limited in focus:

> Answer E is the "obvious" answer for people who try to figure out the correct answer by looking at the first paragraph. But not a lot was mentioned about the ship itself navigating through the rough weather, so this isn't a good answer. Answer D is talked about indirectly, as Hunt's swimming ability is key to him saving Martin Holt. But it's not really focused on here, and there's a much better answer that we can choose. We should eliminate D. Answer B isn't really covered here. The heart of this story is not with the Captain; he's a secondary figure in the case. While his leadership style might have inspired Hunt's natural instinct to save a crewman, it's not the *main* point of the passage. Answer A is a test on the reader's natural instincts when reading this passage. If this seems like an average day aboard a ship, then the reader doesn't seem to be able to put this in perspective of the natural situation. Given the efforts described, the drama of the situation, it should be inferred that, even if you know nothing about boats and sailing, that this is anything but routine. We're left with answer C, which truly covers the main point of capturing this story.

20. Answer: D. Let's look at the dialog around line 48 to set up our situation:

> "Hunt," cried the boatswain, "Hunt risked his life for you."
>
> As the latter was hanging back, Hurliguerly pushed him towards Martin Holt, whose eyes expressed the liveliest gratitude.
>
> "Hunt," said he, "you have saved me. But for you I should have been lost. I thank you."

At this point, Martin Holt and Hunt are back on the ship, and Martin Holt has asked the crew who saved his life. The boatswain identifies

Hunt as the hero, and fellow sailor Hurliguerly pushes Hunt closer to Martin Holt, so that Martin Holt can say thank you in person. The last line of this snippet, the one with the "he," cannot be said *by* Hunt, since it's talking to Hunt. We know from this dialog that it's the person who was saved by Hunt that is talking. That person is Martin Holt, and our answer is D.

21. **Answer: D.** In order to make educated guesses about the personality of a character in the story, it's important to isolate the key instances of that character's actions and interpret them against the rest of the story. In this case, West's "performance" is best captured in lines 20–22:

    "They are lost! both lost!" exclaimed the captain. "The boat, West, the boat!"

    "If you give the order to lower it," answered West, "I will be the first to get into it, although at the risk of my life. But I must have the order."

At this point, Martin Holt is overboard, Hunt has dove in after him, and the crew has already thrown things in the water for Martin to grab. The captain is ordering West to lower the boat. West's response is very telling and the key to answering this question. He's willing to be the first person to get into this boat (presumably a lifeboat), but he's not leaping at the opportunity (no pun intended). He'll follow orders and set an example, but he's clearly not volunteering. It appears that he understands the risks, and is taking a rational approach to the situation. This is *not* a foolish reaction, so we can eliminate answer C. He's obviously stepping up to the task, and as the last line indicates, we know at least some of the sailors report to West, so he's clearly one of the leaders. He's not acting shy, so we can eliminate answer E. We know from the rest of the story that the boat is not lowered and West never had to get inside, as Hunt caught up with Martin Holt and brought him back to the ship. There is no evidence of determination on the part of West, so there's no direct evidence that answer B is correct. So we're down to heroism and responsibility. While West was willing to risk his life by getting in the boat, he made it clear that he needed a direct order in order to do so. While being heroic doesn't require "leaping into the fray," it's clear that he's taking his responsibility as a leader and willing to do the right thing if it's necessary, but nothing further. Answer D is our best choice and it should be the answer you choose.

22. **Answer: E.** Let's pull back and examine the situation in the story around this instance:

   > "At the moment when I struggled up to my feet I caught sight of a **massive substance** which cleft the air and vanished in the whirl of the waves.
   >
   > "Was this a second accident? No! It was a voluntary action, a deed of self-sacrifice. Having finished his task, Hunt had thrown himself into the sea, that he might save Martin Holt."

   The author saw something that cut through the air and landed and got swallowed up in the waves. Because the author is still onboard the Halbrane, it's not logical for the entire ship to be swallowed up by the waves, so we can probably rule out answer C. Likewise, it's probably not "a wave" that's swallowed up by other waves, so we can rule out answer A. The next paragraph gives us the critical clue. At first, the author wonders if what he just saw was a second accident, this massive substance flying by. Instead, he realizes it's a rescue effort, and identifies sailor Hunt as the person who "flew" by him, into the water, after Martin Holt. Therefore, our answer is E. While the mainsail is mentioned in the first paragraph, it's not referred to again, so it's not a logical choice. And while Martin Holt could've been swallowed by the waves, given his location (in the water) at this point in the story, he couldn't have cut through the air; he was already fighting for his life in the ocean.

23. **Answer: A.** This question is another way of asking you what should be added next in the passage. To do this, you need to understand the main point of the passage and in this case, the actions by the players in the story. Because the story revolved around Hunt selflessly jumping into the water to save Martin Holt, an award to reflect this effort should reflect the heroism and self-sacrifice that Hunt undertook in this rescue operation. While he had to be an expert swimmer to survive in those rough waters, that's not why he should be recognized. Likewise, it takes an incredible amount of stamina to survive a raging sea and pull somebody about to drown back to the ship. It also takes an innate amount of navigation to find his missing crewmate through all the waves and foam. However, none of these are the actual reason for receiving an award. It's not like Hunt was competing against his other sailors in these categories or was being tested on his swimming, navigation, or stamina. Here's the final piece: While Hunt probably saw his duties as loyalty to his crew, reflected by his actions at the end of the story, that's not a trait necessarily deserving of an award by the captain. Hunt's act was one of valor, and you should choose answer A.

24. **Answer: D.** Once again, we're asked to add something to the story, but this time, we're asked for the one item among five choices that would *not* be helpful to the crew during this event. The critical part of this question is the end: "**after** Martin Holt was swept offboard." We know the crew was throwing objects toward Holt so he'd have something to hold onto. If they were able to throw a life preserver, that could've helped. As they were trying to locate him, searchlights could've helped the crew fixate on Holt, monitor his condition, and guide people to his location. Additionally, an on-board radar system could give the crew ideas of where the storm was heading, and hopefully Holt's location in the water. If Hunt could've worn a life jacket before jumping, or been able to take an extra life jacket to put on Martin Holt, that would have definitely helped. While real-time weather reports could've helped the crew prepare for the oncoming storm and rough waters, once Holt was swept overboard, there's not much these reports can do to save Holt's life. Our best answer here is D.

25. **Answer: C.** In this case, we're asked to divine the meaning of a word which, to our ears, might not be the most obvious choice. As usual, the best way to puzzle this out is to look at the context of the word choice. Holt has just been pulled from the ocean and asks who saved him. When he is told that it was Hunt, Martin Holt's eyes express the "liveliest" gratitude. Clearly, this is a strong emotion, and A and E do not fit. Holt is grateful, so D—combative—is probably out. And although one meaning of "lively" could be "vivacious," it is clear that Holt is conveying sincere gratitude for having his life unexpectedly saved. C is the strongest answer.

26. **Answer: D.** Here, we're asked to intuitively deduce something from the events of the story. Unless one is familiar with the staffing and operations of a sailing ship, it is better to look at the context of the passage. The key is in the phrase: "So great had been the incline of the schooner that the end of the yard of the mainsail was plunged three or four feet into the crest of a wave." This phrase, plus the general air of emergency that surrounds the passage, indicate that this is not a time of unconcerned normalcy on board. One can deduce that because the author mentions how great the ship was inclined, it must be unusual for the ends of the mainsail to touch the waves. Therefore, B is out. We are given no clues to whether Holt sits here regularly or not, so C and E are both weak answers. Finally, while evidently dangerous—Holt is swept overboard and almost drowns—we have no way of ranking how dangerous a spot it is compared to other duty posts. By process of elimination, D is the best answer.

SECTION IV—Logical Reasoning

1. A	**9.** A	**17.** A
2. B	**10.** D	**18.** A
3. D	**11.** D	**19.** D
4. E	**12.** E	**20.** C
5. C	**13.** B	**21.** E
6. E	**14.** C	**22.** B
7. C	**15.** B	**23.** C
8. B	**16.** D	**24.** E

1. **Choice A is** correct. The statement states that brown bears eat blueberries. Because the hairs of grizzly bears contained a higher ratio of [X] to [Y] than the hair of brown bears, and the higher the ratio of [X] to [Y], the more blueberries the bear had in its diet, the statements strongly support the conclusion that the diet of grizzly bears included at least some blueberries. Choice B is incorrect. The only information presented in the statement is that the hairs of grizzly bears contained a higher ratio of [X] to [Y] than the hair of brown bears. This statement does not provide support for the statement that the blueberries in the diet of brown bears were higher in [X] than the blueberries in the diets of other types of bears. Choice C is incorrect. The only information presented in the statement is that the hairs of grizzly bears contained a higher ratio of [X] to [Y] than the hair of brown bears. This statement does not provide support for the statement the diet of brown bears is richer in [Y] than the diet of grizzly bears. Choice D is incorrect. The only information presented in the statement is that the hairs of grizzly bears contained a higher ratio of [X] to [Y] than the hair of brown bears. This statement does not provide support for the statement the diets of grizzly bears and brown bears both contained less [X] than [Y]. Choice E is incorrect. There is nothing in the statement that indicates that the process of collecting the hairs from the bears somehow altered the ratio of [X] to [Y].

2. **Choice B is** correct. While morally laudable, the writer doesn't make any assumptions about what percentage of losses modern armies can accept. In this specific case, the 20% rate would only cause the general's army to "lose cohesion." Choice A is incorrect. The premise of the

entire passage is that orthopox kills a much greater number of people if they are not vaccinated. The number of people killed by vaccination—while grim indeed—is less, meaning that the infection is less deadly once people are vaccinated. Choice C is incorrect because the writer specifically states that the army's cohesion as a fighting force could be preserved with a 1% casualty rate. Choice D is incorrect. The writer assumes that the general's decision to vaccinate the army is a grim but necessary one. Therefore, no other effective options to avoid the high death toll caused by orthopox can be assumed. Choice E is incorrect, because the writer makes it clear that exposing an unvaccinated army to orthopox would have rendered the entire force ineffective.

3. **Choice D** is correct. The lack of crop pests due to the recent shift of climate and their ability to re-establish themselves in the rice fields will result in a direct impact on the amount of rice grown, resolving the apparent paradox. Choice A is incorrect because it does not resolve the paradox by showing why rice yields will be lower, only that yields of all crops will be higher. Choice B is incorrect. An increased population could result in, say, greater urban development, which could eventually crowd out fields used to grow rice. However, this is a speculative argument at best, therefore not a strong answer. Choice C is incorrect because it actually increases the paradox by adding a strong argument that the rice crops will, in fact, be substantially larger than before. Choice E is incorrect. Even if the monsoon cycle fails next year, the overall trend of lower temperature and humidity over the next centuries will continue the apparent paradox of better climate without a higher rice yield.

4. **Choice E** is correct. This statement upholds the core assumption of the argument: that there are no significant differences between the decade preceding the mandate to the car manufacturers and the 10 years since its passage that could account for the decrease in teen fatalities. Choice A is incorrect because it weakens the argument by providing an alternative explanation to the decrease in teen accident deaths: the fact that teens are driving heavier cars such as SUVs. Choice B is incorrect because it weakens the argument by providing an alternative explanation to the decrease in teen accident deaths: the fact that teens are getting into fewer accidents. Choice C is incorrect because it weakens the argument by providing an alternative explanation to the decrease in teen accident deaths: the fact that there simply aren't as many teen drivers out on the roads to get into accidents in the first place. Choice D is incorrect because it doesn't particularly

strengthen the argument that by mandating the manufacturers to put airbags into "cars driven by teenagers." Rather, it muddies the conclusion by showing that teens stopped driving cars, shifted to pickup trucks, and then back, raising the possibility that another force was coming into play to reduce teen deaths besides the mandate.

5. **Choice C** is correct. The author of the text is basing his conclusion on two groups of data: the teen crash fatality statistics of two different decades. Choice A is incorrect. Although the writer notes that the presentation was convincingly done by the veteran head of the AARG, there is no evidence that the presenter's authority was what swayed the writer to their conclusion. Choice B is incorrect. There is no evidence that the writer consulted public opinion at all here. Choice D is incorrect, as it would have the effect of weakening the conclusion. Choice E is incorrect, as it would have the effect of weakening the conclusion.

6. **Choice E** is correct. This goes to the heart of telephone survey, as it is the deepest flaw in the questioning. Literate respondents who did not read the paper—preferring, for example, to read weekly news magazines—would register on the survey as a "false positive," artificially raising the reported illiteracy rate. Choice A is incorrect. Even though some people may not have told the truth, it is not a flaw that is directly applicable to the questions asked by the survey. Choice B is incorrect, as it is irrelevant to the argument that Metropolis has an extremely high illiteracy rate. Choice C is incorrect because it is a weaker answer than E. This is a flaw in the timing of the survey, not the survey itself. Choice D is incorrect because it is a weaker answer than E. As with C, this is a flaw in the timing of the survey, not the survey itself.

7. **Choice C** is correct because the argument is based on comparing the amount of hydrogen left over on the ring particles. If particles started off with different amounts of hydrogen to begin with, then the argument's validity would be seriously compromised. Choice A is incorrect because it only addresses one of the subjects that is required for the argument—the Oort asteroids. It does not discuss the ringed planets or the level of hydrogen. Choice B is incorrect. It is a *non sequitur* because it has nothing to do with the argument presented about the amount of hydrogen found on ring particles. Choice D is incorrect because it is too general. The argument specifically discusses Oort asteroids and ringed planets, not asteroids in general. Choice E is incorrect. It is a non sequitur because it has nothing to do with the argument presented about the amount of hydrogen found on ring particles.

8. **Choice B** is correct. Timothy's reply indicates that he interpreted Alan's remark to mean that the only superb debaters are people who attended college. Choice A is incorrect. Timothy isn't objecting to the likelihood that college graduates could be better debaters—only that *every* great debater had to have gone to college. Choice C is incorrect. This is a logical inference from Timothy's remark, not Alan's. Choice D is incorrect. This is a good answer, but it is not as strong as B because Timothy isn't making his statement about college = superb debating; he is instead making the contention that professions that don't need college training can also produce great debaters. Choice E is incorrect. This is a logical inference from Timothy's remark, not Alan's.

9. **Choice A** is correct. Both A and the initial statement draw a dubious conclusion from two related statements, concluding that if one condition preceded another, the result is known. Choice B is incorrect. Even though the argument's flaws are very similar to the initial statement, the "will" statement means that it is speculative in nature. Choice C is incorrect—all the statement does is reword itself. Choice D is incorrect because the statement is not flawed; it is contradictory in nature. Choice E is incorrect. As with B, even though the argument's flaws are very similar to the initial statement, the "will" statement means that it is speculative in nature.

10. **Choice D** is correct because the statement is really just self-referential: you have to agree with Hobbes because he felt this way, and you cannot disagree. Choice A is incorrect. It is of no consequence if the author met Hobbes or not so long as they have accurately quoted the words and the context of what Hobbes meant to say. Choice B is incorrect. Even if many scholars think the book is outdated, it does not address the relevance or irrelevance of the book's ideas. Choice C is incorrect because offering a biography of Hobbes is superfluous to what the author is arguing unless he or she is lying about what Hobbes's quote actually supports. Choice E is incorrect. The specifics of what a strong government would do is superfluous to the core of the argument.

11. **Choice D** is correct. The past historical record of commute prices provides the most direct answer to one of the paragraph's most important statements: why **the cost of commuting by automobile continues to rise at more than 15% each year.** Choice A is incorrect because the text only deals with the average cost of projects in

neighboring states; it is impossible to determine whether it logically follows that a specific rail project in Cayuga City would also cause the city council to lay out $40 million. Choice B is incorrect because there is no mention of how the city council arrived at the figure of $40 million. The only speculation that the city council engages in is that they don't **expect the train to run for the next five years.** Choice C is incorrect because if true, it potentially undermines the conclusion of the text—which is that overall ridership of the train will be higher in five years because of the comparatively high cost of commuting by car versus rail. Choice E is good answer and would be correct if not for the stronger answer in D. It shows that the price of gas—a component of the costs of commuting by car—has increased. However, it does not address the fact that other costs of the commute by car (automobile upkeep, tolls, and so forth) could have decreased, resulting in a different result than a 15% increase in the cost of the commute each year.

12. **Choice E** is correct because it follows that if the main source of the commuting workers—the Bell Monte canning company—plans to move before the train's opening, the demand for rail services will be greatly diminished compared to the present. A is incorrect because it does not necessarily follow that a cost overrun will lead to lower ridership. The cost has to be shown as impacting the consumer of the rail services in a negative way for it to be relevant. Choice B is incorrect because it misstates the purpose of having a longer rail line. The purpose of the longer line is not to run more trips throughout the day, but to encourage more commuters to use the rail line as it is more conveniently located. Choice C is a *non sequitur*. That is, there is nothing factually incorrect about the statement but it really doesn't relate to the argument at hand. It is simply a speculative statement that the rail line is likely to open in only four years. Choice D is actually a fairly good answer and would be correct if not for the stronger answer in E. It does follow that a cost overrun leading to higher ticket prices could lead to lower ridership. However, the answer has two flaws that weaken it compared to E. First, it is speculative in nature, and second, it does not show that the higher ticket prices would be more expensive than the cost of commuting by automobile, especially if the cost of that form of commute is going up by 15% each year.

13. **Choice B** is correct. Bob's statement is inherently illogical because it references itself. Choice A is incorrect because it is logical to assume that the more someone likes a food, the more they will eat of it, or the less they will avoid it the way Sally wants to avoid the broccoli her mom may be serving. Choice C is incorrect because all it does is present a fact that Bob is unaware of. Choice D is incorrect because Sally's

truthfulness is secondary to the self-referencing nature of Bob's statement. Choice E is incorrect because the quality of whether broccoli is good for you or not is irrelevant to the validity of Bob's statement.

14. **Choice C** is the best answer because it supports the idea that smokers can pick out strong tastes, thereby developing strong attractions and aversions based on different flavored brands of tobacco. Choice A is incorrect because it is a more broadly drawn statement about how people with food allergies act similarly. Choice B is incorrect. It is irrelevant health information in regard to linking smoking and strong brand preferences and aversions. Choice D is incorrect. This weakens the argument because it implies that smokers wouldn't develop strong preferences and strong aversions to certain brands. Choice E is incorrect. It is a non sequitur.

15. **Choice B** is correct because the argument excludes all explanations of how salmon navigate except for smell. Choice A is incorrect as it does not pick out individual members of the group to draw conclusions about the salmon species in general. Choice C is incorrect. It is a very good answer, but B is stronger because the argument specifically raises alternative explanations and then discards them in favor of its conclusion. Choice D is incorrect. There is no comparison being made between two groups of animals. Choice E is incorrect. The argument does not seek to apply a rule to all species of Pacific salmon when it only talks about Chinook salmon.

16. **Choice D** is correct because the author likens the reckless use of the forest timber to schemes involving the fur trade and nuclear waste. Choice A is incorrect. The article does not state that the author had observed the fur trade and nuclear industry. Choice B is incorrect. The article does not state that the author had worked with the paper and pulp industries. Choice C is incorrect because the author does not cite any authority, but argues against it. Choice E is incorrect. The appeal is very emotional, and does not appeal to common sense.

17. **Choice A** is correct because it implies that no matter how truthful Lynch normally is, that evening his judgment may have been compromised by alcohol. This best explains why the FBI is disregarding his report. Choice B is incorrect because Lynch's accuracy on the stand for an unrelated subject is irrelevant to the FBI's decision. Choices C and D are incorrect because they both strengthen Lynch's assertion that he did in fact see a UFO, which does not explain why the FBI dismissed his observation. Choice E is incorrect. It does not directly explain why the FBI chose to disregard Lynch's statement; it only offers an additional hypothesis as to what Lynch might have seen.

18. **Choice A** is correct. The argument that strict regulation leads to the loss of industry and jobs is directly weakened by showing that this is not the case in neighboring states. Choice B is incorrect. The number of measures passed is not in issue—only the creation and enforcement is claimed to have a negative effect on industry. Choice C is incorrect because it is irrelevant how many people are in specific industries—the argument is that the measures are bad for all industries, who will eventually move out of Ecotopia because of the measures. Choice D is incorrect because it is purely speculative in nature. Choice E is incorrect because it strengthens, not weakens the argument.

19. **Choice D** is correct because it helps the argument logically show the effect of the onerous beach protection measures. Choice A is incorrect. Whether the fines were just or not does not impact the argument of the measure's effect on industry in general. Choice B is incorrect. In fact it could weaken the argument because there may be an alternative reason that business could leave Ecotopia instead of the strict beach protection measures. Choice C is incorrect because it doesn't make clear that Avalon Industries left because of the beach protection measures. Choice E is incorrect because it is too narrow; the argument used these two industries as examples, not as conclusions.

20. **Choice C** is correct because like in the initial text, there are two complementary reasons cited to support a conclusion. Furthermore, the conclusion is expressed in a manner demonstrating a condition that will be invalid because the conclusion is true. Choices A, B, D, E: These choices are all incorrect. Each of these statements contain complementary reasons but are not as close to the original style of reasoning because they do not illustrate the conclusion by demonstrating a condition that will be invalid because the conclusion is true. In each case, they illustrate a condition that will be valid: the tax burden will be higher, the special hazard fee will be charged, or the farm will be taxed at a new rate. Note that answer D attempts to confuse you by throwing in an unrelated fact discussing the first section of an updated nuisance law.

21. **Choice E** is correct. It follows that if companies who concentrate on only one of the two services will succeed, it is because customers don't want the combined services. Choice A is incorrect even though it could be true, because it does not necessarily follow. The two services could actually have a lot in common, but commonality or lack thereof is not the argument—only that if a company tries to do both, then they will not succeed. Choices B and C are incorrect for the same reason: they are *non sequiturs*. That is, there is nothing factually incorrect about the statements themselves, but they really don't relate to the argument at

hand. Choice D is incorrect because it only pertains to part of the argument. The case is made that a company can only be successful at concentrating on one area—it does not specify which!

22. **Choice B** is correct because it shows that doctors do learn about public health in a setting outside of post-graduate training. Choice A is incorrect because it actually reinforces the argument is that it is highly unlikely that medical students get training in how the public health system works, because it is an optional course that students have to request in order to learn. Choice C is incorrect. The argument is about the training of doctors, not who actually provides the care in the current system. Choice D is incorrect because even if it is true, it does not make the conclusion logically incorrect. Choice E is incorrect. The fact that public health is covered in a textbook on surgical practice does not change the fact that many have not taken a full course in public health operations.

23. **Choice C** is correct. In the final sentence it is concluded that this practice is wrong because it would be a violation of the good faith contract we enter into when we hire individuals in other professions. Choice A is incorrect. It is unsupported by the passage. The passage does not state that politicians often lie to their constituents, nor is this the main focus of the passage. The main focus of the passage is to determine not whether they do, but whether they should engage in this practice. Choice B is incorrect, because it is not a conclusion, simply a statement implied by the passage. Choices D and E are incorrect. They are not conclusions; they are premises of the argument.

24. **Choice E** is correct. In this answer choice, Amy disagrees based on the claim that the existence of the opposite of the characteristic cited by Jeannie is evidence that something is not good. Choice A is incorrect. In the interchange in the passage, Jeannie concludes that something should not be done based on a certain characteristic. Amy disagrees, based on the claim that the opposite of that characteristic is evidence that something is not good. In this answer choice, Amy disagrees based on the claim that the existence of that characteristic is evidence that something is good. Choice B is incorrect. In this answer choice, Amy disagrees based on the claim that the existence of the characteristic cited by Jeannie is something that he personally prefers. Choice C is incorrect. In this answer choice, Amy disagrees based on the claim that the existence of the same characteristic cited by Jeannie is evidence that something is not good. Choice D is incorrect. In this answer choice, Amy disagrees based on the claim that the existence of the same characteristic cited by Jeannie is evidence that something is good.

Practice Exam 2

SECTION I—Reading Comprehension

Time—35 minutes

27 Questions

Directions: Each passage in this section is followed by a group of questions to be answered on the basis of what is stated or implied in the passage. For some of the questions, more than one of the choices could conceivably answer the question. However, you are to choose the best answer; that is, the response that most accurately and completely answers the question, and blacken the corresponding space on your answer sheet.

The Cassini spacecraft's two close flybys of Saturn's icy moon Enceladus have revealed that the moon has a significant atmosphere. Scientists, using Cassini's magnetometer instrument for their studies, say the source may be volcanism, geysers, or gases escaping from the surface or the interior.

5

When Cassini had its first encounter with Enceladus on Feb. 17 at an altitude of 1,167 kilometers (725 miles), the magnetometer instrument saw a striking signature in the magnetic field. On March 9, Cassini approached to within 500 kilometers (310 miles) of Enceladus's surface and obtained additional evidence.

10

The observations showed a bending of the magnetic field, with the magnetospheric plasma being slowed and deflected by the moon. In addition, magnetic field oscillations were observed. These are caused when electrically charged (or ionized) molecules interact with the magnetic field by spiraling around the field line. This interaction creates characteristic oscillations in the magnetic field at frequencies that can be used to identify the molecule. The observations from the Enceladus flybys are believed to be due to ionized water vapor.

15

"These new results from Cassini may be the first evidence of gases originating either from the surface or possibly from the interior of Enceladus," said Dr. Michele Dougherty, principal investigator for the Cassini magnetometer and professor at Imperial College in London. In 1981, NASA's Voyager spacecraft flew by Enceladus at a distance of 90,000 kilometers (56,000 miles) without detecting an atmosphere. It's possible detection was beyond Voyager's capabilities, or something may have changed since that flyby.

20

25

This is the first time since Cassini arrived in orbit around Saturn last summer that an atmosphere has been detected around a moon of Saturn, other than its largest moon, Titan. Enceladus is a relatively small moon. The amount of gravity it exerts is not enough to hold an atmosphere very long. Therefore, at Enceladus, a strong continuous source is required to maintain the atmosphere.

30

The need for such a strong source leads scientists to consider eruptions, such as volcanoes and geysers. If such eruptions are present, Enceladus would join two other such active moons, Io at Jupiter and Triton at Neptune. "Enceladus could be Saturn's more benign counterpart to Jupiter's dramatic Io," said Dr. Fritz Neubauer, co-investigator for the Cassini magnetometer, and a professor at the University of Cologne in Germany.

35

Since the Voyager flyby, scientists have suspected that this moon is geologically active and is the source of Saturn's icy E ring. Enceladus is the most reflective object in the solar system, reflecting about 90 percent of the sunlight that hits it. If Enceladus does have ice

40

45   volcanoes, the high reflectivity of the moon's surface might result from continuous deposition of icy particles originating from the volcanoes.

Enceladus's diameter is about 500 kilometers (310 miles), which would fit in the state of Arizona. Yet despite its small size, Enceladus exhibits one of the most interesting surfaces of all the icy satellites.

Source: NASA Press Release 3/16/05: Cassini Finds an Atmosphere on Saturn's Moon Enceladus: http://www.nasa.gov/mission_pages/cassini/media/cassini-031605.html

1. Which one of the following best expresses the main idea of the passage?

   ❑ A. Evidence gathered by the Cassini spacecraft reveals that Saturn's moon, Enceladus, has volcanoes or geysers on its surface or the interior.

   ❑ B. The Cassini spacecraft is more technologically advanced than the Voyager spacecraft.

   ❑ C. Enceladus has one of the most interesting surfaces of Saturn's moons.

   ❑ D. Flybys by the Cassini spacecraft indicate that Saturn's moon, Enceladus, has a significant atmosphere.

   ❑ E. Scientists suspect Cassini is geologically active.

2. According to the passage, why do scientists believe it likely that Enceladus has volcanoes or geysers on its surface or interior?

   ❑ A. The bending of the magnetic field observed indicates the presence of volcanoes or geysers.

   ❑ B. The amount of gravity Enceladus exerts requires a strong continuous source to maintain an atmosphere.

   ❑ C. The Voyager flyby produced evidence that the moon is geologically active.

   ❑ D. Enceladus's high reflectivity is indicative of ice volcanoes.

   ❑ E. Pictures taken by the Cassini spacecraft show an active volcano.

3. Which one of the following best expresses the meaning of "benign," as that word is used in line 37 of the passage?

   ❑ A. Harmless

   ❑ B. Beneficial

   ❑ C. Not malignant

   ❑ D. Mild

   ❑ E. Harsh

4. Which one of the following can be inferred from the passage?

   ❑ A. Enceladus is Saturn's smallest moon.

   ❑ B. Io is more geologically active than Enceladus.

   ❑ C. Enceladus is the only moon of Saturn that has an atmosphere.

   ❑ D. Triton is larger than Titan.

   ❑ E. Io is more active than Triton.

5. According to the passage, what is the cause of the magnetic field oscillations that were observed by the Cassini spacecraft?

❑ A. Magnetospheric plasma being slowed and deflected by the moon

❑ B. Low gravity conditions on Enceladus

❑ C. The interaction of electrically charged or ionized molecules with the magnetic field

❑ D. The high reflectivity of Enceladus's surface

❑ E. Saturn's icy E ring

6. In lines 7–8 of the passage, the author notes that "the magnetometer instrument saw a striking signature." To which one of the following does the phrase "striking signature" refer?

❑ A. The bending of the magnetic field

❑ B. The slowing of magnetospheric plasma

❑ C. The deflection of magnetospheric plasma by the moon

❑ D. Oscillations in the magnetic field

❑ E. Gases escaping from the surface of Enceladus

7. Which one of the following best describes the author's attitude toward the possible discovery of an atmosphere on Enceladus?

❑ A. Disdainful

❑ B. Objective

❑ C. Bubbly

❑ D. Incredulous

❑ E. Timid

The promise of America was born in the 18th century out of the bold conviction that we are all created equal. It was extended and preserved in the 19th century, when our nation spread across the continent, saved the Union, and abolished the awful scourge of

5   slavery.

Then, in turmoil and triumph, that promise exploded onto the world stage to make this the American century. And what a century it has been. America became the world's mightiest industrial power, saved the world from tyranny in two World Wars and a long cold war, and

10   time and again reached out across the globe to millions who, like us, longed for the blessings of liberty.

Along the way, Americans produced a great middle class and security in old age, built unrivaled centers of learning and opened public schools to all, split the atom and explored the heavens, invented the

15   computer and the microchip, and deepened the well-spring of justice by making a revolution in civil rights for African-Americans and all

minorities and extending the circle of citizenship, opportunity, and dignity to women.

20 Now, for the third time, a new century is upon us and another time to choose. We began the 19th century with a choice: to spread our Nation from coast to coast. We began the 20th century with a choice: to harness the industrial revolution to our values of free enterprise, conservation, and human decency. Those choices made all the difference. At the dawn of the 21st century, a free people must now

25 choose to shape the forces of the information age and the global society, to unleash the limitless potential of all our people, and yes, to form a more perfect Union.

As times change, so government must change. We need a new government for a new century, humble enough not to try to solve all

30 our problems for us but strong enough to give us the tools to solve our problems for ourselves; a government that is smaller, lives within its means, and does more with less. Yet where it can stand up for our values and interests around the world, and where it can give Americans the power to make a real difference in their everyday lives,

35 government should do more, not less. The preeminent mission of our new government is to give all Americans an opportunity, not a guarantee but a real opportunity, to build better lives.

Beyond that, my fellow citizens, the future is up to us. Our founders taught us that the preservation of our liberty and our Union depends

40 upon responsible citizenship. And we need a new sense of responsibility for a new century. There is work to do, work that government alone cannot do. Each and every one of us, in our own way, must assume personal responsibility not only for ourselves and our families but for our neighbors and our nation. Our greatest

45 responsibility is to embrace a new spirit of community for a new century. For any one of us to succeed, we must succeed as one America. The challenge of our past remains the challenge of our future: Will we be one nation, one people, with one common destiny, or not? Will we all come together, or come apart?

http://www.clintonfoundation.org/speeches.htm

8. Which one of the following would be the best title for the passage?
- ❑ A. "The Challenges of a New Century"
- ❑ B. "The Promise of America"
- ❑ C. "America the Great"
- ❑ D. "The American Century"
- ❑ E. "The Scourge of Slavery"

9. According to the passage, which century can be defined as the American century?

   ❏ A. the 17th century
   ❏ B. the 18th century
   ❏ C. the 19th century
   ❏ D. the 20th century
   ❏ E. the 21st century

10. The author is likely to disagree with all of the following statements, *except*:

   ❏ A. The United States should never intercede in foreign affairs.
   ❏ B. America would have been better off if nuclear fission have never been discovered.
   ❏ C. The proper role of government is to guarantee its citizens a better life.
   ❏ D. Americans will succeed together or not at all.
   ❏ E. Only white American males should be entitled to vote.

11. Which one of the following most appropriately describes the attitude of the author of the passage?

   ❏ A. Pessimistic
   ❏ B. Condescending
   ❏ C. Exhortatory
   ❏ D. Threatening
   ❏ E. Dictatorial

12. The primary purpose of the second paragraph is to

   ❏ A. Contrast the successes of America in the 20th century with the travails of the 19th century.
   ❏ B. Praise America for its accomplishments in the 20th century
   ❏ C. Question the choices made by America in the 20th century
   ❏ D. Examine the choices facing America as it enters the 21st century
   ❏ E. Exhort readers to embrace changes in government structure

13. The author is likely to agree with all of the following statements *except*:

   ❏ A. The establishment of the Social Security program in the 20th century was positive event.
   ❏ B. A good government should be able to take care of all of its citizens' problems.
   ❏ C. Americans cannot be complacent about the potential dangers of divisiveness among its citizenry.
   ❏ D. Slavery is evil.
   ❏ E. Government spending should decrease.

14. According to the author, why does America need a new government?

❏ A. America needs a new government that does more, not less.

❏ B. America needs a new government to guarantee Americans better lives.

❏ C. America needs a new government because times have changed.

❏ D. America needs a new government to assume responsibility for America's citizens, families, and neighbors.

❏ E. America needs a new government because the existing government has failed to meet the challenges posed in the 20th century.

"The very rich are different from you and me," Nick Carroway observed, in a memorable line from *The Great Gatsby*, a novel by F. Scott Fitzgerald about life among the very wealthy in the 1920s. But when it comes to using the Web, apparently the
5   wealthy are not much different from the rest of us: Ease of use, selection, speed, and trustworthiness are the key factors in the effectiveness of a website for the wealthy, too.

Yet some luxury retailers such as Nieman Marcus and Tiffany have had a difficult time developing an online presence for their wealthy
10   customers. When Nieman Marcus introduced its website in 2000, web designers were awed by the display of graphics and motion. But most customers were turned off because they could not find enough goods for sale, and could not easily navigate the site. Today, Niemanmarcus.com features no animations, no Flash graphics, but
15   much more merchandise neatly arranged by category and designer.

Developing an online marketing approach that increases a company's access to consumers while retaining an image of exclusivity was the challenge faced by the world-renowned jeweler Tiffany & Co. when it redesigned its website in 1999. The company was in the enviable
20   position of being perhaps the most famous jewelry company in the United States. Tiffany's offline marketing communications sought to engender feelings of beauty, quality, and timeless style—all hallmarks of the Tiffany brand. Tiffany's web designers attempted to build a website with many of those same hallmarks, using soft, neutral
25   colors throughout, sparse wording, and pictures that fade slowly onto the screen. The shopping portion of the website shows just one large item, with some smaller photos that can be enlarged by clicking at the bottom of the screen. The website also includes information on buying and caring for jewelry.

30   Critics complain, however, that the Tiffany website has too few products online, the Flash graphics are slow, there are too many animations, and the product line available is poorly organized. While Tiffany claims there are 2,000 products online, finding them and buying them is an arduous process. In a hurry for those for diamond-
35   studded cufflinks? How about a bracelet with gold and red rubies? Unfortunately, there is no search feature on the home page at the Tiffany site, but if you look hard enough, you'll find it on a separate shopping page.

It is clear that online luxury retailers face a difficult time translating
40   their brands and the look and feel of their luxury shops that connote
exclusivity, extravagance, excessive wealth, and entertainment into a
website that the masses will see. According to a study of wealthy web
customers and their hangouts on the Web, many luxury retailers have
emphasized glitzy animations, subtle color schemes, inscrutable
45   menus, and tricky navigation. Mark Aaron, vice president of investor
relations at Tiffany, notes, "Everyone says we have a beautiful site,
and it's what you'd expect from Tiffany. But having said that, we are
aware that we have to continue evolving to make the site more user
friendly."

50   For a contrast to Tiffany, visit the Nordstrom website. Nordstrom.com,
the website of the Washington-based high-end department store
known for service and customer loyalty, is a marvel of simplicity.
There, you will find more than 5,000 products, shown in big clear
pictures and organized in a thoughtful manner. For the time-starved
55   shopper (are the wealthy ever time-starved like the rest of us?),
Nordstrom provides an effective solution for that unusual, designer gift
that you really can't afford, but can't pass up, either.

Source: Excerpt from "Insight on Business: The Very Rich Are Different From You and Me: Neiman Marcus, Nordstrom, and Tiffany & Co." in E-commerce. business.technology.society, Second Edition. © Kenneth C. Laudon and Carol Guercio Traver, 2004; permission granted.

15. Which one of the following most accurately expresses the main point of the passage?
   - ❏ A. The very rich are likely to be different from the reader.
   - ❏ B. Some luxury retailers have had a difficult time developing effective websites.
   - ❏ C. The websites of Neiman Marcus and Tiffany & Co. feature too many graphics.
   - ❏ D. The websites of luxury retailers connote exclusivity, extravagance, and excessive wealth.
   - ❏ E. The wealthy are not much different from the rest of us.

16. Which one of the following can you infer to be false from reading the passage?
   - ❏ A. The author believes that the Tiffany.com website is more effective than the Neimanmarcus.com website.
   - ❏ B. Tiffany & Co. is one of the best-known jewelers in the United States.
   - ❏ C. The Tiffany & Co. brand uses a soft, neutral color.
   - ❏ D. Finding a specific product on the Tiffany.com website can be a difficult process.
   - ❏ E. The Tiffany.com website may be revised.

17. According to the passage, what is the primary reason the Nordstrom.com site is more effective than the Tiffany.com website?

    ❑ A. The Nordstrom.com website has more graphics.

    ❑ B. The Nordstrom.com website features better products.

    ❑ C. The Nordstrom.com website is easier to use.

    ❑ D. The Nordstrom.com website has more animations.

    ❑ E. The graphics on the Nordstrom.com website display more quickly.

18. The author's quotation of the line "The very rich are different from you and me," from the novel *The Great Gatsby* at the beginning of the passage serves which one of the following functions in the passage?

    ❑ A. It supports the author's assertion that the very rich are different from "regular" people.

    ❑ B. It introduces a commonly held view that the author defends in the rest of the passage.

    ❑ C. It highlights, in a somewhat ironic manner, the author's contention that when it comes to using the Web, the wealthy are not much different from other users of the Web.

    ❑ D. It explains why luxury retailers have had a difficult time developing an online presence for their wealthy customers.

    ❑ E. It presents an implicit criticism of the wealthy that the author further develops in the remainder of the passage.

19. You can infer from the passage that all of the following statements about the Neimanmarcus.com website introduced in 2000 are true *except*:

    ❑ A. The website offered less merchandise than the current Neimanmarcus.com website.

    ❑ B. The website featured Flash graphics and animations.

    ❑ C. The website was not well organized.

    ❑ D. The website was well received by web designers.

    ❑ E. The website was considered a success.

20. According to the passage, why have some luxury retailers had a difficult time developing an effective online presence?

    ❑ A. They have not spent enough money.

    ❑ B. They do not know enough about web design.

    ❑ C. They did not understand what their customers wanted in their websites.

    ❑ D. The wealthy do not use the Web for shopping.

    ❑ E. They have failed to create visually attractive websites.

21. Which one of the following best describes the author's tone in the passage?

- ❑ A. Ironic
- ❑ B. Disparaging
- ❑ C. Derisive
- ❑ D. Sardonic
- ❑ E. Acerbic

She was a maiden of rarest beauty, and not more lovely than full of glee. And evil was the hour when she saw, and loved, and wedded the painter. He, passionate, studious, austere, and having already a bride in his art; all light and smiles, and frolicsome as the young fawn;
5   loving and cherishing all things; hating only the art that was her rival; dreading only the pallet and brushes and other untoward instruments which deprived her of the countenance of her husband.

It was thus a terrible thing for this lady to hear the painter speak of his desire to portray even his young bride. But she was humble and
10   obedient, and sat meekly for many weeks in the dark, high turret-chamber where the light dripped upon the pale canvas only from overhead. But he, the painter, took glory in his work, which went on from hour to hour, and from day to day. And he was a passionate, and wild, and moody man, who became lost in reveries; so that he would
15   not see that the light that fell so ghastly In that lone turret withered the health and the spirits of his bride, who pined visibly to all but him. Yet she smiled on and still on, uncomplainingly, because she saw that the painter (who had high renown) took a fervid and burning pleasure in his task, and wrought day and night to depict her who so loved him,
20   yet who grew daily more dispirited and weak.

And some who beheld the portrait spoke of its resemblance in low words, as of a mighty marvel, and a proof not less of the power of the painter than of his deep love for her whom he depicted so surpassingly well. But at length, as the labor drew nearer to its conclusion, there
25   were admitted none into the turret; for the painter had grown wild with the ardor of his work, and turned his eyes from canvas merely, even to regard his wife. And he would not see that the tints that he spread upon the canvas were drawn from the cheeks of her who sat beside him.

30   And when many weeks had passed, and but little remained to do, save one brush upon the mouth and one tint upon the eye, the spirit of the lady again flickered up as the flame within the socket of the lamp. And then the brush was given, and then the tint was placed; and, for one moment, the painter stood entranced before the work which he had
35   wrought; but in the next, while he yet gazed, he grew tremulous and very pallid, and aghast, and crying with a loud voice, "This is indeed Life itself!" turned suddenly to regard his beloved—she was dead.

Source: Excerpt from "The Oval Portrait," by Edgar Allan Poe, 1850.

22. Which one of the following would be the best title for the passage?
    - ❑ A. "The Evil Painter"
    - ❑ B. "The Dutiful Wife"
    - ❑ C. "The Jealous Bride"
    - ❑ D. "The Beautiful Bride"
    - ❑ E. "The Famous Painter"

23. You can infer from the passage that all of the following adjectives can be used to accurately describe the painter *except*:
    - ❑ A. Talented
    - ❑ B. Dedicated
    - ❑ C. Ardent
    - ❑ D. Ascetic
    - ❑ E. Observant

24. Which one of the following best summarizes the author's attitude toward art, as evidenced by the passage?
    - ❑ A. Art can be used as both an instrument of creation and destruction.
    - ❑ B. Art is dangerous.
    - ❑ C. Art is death.
    - ❑ D. Art is an act of love.
    - ❑ E. Art is life.

25. Which one of the following best expresses the meaning of the following sentence from the passage: "And he would not see that the tints which he spread upon the canvas were drawn from the cheeks of her who sat beside him."
    - ❑ A. Due to the dim lighting in the turret-chamber, the painter could not see his paints.
    - ❑ B. The painter was using his wife's rouge as a pigment, but was unaware of this fact.
    - ❑ C. The painter was blind.
    - ❑ D. The painter failed to realize that requiring his wife to sit for weeks and weeks in the dim turret-chamber for the portrait was making her ill.
    - ❑ E. Due to the dim lighting in the turret-chamber, the painter could not see the canvas.

26. The author identifies all of the following as characteristics of the woman described in the passage *except*:
    - ❑ A. Attractive
    - ❑ B Jealous
    - ❑ C Acquiescent
    - ❑ D Cheerful
    - ❑ E Independent

27. Which of the following best expresses the meaning of "countenance," as that word is used in line 7 of the passage?

❑   A. Approval

❑   B Favor

❑   C Support

❑   D Face

❑   E Applause

THIS IS THE END OF THE SECTION.

SECTION II—Logical Reasoning

Time—35 minutes

24 Questions

Directions: The questions in this section are based on the reasoning contained in brief statements or passages. For some questions, more than one of the choices could conceivably answer the question. However, you are to choose the best answer; that is, the response that most accurately and completely answers the question. You should not make assumptions that are by common-sense standards implausible, superfluous, or incompatible with the passage. After you have chosen the best answer, blacken the corresponding space on your answer sheet.

QUESTIONS 1–2

Laura: "Alyssa has shown great musical ability from an early age. Both her mother and father are accomplished harpsichord players who have played duets at Carnegie Hall in the United States before packed audiences. Therefore, it is all but certain that Alyssa will also become a great harpsichord player."

Michael: "I'm not sure that you can realistically make that argument. Alyssa has wowed audiences at her piano recitals, but she's never shown that she could learn to play the harpsichord."

1. Laura's conclusion is strengthened the most if you assume which one of the following is true?

   ❑ A. Alyssa's aunt Florence has already played harpsichord before packed audiences all over Europe.

   ❑ B. Alyssa's younger sister Veronica has already played harpsichord before packed audiences all over Europe.

   ❑ C. At the age of nine, Alyssa wowed music fanciers by being the youngest person since Mozart to compose an entire concerto consisting of harpsichord duets.

   ❑ D. World-class ability to play the harpsichord is the result of a mix of factors, including exposure to the instrument, international travel, and genetics.

   ❑ E. The ability to play the harpsichord at the professional level is exclusively determined by family background.

2. Michael's reply to Laura indicates that he is relying upon which assumption?

   ❑ A. The audiences at the piano recitals are not as sophisticated as the ones at Carnegie Hall.

   ❑ B. Laura is not the best judge of a child's musical ability.

   ❑ C. Alyssa's learning to play the piano precludes her from learning how to play other instruments at a world-class level.

   ❑ D. The piano and the harpsichord are completely different and unrelated instruments.

   ❑ E. The harpsichord is the most technically challenging instrument to learn in the field of music.

3. When cholera began to kill hundreds of London residents in the summer of 1854, Dr. John Snow, a London medical practitioner from an extremely humble background, felt that the still-controversial "germ theory" was the best one for explaining the outbreak. Of course, he faced a certain amount of ridicule. The tiny "animalcules" that had been observed under a microscope were certainly fascinating, but there was no hard evidence that they did anything to the human body. Obviously, his fellow citizens and scientists in Victorian England cared nothing for the scientific method.

Which one of the following is the strongest criticism of the preceding statement?

   ❑ A. The statement makes a base appeal to emotion and intellectual snobbery.

   ❑ B. The author fails to note that the scientific method hadn't been developed yet in 1854.

   ❑ C. The author did not live during the reign of Queen Victoria and so lacks the perspective to properly judge Dr. Snow's fellow citizens and scientists.

   ❑ D. The author fails to take into account that Snow's fellow citizens and scientists only disregarded the doctor's opinion because he was from a humble background.

   ❑ E. The statement does not acknowledge how incredibly controversial the germ theory was in 1854.

4. While on the stand in the *Smith v. Center City Hospital* trial, Anderson claimed that he saw Smith break into the hospital's drug storage area and steal cases of expensive medications. Anderson claimed he had a perfect vantage point to witness the theft because he had been admitted to the hospital for the removal of his appendix and was recovering in the room next door to the drug storage area. Following his highly detailed and insightful testimony as to what he saw and heard during the theft, Anderson was immediately charged with perjury for lying on the stand.

Which one of the following, if true, best resolves the discrepancy between the apparent quality of the witness's testimony and the court charging him with perjury?

- ❑ A. Anderson had never been admitted to Center City Hospital before the incident in question, and was therefore completely unfamiliar with the building's layout.
- ❑ B. Anderson's room offers only the tiniest sliver of a view into the drug storage area.
- ❑ C. Anderson wears a hearing aid; without the aid, he is almost completely deaf.
- ❑ D. Anderson is 95 years old and suffers from advanced Alzheimer's disease, which affects his memory.
- ❑ E. Anderson had just been released from surgery on his appendix, and had been anesthetized.

5. While out on his nightly patrol, a policeman comes across a drunk intently searching the ground under a lit streetlamp. When he inquires what the drunk is looking for, the reply is, "My keys, I lost them down that dark alley over there." The policeman is taken aback and asks, "Why are you looking over here, when you lost your keys in a different location?" The drunk straightens up and replies, "Why, because the light is better over here."

This style of reasoning most closely parallels which one of the following arguments?

- ❑ A. We shouldn't use a pendulum to find oil on Eugene Mountain because we need a more accurate tool. We should only search for oil with an automobile's oil dipstick.
- ❑ B. We cannot find the Spanish doubloons on the beach because they would have already been picked up by curious bathers. We should only search for the doubloons where no one is bathing, such as the desert.
- ❑ C. We cannot search for the derelict submarine in the area it sunk, because the water is too turbid. We should only search where the water is clear enough that we can find the sub.
- ❑ D. We lost our keys that night we were out drinking in Miami. If we want to find our keys again, we'd better fly back to Miami and get drunk.
- ❑ E. We can't treat the patient with anti-venom for his snakebite because we're out of the serum. We should use the anti-venom for spider bite on the patient because we don't have anything else handy.

6. Proven liquid natural gas (LNG) reserves in the country of Baikalistan are at the same level as they were a decade ago. Proven reserves are the amount of natural gas considered extractable from known fields, and given ready supply of energy, the annual consumption of domestically produced LNG in the capital city of Kahlk has actually increased. However, over this same period, no new natural gas fields of any consequence have been discovered.

Which one of the following, if true, best reconciles the discrepancy described earlier?

- ❏ A. Over the past decade the annual consumption of imported LNG has increased more rapidly than that of domestic liquid natural gas in Baikalistan.
- ❏ B. Conservation measures have lowered the rate of growth of domestic LNG consumption from what it was a decade ago.
- ❏ C. Liquid natural gas exploration in Baikalistan has slowed due to increased concern over the environmental impact on the local caribou and spotted swallow.
- ❏ D. Due to technological advances over the last decade, much liquid natural gas previously considered unextractable—such as that in shale oil sand—is now considered extractable.
- ❏ E. Consumption of LNG has increased because prices have dropped as more domestically produced LNG has entered the market.

7. The International Space Station is a beacon of science and reason in the blackest night of nationalistic barbarism. Instead of competing to be the first nation to gain the "high ground" on the others, the station harnesses our common desire as humans to soar above the atmosphere together. I should know. And as the chief scientist on board the station for the last decade, I can confidently state that we can—and will—continue to make progress so long as we are sufficiently funded. The years I've spent budgeting each item allow me to make sure that every dollar is well spent, so that instead of "bang for the buck," you'll get an "explosion for the penny."

The chief scientist on the space station makes her case by

- ❏ A. A direct appeal to authority other than herself.
- ❏ B. By drawing the conclusion from an analogy.
- ❏ C. Deriving the conclusion from direct experience.
- ❏ D. Deriving the conclusion from indirect observation.
- ❏ E. Directly appealing to emotion and sentimentality.

QUESTIONS 8–9

The idea of "consumer sovereignty" is that the consumer is the force that drives the development of a given product over time, not slick marketing. And the ongoing evolution of the granola bar is proof positive that the consumer is indeed king. In the 1970s, the first bars of rolled oats, grain, and dried fruit were sold as healthy treats. However, only the truly dedicated would eat them because they had the taste and texture of tree bark. As the decades passed, consumers "voted" with their dollars, making sweeter and softer versions of the granola bar the top sellers. Manufacturers responded to the demands of the market and, far from being healthy, today's granola bar is filled with puffed rice, sticky corn syrup, chocolate chips, and as likely as not will be covered with a layer of gooey fudge.

8. Which one of the following statements, if true, most substantially strengthens the preceding argument?

   ❑ A. Despite a $50 million ad campaign by the best agency in the business, the Happy Camper granola brand, which makes a 1970s style of bar, has lost four-fifths of its market share over the last two decades.

   ❑ B. In a fascinating news series, it was revealed that consumer complaints about granola bars being filled with puffed rice and chocolate were rampant. Over half of the complaints across the U.S. requested that the old bars, made with dried fruit and rolled oats, be brought back.

   ❑ C. In a blind taste test, people strongly preferred the taste of fudge over the taste of grain, dried fruit, and rolled oats.

   ❑ D. Four granola bars are sold nationwide with the exact same mix of ingredients. The brand labeled "Tasty" regularly outsells the next three brands, "Soggy," "Moldy," and "Ick" by a factor of 10.

   ❑ E. Thanks to the "green revolution," the development of disease-resistance strains of rice, corn, and cacao beans (the main component of chocolate) caused the price of each of these agricultural products on the world market to drop by over 60 percent.

9. Which one of the following, if true, most substantially weakens the preceding argument?

   ❑ A. After defining chocolate as a vegetable, Congress mandated that granola bars sold in the U.S. had to contain large amounts of chocolate to address worries over outbreaks of scurvy.

   ❑ B. In the 1970s, movie star Arnie Schwartz regularly told his fan club about the health benefits of traditionally made granola bars. But starting in 1981, Schwartz began to tell his fans that they should eat granola bars made by companies that added chocolate chips or chocolate coatings to their recipes.

   ❑ C. Sales figures consistently show that when Americans travel abroad to places as distantly removed from the U.S. market as India and Japan, they will purchase 1970s-style granola bars and not the less healthy kind that are manufactured today.

   ❑ D. Between 1970 and 1990, the amount of chocolate that the average American consumed in a year increased from 45 pounds to an amazing 278 pounds.

   ❑ E. While it's true that today's granola bar is filled with puffed rice, sticky corn syrup, chocolate chips, and fudge, according to nutritionist Sedmont Witz, this is simply indicative of the evolving American diet. Today, the average American's dinner consists of a bowl of puffed rice, sticky corn syrup, chocolate chips, and a heaping layer of gooey fudge.

10. Company Accountant: "We have to switch more production lines to make standard whitewall tires. The type of rubber we have to buy in order to make our sister line of all-weather radial tires is more expensive, and cuts into our profits."

Plant Manager: "Our all-weather radial tire sells better than the white-wall tire because it's higher quality. People are more interested in the safety offered by an all-weather tire than the looks of the whitewall, so we'll sell more units and make up the profit that way."

What is the point of contention between the company accountant and the plant manager?

- ❑ A. Whether the tire company is making enough profit to stay afloat.
- ❑ B. Whether the company should be concentrating on making more radial or whitewall tires.
- ❑ C. Whether the customer's buying preferences should be taken in account in deciding which production lines should be allocated to what kind of tire.
- ❑ D. Whether the radial or the whitewall tire performs better in rain, ice, and snow.
- ❑ E. Whether producing the all-weather radial tire is more expensive than making the whitewall tire.

11. According to behavioral scientists at the University of Canmore, research has shown that the average American sees at least 50 acts of violence involving firearms on television per week while the average Canadian sees only 25. In 1994, twice as many Americans than Canadians were victims of gun violence. One may therefore conclude that the seeing more violence involving firearms on American television was responsible for the greater number of violent deaths involving firearms in the U.S. versus Canada.

Which of the following conditions, if true, does not serve to weaken the scientists' conclusion?

- ❑ A. The population of Canada is half the size of the United States.
- ❑ B. Canadian culture has a strong streak of pacifistic behavior.
- ❑ C. The population of Canada is exactly the same as that of the United States.
- ❑ D. Canadians own half as many guns as Americans.
- ❑ E. Gun permits are extremely difficult to get in Canada due to a bloated bureaucratic system.

12. Last Tuesday, Senator Dorothy Papin made a strong case that she should be her political party's next Presidential nominee. At a press conference, she said, "According to the latest Gallup Poll, 6 out of 10 Americans are ready to vote for a woman for the highest office in our country. This is a clear indication that I would be the strongest candidate." Senator Papin's immediate rival for the nomination, Governor William Griffith, issued an immediate rebuttal to the Senator's Statement.

Assuming that each of the following rebuttals to the Senator's claim is true, which rebuttal is the weakest?

❑   A.   "Senator Papin fails to point out that when the Gallup Poll asked specifically whether Americans were ready to vote Dorothy Papin in as president, the numbers dropped to 4 in 10."

❑   B.   Senator Papin mistakenly assumes that everyone who took the Gallup Poll is also eligible to vote. The Gallup Poll does not screen for voter eligibility."

❑   C.   "Senator Papin fails to point out that the results of Gallup Polls are notoriously volatile. Six months from now, the number of people favorably disposed toward a woman candidate is likely to decrease."

❑   D.   "Senator Papin mistakenly assumes that the poll indicates that 6 out of 10 people will vote for her simply because she is a woman."

❑   E.   "Senator Papin fails to point out that 4 out of 10 people polled are not ready to vote for a woman. No such disadvantage exists for male candidates for president."

13. Dallard Explorations uses robot submersibles to do underwater archaeology. Their most recent discovery, more than 40 feet below the surface of the Black Sea, has been the remains of a prehistoric stone house, pilings to support a pier, and stacks of sealed amphorae, or clay containers, which were commonly used to ship wine or olive oil.

The preceding information most strongly supports which one of the following?

❑   A.   The Black Sea was at a higher level in the past than it is now.

❑   B.   The Black Sea was at a lower level in the past than it is now.

❑   C.   The Black Sea's average level has varied greatly over the centuries.

❑   D.   Since the amphorae are sealed, recovering and opening them will tell us whether or not wine and olive oil was shipped in prehistoric times.

❑   E.   Since the amphorae are sealed, recovering and opening them will tell us whether or not wine or olive oil was shipped in prehistoric times.

14. Nobody has seen a live pterodactyl, or winged flying reptile, because they lived in the Jurassic era of 200 million years ago. Yet it is certain that they were able to glide on the spiraling hot thermals of air that formed in what is now the Big Bend region of Texas, much the way today's birds do. Although they did not have feathers, pterodactyls had to overcome the same problems of weight and lift as today's birds. The weight problem was solved with the evolution of hollow bones, and lift was supplied by masses of leathery skin stretched on extended finger bones to create primitive but effective wings.

The article seeks to do which one of the following?

☐ A. Derive a general conclusion about all members of a group from facts known about a representative member of that group.

☐ B. Establish the validity of one explanation for a phenomenon by excluding alternative explanations.

☐ C. Support, by describing a suitable mechanism, the hypothesis that a certain phenomenon can occur.

☐ D. Conclude that members of two groups are likely to share a certain ability because of other characteristics they share.

☐ E. Demonstrate that a general rules applies in a particular case.

15. The "heckler's veto" is the most insidious threat to free speech on our college campus. Farrago University's administration can decide to censor any speech given on school grounds if they feel that disruptions may occur. But instead of protecting the speech givers, who would stimulate debate, the administration in essence allows any disruptive individual to shut down what might be an enlightening (if controversial) discussion.

Which of the following is the best example of the argument's conclusion that the "heckler's veto" allows potentially disruptive individuals to effectively censor a speaker?

☐ A. At Bandolier College, the administration banned the appearance of a radical environmental speaker on the grounds that he had failed to get a permit to lease the campus square for a gathering.

☐ B. At Grand Valley University, the administration shut down a pro-diversity commentator because the sale of any food items at a speaker's event would convert political commentary into forbidden campus commerce.

☐ C. At Southwestern University, the administration shut down a speech by an antiwar activist because the leaflets that were distributed to promote her were denounced as unfair marketing.

☐ D. At South Texas College, the administration banned a satirical speech making fun of the funding of college sports over liberal arts on the grounds that it would make it harder to recruit top football players.

☐ E. At Tucson Tech University, the administration barred a planned speech by a pro-trade speaker because the local chapter of anti-globalist activists promised to drown out the speech with loud music.

16. A conference of national marketers and members of the state senate of North Dakota came up with a startling proposal to increase revenue generated by tourism, retirees, and industries looking to relocate. The problem, according to the conference, was that the "North" in North Dakota created an image in people's minds that the state was cold, remote, and foreboding. Instead, if they could change the state's name to "Upstate Dakota," the image would be much more positive in nature, leading to an upswing in generated revenue.

Which of the following arguments most closely parallels the one used by the marketers and the North Dakota state senate?

❑ A. The scare over cockroaches can be solved if we simply call the insect by the less threatening name "palmetto bug."

❑ B. Premium ice-cream sales can be increased if we simply call the brand "Ultra-Premium ice cream."

❑ C. We can avoid blaming the loss of the rocket due to a system failure by calling the flaw an "onboard anomaly."

❑ D. We can outsell our competitor's "Slippy Lube" product by calling our own product "Super Slippy Lube."

❑ E. We can avoid a panic by calling the people who died in the epidemic as "metabolically challenged."

17. The "dismal science" of economics—specifically, trade—may be the reason that Homo Sapiens displaced Neanderthal man. To see if trade might be enough to account for the dominance of Homo Sapiens, a computer model was created to capture the relevant variables such as fertility, mortality rates, hunting efficiency, skills in making objects, and the ability to trade. The model showed average Homo Sapiens getting more meat, which drove up fertility and thus increased the population. Since the supply of meat was finite, that left less for the non-trading Neanderthals, and their population declined.

Which of the following archeological finds would logically weaken this argument?

❑ A. A Neanderthal religious site is found with cave paintings that clearly show Homo Sapiens being chased out of the surrounding grasslands and steppe by the Neanderthals.

❑ B. A Neanderthal burial site is found containing ornamental objects created by Homo Sapiens such as beads and fertility goddess figurines.

❑ C. A Neanderthal religious site is found, showing cave paintings that are far more abstract and intricate than those made by Homo Sapiens.

❑ D. A Neanderthal burial site is excavated containing flint arrowheads and obsidian-tipped spears that show more sophisticated craftsmanship than those made by Homo Sapiens.

❑ E. A religious site built by Homo Sapiens is found with cave paintings that clearly show the Neanderthals being chased out of the surrounding grasslands and steppe.

18. All video store clerks like some of their customers. No video store clerk likes all of their customers.

If the preceding statements are true, then all of the following must be true *except*:

❑ A. Most video store clerks like most of their customers.

❑ B. Some video store clerks like some of their customers.

❑ C. No video store clerks dislikes all of their customers.

❑ D. No video store clerks likes all of their customers.

❑ E. All video store clerks dislike some of their customers.

19. The vendors who supply our cookie dough must be lying to us about keeping their prices the same. This year the bakery's expenses must have been higher than ever, because I earned less profit than last year.

    All of the following point to an error in reasoning in this passage *except*:

    ❑ A. The cost of raw material (that is, cookie dough) wasn't the year's only expense.

    ❑ B. This year's tax deductions may have been smaller than last year's.

    ❑ C. The number of people on staff increased from four to six, so the amount of money spent on payroll may have increased.

    ❑ D. Vendors are known for being vague about the rates they charge for cookie dough.

    ❑ E. Th is year's sales may have been smaller than last year's.

20. Conclusive proof that earth has endured what climatologists call the "Little Ice Age" can be seen in the work of Pieter Brueghel the Younger, a Flemish painter who lived in the 1500s. Compared to the works of his father, which featured sun-drenched oil paintings of city terraces and verandas, Brueghel the Younger's work shows Europeans coping with frigid winters by huddling indoors and inventing new games to take advantage of the ice-covered lakes, such as ice skating.

    Which of the following facts, if true, strengthens the conclusion that Brueghel was, in fact, painting the onset of the "Little Icc Age"?

    ❑ A. Breughel's home town recorded an astonishing three-foot snowfall in April, 1574, when the artist was only 10 years old.

    ❑ B. Examination of tree rings all over Europe confirms that temperatures dipped an average of seven degrees between 1450 and 1600.

    ❑ C. Painters all over the Low Countries of Europe in the 1590s were painting scenes of Europeans bundling up against the chill or going out ice skating.

    ❑ D. Cold-weather gear such as skis and parkas were invented in Europe in the 1500s.

    ❑ E. After the invention of the chimney in 1550, Europeans began spending more time indoors than outside in all seasons.

QUESTIONS 21–22

When tall-masted sailing ships like the nineteenth-century China clippers regularly plied the sea lanes with small but incredibly precious cargo such as ambergris, tea, rum, and semiprecious gems, the sailing men were paragons of efficiency. They were acutely aware that their cargo was often perishable, and a rotten cask of rum was as good as throwing money overboard. Their officers also maintained the men's sharp edge by liberal use of the lash to keep them disciplined. Today's corporate managers could learn a thing or two from those old sailing ship officers about how to treat employees as they sail their corporate vessels on the sea of commerce.

21. The author of this piece relies on which two assumptions to make his argument about why the clipper's sailors were paragons of efficiency?

   ❑ A. Sailors in the 1800s were naturally lazy spendthrifts.

   ❑ B. Sailors in the 1800s were motivated by the dual prospect of receiving both discipline and wages.

   ❑ C. Sailors in the 1800s preferred to avoid the lash and were concerned about the perishable nature of their cargo.

   ❑ D. Sailors in the 1800s shared in the profits earned by the ship and preferred to avoid the lash.

   ❑ E. Sailors in the 1800s were willing to endure being lashed by officers so long as they were well paid.

22. Which of the following statements, if true, would most seriously call into question the author's assertion that today's corporate managers should use the same methods as the 1800s naval officers if they want an efficient staff?

   ❑ A. Today's workers do not share in the company's profits, though they do not mind being physically disciplined.

   ❑ B. Today's workers object to being physically disciplined when the company doesn't share the profits out equally.

   ❑ C. Today's workers do not share in the company's profits and they object to being physically disciplined.

   ❑ D. Today's workers share in the company's profits though they object to being physically disciplined.

   ❑ E. Today's workers will endure physical discipline so long as they are paid their wages promptly and regularly.

23. Lisa: The First Amendment to the Constitution states that free speech is protected.

   Since my mom grounded me last week for insulting my younger brother, she was violating my Constitutional rights!

   Jodi: Lisa, according to the First Amendment, the government shall make no law that curtails free speech. Your mom hardly counts as a government agency, so she's not running afoul of the Constitution.

   Jodi has weakened Lisa's argument by doing which one of the following?

   ❑ A. By challenging the accuracy of Lisa's analogy.

   ❑ B. By attacking Lisa's character.

   ❑ C. By providing evidence that challenges her conclusion.

   ❑ D. By demonstrating a historical precedent.

   ❑ E. By showing that Lisa's argument is circular.

24. Darrell: I hear that Mom and Dad are thinking about raising Audrey's and Noah's allowance by $1.00 a week. That would make their allowance higher than mine. Because I'm older than they are, it's not fair that their allowances are raised unless mine is also raised to at least what theirs is.

    Xander: Your twin sister Elana is the same exact age as you and gets the same allowance. It wouldn't be fair to raise your allowance unless Elana's allowance is also raised.

    Which one of the following most helps to justify both Darrell's and Xander's arguments?

    ❏ A. In order to be fair, parents must always pay their children an allowance related to the number of chores they do every day.

    ❏ B. In order to be fair, parents must never pay one child a higher allowance than another unless the first child is older than the other child.

    ❏ C. In order to be fair, parents must always pay one child a higher allowance than another if the first child is older than the other child.

    ❏ D. In order to be fair, parents must pay their children an allowance related to how well they behave.

    ❏ E. In order to be fair, parents must pay the same allowance to children to all children who perform the same chores.

THIS IS THE END OF THE SECTION.

SECTION III—Logical Reasoning

Time—35 minutes

24 Questions

Directions: The questions in this section are based on the reasoning contained in brief statements or passages. For some questions, more than one of the choices could conceivably answer the question. However, you are to choose the best answer; that is, the response that most accurately and completely answers the question. You should not make assumptions that are by common-sense standards implausible, superfluous, or incompatible with the passage. After you have chosen the best answer, blacken the corresponding space on your answer sheet.

1. Dan: Weinacht University is having a difficult year in its fundraising drive. From the figures that I'm looking at, the number of new donors is down by half, and the amounts they're giving are at least $500 less per person than the old donors.

   Joyce: You must be kidding—this is a banner year for Weinacht University. My figures show that our average donation is up by $250, and the total amount raised for the school is up over 10 percentage points from last year.

   Which of the following statements does not help to reconcile the apparent contradiction in what Dan and Joyce see in their figures?

   ❑ A. Although the number of new donors is down by half, the amount given by the total number of donors is up.

   ❑ B. Although the amount given by the new donors is less, this is made up for by the higher level of giving done by the old donors.

   ❑ C. The number of new donors, though joining at lower numbers than in years past, is much greater than the number of old donors.

   ❑ D. Although the number of new donors is down by half, the number of new donors with their lower donations is not enough to reduce the average amount given in total.

   ❑ E. An extremely large donation by a single new donor could have inflated the total given so that while the average was down, the total amount raised is up.

2. The following was seen on a political poster in Capitol City:

Are you tired of seeing your money going to Big Water projects? Are you sick of the sky-high levels of bureaucratic waste in Capitol City? Over 10 percent of our city budget is going into slush funds that need to be looked at by unbiased accountants. And May Chin-Lee has the experience to do something about it from her 10 years in private practice. Are you a responsible citizen? Then vote in Chin-Lee for Capital City treasurer.

This campaign ad makes its case by primarily

- ❏ A. Appealing to authority.
- ❏ B. Drawing the conclusion from an analogy.
- ❏ C. Drawing its conclusion from the presentation of evidence
- ❏ D. Deriving the conclusion by eliminating all other hypotheses.
- ❏ E. Appealing to emotion.

QUESTIONS 3–4

Easily the best musical to pay tribute to the grand vistas and easy lifestyle of the peoples of Adak Island, the songs in *North Pacific* by Hodgers and Rammerstein are a celebration of life. The unique sound of this musical is created by the fusion of the two musical traditions brought together by the efforts of the songwriters—Hodgers's pulsing rhythm of American street music and Rammerstein's use of Scottish bagpipes as accompaniment.

3. Which of the following, if true, most weakens the article's conclusion about the musical's unique sound?
- ❏ A. Hodgers knows very little about American street music.
- ❏ B. Rammerstein isn't Scottish.
- ❏ C. *North Pacific* isn't about the peoples of Adak Island at all.
- ❏ D. Hodgers and Rammerstein never composed anything together.
- ❏ E. Hodgers and Rammerstein dislike each other personally.

4. Which of the following, if true, most strengthens the article's conclusion about the musical's unique sound?
- ❏ A. Hodgers and Rammerstein respect each other's musical talents in their area of expertise.
- ❏ B. Hodgers and Rammerstein have produced other musicals that featured fusions of different cultures' music.
- ❏ C. Hodgers and Rammerstein are good friends and their families have gone on tropical vacations together to Adak Island.
- ❏ D. Hodgers and Rammerstein have never visited Adak Island and know nothing of its cultures.
- ❏ E. Hodgers and Rammerstein are both prima donnas and often stormed off the stage when one criticized the other.

5. It's ironic that the Anzarian military ended up using the K-10 as their standard infantry weapon while the Umbrian guerillas could only buy the Schmeisser machine gun on the black market, making it their weapon of choice. The guerillas chose to specialize in sniping from a distance—which the K-10's rifle sights would have been perfect for. The Anzarian army by contrast could have used the Schmeisser's double-barrel grenade launcher for clearing underbrush as they began their trademark frontal assaults.

The preceding argument relies on which of the following assumptions?

❑ A. That Anzarian tactics required silent, accurate weapons while the Umbrian methods required greater firepower.

❑ B. That Umbrian tactics were ineffective because they required stealth, not greater firepower.

❑ C. That Umbrian tactics required silent, accurate weapons while the Anzarian methods required greater firepower.

❑ D. That Anzarian tactics were ineffective because they required greater firepower when they could have used stealth.

❑ E. Both Anzarian and Umbrian armies were incompetent when choosing the weapon that would have benefited them most.

6. In the country town of Elmhurst, the commuter train generally arrives on time. In urban downtown of the city of Irvine, it generally arrives late. In Belmont, a small farming community, the commuter train generally arrives late. However, in the downtown city district of El Segundo, the commuter train generally arrives on time.

Which one of the following most clearly expresses the main point in the preceding passage above?

❑ A. Whether the commuter train runs on time or not is not solely an urban or rural phenomenon.

❑ B. The train normally runs on time more often in rural communities.

❑ C. The train normally runs on time more often in urban communities.

❑ D. Trains run into all sorts of problems no matter if the setting is urban or rural.

❑ E. Whether the commuter train runs on time or not depends at least in part on the urban versus rural environment.

7. "Brevity is the soul of wit." Haiku, a Japanese form of poetry, is extremely brief because it uses only three lines, in a pattern containing five, seven, and five syllables. Thus, haiku is the wittiest form of poetry.

This style of reasoning most closely parallels which one of the following arguments?

❏ A. "It's better to light a candle than to curse the darkness." Thus, to take the better course of action, one should light a candle immediately.

❏ B. "Thirty days hath September, April, June, and November." The current month is February. Thus, there aren't thirty days in this month.

❏ C. "An event is rare if it happens once in a blue moon." Today there was an eclipse of the sun, which only happens once per century. Thus, an eclipse like this happens only once in a blue moon.

❏ D. "Red sky in the morning" means sailors should take warning. The sky was red this morning. Thus if you were a sailor, you'd have to take warning.

❏ E. "Don't look a gift horse in the mouth." Thus, if you ever get a horse as a gift, then you'd better not open its mouth to look inside.

QUESTIONS 8–9

Oil Rig Geologist: "There's a better than even chance that we'll be able to tap into a new deposit of crude below the shale layer if we start drilling from the North Sea platform immediately. It's risky, but not only will we be able to profit from the current high prices we can charge, but we'll beat our competitors to market.

Oil Rig Driller: "We're sure to make a bundle, and we'll be two months ahead of anyone else, but it's still ice storm season out on the North Sea. There's a higher risk of accidents if we drill now, and if the core buckets freeze over, the whole line will snap. And if you're wrong about that shale, we could end up dulling the drill bit. Then we'll never earn a dime, and the competition will eat our lunch."

8. What is the point of contention between the geologist and the driller?

❏ A. Whether there are risks involved in the proposed drilling operation.

❏ B. Whether the drilling will in fact earn the company a great deal of money.

❏ C. Whether the risk of accidents is higher in the North Sea.

❏ D. Whether the drilling will in fact allow them to beat the competition to market.

❏ E. Whether or not to drill for the new deposit of crude right away.

9. Which of the following conditions, if true, would most weaken the geologist's case to drill immediately?

❏ A. Shale oil deposits are notoriously difficult to find.

❏ B. Shale oil deposits are notoriously difficult to tap.

❏ C. Core buckets are notorious for freezing over in ice storm season.

❏ D. Drill bits are notorious for becoming dull when used for drilling.

❏ E. Oil rig accidents are notorious for being deadly.

10. Bruce loves mild winters and hot, dry summers. This is what is known in meteorological circles as the "Mediterranean" climate, which absolutely determines where bananas can be grown. It is therefore logical to conclude that Bruce will want to live wherever in the world where bananas can be grown.

Which of the following facts, in true, would best strengthen this conclusion?

- ❑ A. Bananas also thrive in hot subtropical climates with wet, sticky summers and no winter at all.
- ❑ B. Bruce refuses to live anywhere there is snow or frost on even one day of the year.
- ❑ C. Bruce values the Mediterranean climate over growing bananas.
- ❑ D. The rainforest zone in equatorial Africa is considered the best place to grow bananas in the world.
- ❑ E. Bruce likes to live where one can ski in the winter.

11. Cartoonist Thomas Nast is perhaps best known for his wickedly sharp editorial cartoons targeting Mayor "Boss" Tweed and New York's corrupt Tammany Hall. When Nast portrayed Tweed and the Tammany Ring pointing at each other in answer to the question, "Who stole the people's money?" Tweed demanded, "Stop them damned pictures. I don't care what the papers write about me. My constituents can't read. But, damn it, they can see pictures."

Which of the following assumptions is Tweed relying on when he makes his demand?

- ❑ A. Some of his constituents are illiterate but vote on the basis of persuasive images.
- ❑ B. Some of his constituents read newspapers where unflattering editorial cartoons are printed.
- ❑ C. Some of his constituents are illiterate and won't vote on the basis of persuasive images.
- ❑ D. Some of his constituents read unflattering editorial cartoons when they are printed in the newspapers.
- ❑ E. Some of his constituents are literate but vote on the basis of persuasive images.

12. Interest rates on the Nacirema Express credit card are often higher for people from the state of Gotham that for other states. To justify these rates, Nacirema Express claims that a greater percentage of Gotham residents and businesses default on their credit card bills than from any other state. If this is true then Nacirema Express would undoubtedly save money if they refused to issue credit cards in the state of Gotham altogether.

The reasoning in the argument is flawed because

- ❑ A. The argument fails to consider whether irresponsible businesses based in the state of Gotham are hurting Nacirema Express fiscally.
- ❑ B. The argument accepts without question that Nacirema Express has the right to charge different rates based on the cardholder's state affiliation.
- ❑ C. The argument ignores the possibility that fiscally irresponsible people and businesses have a preference for living in the state of Gotham.
- ❑ D. The argument does not specify precisely whether the losses incurred on Gotham accounts eliminates all fiscal benefit.
- ❑ E. The argument makes an unsupported assumption that businesses in the state of Gotham are fiscally irresponsible, when it's really the individual personal credit card holders in Gotham that are to blame.

13. Two newly discovered fossils of crocodile-like amphibians that lived more than 250 million years ago suggest the animal world was more diverse back then than thought. The species, named Aegyptile and Sarastega, were found in middle of the Sahara Desert. Although the two amphibians are the size of today's crocodiles, the finely preserved rock shows that the amphibians had the same thin, permeable skin as salamanders today, meaning that they could quickly dehydrate out once out of the water.

Which of the following could one logically conclude from the article?

- ❑ A. Water must have been present in the Sahara 250 million years ago.
- ❑ B. The sands of the Sahara desert must have receded 250 million years ago.
- ❑ C. The two animals discovered must have dehydrated in the desert before turning into fossils.
- ❑ D. The two animals discovered must have been directly related to today's salamanders.
- ❑ E. The two animals discovered show reptiles must be been related to today's salamanders.

14. Grace: So much bauxite ore is being mined that we may run out of aluminum by 2010. In order to ensure that we don't run out of aluminum, we should require sanitation companies to separate out trash so that they can send bulk shipments of used soda cans to recycling centers.

Tammy: There are already too many aluminum cans for existing recycling centers to process, and simply requiring sanitation companies to send more cans to the centers will not solve the impending shortage of aluminum.

Which one of the following most accurately describes how Tammy's response is related to Grace's argument?

- ❑ A. It presents a consideration that undercuts an assumption on which Grace's argument depends.
- ❑ B. It analyzes an undesirable result of undertaking the course of action that Grace recommends.
- ❑ C. It defends an alternative solution to the problem that Grace describes.
- ❑ D. It argues that Grace has mistaken an unavoidable trend for an avoidable one.
- ❑ E. It provides information that is inconsistent with an explicitly stated premise in Grace's argument.

15. In the past 20 years, engineers and scientists have turned more and more to nature for design inspiration. Their newly emerging field is called biomimetics. For example, seaweed-eating mollusks called abalone create a brick-like tile structure for their shells that is extremely tough. Abalone shell cannot stop a bullet, but careful examination of the steps taken by abalone to make their shells may help biomimetic scientists develop lightweight and effective body armor for the police.

Which of the following statements could be logically deduced from the article's conclusion?

- ❑ A. Today's body armor is much tougher than abalone shell because body armor can already stop bullets.
- ❑ B. Mimicking the brick-like structure of the abalone shell is the key to producing new lightweight and effective body armor.
- ❑ C. The full potential for biomimetic applications are untapped.
- ❑ D. The brick-like structure of the abalone shell is not what gives the shell its great strength.
- ❑ E. Without nature, engineers and scientists will not be inspired to create new designs.

16. Only about a thousand priceless Ayre cellos are thought to exist today. The old theory was that their pure sound resulted from their rare wood varnish. However, the new theory that has replaced the old one within the musical community is that the sound results from the wood being immersed in water. Historical records show that the wood for these cellos was cut and floated downriver to London, soaking up the rich broth of minerals in the river.

Which of the following statements, if true, would best help link the ideas presented in the article as the cause of the Ayre cello's pure sound?

- [ ] A. Micrographs taken of Ayre cello wood reveal that forms of fungus grew on the surfaces, creating an extremely reflective surface.
- [ ] B. Photographs of the wood show that it was cut with a special saw, which warped the wood in a unique manner.
- [ ] C. Micrographs taken of Ayre cello wood reveal that rare water bugs drilled holes in the wood, which created microscopic echo chambers.
- [ ] D. Photographs of the wood show that it was treated with varnish from a type of elm tree that is extinct today before being floated downstream.
- [ ] E. Micrographs taken of Ayre cello wood reveal large quantities of finely ground minerals in the wood, which created microscopic echo chambers.

17. The city of Ravenswood wants to attract more single workers. An esteemed urban planner made an extremely detailed presentation arguing that Ravenswood needed to expand late-night dance clubs, spotlight local artist galleries, and use hip techno music in local shopping malls. The presentation highlighted how nearby Neon City, which had followed this plan, had kept their economy booming with this method. The presentation was unanimously rejected by the planning council.

    Which one of the following, if true, best resolves the discrepancy between the accuracy of the presentation and the council's conclusion to reject it?

    - [ ] A. Neon City, which followed the presentation's plan, has a booming economy but as a result also has triple the crime rate.
    - [ ] B. The presentation relied on a causal link between attendance at galleries, dance clubs, and economic growth.
    - [ ] C. The presentation neglected to mention that Neon City's economic strength may have had other causes than its dance clubs, artist galleries, and hip techno music.
    - [ ] D. The presentation's statistics skipped over the years that Neon City had a recession.
    - [ ] E. Neon City, which followed the presentation's plan, has a booming economy but also has the greatest number of homeless people as a result.

18. Medium-size parrots such as conures show high levels of cognitive intelligence. For example, researchers at Presnell U. have videotaped a pair of green sun conures named Cactus and Yucca figuring out complex cage locks and teaching other birds to do the same. Thus while parrots might learn by linking the act of performing a task with getting a reward, it seems likely that they also engage in imitative learning.

The article seeks to do which one of the following?

☐ A. Derive a general conclusion about all members of a group from facts known about representative members of that group.

☐ B. Establish the validity of one explanation for a phenomenon by excluding alternative explanations.

☐ C. Support, by describing a suitable mechanism, the hypothesis that a certain phenomenon can occur.

☐ D. Demonstrate that a general rules applies in a particular case.

☐ E. Conclude that members of two groups are likely to share certain ability because of other characteristics they share.

19. Keri: Strong, swift punishment for criminals is the most effective way to reduce crime in this country. For example, anyone who might be thinking of burglarizing someone's house would definitely think twice if they had to go to jail for 10 or more years.

Phil: Strong punishment can't be the most effective way to reduce crime. Burglary only accounts for five percent of all crime committed. What about deterring assault, robbery, or arson?

Phil's reply to Keri demonstrates that he has taken Keri's remark to mean which of the following?

☐ A. Only certain criminals will think twice if they have to go to jail for 10 or more years.

☐ B. That strong, swift punishment won't only deter the crimes of assault, robbery, or arson.

☐ C. That strong, swift punishment will only deter the crime of burglary.

☐ D. Strong punishment can't be an effective way to reduce crime.

☐ E. Strong punishment can be an extremely effective way to reduce all forms of crime.

20. Recent studies show that the weight of the average citizen of the country of Cambria has increased by 12 pounds in the past decade. This lends support to the view that the modern western diet, which has only come to Cambria in the last nine years, is one that naturally tends to make people heavier.

The argument would be strengthened if which of the following are true?

☐ A. Highly exacting and accurate statistical studies were done among Cambrian citizens, analyzing which foods were eaten and in what quantities.

☐ B. Foods found in the western diet are naturally high in fat.

☐ C. The average weight of citizens in neighboring countries who haven't adopted the Western diet is increasing at the same rate as in Cambria.

☐ D. The average weight of citizens in neighboring countries who have adopted the Western diet is increasing at the same rate as in Cambria.

☐ E. There is no such thing as an average Cambrian citizen.

QUESTIONS 21–22

Civilizations from Sub-Saharan Africa through Mesopotamia chose to use symbols to represent wealth. Obviously, it was much easier to use a string of trade beads, which could be worn in corded bunches around the neck, than to bring along a herd of cattle, a sheaf of wheat, or a sack of gold dust. Universal acceptance of beads and eventually coins came about when rare but beautiful gold flake started to be worked into the beads, providing consistent valuations across cultures from Greece to India. In short, before early societies had invented an easily standardized and portable method of representing monetary value, beads played the key role in wealth accumulation.

21. Which one of the following statements, if true, most substantially strengthens the preceding argument?

☐ A. An ancient vault in Mesopotamia is found describing the contents as the "wealth of the kingdom." When the vault is opened it is full of trade beads.

☐ B. Cords of beads have been found in grave sites all over the Eastern Mediterranean, both of local and foreign manufacture.

☐ C. Cords of beads are indeed much easier to tote around than a sheaf of wheat, since the former weighs a fraction of the latter.

☐ D. Cords of beads are easier to conceal on one's person compared to a sack of gold dust, meaning that beads were an easier way to protect one's wealth in a time without effective police.

☐ E. Trade beads have been found in archeological digs from Africa to China. Often times they are found to have come from over 1,000 miles away.

22. Which one of the following, if true, most substantially weakens the preceding argument?

☐ A. Ancient records from the Bantu people in Africa show that a sack of gold dust could buy 20 cows, but a single strand of trade beads could only buy a single cow.

☐ B. A single wheat sheaf was harder to carry around than beads until 500 BC, when the invention of the ox-driven wheeled cart made it easier to haul bunches of wheat over long distances.

☐ C. Counterfeit gold flake originating in Asia Minor in 300 BC caused a disastrous economic crash, because people couldn't trust the metal and thus couldn't trust the value of the trade beads.

☐ D. During the reign of the third Egyptian Pharaoh, records indicate that a barbarian people raided the treasury and stole 40 sacks of gold dust.

☐ E. Recent archeological finds show that trade beads are commonly found in religious centers while metal disks, precursor to coins, are found in royal treasuries.

23. Lorraine bought a new tofu fryer at Sven's Tofu Fry Mart last week. After bringing the tofu fryer home and trying to cook a batch, she discovered that the lard melter was broken so the tofu could not be fried. Lorraine concluded that Sven's Tofu Fry Mart intentionally sells all types of defective kitchen appliances to its customers.

The preceding argument is flawed for which of the following reasons?

- ❑ A. It overlooks the possibility that the tofu fryer manufacturer may have shipped defective tofu fryers to the Fry Mart without Sven's knowledge.
- ❑ B. It directly attacks the character of the owner of Sven's Tofu Fry Mart.
- ❑ C. It mistakenly assumes that the lard melter is an integral part of the fryer.
- ❑ D. It assumes without justification that all tofu fryers that are sold are functionally sound.
- ❑ E. It appeals to governmental authority.

24. Motorboat Salesman: This 2003 Celeste Doria is the best boat I have for sale. It only has 30,000 nautical miles on it, it still gets 35 miles to a gallon, and the body doesn't have a scratch on it. I can offer it for only $100,000, and I'm telling you, you would be a fool to pass it up. You can go to any other motorboat seller in the country and you won't see another 2003 Celeste Doria in better condition selling for less.

Which of the following, if true, casts the most doubt on the claim made by the motorboat salesman?

- ❑ A. The motorboat salesman has an available 2000 Celeste Doria with 50,000 miles for only $80,000.
- ❑ B. The motorboat lot down the street from the motorboat salesman has a 2003 Celeste Doria with 25,000 miles and no body damage that gets 37 miles to a gallon for $90,000.
- ❑ C. The motorboat lot across town has a 2003 Celeste Doria with 18,000 miles and some minor body damage that gets 36 miles to a gallon for $90,000.
- ❑ D. All motorboats should be tested by independent mechanics to verify the information that is provided about those vehicles by motorboat salesman.
- ❑ E. The motorboat salesman has an available 2003 Gliding Dutchman boat with 30,000 miles and no body damage that gets 35 miles to a gallon for $97,500.

THIS IS THE END OF THE SECTION.

SECTION IV—Analytical Reasoning

Time—35 minutes

24 Questions

Directions: Each group of questions in this section is based on a set of conditions. In answering some of the questions, it may be useful to draw a rough diagram. Choose the response that most accurately and completely answers each question and blacken the corresponding space on your answer sheet.

QUESTIONS 1–6

At the Kentucky Horse Park (KHP), there are not less than three and not more than five of seven possible different breeds of horses present—Thoroughbreds, Morgans, Hanoverians, Oldenbergs, Arabians, Quarter Horses, and Standardbreds, in accordance with the following conditions:

❑ If Standardbreds are present, Hanoverians are not.

❑ If Thoroughbreds are present, Arabians are not.

❑ If both Morgan and Oldenbergs are present, Standardbreds are present.

❑ If Thoroughbreds are not present in the KHP, then neither are Quarter Horses, but Morgans and Oldenbergs are both present.

1. If Arabians are present in the KHP, then which one of the following must be true?

❑ A. There are three breeds of horses present in the KHP.

❑ B. There are no Quarter Horses present in the KHP.

❑ C. Neither Thoroughbreds nor Hanoverians are present in the KHP.

❑ D. Neither Thoroughbreds nor Oldenbergs are present in the KHP.

❑ E. Neither Morgans nor Hanoverians are present in the KHP.

2. If Thoroughbreds are not present in the KHP, then which one of the following must be true?

❑ A. Hanoverians are not present in the KHP.

❑ B. Oldenbergs are not present in the KHP.

❑ C. Standardbreds are not present in the KHP.

❑ D. Arabians are present in the KHP.

❑ E. Quarter Horses are present in the KHP.

3. Which one of the following could be a complete and accurate list of the types of horses present in the KHP?

❑ A. Thoroughbreds, Hanoverians, and Standardbreds

❑ B. Thoroughbreds, Morgans, and Oldenbergs

❑ C. Thoroughbreds, Morgans, Arabians, and Quarterhorses

❑ D. Arabians, Morgans, Oldenbergs, and Standardbreds

❑ E. Thoroughbreds, Hanoverians, Oldenbergs, Quarter Horses, and Standardbreds

4. If neither Hanoverians nor Thoroughbreds are present in the KHP, which one of the following could be true?

❑ A. Morgans are not in the KHP.

❑ B. Quarter Horses are present in the KHP.

❑ C. Standardbreds are not present in the KHP.

❑ D. There are four breeds of horses present in the KHP.

❑ E. There are five breeds of horses present in the KHP.

5. Which one of the following could be true?

❑ A. Neither Thoroughbreds nor Morgans are present in the KHP.

❑ B. Neither Thoroughbreds, Quarter Horses, nor Standardbreds are present in the KHP.

❑ C. Neither Morgans nor Quarter Horses are present in the KHP.

❑ D. Neither Hanoverians nor Standardbreds are present in the KHP.

❑ E. Neither Oldenbergs nor Quarter Horses are present in the KHP.

6. Each of the following could be a partial list of the breeds of horses in the KHP except:

❑ A. Oldenbergs and Quarter Horses

❑ B. Oldenbergs and Standardbreds

❑ C. Thoroughbreds, Morgans, and Oldenbergs

❑ D. Thoroughbreds, Hanoverians, Oldenbergs

❑ E. Morgans, Hanoverians, and Oldenbergs

QUESTIONS 7–12

On the third Thursday of every month, eight Labrador Retriever puppies (Archie, Benjy, Colby, Daisy, Emmet, Fancy, Gilly, and Hank) from the Guiding Eyes for the Blind visit the veterinarian's office for their monthly checkup. Each puppy is either a black lab or a yellow lab. The puppies each arrive at the office at a different time. The following conditions apply:

Gilly arrives at the vet's office before Fancy but after Archie.

Colby arrives at the vet's office before Gilly.

Benjy arrives at the vet's office after Archie but before Fancy.

Fancy arrives at the vet's office before Daisy.

7. If Colby arrives after Benjy, which one of the following must not be true?

   ☐ A. Archie is the second of the puppies to arrive at the vet's office.

   ☐ B. Benjy is the fifth of the puppies to arrive at the vet's office.

   ☐ C. Colby is the third of the puppies to arrive at the vet's office.

   ☐ D. Daisy is the sixth of the puppies to arrive at the vet's office.

   ☐ E. Fancy is the seventh of the puppies to arrive at the vet's office.

8. Of the eight puppies, what is the maximum number of puppies that could have arrived at the vet's office before Archie?

   ☐ A. None

   ☐ B. One

   ☐ C. Two

   ☐ D. Three

   ☐ E. Four

9. If Emmet arrives at the vet's office first, Colby arrives fourth and Hank arrives last, and Benjy is a black lab, which one of the following *cannot* be a yellow lab?

   ☐ A. Archie

   ☐ B. Colby

   ☐ C. Gilly

   ☐ D. Fancy

   ☐ E. Hank

10. If Hank arrived at the vet's office before Colby but after Emmet, which one of the following could be true?

   ☐ A. Gilly arrived at the vet's office before Hank.

   ☐ B. Benjy arrived at the vet's office before Emmet.

   ☐ C. Daisy was not the last puppy to arrive at the vet's office.

   ☐ D. Fancy arrived at the vet's office before Hank.

   ☐ E. Fancy was not the seventh of the puppies to arrive at the vet's office.

11. Which one of the following must be true?

   ☐ A. At least two puppies arrived at the vet's office before Colby.

   ☐ B. At least five puppies arrived at the vet's office before Emmet.

   ☐ C. At least four puppies arrived at the vet's office before Fancy.

   ☐ D. At least three puppies arrived at the vet's office before Gilly.

   ☐ E. At least two puppies arrived at the vet's office before Hank.

12. What are the minimum and maximum number of puppies, respectively, that could have arrived before Gilly?

- ❑ A. One, five
- ❑ B. Two, five
- ❑ C. Three, five
- ❑ D. One, six
- ❑ E. Two, six

QUESTIONS 13–18

The members of the Environmental Litigation department at Primrose Mendel, a small New York City law firm, are moving to a new floor. You have been given the task of assigning the members of the department to new rooms. The department has two partners, Chris and Greg; three senior associates, Ann, Ross, and Lee; and two new junior associates, Devon and Pat. There are seven consecutive rooms (rooms 1933 to 1939) available along the left side of a straight hallway. Rooms 1933 and 1939 are somewhat smaller than the other rooms. The room assignments must conform to the following conditions:

Due to client confidentiality concerns, neither of the new junior associates can be given a room next to a partner.

Neither of the partners can be assigned to Room 1933 or Room 1939.

Greg, who smokes, cannot be assigned to a room next to Ross, who is allergic to smoke.

Pat cannot be assigned to a room next to Devon unless Ross is also assigned a room next to Devon.

13. If Chris and Greg are assigned rooms with one room (Room X) between them, which one of the following is a list of department members that could be assigned to Room X?

- ❑ A. Ann or Ross
- ❑ B. Ann or Lee
- ❑ C. Ann or Devon
- ❑ D. Ross or Pat
- ❑ E. Lee or Devon

14. Which one of the following room assignments for Ross, Pat, and Devon is possible?

- ❑ A. Ross, 1935; Pat, 1934; Devon, 1933
- ❑ B. Ross, 1936; Pat, 1934; Devon, 1933
- ❑ C. Ross, 1936; Pat, 1935; Devon, 1933
- ❑ D. Ross, 1938; Pat, 1935; Devon, 1936
- ❑ E. Ross, 1937; Pat, 1938; Devon, 1939

15. What is the maximum number of rooms that could exist between the rooms to which Chris and Greg are assigned?

❑ A. One
❑ B. Two
❑ C. Three
❑ D. Four
❑ E. Five

16. If Ross is assigned to Room 1936, which one of the following must be assigned to either Room 1935 or Room 1937?

❑ A. Chris
❑ B. Greg
❑ C. Ann
❑ D. Devon
❑ E. Pat

17. Which one of the following *cannot* be assigned Room 1936?

❑ A. Chris
❑ B. Greg
❑ C. Ann
❑ D. Lee
❑ E. Devon

18. If Chris and Greg are not assigned rooms that are next to each other, which one of the following *cannot* be assigned to Room 1939?

❑ A. Pat
❑ B. Devon
❑ C. Lee
❑ D. Ross
❑ E. Ann

QUESTIONS 19–24

The results of a student survey of pizza places within a 5-mile radius of College U. have just been released. The survey ranks seven pizza places (Artisan, Baci, Capri, Donato, Enzio, Forni, and Gigi) from best (highest) to worst (lowest). There were no ties. The ranking is in accordance with the following conditions:

Capri ranks higher than Artisan but lower than Donato.

Baci ranks higher than Gigi but lower than Forni.

If Enzio ranks higher than Capri, Baci ranks higher than Enzio.

If Capri ranks higher than Enzio, Enzio ranks higher than Baci.

19. Which one of the following is the lowest ranking that Baci could have?
   - ❑ A. Second highest
   - ❑ B. Third highest
   - ❑ C. Fourth highest
   - ❑ D. Fifth highest
   - ❑ E. Sixth highest

20. Which one of the following could be an accurate ranking of the pizza places, from best to worst?
   - ❑ A. Forni, Baci, Enzio, Capri, Gigi, Donato, Artisan
   - ❑ B. Donato, Capri, Forni, Baci, Enzio, Gigi, Artisan
   - ❑ C. Forni, Baci, Enzio, Donato, Gigi, Capri, Artisan
   - ❑ D. Forni, Donato, Baci, Gigi, Capri, Enzio, Artisan
   - ❑ E. Donato, Capri, Baci, Enzio, Gigi, Forni, Artisan

21. If Baci ranks lower than Artisan, which one of the following must be true?
   - ❑ A. Artisan ranks higher than Forni.
   - ❑ B. Enzio ranks higher than Gigi.
   - ❑ C. Capri ranks higher than Forni.
   - ❑ D. Forni ranks higher than Enzio.
   - ❑ E. Forni ranks higher than Capri.

22. If Gigi ranks higher than Donato, then which one of the following could be ranked fifth highest?
   - ❑ A. Forni
   - ❑ B. Baci
   - ❑ C. Enzio
   - ❑ D. Gigi
   - ❑ E. Capri

23. If Forni is ranked third highest, then which one of the following *cannot* be true?
   - ❑ A. Baci is ranked fifth highest.
   - ❑ B. Baci is ranked sixth highest.
   - ❑ C. Artisan is ranked fourth highest.
   - ❑ D. Capri is ranked fifth highest.
   - ❑ E. Enzio is ranked fifth highest.

24. Which one of the following *cannot* be true?
   - ❑ A. Capri ranks second highest.
   - ❑ B. Gigi ranks third highest.
   - ❑ C. Artisan ranks third highest.
   - ❑ D. Donato ranks fifth highest.
   - ❑ E. Enzio ranks sixth highest.

Answer Key for Practice Exam 2

SECTION I—Reading Comprehension

1. D
2. B
3. D
4. B
5. C
6. D
7. B
8. A
9. D

10. D
11. C
12. B
13. B
14. C
15. B
16. A
17. C
18. C

19. E
20. C
21. A
22. B
23. E
24. A
25. D
26. E
27. D

1. **Choice D** is correct. In this passage, the main idea is expressed in the very first sentence (note that this is not always the case): That evidence gathered in two flybys by the Cassini spacecraft indicate that Saturn's moon Enceladus, has a significant atmosphere. The remainder of the passage describes the potential sources for this atmosphere, and provides further detail on the evidence leading scientists to this conclusion. Choice A is incorrect. The evidence gathered by Cassini indicates that there *may* be volcanoes or geysers on Enceladus's surface or interior, but this is not yet definite. Note the use of qualifying terms throughout the passage, such as "may be volcanism" (line 4), "believed to be due to…" (line 18), and "If such eruptions are present…" (line 34). Choice B is incorrect. Although you can infer from the passage that the Cassini spacecraft is more technologically advanced than the Voyager spacecraft (see line 25, "It's possible detection was beyond Voyager's capabilities"), this is not the main idea of the passage. Choice C is incorrect. Although the passage does state that "Enceladus exhibits one of the most interesting surfaces of all the icy satellites" (lines 47–48), this is an editorial observation by the author of the passage, and is not the main idea. Choice E is incorrect. While it is true that scientists suspect that Enceladus is geologically active, the main focus of the passage is evidence gathered by Cassini that Enceladus has an atmosphere.

2. **Choice B** is correct. The passage states that the amount of gravity Enceladus exerts is not enough to hold an atmosphere for long, and that therefore, a strong continuous source is required to maintain the atmosphere, leading scientists to consider eruptions, such as volcanoes and geysers (lines 33–34). Choice A is incorrect. While the Cassini flyby recorded evidence of the bending of the magnetic field, this in and of itself is not is not evidence that the moon has volcanoes or geysers on its surface or interior. Choice C is incorrect. Since the Voyager flyby, scientists have suspected that Enceladus is geologically active (lines 40–41), but the Voyager flyby did not produce any direct evidence of such. Choice D is incorrect. Enceladus's high reflectivity *may* be indicative of ice volcanoes, but this is not why scientists believe it likely that Enceladus has volcanoes or geysers on its surface or interior. Choice E is incorrect. The passage does not state that the Cassini spacecraft took pictures of an active volcano on Enceladus.

3. **Choice D** is correct. Mild is the best choice for the meaning of the word *benign*, as it is used in the context of the passage. The key indicator is the inferred comparison between the moon Io (referred to as "dramatic") and Enceladus. In such a situation, the appropriate definition is a word that is an antonym, as mild is to dramatic. Choice A is

incorrect. Although "harmless" is a possible meaning of the word benign, it is not an appropriate meaning in the context of the passage. Choice B is incorrect. Although "beneficial" is a possible meaning of the word benign, it is not an appropriate meaning in the context of the passage. Choice C is incorrect. Although "not malignant" is a possible meaning of the word benign, it is not an appropriate meaning in the context of the passage. Choice E is incorrect. Harsh is not an appropriate definition of benign.

4. **Choice B** is correct. You can appropriately infer from Dr. Fritz Neubauer's statement that "Enceladus could be Saturn's more benign counterpart to Jupiter's dramatic Io" (lines 36–37) that Io is more geologically active than Enceladus. Choice A is incorrect. Although the passage states that Enceladus is a relatively small moon (lines 29–30), no information is given about its size relative to other moons of Saturn. Choice C is incorrect. The passage states in lines 27–29 that an atmosphere had previously been detected around Saturn's moon, Titan. Choice D is incorrect. No information is presented in the passage about the size of Triton relative to the size of Titan. Choice E is incorrect. Although both Io and Triton are mentioned as active moons (lines 35–36), the passage gives no information about the relative activity of Io versus Triton.

5. **Choice C** is correct. According to the passage, magnetic field oscillations are caused when electrically charged (or ionized) molecules interact with the magnetic field by spiraling around the field line (lines 13–15). Choice A is incorrect. The slowing and deflection of magnetospheric plasma is related to the bending of the magnetic field, not magnetic field oscillations (see lines 12–13). Choice B is incorrect. Low gravity conditions on Enceladus's surface are unrelated to magnetic field oscillations. Choice D is incorrect. The high reflectivity of Enceladus's surface is unrelated to magnetic field oscillations. Choice E is incorrect. Saturn's icy E ring (lines 40–41) is not a causative fact in the creation of magnetic field oscillations.

6. **Choice D** is correct. In line 16 of the passage, the author uses the term "characteristic" to refer to oscillations in the magnetic field. The author also notes that these characteristic oscillations in the magnetic field can be used to identify a particular molecule. Thus, both elements of the definition of the phrase "striking signature" (distinctive characteristic indicating identity) as it is used in the passage, are fulfilled. Choice A is incorrect. While it is true that Cassini's observations showed a bending of the magnetic field (line 11 of the passage), this is not the "striking signature" to which the phrase is referring. A

"striking signature," as that phrase is used in the passage, is a distinctive characteristic indicating identity. Unlike with respect to Choice D, the author does not state that the bending of the magnetic field is indicative of some specific finding. Choice B is incorrect. While it is true that Cassini's observations showed the slowing of magnetospheric plasma (line 12 of the passage), this is not the "striking signature" to which the phrase is referring. A "striking signature," as that phrase is used in the passage, is an a distinctive characteristic indicating identity. Unlike with respect to Choice D, the author does not state that the slowing of magnetospheric plasma is indicative of a specific finding. Choice C is incorrect. While it is true that Cassini's observations showed the deflection of magnetospheric plasma by the moon (line 12 of the passage), this is not the "striking signature" to which the phrase is referring. A "striking signature," as that phrase is used in the passage, is a distinctive characteristic indicating identity. Unlike with respect to Choice D, the author does not state that the deflection of magnetospheric plasma by the moon is indicative of a specific finding. Choice E is incorrect. Nowhere in the passage does the author state that Cassini observed gases escaping from the surface of Enceladus.

7. **Choice B** is correct. The author's attitude toward the possible discovery of an atmosphere on Enceladus can best be described as objective (that is, not influenced by personal or emotional preferences, but rather based on observable evidence). Choice A is incorrect. Nothing the author writes is indicative of a disdainful (that is, an attitude of haughty contempt) attitude toward the possible discovery of an atmosphere on Enceladus. Choice C is incorrect. While the author's attitude toward the possible discovery of an atmosphere on Enceladus can possibly be described as enthusiastic to a certain extent, to describe it as bubbly (that is, zestfully enthusiastic) is too strong. Choice D is incorrect. Nothing that the author writes is indicative of an incredulous (that is, highly skeptical or disbelieving) attitude toward the possible discovery of an atmosphere on Enceladus. Choice E is incorrect. Nothing that the author writes is indicative of a timid attitude toward the possible discovery of an atmosphere on Enceladus.

8. **Choice A** is correct. The "Challenges of a New Century" is the best title for the passage because the primary focus of the passage is on the choices and challenges that face American citizens at the dawn of the 21st century (see lines 28–29; 44–45). Choice B is incorrect. The "Promise of America" is not the best choice for the title of the passage. Although the author mentions the "promise of America" in the first and second paragraphs, it is not the focus of the passage. Choice C is incorrect. "America the Great" is not the best choice for the title of the

passage. Although the author clearly believes that America has achieved greatness in the past (see the second and third paragraphs), the focus of the passage relates to the choices that Americans must make at the dawn of the 21st century to "form a more perfect Union." (line 27). Choice D is incorrect. "The American Century" is not the best choice for the title of the passage. The author refers in line 7 to "the American century," which the reader may infer is a reference to the 20th century. Although the author mentions the achievements of the 20th century, the focus of the passage is primarily on the challenges facing America as it enters the 21st century. Choice E is incorrect. The "Scourge of Slavery" is not the best choice for the title of the passage. Although the scourge of slavery is mentioned in the passage (lines 4–5), it is not the primary focus of the passage.

9. **Choice D** is correct. In lines 6–7, the author states "that promise exploded onto the world stage to make this the American century." Although the passage does not provide a date for when it was made, line 24, which refers to "at the dawn of the 21st century," and lines 41 and 45, which refer to "a new century" in the context of the discussion of the future, allow the reader to infer that the phrase "this century" refers to the 20th century. Choice A is incorrect. The passage does not mention the 17th century. Choice B is incorrect. The passage identifies the 18th century as when the "promise of America" was born, not as the "American century." Choice C is incorrect. The passage notes that the "promise of America" was extended and preserved in the 19th century, but does not identify it as the "American century." Choice E is incorrect. The passage refers to the "dawn of the 21st century," and so on (see previous discussion), as a future event, allowing the reader to infer that the phrase "this century" refers to the 20th century, not the 21st century.

10. **Choice D** is correct. In the last paragraph of the passage, the author states in lines 46–47, "For any one of us to succeed, we must succeed as one America." Choice A is incorrect. In lines 8–9 ("America saved the world from tyranny in two World Wars...") and lines 32–33 ("where it [America] can stand up for our values and interests around the world.... Government should do more, not less"), the author writes approvingly of the intercession of the United States in foreign affairs. Choice B is incorrect. In the third paragraph, the author writes approvingly of the splitting of the atom as an accomplishment of Americans during the 20th century. Choice C is incorrect. In lines 35–37, the author states specifically that the mission of government is to give all Americans an opportunity to build a better life, rather than a guarantee of a better lives. Choice E is incorrect. In the third

paragraph of the passage, the author writes approvingly of the revolution in civil rights for African-Americans and all minorities, and extending the circle of citizenship to women, and as such is likely to disagree that only white American males should vote.

11. **Choice C** is correct. Exhortatory is the best choice to describe the attitude of the author. To exhort is to urge someone, by a strong or stirring argument. On several occasions, the author exhorts the reader to meet the challenges posed by the coming 21st challenges and work together to create a "more perfect Union." Choice A is incorrect. There is nothing in the passage that suggests that the author is pessimistic about the future. Choice B is incorrect. The author speaks to the reader in an inclusive manner, through the use of the words "we" and "us," and as such, does not set himself/herself above the reader, as would someone speaking in a condescending way. Choice D is incorrect. Although the author challenges readers, nothing in the passage can be construed as threatening. Choice E is incorrect. By using language such as "the future is up to us" (line 38), and "a free people must now choose" (lines 24–25), the author exhibits a democratic as opposed to dictatorial attitude.

12. **Choice B** is correct. The main purpose of the second paragraph in the passage is to praise America for its accomplishments in the 20th century. Choice A is incorrect. While the second paragraph is the passage mentions the successes of America in the 20th century, it does not contrast those successes with any events of the 19th century. Choice C is incorrect. Nothing in the second paragraph of the passage questions the choices made by America in the 20th century. Choice D is incorrect. Nothing in the second paragraph of the passage relates to examining the choices facing America as it enters the 21st century. Choice E is incorrect. While the passage does, in fact, exhort readers to embrace change in government structure, this occurs in the fifth paragraph, not the second.

13. **Choice B** is correct. The author is likely to disagree with the statement that "A good government should be able to take care of all of its citizens' problems" because in lines 41–42 he/she notes that "There is work to do, work that government alone cannot do" and in lines 42–44, notes that each person must assume personal responsibility. In lines 29–30, the author calls for a new Government "humble enough not to try to solve all our problems for us...." Choice A is incorrect. The author is likely to agree that the establishment of the Social Security program in the 20th century was a positive event because he/she lists the production of "security in old age" (lines 12–13) as one

of the accomplishments of Americans. Choice C is incorrect. The author is likely to agree that Americans cannot be complacent about the potential dangers of divisiveness among its citizenry, noting in lines 46–47 that "For any one of us to succeed, we must succeed as one America." The author is likely to agree that slavery is evil, as he/she refers to the abolition of the "awful scourge of slavery" in a positive manner in lines 4–5). The author is likely to agree with the statement that government spending should decrease, as in lines 31–32, the author states that we need a new government "that is smaller, lives within its means and does more with less."

14. **Choice C** is correct. In line 28, the author explicitly states that "as times change, so government must change." Choice A is incorrect. This is how a new government might act, not why a new government is needed. Furthermore, the author states in the fifth paragraph that government should do more, not less only in certain prescribed circumstances ("where it can stand up for our values and interests around the world, and where it can give Americans the power to make a real difference in their everyday lives"). Choice B is incorrect. This is how a new government might act (and only under certain very prescribed circumstances), not why a new government is needed. Furthermore, in lines 35–37, the author states that the preeminent mission of our new government is to give all Americans an opportunity, not a guarantee, to build better lives. Choice D is incorrect. This is how a new government might act, not why a new government is needed. Furthermore, in the sixth paragraph, the author explicitly states that individuals, not government, must assume personal responsibility for themselves, their families, and their neighbors. Choice E is incorrect. Unlike choices A, B, and D, this choice (like choice C) offers a reason why a new government is needed. However, the reasoning offered by choice E is incorrect. In paragraphs two and three, the author indicates that he believes that the existing government has met the challenges posed in the 20th century.

15. **Choice B** is correct. The main point of the passage is that some luxury retailers (such as Neiman Marcus and Tiffany & Co.) have had a difficult time developing effective websites. This is explicitly stated in the first line of the second paragraph and is the focus of the second, third, fourth, and fifth paragraphs. Choice A is incorrect. Although line 1 of the passage states "The very rich are different from you and me" (quoting the novel *The Great Gatsby*), this is not the main point of the passage, and in fact, this assertion is directly controverted by lines 4–5 of the passage, in which the author states that "when it comes to using the Web, apparently the wealthy are not much different from the rest

of us." Choice C is incorrect. Although it is probable that the author believes that the initial website of Neiman Marcus and the current website of Tiffany & Co. feature too many graphics, this is not the main point of the passage. Choice D is incorrect. The passage states that the luxury retailers have had a difficult time translating the look and feel of their *luxury shops*, which connote exclusivity, extravagance, excessive wealth, and entertainment, into a website. Choice E is incorrect. While the passage states that in some ways (with respect to using websites), the wealthy are "not much different from the rest of us," this is not the main point of the passage.

16. **Choice A** is correct. You can infer that the author believes that the Neimanmarcus.com website is more effective than the Tiffany.com website by contrasting the approving tone of lines 13–15 with the disapproving tone of the fourth paragraph, which details a number of negative characteristics of the Tiffany.com site. Choice B is incorrect. The passage refers to Tiffany in line 18 as "world-renowned" and states in lines 19–21 that Tiffany is "in the enviable position of being perhaps the most famous jewelry company in the United States." Therefore you can infer from this statement that Choice B is not false. Choice C is incorrect. In lines 23–25, the passage refers to the fact that Tiffany's web designers attempted to build a website using soft neutral colors. Therefore, you can infer from this statement that choice C is not false. Choice D is incorrect. The fourth paragraph of the passage (lines 36–37) states that there is no search feature on the home page at the Tiffany site. You can infer from this fact that Choice D is not false. Choice E is incorrect. In the fifth paragraph of the passage (lines 47–49), a Tiffany spokesperson is quoted as saying "we are aware that we have to continue evolving to make the site more user friendly." You can infer from this quotation that Choice E is not false.

17. **Choice C** is correct. In line 52, the author approvingly states that the Nordstrom.com website is a "marvel of simplicity," and in lines 53–54, that Nordstrom's 5,000 products are "shown in big clear pictures and organized in a thoughtful manner," from which the reader can infer that it is easier to use. In line 5, "ease of use" is listed as a key factor with respect to the effectiveness of a website. Choice A is incorrect. While it is likely that the Nordstrom.com website includes more graphics than the Tiffany.com website (according to lines 53–54, it has "over 5,000 products, shown in big clear pictures"), nowhere in the passage does the author indicate that the number of graphics is in anyway related to the effectiveness of a website. Choice B is incorrect. The author nowhere comments on the relative merits of the various products offered by Nordstrom.com compared to those offered by

Tiffany.com. Choice D is incorrect. There is no information in the passage about the number of animations on the Nordstrom.com website. In addition, you can infer from several statements in the passage that, if anything, the number of animations on a website tends to correlate in a negative manner to the effectiveness of a website (see lines 14, 31, 44). Choice E is incorrect. Although in line 6, speed is mentioned as a key factor in the effectiveness of a website, the passage does not comment on the speed at which the graphics on the Nordstrom.com website display.

18. **Choice C** is correct. The author's quotation of the line "The very rich are different from you and me," from the novel *The Great Gatsby* at the beginning of the passage serves to highlight, in a somewhat ironic manner, the author's contention that when it comes to using the Web, the wealthy are not much different from other users of the Web. Choice A is incorrect. One of the main points of the passage is that with respect to the use of the Web, the very rich are in fact very similar to "the rest of us." Choice B is incorrect. The author does not defend the view that "the very rich are different from you and me" in the rest of the passage, and in fact, contradicts that view in lines 4–5. Choice D is incorrect. The sentiment expressed by the quotation does not explain why luxury retailers have had a difficult time developing an online presence for their wealthy customers. Choice E is incorrect. The quotation does not present an implicit criticism of the wealthy, nor does the author further develop any such criticism in the remainder of the passage.

19. **Choice E** is correct. You can infer that the statement that the Neimanmarcus.com website introduced in 2000 was considered a success is false by the fact that, as noted in line 12, "most customers were turned off" and the further implication from lines 13–15 that Neiman Marcus subsequently significantly revised the website and that today it "features no animations, no Flash graphics, but much more merchandise neatly arranged by category and designer." Choice A is incorrect. You can infer that the statement that the Neimanmarcus.com website introduced in 2000 offered less merchandise than the current Neimanmarcus.com website is true because in lines 13–15, the author states that "Today, Neimanmarcus.com features…much more merchandise." Choice C is incorrect. You can infer that statement that the Neimanmarcus.com website introduced in 2000 featured animations and Flash graphics is true because in lines 10–11, the author notes that "Web designers were awed by the display of graphics and motion" and in lines 13–15, the author implies that in contrast "Today, Neimanmarcus.com features no animations, no Flash graphics…"

Choice C is incorrect. You can infer that the statement that the Neimanmarcus.com website introduced in 2000 was not well organized is true because in lines 11–13, the author notes that "most customers were turned off because they...could not easily navigate the site." In lines 13–15, the author implies that in contrast, "Today, Neimanmarcus.com features...merchandise neatly arranged by category and designer." Choice D is incorrect. You can infer that the statement that the Neimanmarcus.com website introduced in 2000 was well received by web designers is true by the statement in lines 10–11 of the passage that "Web designers were awed by the display of graphics and motion."

20. **Choice C** is correct. In lines 43–45, the passage states that "many luxury retailers have emphasized glitzy animations, subtle color schemes, inscrutable menus, and tricky navigation" in an effort to translate their offline brands onto the Web, but in fact, what they have failed to understand is that what their customers value most is "ease of use, selection, speed, and trustworthiness" (lines 5–7), just like "the rest of us." Choice A is incorrect. The passage does not discuss the amount of money spent to create websites as a factor in their effectiveness. Choice B is incorrect. The passage does not state that luxury retailers do not know enough about website design. Choice D is incorrect. The passage does not state that the wealthy do not use the Web for shopping. Choice E is incorrect. The passage notes that both the Neimanmarcus.com and Tiffany.com websites were visually attractive.

21. **Choice A** is correct. Irony involves an incongruity between what might be expected and what actually occurs. In the first line of the passage, the author includes a quotation that "the very rich are different from you and me," which is a commonly held belief (and also held, apparently, by some luxury brand retailers, who then spent presumably large amounts of money to create websites designed to appeal to them). The irony presented by the author is that, in fact, the very rich are not so different "from you and me" when it comes to websites. Choice B is incorrect. Nothing the author has written in the passage evinces a disparaging (that is, disrespectful or belittling) tone. Choice C is incorrect. Nothing the author has written in the passage exhibits a derisive (that is, mocking or jeering) tone. Choice D is incorrect. Nothing the author has written in the passage has a sardonic (that is, scornful or cynically mocking) tone. Choice E is incorrect. Nothing the author has written in the passage manifests an acerbic (that is, sharp or biting) tone.

22. **Choice B** is correct. "The Dutiful Wife" is the best title for the passage among the choices presented. In line 10, the author refers to the woman in the passage as "obedient" and in line 17, notes that the bride "smiled on and still on, uncomplainingly" as she sat for her portrait, despite the fact that her health and spirits were withering. This dutifulness then becomes a main factor in the outcome of the story. Choice A is incorrect. Although in lines 2–3 of the passage, the author writes "evil was the hour when she saw, and loved, and wedded the painter," the author does not portray the painter himself as evil. Choice C is incorrect. Although the author describes the bride as jealous of her husband's art, she put that jealousy aside in order to sit for a portrait, as her husband desired. Her jealousy of his art is not a central aspect of the passage. Choice D is incorrect. Although the woman in the passage is described in several lines by the author as beautiful (lines 1, 4), her beauty is not the main focus of the passage. Choice E is incorrect. Although the author refers to the artist as having "high renown" (line 18), this fact is not particularly relevant to the passage.

23. **Choice E** is correct. Although one might assume that a painter must be observant in order to paint, in several instances, the author notes the painter's failure to observe his wife's true condition. (In lines 14–16, he is referred to as "lost in reveries; so that he would not see that the light which fell so ghastly...withered the health and spirits of his bride;" and in lines 27–29 that he "would not see that the tints which he spread upon the canvas were drawn from the cheeks of her who sat beside him.") Choice A is incorrect. You can infer that the painter is talented from lines 21–24 in which the author reports that some who beheld the portrait spoke of it as a "mighty marvel" and, and that he depicted his wife "so surpassingly well." Choice B is incorrect. You can infer that the painter is dedicated from lines 12–13, in which the author describes the painter as "taking glory in his work, which went on from hour to hour and from day to day." Choice C is incorrect. You can infer that the painter is ardent from the author's description of him as passionate in lines 3 and 13. Choice D is incorrect. You can infer that the painter is ascetic from the author's description of him as austere in line 3.

24. **Choice A** is correct. The passage illustrates how an artist can both create art (the portrait) and yet destroy something at the same time (as illustrated by the death of the artist's wife as a result of the painting of the portrait). Of the available choices, this choice best summarizes the author's attitude toward art, as evidenced by the passage. Choice B is incorrect. While it is true that one may infer from the passage that the

author believes that art can be dangerous, this choice fails to encompass the creative aspect of art that is also present in the passage, and therefore is an inferior choice compared to choice A. Choice C is incorrect. While it is true that one may infer from the passage that the author believes that art can lead to death, this choice fails to encompass the creative aspect of art that is also present in the passage, and therefore is an inferior choice compared to choice A. Choice D is incorrect. While it is true that one may infer from the passage that the author believes that art is an act of love (as illustrated by the wife's love for her husband, and presumably the husband's love for his wife), this choice fails to encompass the destructive aspect of art that is alluded to in the passage, and therefore is an inferior choice compared to choice A. Choice E is incorrect. While it is true that one may infer from the passage that the author believes that art is an act of love (as illustrated by the wife's love for her husband, and presumably the husband's love for his wife), this choice fails to encompass the destructive aspect of art that is alluded to in the passage, and therefore is an inferior choice compared to choice A.

25. **Choice D is correct.** The sentence in question is an allusion to the fact that the painter, in his absorption with his work, failed to realize that requiring his wife to sit for weeks and weeks in the dim turret-chamber for the portrait was making her ill. Choice A is incorrect. The sentence in question is an allusion to the fact that the painter in his absorption with his work, failed to realize that his wife was ill. It does not refer to a literal failure to see paint. Choice B is incorrect. The sentence in question is an allusion to the fact that the painter in his absorption with his work, failed to realize that his wife was ill. It should not be read literally to mean that the painter was using his wife's rouge as a pigment. Choice C is incorrect. The sentence in question is an allusion to the fact that the painter in his absorption with his work, failed to realize that his wife was ill. Nowhere in the passage does the author suggest that the painter was blind. Choice E is incorrect. The sentence in question is an allusion to the fact that the painter in his absorption with his work, failed to realize that his wife was ill. It does not refer to a literal failure to see the canvas.

26. **Choice E is correct.** From the author's description of the woman in the passage, she cannot be characterized as independent, given her "obedience" and "meekfulness" in complying with her husband's wishes for her to sit for the portrait. Choice A is incorrect. In lines 1 and 4–5, the author describes the woman as "a maiden of rarest beauty." Therefore, one can infer that she could be characterized as attractive. Choice B is incorrect. In line 5, the author describes the woman as

"hating only the art that was her rival," from which one can infer that she was jealous of her husband's devotion to his art. Choice C is incorrect. In lines 9–10, the author describes the woman as humble and obedient and that she sat "meekly." Therefore, one can infer that she could be characterized as acquiescent. Choice D is incorrect. In lines 1 and 5, the author describes the woman as "full of glee," from which one can infer that she was cheerful.

27. **Choice D** is correct. A primary meaning of the word countenance is as a reference to someone's face or appearance. Face is the best choice of the meaning of the word as it is used in the context of the passage. Choice A is incorrect. Although countenance, when used as a verb, may mean "to approve," approval is not an appropriate meaning for the word in the context of this passage. Choice B is incorrect. Although countenance, when used as a verb, may mean "to favor," favor is not an appropriate meaning for the word in the context of this passage. Choice C is incorrect. Although countenance, when used as a verb, may mean "to support," support is not an appropriate meaning of the word in the context of this passage. Choice E is incorrect. Although countenance, when used as a verb, may mean "to applaud," applause is not an appropriate meaning for the word in the context of this passage.

SECTION II—Logical Reasoning

1. E	**9.** A	**17.** B
2. D	**10.** B	**18.** A
3. B	**11.** C	**19.** D
4. E	**12.** C	**20.** B
5. C	**13.** B	**21.** D
6. D	**14.** D	**22.** C
7. C	**15.** E	**23.** C
8. A	**16.** A	**24.** B

1. **Choice E** is correct. Laura's extensive citing of Alyssa's family background makes it clear that she is relying on this as proof that Alyssa will be an excellent harpsichord player. Choice A is incorrect. While Alyssa's aunt is a member of the extended family, Laura's argument centers on the fact that Alyssa's parents are talented at the harpsichord.

Choice B is incorrect. This is an attempt to fool you into the same logical error as in Choice A by supplying a member of the immediate family. However, Laura's argument centers on the fact that Alyssa's parents are talented at the harpsichord, not Alyssa's siblings. Choice C is incorrect. While this highlights Alyssa's talents, notice that it's in the area of composing harpsichord music, not playing the instrument. Because Laura's conclusion is that Alyssa will be a great player, we have to set this choice aside. Choice D is incorrect. While a strong answer, it loses out to E because it encompasses areas outside of Laura's argument. For example, Laura never cites international travel or Alyssa's exposure to harpsichord music, only the girl's family background.

2. **Choice D** is correct. Michael has assumed that just because Alyssa knows how to play piano, it is unlikely that she can transfer that skill to the harpsichord. Choice A is incorrect. Michael's argument does not rely upon the ability of one audience to judge musical talent over the other. Choice B is incorrect. Laura's talent at judging Alyssa's musical ability is not at issue here. Choice C is incorrect. Michael makes no mention about "other instruments." His argument is solely concerned with the piano and harpsichord. Choice E is incorrect. While tempting, it is not as strong an answer as D because Michael does not base his argument on the difficulty level in learning how to play any other instrument versus the harpsichord.

3. **Choice B** is correct. It perfectly targets the author's conclusion—that the Victorians didn't care about the scientific method. If the method hadn't been developed yet, it would have been impossible for them to care about it in the first place. Choice A is incorrect. While portions of the statement can be read as emotionally charged—and indeed, looking down on Victorian England, it is not germane to the author's assertion that the Victorians did not care about the scientific method. Choice C is incorrect. The claim about lack of perspective is weaker than the choice in B, which directly refutes the author's main conclusion. Choice D is incorrect. The author does not base his conclusion on the implication that the Victorians dismissed Snow's conclusions based on his "humble" origins. Choice E is incorrect. The degree to which the germ theory was controversial is not directly relevant to the passage.

4. **Choice E** is correct. While choices B, C, and D are reasonable because they set up conditions which call the accuracy of Anderson's testimony into question, E is by far the strongest. If Anderson was anesthetized during Smith's supposed break-in, it would have been impossible—not just difficult—for him to have seen or heard anything. Therefore, he

was not honestly mistaken in anything he heard or saw—he was flat out lying. Choice A is incorrect because Anderson's familiarity with the way the building was laid out is irrelevant to his ability to perceive what was happening in the next room. Choice B is incorrect. As shown in the discussion of Choice E, it is a reasonable answer but not as complete and strong as E. Choice C is incorrect. As shown in the discussion of Choice E, it is a reasonable answer but not as complete and strong as E. Choice D is incorrect. As shown in the discussion of Choice E, it is a reasonable answer but not as complete and strong as E.

5. **Choice C** is correct because it most closely matches the illogical reasoning in the statement; regardless of the location that the sought object resides, the search area should be determined by the degree of visibility. Choice A is incorrect. Essentially, the argument is that since one tool is ineffective, a different (if equally ineffective) tool should be used. Choice B is incorrect because although it comes close to matching the illogical reasoning in the initial statement, the conclusion is not determined by the degree of visibility in an area but instead by the unlikelihood that anyone else had searched in the area before. Choice D is incorrect because the argument simply states that by re-creating the conditions of the loss, an object can be found. Choice E is incorrect. The argument is based on the notion that because the best remedy is unavailable, something—anything—else should be tried. Luckily, it's unlikely that too many doctors actually reason like this.

6. **Choice D** is correct. If true, then the advances in technology would allow more LNG to be pumped from existing sources, thereby increasing supply without increasing the number of discovered reserves. Choice A is incorrect because it does not address the core question: why the annual consumption of domestically produced LNG is higher. Consumption levels of imported LNG are not relevant to the question. Choice B is incorrect, and a very clever trap for those not reading carefully. B talks about lowering the rate of growth of LNG consumption. It does not address why the total amount of consumption has increased, only how conservation has "decreased the rate of the increase." Choice C is incorrect because it answers only part of the question. It answers why no new LNG fields of any consequence have been discovered, but it doesn't explain why consumption has increased. Choice E is incorrect because it is a variant of C. Lower prices can help explain why more people are buying natural gas. But if there are no newly discovered reserves of any significance, it doesn't explain how more domestically produced LNG has entered the market in the first place.

7. **Choice C** is correct. The argument's conclusion is that funding should continue because it will be well spent. The premise is that the money will be well spent because the chief scientist has a great deal of direct experience managing the budget. Choice A is incorrect because the author does not cite any authority, save herself. Choice B is incorrect because the author does not use analogy for the argument, but more for a choice bit of imagery. Choice D is incorrect. The argument is drawn from direct experience with handling the budget, not observation of any kind. Choice E is incorrect. The appeal is emotional, but the emotion is used only to fuel the premise that the space station is a worthy project. It does not touch on the conclusion, which is that the chief scientist's experience is why the money will be well spent.

8. **Choice A** is correct. Even though a granola bar company spent a great deal of money to persuade consumers to eat the 1970s-style bars, the consumers apparently chose to disregard the commercials and continue to eat the bars with sweeter, softer ingredients. Choice B is incorrect. Because consumers are complaining about their choices in the granola bar department, it would appear that consumer preferences are being ignored, which would weaken the argument that consumers are king. Choice C is incorrect. Even though it shows that it would be likely that the 1970s bars would be at a disadvantage taste-wise, it does not demonstrate that consumer preference outweighs slick marketing in choosing a granola bar. Choice D is incorrect. This answer shows that consumers are, in fact, influenced by marketing, because identically made bars will sell differently based on how appetizing their name(s) are. Choice E is incorrect because it shows why manufacturers might choose to manufacture items with rice, corn, and chocolate products instead of the ingredients used in 1970s-style bars (rolled oats, grains, dried fruit). If anything, it might serve to weaken the consumer sovereignty argument because the consumer's choices aren't driving the change in granola bars; the companies making the bars are making the changes based on the cheapness of available ingredients.

9. **Choice A** is correct because unlike the other answers, Congress's actions entirely removed the consumer's choice in the matter. This essentially "de-thrones" consumer sovereignty even though no marketing was used. Additionally, this is a good example of how "truth" and "logic" are not the same thing on the LSAT. The idea of Congress using chocolate to combat scurvy is ludicrous—but in the context of the question, because we are asked to assume that it is true, it logically follows that the idea of the consumer as king is drastically weakened. Choice B is incorrect even though it implies that consumers are indeed swayed by the slick marketing, this time provided by actor Arnie

Schwartz. However, Arnie is pitching various kinds of bars to a smaller subset of the population—his fan base. Therefore, Choice A is stronger because it completely negates consumer choice instead of only weakening it slightly. Choice C is incorrect. Because consumers behave differently when they go abroad, this implies that their wishes at home are not driving the change in how granola bars are made. However, as in Choice B, international travelers only represent a subset of the population, and other factors could be at work (for example, stores in other parts of the world may only commonly carry 1970s-style bars). Choice A is still a stronger answer. Choice D is incorrect because although this is an interesting fact, it only applies in a tangential manner to the argument at hand. It could be that chocolate consumption is up for a number of reasons, ranging from a drop in the price of chocolate to an increase in the popularity of cocoa powder in baked goods. Choice E is incorrect. The implication is that granola bars changed their ingredient mix because the average American normally eats substances like fudge, rice, corn syrup, and chocolate. If anything, this strengthens the idea that consumers are the driving force behind the change in how granola bars are made today.

10. **Choice B** is correct. The key point of contention between the two people is whether the company should make more of one type of tire than the other. Choice A is incorrect. While both people are concerned about the amount of profit made on sales of tires, neither appears to be concerned about the company staying in the black. Choice C is incorrect. The plant manager explicitly indicates that she believes that the customer will show a clear preference for the radial tire for reasons of performance over looks. Choice D is incorrect. The accountant isn't questioning the performance of either tire, just that one kind is more expensive to make than the other. Choice E is incorrect. The accountant makes it very clear that the radial tire is more expensive to produce, cutting into the profit per tire sold.

11. **Choice C** is correct. If the populations of both countries are equal, then it definitely shows that for some reason, twice as many Americans were victims of gun violence than Canadians. Because this correlates exactly with the amount of gun violence seen on the TV, there is an implied link. Choice A is incorrect. If Canada's population is only half that of the U.S., then on a per capita basis, the rate of gun violence is exactly the same in both countries, weakening the conclusion that the amount of gun violence seen on TV is a factor. Choice B is incorrect. If Canada's culture is more naturally peace-loving than American culture, it would weaken the argument that television violence that is the determining factor. Choice D is incorrect. If Canada's level of gun

ownership is only half that of the U.S., then a lower rate of gun violence could be due to fewer guns being available in the country, weakening the conclusion that the amount of gun violence seen on TV is a factor. Choice E is incorrect because if gun permits are difficult to get in Canada, then it is possible that the lower rate of gun violence is simply because it's difficult for people to get their hands on a firearm.

12. **Choice C** is correct. The rebuttal is completely speculative because the volatility of the Gallup Poll could mean that support for a female candidate could drastically increase as well as decrease. Choice A is incorrect. This rebuttal is right on target—the public may be willing to vote for a woman candidate in general, but not for a specific woman— in this case, Senator Papin. Choice B is incorrect because Governor Griffith properly points out that if a substantial percentage of the polled subjects are also ineligible to vote—for example, if the poll respondent was underage—then the overall support for a female candidate would be different than what was tabulated. Choice D is incorrect. Governor Griffith makes the point that while the majority public may be willing to vote for a woman candidate in general, they may not be willing to vote for a specific candidate specifically because she is female. Choice E is incorrect because it addresses the other side of the poll—that there exists a substantial minority of Americans who for one reason or another are not ready for a woman candidate.

13. **Choice B** is correct. The fact that the ancient house was built in a spot where a shoreline used to be—and is now 40 feet underwater—strongly indicates that the Black Sea is higher now than it used to be. Choice A is incorrect. This is contraindicated by the findings of a house built below today's sea level. Choice C is incorrect because although the house's location shows the level has fluctuated, the only evidence is that the level was lower in the past, not that it has gone up and down over time. B is a stronger answer. Choices D and E are incorrect, because the statement tell us that it's already known that both wine and olive oil were shipped in prehistoric times. Raising these objects won't tell us anything that isn't already known.

14. **Choice D** is correct. The article puts forward the conclusion that because birds and pterodactyls share hollow bones and wing structures, that they could have ridden thermals of hot air. Choice A is incorrect because the article begins by stating that no one has seen a live pterodactyl; thus it explicitly discounts facts known about a representative member of a group. Choice B is incorrect. The article doesn't exclude alternative explanations for its conclusion. Choice C is incorrect because the article doesn't propose a hypothesis about how any certain

phenomenon occurs. Choice E is incorrect because the article doesn't lay out a general rule to apply in any specific case.

15. **Choice E** is correct because it is the only example of where the "heckler's veto" is actually exercised. The activist chapter has promised to be disruptive at the speech; thus in order to prevent the disruption, the administration opted to allow the speaker to be censored as opposed to protecting the speaker from the planned disturbance. Choice A is incorrect. The administration here is not exercising the heckler's veto because it is not concerned with potential disruption by unruly individuals but a leasing permit. Choice B is incorrect. The administration here is not exercising the heckler's veto because it is not concerned with potential disruption by unruly individuals but the fine dividing line between political speech and commerce. Choice C is incorrect because the administration here is not exercising the heckler's veto. Southwestern U. is not concerned with potential disruption but the issue of fairness in the promotion of the speech. Choice D is incorrect. Here, the administration it is not concerned with potential disruption by unruly individuals but by the potential difficulty in recruiting athletes should the satire cause controversy beyond the bounds of the campus.

16. **Choice A** is correct because like the North Dakota proposal, the "problem" will be solved by replacing a negative-sounding name with a more positive one. Choice B is incorrect. The change in description is not to eliminate a negative but to enhance a positive. A is a stronger answer. Choice C is incorrect because it seeks to solve the problem by using a more bureaucratically obscure description for the failure. Choice D is incorrect. The change in description is not to eliminate a negative but to copy and "one-up" a competitor's name. A is a better answer. Choice E is incorrect because it substitutes a fictional medical euphemism for "death."

17. **Choice B** is correct because the presence of ornamental objects in a Neanderthal grave site is strong evidence that trade existed between the two cultures, which weakens the argument's premise that trade was an advantage exclusive to Homo Sapiens. Choices A and E are incorrect. The one-time dominance of one species over another is not central to the argument, because trade is supposed to be the defining factor in the dominance of Homo Sapiens. Choice C is incorrect because the relative sophistication of art is not central to the argument, because trade is supposed to be the defining factor in the dominance of Homo sapiens. Choice D is incorrect. The relative sophistication of tools in either species is not central to the argument, because trade was the defining factor in the dominance of Homo Sapiens.

18. **Choice A** is correct. All the two starting statements imply is that all of the clerks like at least one or more of their customers. It does not logically follow that the majority (most) of the clerks like the majority (most) of their customers. Choice B is incorrect as it follows logically that at least some of the clerks like some of their customers, because it is stated that all of the clerks like at least some of the customers. Choice C is incorrect because this is borne out by the statement that "All video store clerks like some of their customers." Choice D is incorrect because this choice is stated verbatim previously. Choice E is incorrect because it follows logically that since no video store clerk likes all of their customers, all of the clerks have to dislike some (at least one) of his or her customers.

19. **Choice D** is correct because it does not directly refute the statement's error, and in fact provides a corroborating premise that strengthens (weakly) the passage's reasoning. Choice A is incorrect. The fact that other expenses may be to blame does point directly to an error in the passage's reasoning. Choice B is incorrect because fewer tax deductions could translate into higher costs and thus lower profits. Thus, choice B does point to an error in the passage's reasoning. Choice C is incorrect. The fact that greater payroll expenses could translate into lower profits points to an error in the passage's reasoning. Choice E is incorrect. The fact that lower sales could translate into lower profits does point to an error in the passage's reasoning.

20. **Choice B** is correct. The dip in temperatures recorded in tree rings is strong evidence that Brueghel was painting a significant change in the climate. Choice A is incorrect. If anything, the fact that the snowfall was "astonishing" shows that the climate was normally warmer, not cooler. Choice C is incorrect because it is possible that painters were responding to other forces than climate change. For example, if winter pictures had come into vogue, artists would have painted winter scenes for clients, no matter the weather outside. B is a stronger answer because it is based purely on physical evidence. Choice D is incorrect. The fact that pieces of cold weather gear were invented in and of themselves doesn't logically mean that the climate was growing colder all over Europe. Choice E is incorrect. The chimney, by providing more light and warmth at night, may have been the reason for Europeans staying inside, not the existence of a Little Ice Age.

21. **Choice D** is correct because the author makes it clear that the crew was motivated toward efficiency by two forces: profit from the cargo and discipline by the officers. The first is indicated by showing that the crew considered a lost cargo "throwing money overboard." The second

is the reference to the lash (punishment) for discipline. The principle for obedience via punishment is that a certain type of behavior is mandated to avoid receiving punishment. Therefore, sailors were obedient in order to avoid a lashing, as opposed to reacting positively to gain physical punishment. Choice A is incorrect. It is irrelevant to the author's argument what the qualities of the crew was without their sources of motivation. Choice B is incorrect because "wages" are money paid for time served. The passage clearly implies that the sailors were motivated via the profit from their cargo. Otherwise, they would not care about the fate of the cargo. For example, if they spent six months at sea and the cargo was washed overboard, they would have still been paid the same amount of money had they been wage earners. Choice C is incorrect because D is a stronger answer. C correctly notes that the crew was concerned about the loss of cargo; but D gives us the ultimate motivation, which was monetary. Choice E is incorrect. D is a stronger answer because it goes more to the heart of what really motivated the sailors—profit and avoiding discipline. E implies that the discipline, while not welcome, was just part of the job that the sailors were willing to endure so long as they earned their pay.

22. **Choice C** is correct. If today's workers don't get a share of the company's profits and they refuse to be physically disciplined, it is a direct refutation of the two motivating factors that made the 1800s sailors efficient. Choice A is incorrect. If today's workers accept physical discipline, even if they don't get to share profits, then at least one of the two motivating forces of the 1800s sailors is in place. Choice B is incorrect because it implies that today's workers don't mind being physically disciplined so long as they get to share profits fairly. If that is the case, then the two motivating forces of the 1800s sailors are still valid and the author's case is actually strengthened. Choice D is incorrect. Even if today's workers refuse to be physically disciplined, if they get to share profits then at least one of the two motivating forces of the 1800s sailors is in place. Thus D is a weaker answer than C. Choice E is incorrect. If today's workers tolerate being physically disciplined, even if they only get hourly wages and don't get to share profits, then one of the two motivating forces of the 1800s sailors is in place. Therefore E is a weaker answer than C.

23. **Choice C**. is correct. Jodi has weakened Lisa's argument by providing evidence (that is, that the First Amendment only applies to government action) that refutes Lisa's conclusion. Choice A is incorrect because Lisa didn't use an analogy when she made her argument. Choice B is incorrect because Jodi has not attacked Lisa's character. Choice D is

incorrect. Jodi did not rely on a historical precedent to refute Lisa's argument. Choice E is incorrect. Lisa's argument is not circular, nor does Jodi attempt to characterize it as circular.

24. **Choice B** is correct. Both Darrell and Xander's arguments are based on the grounds that in order to be fair, parents must never pay a child a higher allowance than another unless the first child is older than the other child. Darrell objects to his younger siblings getting a higher allowance than he; Xander objects to Darrell getting a higher allowance than Elana because Darrell is not older than Elana. Choice A is incorrect. The number of chores performed each day is irrelevant to the arguments, which focus on the relationship of age to amount of allowance paid. Choice C is incorrect. Although this answer choice focuses on the relationship of age to amount of allowance paid, it does not support Darrell's argument. Darrel does not insist on being paid more than younger siblings, just the same amount. Choice D is incorrect. The behavior of children is irrelevant to the arguments, which focus on the relationship of age to amount of allowance paid. Choice E is incorrect. The type of chores performed is irrelevant to the arguments, which focus on the relationship of age to amount of allowance paid.

THIS IS THE END OF THE SECTION.

SECTION III—Logical Reasoning

1. C	**9.** B	**17.** D
2. E	**10.** B	**18.** A
3. D	**11.** A	**19.** C
4. B	**12.** D	**20.** D
5. C	**13.** A	**21.** A
6. A	**14.** A	**22.** E
7. C	**15.** B	**23.** A
8. E	**16.** E	**24.** B

1. **Choice C** is correct. If the number of new donors is much greater than the old ones, then it makes it more difficult to reconcile the fact that the total average donation is up, let alone the total amount given to the university. Choice A is incorrect. If the total amount given is up, then that would offset the lower number of new donors contributing to the university. Choice B is incorrect because this is an adequate explanation for the contradiction—with the older donors giving more, the average and total donations would also be higher. Choice D is incorrect. If there aren't enough new donors to offset the higher averages and total, then this is an adequate explanation for the contradiction. Choice E is incorrect because a single large donation could be an adequate explanation for the contradiction in data between Dan and Joyce.

2. **Choice E** is correct. While some evidence and experience of the candidate is presented, this is primarily an emotional appeal in its attempts to stir up voter anger and feelings of civic responsibility. Choice A is incorrect because the author does not cite any authority. Choice B is incorrect because the poster does not use analogy for the argument. Choice C is incorrect. The ad presents a piece of evidence in the citing of the percentage of the budget going to slush funds, but the primary focus is to stir up emotion. Choice D is incorrect because the poster does not cite or eliminate any other hypotheses at all.

3. **Choice D** is correct. If Hodgers and Rammerstein didn't work together, their "efforts" couldn't have produced the fusion of sound noted in the article. Choice A is incorrect. It is irrelevant how much Hodgers knows about street music when it comes to the argument of the fusion of two musical traditions. Choice B is incorrect. Rammerstein's ethnic background is irrelevant when it comes to the argument of the fusion of two musical traditions. Choice C is incorrect. The argument does not rely on the subject matter of the musical, only the origin of its unique sound. Choice E is incorrect because even if the two composers disliked each other, it implies that they worked together in the first place, which strengthens the argument that their work together produced the fusion of sound.

4. **Choice B** is correct. If Hodgers and Rammerstein have produced other musical shows that featured fusions of different cultures' music, it is logical to imply that their work "fused" the two musical traditions in *North Pacific*. Choice A is incorrect. Even if they respected each other,

it is not clear that they worked together before or on *North Pacific*. B is a stronger answer. Choice C is incorrect because though they may be great friends, there is no evidence presented that they collaborated together musically. Thus B is a stronger answer. Choice D is incorrect. It is irrelevant how much Hodgers or Rammerstein knew about Adak's cultures when working on the musical. Choice E is incorrect because if the two couldn't work together due to problems with each other's ego, the conclusion of the article is weakened, not strengthened.

5. **Choice C** is correct. Umbria required accuracy while the Anzarians required greater firepower. Choice A is incorrect because it reverses the needs of the two military outfits. Choices B and D are incorrect because the article does not rely upon the relative effectiveness or ineffectiveness of the choices of the two military groups. Choice E is incorrect. While arguably true, C is a stronger answer because it more directly answers which premises the argument relies upon for its conclusion.

6. **Choice A** is correct because the evidence presented shows no correlation between the types of community the train services and its tendency to be on time. Choice B is incorrect. The fact that the train is late into rural Belmont contradicts this answer. Choice C is incorrect. The fact that the train is late into the urban setting of Irvine contradicts this. Choice D is incorrect. Although the answer correctly dismisses the environment as a factor, it is too broadly drawn to accurately depict the passage's main point. Choice A is a stronger answer. Choice E is incorrect because the evidence contradicts it.

7. **Choice C** is correct. It parallels the initial argument most closely in structure by taking a saying, applying it to a condition, and concluding that the saying applies to the condition. Choice A is incorrect. It simply states a saying and then recommends an action. Choice B is incorrect. Although it closely parallels the initial argument in structure by taking a saying and applying it to a condition, it concludes that the saying does *not* apply to the condition in question. C is a stronger answer. Choices D and E are incorrect in that they are both speculative: "if you were a sailor," and "if you ever get a horse as a gift." C is the stronger answer.

8. **Choice E** is correct. All the premises that the geologist and the driller trade relate to the central question of whether or not drilling should take place at this time, given that it is ice storm season. Choice A is incorrect. The fact that risks exist is acknowledged but is not the central issue, which is whether to drill. Choice B is incorrect because it is clear that if the drilling is successful, they will earn a great deal of

money. The central issue is whether the drilling should, in fact, take place at this time. Choice C is incorrect as it does not address the central issue of whether to drill. Choice D is incorrect because it is clear that if the drilling is successful, they will beat the competition. The central issue is whether the drilling should, in fact, take place.

9. **Choice B** is correct. At issue is whether or not to drill for the deposit. If the deposit is reached but it is difficult to tap the oil, the risks are not compensated for by the advantages of drilling. Choice A is incorrect because it is not at issue; it is clear that the oil deposit has been located. Choices C and D are incorrect because they are risks, but do not weaken the central issue of whether to drill or not. Choice E is incorrect as it is irrelevant to the arguments presented.

10. **Choice B** is correct. Because Bruce likes mild winters, he won't want to live where there's snow—in short, he wants to live where bananas can be grown. Choice A is incorrect. Because Bruce likes dry summers, it is unlikely that he would like to live where bananas are grown in subtropical climates. Choice C is incorrect. Bruce's preference of climate over bananas is irrelevant because the conclusion is that his preference and the presence of bananas are linked. Choice D is incorrect because it is irrelevant to the argument of where Bruce wants to live. Choice E is incorrect because it weakens the conclusion.

11. **Choice A** is correct. Tweed is concerned that some of his constituents can't read, but may vote on the basis of a cartoon that portrays him and the Tammany Ring as corrupt. Choice B is incorrect because Tweed is specifically concerned about illiterates being persuaded by cartoons. Choice B is too broadly based and thus A is a stronger answer. Choice C is incorrect. Tweed isn't concerned if his constituents are not influenced to change their vote on the basis of a cartoon that portrays him and the Tammany Ring in an unflattering manner. Choice D is incorrect. Tweed is concerned with the cartoons being persuasive, not that they are printed in the first place. Choice E is incorrect. Tweed isn't concerned if the literate portions of his constituency are influenced to change their vote on the basis of a cartoon that portrays him and the Tammany Ring in an unflattering manner. It can be inferred that literate members of his constituency would be influenced by unflattering articles, not cartoons.

12. **Choice D** is correct. If Nacirema Express is earning a profit from its Gotham operations, then they could lose money, not save it, if they refused to issue credit in the state. Choice A is incorrect because it is too narrowly drawn. The argument does not make the assumption that the businesses or personal creditors are hurting Nacirema Express

worse than the other. Choice B is incorrect. The right of Nacirema
Express to charge different rates is irrelevant to the main argument.
Choice C is incorrect. The argument does raise this premise, which is
the reason that Nacirema Express is charging higher rates in Gotham.
Choice E is incorrect. The argument does not make the assumption
that one group of creditors is to blame versus the other.

13. **Choice A** is correct because it logically explains why two water-
dependent species could have been found in what is today a desert.
Choice B is incorrect because it focuses on the stability of the desert's
location, not the requisite issue that water must have been present for
there to be salamander-like animals present. Choice C is incorrect.
This is an unsupported assumption because no facts in the article indicate that this happened. Choice D is incorrect. The fossilized animals
had salamander-like skin, which does not automatically imply that the
animals were directly related. Choice E is incorrect. This is an unsupported assumption because no facts in the article indicate that reptiles
were related to amphibians.

14. Choice A is correct because Tammy's response undercuts Grace's
assumption that requiring recycling will avert the impending aluminum
shortage. Choice B is incorrect because Tammy's reply does not focus
on an unintended result. Choice C is incorrect. Tammy does not offer
an alternative solution to the problem of the impending shortage of
aluminum. Choice D is incorrect because Tammy doesn't argue with
grace about any sort of trend. Choice E is incorrect because Tammy
doesn't provide information that contradicts any of Grace's premises.

15. **Choice B** is correct. It can be logically deduced that because the article discusses examining how abalone make their shells is key to producing new body armor, it is the structure of the shell that is important.
Choice A is incorrect because while it can be inferred from the facts in
the article, it does not contribute to the conclusion that abalone will
help create new body armor. Choice C is incorrect. This is a restate-
ment of the article's claim that biomimetic is a brand-new field—by
definition, untapped. Choice D is incorrect because it contradicts a fact
from the article. Choice E is incorrect. While the article states that
nature is a form of inspiration, it does not logically follow that without
nature, scientists and engineers completely lack inspiration.

16. **Choice E** is correct because it is the only choice that correctly links
the minerals in the water with the reason that the soaking contributed
to their pure sound. Choices A and C are incorrect because neither
fungus, warping, nor water bugs are ever mentioned in the facts as part
of the cello's manufacturing or transport process. Choice B is incorrect

because it does not involve immersion in water, so the choice cannot help to link the immersion to the pure sound of the instrument. Choice D is incorrect because it refers back to the older, discredited theory of varnish.

17. **Choice D** is correct. This would be a key omission in the argument that the presentation's methods lead logically to economic growth. Choice A is incorrect because it cites an unintended result of economic growth, not a reason to dismiss the presentation's conclusions. Choice B is incorrect because it simply restates the premises of the presentation's argument. Choice C is incorrect. While the presentation may not have presented alternative theories as to Neon City's success, Choice C does not weaken the conclusion presented. D is a stronger answer. Choice E is incorrect because as in choice A, it cites a result of economic growth, not a reason to dismiss the presentation's conclusions.

18. **Choice A** is correct. The article seeks to derive the conclusion that conures have a high level of cognitive intelligence from the actions of the sun conures Cactus and Yucca. Choice B is incorrect. The article doesn't exclude alternative explanations for its conclusion. Choice C is incorrect because the article doesn't propose a hypothesis about how a certain phenomenon occurs. Choice D is incorrect because the article doesn't lay out a general rule to apply to a specific case. Choice E is incorrect because the article lists characteristics for only one group: medium-size parrots called conures.

19. **Choice C** is correct. Phil's objection is that Keri's statement is wrong because only burglars will be deterred, while other criminal acts will not be deterred. Choice A is incorrect as Phil's objection specifically points to burglary as the only crime that will be affected by deterrence. Choice C is more specific and therefore a stronger answer. Choices B and C are incorrect. These are Phil's assertions, not his interpretations of Keri's argument. Choice E is incorrect. Phil's interpretation of Keri's argument is that she is only talking about reducing the crime of burglary.

20. **Choice D** is correct because it provides evidence that people exposed to the same diet across different countries are also gaining weight. Choice A is incorrect. All it does is point out that the methodology used to support the study is likely to be accurate. Choice B is incorrect. It simply states one of the qualities of the western diet. Choice C is incorrect. If neighboring peoples are gaining weight at the same rate without adopting the western diet, then something else must be to blame and the conclusion is weakened. Choice E is incorrect as it is a statement that simply claims the results of the studies are meaningless.

21. **Choice A** is correct because it directly strengthens the conclusion that trade beads were the main symbol of wealth in the ancient world. Choice B is incorrect because it strengthens the premise that beads were used for trade, but it doesn't strengthen the conclusion that they were used to symbolize the accumulation of wealth. Choices C and D are incorrect because they strengthen the premises that beads were easier forms of wealth to transport due to weight and security, but it fails to strengthen the conclusion of the passage that beads were used to accumulate wealth. Choice E is incorrect because as in Choice B, it strengthens the premise that beads were used for long-distance trade, but it doesn't strengthen the conclusion that they were used to symbolize the accumulation of wealth.

22. **Choice E** is correct. If beads are found in religious centers while disks are found in treasuries, it implies that beads were actually traded for primarily religious or spiritual purposes. This directly weakens the article's conclusion that beads were used to accumulate wealth. Choice A is incorrect because it shows that the value of a number of beads versus gold dust may have been unequal, but it doesn't refute the idea of beads as the primary way to accumulate wealth. Choice B is incorrect. It only serves to weaken the premise that beads were an easier form of wealth to transport due to weight. Choice C is incorrect because it describes a crash caused by the devaluation of the main source of wealth, the gold foil in the trade beads. This strengthens, not weakens, the conclusion that beads were the main form used to symbolize the accumulation of wealth. Choice D is incorrect because it is weaker than E. While it implies that gold dust was in the treasury, it does not directly refute the idea that beads were the main counter used to demonstrate wealth.

23. **Choice A** is correct. Lorraine does not consider the possibility that Sven's Tofu Fry Mart may have been unaware of the defects and thus was not intentionally selling bad tofu fryers. Choice B is incorrect because Sven's character is not directly attacked. Choice C is incorrect. Because the tofu could not be fried, it is reasonable that the melter is integral. Choice D is incorrect because it is too specific; her argument is that Sven's sells "all types" of defective appliances. Choice E is incorrect because Lorraine doesn't appeal to the government over this issue.

24. **Choice B** is correct. Based on the salesman's claims, showing one example of another motorboat lot where a 2003 Celeste Doria is in better condition and selling for a lower price weakens his argument most seriously. Choice A is incorrect because the boat in question is not the same—it's a 2000 model. Choice C is incorrect because the

condition of the boat in question is not the same—it has body damage. Choice D is incorrect because while correct, it doesn't seriously weaken the salesman's claims. Choice E is incorrect because it is a completely different model of boat being offered.

SECTION IV—Analytical Reasoning

1. C	9. C	17. E
2. A	10. B	18. D
3. D	11. C	19. E
4. D	12. B	20. C
5. D	13. B	21. B
6. E	14. C	22. C
7. B	15. A	23. D
8. D	16. A	24. E

QUESTIONS 1–6

At the Kentucky Horse Park (KHP), there are not less than three and not more than five of seven possible different breeds of horses present—Thoroughbreds, Morgans, Hanoverians, Oldenbergs, Arabians, Quarter Horses, and Standardbreds, in accordance with the following conditions:

If Standardbreds are present, Hanoverians are not.

If Thoroughbreds are present, Arabians are not.

If both Morgan and Oldenbergs are present, Standardbreds are present.

If Thoroughbreds are not present in the KHP, then neither are Quarter Horses, but Morgans and Oldenbergs are both present.

1. **Choice C** is correct. The first condition offers no information relevant to the question. The second condition tells you that if there are Arabians present in the KHP, Thoroughbreds are not. If there are no Thoroughbreds at the KHP, then under the fourth condition, there are no Quarter Horses present either. If there are no Thoroughbreds and Quarter Horses in the KHP, then both Morgans and Oldenbergs are present. This information enables you to eliminate both Choices D and E. You already know from the preceding analysis that Choices A

and B are not true. Therefore, by process of elimination you can determine that Choice C is the correct answer. Choice A is incorrect. The second condition tells you that if there are Arabians present in the KHP, Thoroughbreds are not. If there are no Thoroughbreds at the KHP, then under the fourth condition, there are no Quarter Horses present either. If there are no Thoroughbreds and Quarter Horses in the KHP, then both Morgans and Oldenbergs are present. If both Morgans and Oldenbergs are present, then Standardbreds are present, for a total of at least four breeds. Choice B is incorrect. The second condition tells you that if there are Arabians present in the KHP, Thoroughbreds are not. If there are no Thoroughbreds at the KHP, then under the fourth condition, there are no Quarter Horses present either. Choice D is incorrect. See earlier discussion. Choice E is incorrect. See earlier discussion.

2. **Choice A** is correct. If Thoroughbreds are not present in the KHP, then under the fourth condition, both Morgans and Oldenbergs are present. This makes Choice B incorrect, If both Morgans and Oldenbergs are present, then under the third condition, Standardbreds are also present. This makes Choice C incorrect. It is impossible to determine whether Choice D is true or not. (The second condition tells you that if Thoroughbreds are present, Arabians are not, but does not tell you whether or not Arabians are present if Thoroughbreds are not.) Therefore Choice D cannot be correct. The fourth condition tells you that if Thoroughbreds are not present in the KHP, then neither are Quarter Horses, so Choice E is incorrect. Finally, the first condition tells you that if Standardbreds are present, Hanoverians are not present, making Choice A the correct answer. Choice B is incorrect. See preceding discussion. Choice C is incorrect. See preceding discussion. Choice D is incorrect. See preceding discussion. Choice E is incorrect. See preceding discussion.

3. **Choice D** is correct. None of the conditions are contradicted by this list of possible breeds of horses in the KHP. Choice A is incorrect. The first condition tells you that if Standardbreds are present, Hanoverians are not. Therefore Choice A can be eliminated because it posits that both Standardbreds and Hanoverians are present in the KHP, thereby contradicting the first condition. Choice B is incorrect. The third condition tells you that if both Morgans and Oldenbergs are present in the KHP, then Standardbreds are also present. Choice B can be eliminated because it posits that there are Morgans, Oldenbergs, and Thoroughbreds in the part. By failing to include Standardbreds, this answer contradicts the third condition. Choice C is incorrect. The second condition tells you that if Thoroughbreds are present in the KHP,

Arabians are not. Because Choice C includes both Thoroughbreds and Arabians, it cannot be correct. Choice E is incorrect. Like Choice A, it violates the first condition by including both including both Thoroughbreds and Standardbreds.

4. **Choice D** is correct. Morgans, Oldenbergs, Arabians, and Standardbreds could be in the KHP without contradicting any of the conditions of the scenario or this question. Choice A is incorrect. According to the fourth condition, if Thoroughbreds are not present in the KHP, then Morgans are present. Choice B is incorrect. According to the fourth condition, if Thoroughbreds are not present in the KHP, then neither are Quarter Horses. Choice C is incorrect. According to the fourth condition, if Thoroughbreds are not present in the KHP, then Morgans and Oldernbergs are both present. According to the third condition, if both Morgans and Oldenbergs are present, then Standardbreds are also present. Choice E is incorrect. According to the fourth condition, if Thoroughbreds are not present in the KHP, then neither are Quarter Horses, but both Morgan and Oldenbergs are present. According to the third condition, if both Morgans and Oldenbergs are present then Standardbreds are also present. That accounts for three breeds: Morgans, Oldenbergs, and Standardbreds. The first condition provides that if Standardbreds are present Hanoverians are not. Therefore, in this question scenario, it is not possible that there could be five breeds of horses in the KHP.

5. **Choice D** is correct. While the first condition tells you that if Standardbreds are present, Hanoverians are not, it tells you nothing about the situation in which Standardbreds are not present. This is the only choice of those listed that could be true. Choice A is incorrect. According to the fourth condition, if Thorougbreds are not present in the KHP, then Morgans are present. Choice B is incorrect. According to the fourth condition, if Thoroughbreds are not present in the KHP, then neither are Quarter Horses, but Morgans and Oldenbergs are both present. If both Morgans and Oldenbergs are present, then, according to the third condition, Standardbreds are present also. Choice C is incorrect. According to the fourth condition, if Quarter Horses are not present in the KHP, then Morgans are present. Choice E is incorrect. According to the fourth condition, if Quarter Horses are not present in the KHP, Oldenbergs are present.

6. **Choice E** is correct. Under the third condition, if both Morgans and Oldenbergs are present, then Standardbreds are also present. If Standardbreds are present, under the first condition, Hanoverians are not present. Therefore Morgans, Hanoverians, and Oldenbergs cannot

be an accurate partial listing of the breeds in the KHP, making Choice E the correct answer. Choice A is incorrect. The fourth condition tells you only that if Thoroughbreds are not present, then neither are Quarter Horses, but that Morgans and Oldenbergs are present. It does not tell you that if Quarter Horses are present, Morgans and Oldenbergs are not present. Therefore, Choice A could be a possible partial listing of breeds in the KHP. Choice B is incorrect. The third condition tells you that if Oldenbergs (together with Morgans) are present, Standardbreds are also present. Therefore, Choice B could be a possible partial listing of breeds in the KHP. Choice C is incorrect. As with Choice A, the fourth condition tells you only that if Thoroughbreds are not present, then Morgans and Oldenbergs are both present. It does not tell you that if Thoroughbreds are present, Morgans and Oldenbergs are not. Therefore choice C could be a possible partial listing of breeds in the KHP. Choice D is incorrect. As with the previous Choices A and C, the fourth condition tells you only that if Thoroughbreds are not present, then Oldenbergs are present. It does not tell you that if Thoroughbreds are present, Oldenbergs are not. Therefore, it is possible that both Thoroughbreds and Oldenbergs are present. With respect to the presence of Hanoverians, note that in the third condition, the presence of both Morgans and Oldenbergs is required to indicate that Standardbreds are present, which would then, under the first condition, preclude the presence of Hanoverians. However, as noted earlier, the fact that Thoroughbreds and Oldenbergs are present tells you nothing as to whether Morgans are also present, and therefore it is possible that Thoroughbreds and Oldenbergs are present without Morgans also being present. Therefore the third condition would not come into play, and it is possible that Thoroughbreds, Oldenbergs, and Hanoverians could all be present together without any condition being violated.

QUESTIONS 7–12

On the third Thursday of every month, eight Labrador Retriever puppies (Archie, Benjy, Colby, Daisy, Emmet, Fancy, Gilly, and Hank) from the Guiding Eyes for the Blind visit the veterinarian's office for their monthly checkup. Each puppy is either a black lab or a yellow lab. The puppies each arrive at the office at a different time. The following conditions apply:

Gilly arrives at the vet's office before Fancy but after Archie.

Colby arrives at the vet's office before Gilly.

Benjy arrives at the vet's office after Archie but before Fancy.

Fancy arrives at the vet's office before Daisy.

EXPLANATION:

The first condition tells you the following about the order of arrival of the puppies at the vet's office:

Archie

Gilly

Fancy

The second condition tells you that Colby arrived before Gilly, but does not tell you whether or not he arrived before Archie. So at this point, either one of the following orders is possible:

Alternative #1	Alternative #2
Colby	Archie
Archie	Colby
Gilly	Gilly
Fancy	Fancy

The third condition tells you that Benjy arrived after Archie but before Fancy, but does not tell you whether or not he arrived before or after Gilly, or before or after Colby. So now the following are possibilities:

#1	#2	#3	#4	#5
Colby	Colby	Archie	Archie	Archie
Archie	Archie	Colby	Colby	Benjy
Benjy	Gilly	Benjy	Colby	Colby
Gilly	Benjy	Gilly	Gilly	Gilly
Fancy	Fancy	Fancy	Benjy	Fancy

The fourth condition tells you that Fancy arrives before Daisy, providing the following alternatives:

#1	#2	#3	#4	#5
Colby	Colby	Archie	Archie	Archie
Archie	Archie	Colby	Colby	Benjy
Benjy	Gilly	Benjy	Gilly	Colby
Gilly	Benjy	Gilly	Benjy	Gilly
Fancy	Fancy	Fancy	Fancy	Fancy
Daisy	Daisy	Daisy	Daisy	Daisy

No information is provided about the relative arrival time of Emmet or Hank.

If you now provide that Colby arrives after Benjy, but keep all of the other conditions intact, the relative order must be as follows as set forth in alternative #5 immediately preceding, to wit:

1. Archie

2. Benjy

3. Colby

4. Gilly

5. Fancy

6. Daisy

Although no information is provided about when Emmet or Hank arrived, you know that at most the arrival order of all of the others dogs can only shift down one or two spots from the order shown previously.

With this information mapped out, you can proceed to answer Question 7.

7. **Choice B** is correct. Benjy can either be the second, third, or fourth puppy to arrive at the vet's office. Because he cannot be the fifth to arrive, this choice is cannot be true and therefore is the correct answer. Choice A is incorrect. Archie can be anywhere from the first, second, or third puppy to arrive at the vet's office, so this choice might be true, and therefore is incorrect. Choice C is incorrect. Colby can be the third, fourth, or fifth puppy to arrive at the vet's office, so this answer might be true and therefore is incorrect. Choice D is incorrect. Daisy can be the sixth, seventh, or eight puppy to arrive at the vet's office, so this answer might be true and therefore is incorrect. Choice E is incorrect. Fancy can be the fifth, sixth, or seventh puppy to arrive at the vet's office, so this answer might be true and therefore is incorrect.

8. **Choice D** is correct. You know from the analysis set forth for Question 7 that Colby may have arrived at the vet's office before Archie, and that it is also possible that Emmet and/or Hank arrived there before Archie as well. Therefore, the maximum number of puppies that could have arrived at the vet's office before Archie is three. Choice A is incorrect. The maximum number of puppies that could have arrived at the vet's office before Archie is three (see earlier discussion for Choice D). Choice B is incorrect. The maximum number of

puppies that could have arrived at the vet's office before Archie is three (see earlier discussion for Choice D). Choice C is incorrect. The maximum number of puppies that could have arrived at the vet's office before Archie is three (see earlier discussion for Choice D). Choice E is incorrect. The maximum number of puppies that could have arrived at the vet's office before Archie is three (see earlier discussion for Choice D).

9. **Choice C** is correct. Gilly is a black lab. You arrive at this answer by using the following analysis to check the validity of each of the given answers. The only order of arrival that fits the conditions and this scenario is the following:

   1. Emmet

   2. Archie

   3. Benjy

   4. Colby

   5. Gilly

   6. Fancy

   7. Daisy

   8. Hank

Once you know that Benjy is a black lab, you can construct the following color chart:

   1. Emmet—black

   2. Archie—yellow

   3. Benjy—black

   4. Colby—yellow

   5. Gilly—black

   6. Fancy—yellow

   7. Daisy—black

   8. Hank—yellow

Choice A is incorrect. As you can see, Archie is a yellow lab. Choice B is incorrect. Colby is a yellow lab. Choice D is incorrect. Fancy is a yellow lab. Choice E is incorrect. Hank is a yellow lab.

10. **Choice B** is correct. Although you do not know exactly when Benjy arrived, it is possible that he arrived at the vet's office before Emmet. Therefore, this answer could be true and as a result is the correct choice. You arrive at this answer by using the following analysis to check the validity of each of the given answers. If Hank arrived at the vet's office before Colby but after Hank, you can determine the relative order of arrivals as follows:

Emmet

Hank

Colby

Gilly

Fancy

Daisy

Note that you do not have enough information to determine exactly when Archie and Benjy arrived; however, you do know that they both arrived before Fancy. Choice A is incorrect. From the previous, you can determine that Hank arrived at the vet's office before Gilly, and therefore Choice A cannot be true. Choice C is incorrect. As noted previously, although you do not know exactly when Archie and Benjy arrived, you do know that they both arrived before Fancy and therefore before Daisy. Daisy is the last to arrive at the office, and therefore this answer cannot be true. Choice D is incorrect. From the previous, you can determine that Hank arrived at the vet's office well before Fancy, and therefore this answer cannot be true. Choice E is incorrect. As noted previously, although you do not know exactly when Archie and Benjy arrived, you do know that they both arrived before Fancy. As a result, Fancy is the seventh of the puppies to arrive at the vet office, and therefore this answer cannot be true.

11. **Choice C** is correct. You arrive at this answer by using the following analysis to check the validity of each of the given answers. As you already know from the analysis you performed in the process of answering Question 7, the conditions accompanying the scenario do not provide any information about the timing of the arrival of Hank or Emmet at the vet's office. Therefore, you can eliminate answers B and E as incorrect, because neither of them "must be true" based on the scenario and conditions. From re-examining the chart you constructed to answer Question 7

#1	#2	#3	#4	#5
Colby	Colby	Archie	Archie	Archie
Archie	Archie	Colby	Colby	Benjy
Benjy	Gilly	Benjy	Gilly	Colby
Gilly	Benjy	Gilly	Benjy	Gilly
Fancy	Fancy	Fancy	Fancy	Fancy
Daisy	Daisy	Daisy	Daisy	Daisy

you see that Colby may have been the first puppy to arrive at the vet's office (alternative #1 and #2). ThereforeC A is incorrect. You can also see that it possible that only two puppies arrived at the vet's office before Gilly (alternatives #2 and #4), making Choice D incorrect. Therefore you know from process of elimination that Choice C must be the correct answer. Examining the chart, you can see that no matter which alternative is examined, and no matter when Emmet and Hank arrived at the vet's office (one or both either before or after Fancy), at least four puppies arrived at the vet's office before Fancy. Therefore Choice A is incorrect. See previous discussion. Choice B is incorrect. See previous discussion. Choice D is incorrect. See previous discussion. Choice E is incorrect. See previous discussion.

12. **Choice B** is correct. You arrive at this answer by using the following analysis to check the validity of each of the given answers. From re-examining the chart you constructed to answer Question 7

#1	#2	#3	#4	#5
Colby	Colby	Archie	Archie	Archie
Archie	Archie	Colby	Colby	Benjy
Benjy	Gilly	Benjy	Gilly	Colby
Gilly	Benjy	Gilly	Benjy	Gilly
Fancy	Fancy	Fancy	Fancy	Fancy
Daisy	Daisy	Daisy	Daisy	Daisy

you can see under the conditions set forth in the scenario, the *minimum* number of puppies that could have arrived before Gilly under all possible alternatives is two. Therefore you can immediately eliminate Choices A, C, and D. You must now decide between Choices B and E. Looking at the chart, you can see that if Emmet and Hank both arrived at the vet's office before Gilly, the *maximum* number of puppies that could have arrived before Gilly under all possible alternatives is five.

Therefore Choice B is the correct choice. There is no possible alternative under which six puppies could have arrived before Gilly, so choice E is incorrect. Choice A is incorrect. See previous discussion. Choice C is incorrect. See previous discussion. Choice D is incorrect. See previous discussion. Choice E is incorrect. See previous discussion.

QUESTIONS 13–18

The members of the Environmental Litigation department at Primrose Mendel, a small New York City law firm, are moving to a new floor. You have been given the task of assigning the members of the department to new rooms. The department has two partners, Chris and Greg; three senior associates, Ann, Ross, and Lee; and two new junior associates, Devon and Pat. There are seven consecutive rooms (rooms 1933 to 1939) available along the left side of a straight hallway. Rooms 1933 and 1939 are somewhat smaller than the other rooms. The room assignments must conform to the following conditions:

Due to client confidentiality concerns, neither of the new junior associates can be given a room next to a partner.

Neither of the partners can be assigned to Room 1933 or Room 1939.

Greg, who smokes, cannot be assigned to a room next to Ross, who is allergic to smoke.

Pat cannot be assigned to a room next to Devon unless Ross is also assigned a room next to Devon.

13. **Choice C** is correct. The question asks for a list of the people in the Environmental Litigation department who could possibly be given a room between Chris and Greg. The scenario tells you that Chris and Greg are partners. The first condition then tells you that neither Pat or Devon, who are junior associates, can be given a room next to a partner (Chris or Greg). Therefore, you can immediately eliminate choices C, D, and E, because each one of these choices includes either Pat or Devon. You must now decide between Choice A and Choice B. The third condition tells you that Ross (who is listed in Choice A) is allergic to smoke and therefore cannot be given a room next to Greg, who smokes. Therefore, you can eliminate Choice A as incorrect. Choice C, by process of elimination, must be the correct choice. Choice A is incorrect. See previous discussion. Choice B is incorrect. See previous discussion. Choice D is incorrect. See previous discussion. Choice E is incorrect. See previous discussion.

14. **Choice C is correct.** In this choice, Devon's and Pat's rooms (Rooms 1933 and 1935) are not next to one another. The fourth condition only addresses where Ross's room must be if Devon's and Pat's room are next to each other, and says nothing about where it may be if they are not. Therefore, this could be a possible room assignment for Ross, Pat, and Devon. Under the fourth condition, if Pat's and Devon rooms are next to each other, Ross *must* be assigned to the room next to Devon. This enables you to automatically eliminate all choices (Choices A, B, D, and E) that violate this condition. You are therefore left with only one possible choice, C. Choice A is incorrect. In this choice, Devon and Pat's rooms are next to each other (Rooms 1933 and 1934), but Ross's room (1935) is next to Pat, not Devon, thereby violating the fourth condition. Choice B is incorrect. In this choice, Devon's and Pat's rooms are again next to each other (Rooms 1933 and 1934), but Ross's room (Room 1936) is not next to Devon's. Choice D is incorrect. In this choice, Devon's and Pat's rooms are next to each other (Rooms 1935 [Pat] and 1936 [Devon]), but Ross's room (Room 1938) is not next to Devon's room. Choice E is incorrect. In this choice, Devon's and Pat's rooms are again next to each other (Rooms 1938 [Pat] and 1939 [Devon]), but Ross's room (1937) is next to Pat's room, not Devon's room.

15. **Choice A is correct.** The second condition tells you that neither Chris nor Greg can be assigned to Rooms 1933 or 1939. Therefore, under this condition, the farthest apart that Chris and Greg could be is three rooms (if Chris is in Room 1934 and Greg is in Room 1938, or vice versa). Therefore, you can immediately eliminate Choices D and E as incorrect. Under the first condition, you know that neither of the junior associates (Devon or Pat) can be assigned a room next to Chris or Greg. So in this scenario (three rooms separating Chris and Greg), Rooms 1933, 1935, 1937, and 1939 must be assigned to senior associates. Here you face a problem, however. There are only three senior associates, not four. Therefore, you now know that there must be less than three rooms Chris and Greg, and that Choice C is incorrect. What if only two rooms separated Chris and Greg (choice B)? In this situation (Chris in Room 1935 and Greg in Room 1938, or vice versa), you still face the same restrictions imposed by the first condition. Rooms 1934, 1936, 1937, and 1939 must be assigned to senior associates, but once again, there are four rooms and only three senior associates, and therefore Choice B is incorrect. By process of elimination, you are left with Choice A as the only correct choice. By leaving only

one room between Chris and Greg (Chris in Room 1935 and Greg in Room 1937, or vice versa) you can place Ross next to Chris in Room 1934 (because he cannot be placed next to Greg), Lee and Ann in the rooms next to Greg (Rooms 1936, and 1938), and Pat and Devon in the end rooms 1933 and 1939. In this lineup, none of the conditions are violated. Choice B is incorrect. See previous discussion. Choice C is incorrect. See previous discussion. Choice D is incorrect. See previous discussion. Choice E is incorrect. See previous discussion.

16. **Choice A** is correct. As illustrated by the following table, if Ross is in Room 1936, Chris must be assigned to either Room 1935 or 1937 in order to fulfill all of the conditions given as part of the scenario. You can immediately eliminate Choice B, since the third condition states that Greg cannot be assigned a room next to Ross. You also know from the second condition that Greg cannot be in Rooms 1933 or 1939. That leaves two possible rooms for Greg, either Room 1934 or Room 1938. Let's examine the case in which Greg is assigned to Room 1934 first. This means that neither Devon nor Pat can be assigned to Rooms 1933 or 1935, because they cannot be next to a partner. This then leaves as Ann or Lee as possible occupants of Room 1933. In Room 1935, possible occupants include Chris or whichever of Ann or Lee is not in Room 1933. How can you decide which of these two is possible? Consider that if Chris is not in Room 1935, then he must be in either Room 1937 or 1938. If Chris is in Room 1937, then he would have to be next to either Devon or Pat in Rooms 1938 and 1939, which would violate the first condition, so from this, you know that Chris must be assigned to Room 1935.

1933	1934	1935	1936	1937	1938	1939
Not Greg	**Greg**	Not Greg	**Ross**	Not Greg	Not Greg	Not Greg
Not Chris		Not Devon		Ann or Lee?	Ann or Lee?	Not Chris
Not Devon		Not Pat		Devon?	Devon?	Ann or Lee?
Not Pat		**Chris**		Pat?	Pat?	Devon?
Ann or Lee?						Pat?

If Greg is assigned to Room 1938 instead, the following results (a mirror image of the previous table):

1933	1934	1935	1936	1937	1938	1939
Not Greg	Not Greg	Not Greg	**Ross**	Not Greg	**Greg**	Not Greg
Not Chris	Ann or Lee?	Ann or Lee?		Not Devon		Not Chris
Ann or Lee?	Devon?	Devon?		Not Pat		Not Devon
Devon?	Pat?	Pat?		**Chris**		Not Pat
Pat?						Ann or Lee?

Choice B is incorrect. As illustrated by the previous tables, if Ross is in Room 1936, Greg cannot be in Room 1935 or 1937 without violating the third condition. Greg must be in either Room 1934 or 1938.

Choice C is incorrect. As illustrated by the previous tables, if Ross is in Room 1936 then Ann could be in Rooms 1935 or 1937, but she could also be in a different room (Room 1933 or 1939) without violating any of the conditions. Choice D is incorrect. As illustrated by the previous tables, if Ross is in Room 1936, then Devon could be in Rooms 1935 or 1937, but he could also be in a different room (1937, 1938, or 1939 if Greg is in Room 1934, or in Room 1933, 1934, or 1935 if Greg is in Room 1938) without violating any of the conditions. Choice E is incorrect. As illustrated by the previous tables, if Ross is in Room 1936, then Pat could be in Rooms 1935 or 1937, but he could also be in a different room (1937, 1938, or 1939 if Greg is in Room 1934, or in Room 1933, 1934, or 1935 if Greg is in Room 1938) without violating any of the conditions.

17. **Choice E** is correct. By process of elimination, you can determine that Devon cannot be assigned to Room 1936. You already know from completing Question 15 that either Ann or Lee could be placed in Room 1936 without violating any of the conditions of the scenario, so you can immediately eliminate Choices C and D as incorrect. The second condition tells you that neither Chris nor Greg can be assigned to Rooms 1933 or 1939. Therefore, the pool of available rooms to which they may be assigned includes Room 1936. If you assign either Chris or Greg to this room, you can create the following room assignments without violating any of the conditions:

1933	1934	1935	1936	1937	1938	1939
Devon	Ross	Ann	Chris or Greg	Greg or Chris	Lee	Pat

Therefore either Chris or Greg could be assigned to Room 1936, allowing you to eliminate both Choices A and B. By process of elimination, Choice E must be the correct choice. Choice A is incorrect.

Chris could be assigned to Room 1936 without violating any of the conditions of the scenario. See previous discussion. Choice B is incorrect. Greg could be assigned to Room 1936 without violating any of the conditions of the scenario. See previous discussion. Choice C is incorrect. Ann could be assigned to Room 1936 without violating any of the conditions of the scenario. See previous discussion. Choice D is incorrect. Lee could be assigned to Room 1936 without violating any of the conditions of the scenario. See previous discussion.

18. **Choice D** is correct. By process of elimination you can determine that Ross cannot be assigned to Room 1939 without violating the conditions of the scenario. From the first condition, you know that neither Devon nor Pat can be given a room next to Chris or Greg (which means that either Ross, Ann, or Lee must be in those rooms). From the second condition, you know that neither Chris nor Greg can be assigned to Room 1933 or 1939. From the third condition, you know that Ross cannot be assigned a room next to Greg. From the fourth condition, you know that Pat cannot be assigned a room next to Devon unless Ross is also assigned a room next to Devon. If Chris and Greg are not assigned to adjacent rooms, the first possible rooms that Chris and Greg could be assigned would be to Rooms 1934 and 1936. You then have the following possible room assignment:

1933	1934	1935	1936	1937	1938	1939
Not Chris	Greg	Not Chris	Chris	Not Greg	Devon	Not Chris
Not Greg		Not Devon		Not Devon		Not Greg
Not Devon		Not Pat		Not Pat		Pat
Not Pat		Not Ross		Ross		
Not Ross		Ann or Lee				
Lee or Ann						

Note that it is not possible to place Chris in Room 1934 and Greg in 1936 without violating the conditions of the scenario. That is, if Ross is placed in Room 1933 so that he is not next to Greg, then the only available rooms for Devon and Pat would be Rooms 1938 and 1939. But Pat cannot be assigned to a room next to Devon unless Ross is also assigned to a room next to Devon (the fourth condition), and this is not possible under the third condition.

The next possible room assignments for Chris and Greg are Rooms 1935 and 1937, with the following possible alignment:

1933	1934	1935	1936	1937	1938	1939
Not Chris	Not Devon	Chris	Not Greg	Greg	Not Chris	Not Chris
Not Greg	Not Pat		Not Devon		Not Devon	Not Greg
Devon or Pat	Not Greg		Not Pat		Not Pat	Pat or Devon
	Ross		Not Ross		Not Ross	
			Ann or Lee		Lee or Ann	

and its mirror image:

1933	1934	1935	1936	1937	1938	1939
Not Chris	Not Chris	Greg	Not Greg	Chris	Not Devon	Not Chris
Not Greg	Not Devon		Not Devon		Not Pat	Not Greg
	Not Pat		Not Pat		Not Greg	
Devon or Pat	Not Ross		Not Ross		Ross	Pat or Devon
	Ann or Lee		Lee or Ann			

The final possible set of room assignments for Chris and Greg are Rooms 1936 and 1938, with the following alignment:

1933	1934	1935	1936	1937	1938	1939
Not Chris	Devon	Not Greg	Chris	Not Greg	Greg	Not Chris
Not Greg		Not Devon		Not Devon		Not Greg
Pat		Not Pat		Not Pat		Not Devon
		Ross		Not Ross		Not Pat
				Ann or Lee		Not Ross
						Not Ross
						Lee or Ann

Note that it is not possible to place Greg in Room 1936 and Chris in Room 1938 without violating the conditions of the scenario. From this analysis, you can see that Lee, Ann, Devon, and Pat can all be successfully assigned to Room 1939. Therefore, you can eliminate Choices A,

B, C, and E as incorrect, leaving you with Choice D as the correct answer. Choice A is incorrect. As seen from the previous analysis, if Chris and Greg are not assigned rooms that are next to each other, Pat can be assigned to Room 1939 without violating any of the conditions of the scenario. Choice B is incorrect. As seen from the previous analysis, if Chris and Greg are not assigned rooms that are next to each other, Devon can be assigned to Room 1939 without violating any of the conditions of the scenario. Choice C is incorrect. As seen from the previous analysis, if Chris and Greg are not assigned rooms that are next to each other, Lee can be assigned to Room 1939 without violating any of the conditions of the scenario. Choice E is incorrect. As seen from the previous analysis, if Chris and Greg are not assigned rooms that are next to each other, Ann can be assigned to Room 1939 without violating any of the conditions of the scenario.

QUESTIONS 19–24

The results of a student survey of pizza places within a 5-mile radius of College U. have just been released. The survey ranks seven pizza places (Artisan, Baci, Capri, Donato, Enzio, Forni, and Gigi) from best (highest) to worst (lowest). There were no ties. The ranking is in accordance with the following conditions:

Capri ranks higher than Artisan but lower than Donato.

Baci ranks higher than Gigi but lower than Forni.

If Enzio ranks higher than Capri, Baci ranks higher than Enzio.

If Capri ranks higher than Enzio, Enzio ranks higher than Baci.

19. **Choice E is correct.** It is possible that Baci could be ranked as low as sixth (if Artisan is ranked above it). Under the second condition, Gigi is ranked lower than Baci so it is not possible for Baci to ranked seventh. Looking at your answer choices, you can see that the correct choice is Choice E. You arrive at this answer by using the following analysis to check the validity of each of the given answers. First, examine the conditions to see what they tell you about the possible relative rankings of the various pizza places. From the first condition, you can see that

Donato

Capri

Artisan

The second condition tells you

Forni

Baci

Gigi

At this point, you still have no information about where in the list of seven pizza places these two sets of rankings appear, or whether any of the other four pizza places are interposed between any of the pizza places ranked. The third and fourth conditions concern the relative ranking of a set of three pizza places: Enzio, Capri, and Baci. The third condition tells you that if Enzio ranks higher than Capri, Baci ranks higher than Enzio, so therefore

Baci

Enzio

Capri

The fourth condition tells you that if Capri ranks higher than Enzio, Enzio ranks higher than Baci. Therefore, under all conditions, you now know that Enzio is always ranked somewhere between Baci and Capri; either

Capri

Enzio

Baci

or

Baci

Enzio

Capri

Note that third and fourth conditions are mutually exclusive; that is, if the third condition is the case, then the fourth condition is not, and vice versa. Combining condition 1 (which mentions Capri) with condition 3 (which also mentions Capri) together provides the following possible rankings in the situation in which Enzio ranks higher than Capri:

Donato	Baci	Baci
Baci	Donato	Enzio
Enzio	Enzio	Donato
Capri	Capri	Capri
Artisan	Artisan	Artisan

Adding condition 2 to conditions 1 and 3 (which mentions Baci) presents the following possibilities with respect to the location of Forni:

Donato	Forni	Forni	Forni
Forni	Donato	Baci	Baci
Baci	Baci	Donato	Enzio
Enzio	Enzio	Enzio	Donato
Capri	Capri	Capri	Capri
Artisan	Artisan	Artisan	Artisan

Gigi could be located anywhere after Baci all the way to the bottom of the list; therefore, all of the following sets of orders are possibilities:

1A	1B	1C	1D
Donato	Donato	Donato	Donato
Forni	Forni	Forni	Forni
Baci	Baci	Baci	Baci
Gigi	Enzio	Enzio	Enzio
Enzio	Gigi	Capri	Capri
Capri	Capri	Gigi	Artisan
Artisan	Artisan	Artisan	Gigi

2A	2B	2C	2D
Forni	Forni	Forni	Forni
Donato	Donato	Donato	Donato
Baci	Baci	Baci	Baci
Gigi	Enzio	Enzio	Enzio
Enzio	Gigi	Capri	Capri
Capri	Capri	Gigi	Artisan
Artisan	Artisan	Artisan	Gigi

3A	3B	3C	3D	3E
Forni	Forni	Forni	Forni	Forni
Baci	Baci	Baci	Baci	Baci
Gigi	Donato	Donato	Donato	Donato
Donato	Gigi	Enzio	Enzio	Enzio
Enzio	Enzio	Gigi	Capri	Artisan
Capri	Capri	Capri	Gigi	Gigi
Artisan	Artisan	Artisan	Artisan	

4A	4B	4C	4D	4E
Forni	Forni	Forni	Forni	Forni
Baci	Baci	Baci	Baci	Baci
Gigi	Enzio	Enzio	Enzio	Enzio
Enzio	Gigi	Donato	Donato	Donato
Donato	Donato	Gigi	Capri	Capri
Capri	Capri	Capri	Gigi	Artisan
Artisan	Artisan	Artisan	Artisan	Gigi

You can create a similar set of charts for the situation referred to in the fourth condition, in which Capri is ranked higher than Enzio. Combining conditions 1, 2, and 4, you know the following:

Donato

Capri

Enzio

Baci

Gigi

You can also determine that Forni could be ranked anywhere from the top of the list to just in front of Baci, and that Artisan could be ranked anywhere from between Capri and Enzio to last on the list. It is possible that Baci could be ranked as low as sixth (if Artisan is ranked above it). Under the second condition, Gigi is ranked lower than Baci so it is not possible to Baci to ranked seveth. Looking at your answer choices, you can see that the correct choice is Choice E. Choice A is incorrect. Baci could be ranked lower than second highest (see previous discussion). Choice B is incorrect. Baci could be ranked lower than third highest (see previous discussion.) Choice C is incorrect. Baci could be ranked lower than fourth highest (see previous discussion.) Choice D is incorrect. Baci could be ranked lower than fifth highest (see previous discussion).

20. Which one of the following could be an accurate ranking of the pizza places, from best to worst?

   ❑ A. Forni, Baci, Enzio, Capri, Gigi, Donato, Artisan
   ❑ B. Donato, Capri, Forni, Baci, Enzio, Gigi, Artisan
   ❑ C. Forni, Baci, Enzio, Donato, Gigi, Capri, Artisan
   ❑ D. Forni, Donato, Baci, Gigi, Capri, Enzio, Artisan
   ❑ E. Donato, Capri, Baci, Enzio, Gigi, Forni, Artisan

Choice C is correct. You arrive at this answer by using the following analysis to check the validity of each of the given answers. Start by examining all of the choices to see whether any are eliminated because they violate one of the conditions stated in the scenario. In doing so, you can see that Choice A violates the first condition, which provides that Capri ranks lower than Donato. You can also see that Choice E violates the second condition, which provides that Baci ranks lower than Forni. So Choices A and E can immediately be eliminated. You must now choose between Choices B, C, and D. None of these choices violate the third condition. However, both choices B and D violate the fourth condition, which states that if Capri ranks higher than Enzio, Enzio ranks higher than Baci. In both of these choices, Capri ranks higher than Enzio, but Enzio does not rank higher than Baci. Therefore, by process of elimination, Choice C is the correct choice. Choice A is incorrect because it violates the first condition (see previous discussion). Choice B is incorrect because it violates the fourth condition (see previous discussion). Choice D is incorrect because it violates the fourth condition (see previous discussion). Choice E is incorrect because it violates the second condition (see previous discussion).

21. If Baci ranks lower than Artisan, which one of the following must be true?

   ❑ A. Artisan ranks higher than Forni.
   ❑ B. Enzio ranks higher than Gigi.
   ❑ C. Capri ranks higher than Forni.
   ❑ D. Forni ranks higher than Enzio.
   ❑ E. Forni ranks higher than Capri.

Choice B is correct. By examining the charts above, you can see that under all possible rankings in which the fourth condition is involved,

Enzio must rank higher than Gigi. You can answer this question by examining the charts above. You can see this must be a situation in which the fourth condition is in effect, because Baci cannot rank lower than Artisan if the third condition were the case. You can easily see that the only choice that **must** be true is choice B. Choice A is incorrect. By examining the charts above, you can see that it is possible for Artisan to rank lower than Forni if Baci ranks lower than Artisan, as follows:

Forni

Donato

Capri

Artisan

Enzio

Baci

Gigi

Choice C is incorrect. By examining the charts above, you can see that it is possible for Capri to rank lower than Forni if Baci ranks lower than Artisan, as follows:

Forni

Donato

Capri

Enzio

Artisan

Baci

Gigi

Choice D is incorrect. By examining the charts above, you can see that it is possible for Forni to rank lower than Enzio if Baci ranks lower than Artisan, as follows:

Donato

Capri

Enzio

Forni

Artisan

Baci

Gigi

Choice E is incorrect. By examining the previous charts above, you can see that it is possible for Forni to rank lower than Capri if Baci ranks lower than Artisan, as follows:

> Donato
>
> Capri
>
> Forni
>
> Enzio
>
> Artisan
>
> Baci
>
> Gigi

22. If Gigi ranks higher than Donato, then which one of the following could be ranked fifth highest?
   - ❑ A. Forni
   - ❑ B. Baci
   - ❑ C. Enzio
   - ❑ D. Gigi
   - ❑ E. Capri

Choice C is correct. If Gigi ranks higher than Donato, Enzio could be ranked fifth highest. If Gigi ranks higher than Donato, you can use the first two conditions to establish the following ranking:

> Forni
>
> Baci
>
> Gigi
>
> Donato
>
> Capri
>
> Artisan

You also know from the third and fourth conditions that under all conditions, Enzio must be ranked between Baci and Capri. There are, therefore, three possible rankings:

Forni	Forni	Forni
Baci	Baci	Baci
Enzio	Gigi	Gigi
Gigi	Enzio	Donato
Donato	Donato	Enzio
Capri	Capri	Capri
Artisan	Artisan	Artisan

Looking at your answer choices, you can see that the only one of the choices that could be ranked the fifth highest is C, Enzio. Choice A is incorrect. If Gigi ranks higher than Donato, Forni could not be ranked fifth highest (see previous discussion). Choice B is incorrect. If Gigi ranks higher than Donato, Baci could not be ranked fifth highest (see previous discussion). Choice D is incorrect. If Gigi ranks higher than Donato, Gigi could not be ranked fifth highest (see previous discussion). Choice E is incorrect. If Gigi ranks higher than Donato, Capri could not be ranked fifth highest (see previous discussion).

23. If Forni is ranked third highest, then which one of the following *cannot* be true?

   ❏   A. Baci is ranked fifth highest.
   ❏   B. Baci is ranked sixth highest
   ❏   C. Artisan is ranked fourth highest.
   ❏   D. Capri is ranked fifth highest.
   ❏   E. Enzio is ranked fifth highest.

Choice D is the correct answer by process of elimination. You can see from your charts that if the third condition is in effect, Forni is not ranked lower than second. Therefore, this must be a situation in which the fourth condition is in effect. Here you can see that if Forni is ranked third; the following are possible rankings:

Donato	Donato	Donato	Donato
Capri	Capri	Capri	Capri
Forni	Forni	Forni	Forni
Artisan	Enzio	Enzio	Enzio
Enzio	Artisan	Baci	Baci
Baci	Baci	Artisan	Gigi
Gigi	Gigi	Gigi	Artisan

Choices A, B, C, E: These choices are all incorrect. From examining this chart, you can see that rankings listed in Choices A, B, C, and E are possibilities, and are therefore incorrect. Therefore, by process of elimination, Choice D is the correct answer. You can also confirm this answer by looking at the chart and observing that in all of the possible rankings Capri is listed in second place.

24. Which one of the following *cannot* be true?

- ❏ A. Capri ranks second highest.
- ❏ B. Gigi ranks third highest.
- ❏ C. Artisan ranks third highest.
- ❏ D. Donato ranks fifth highest.
- ❏ E. Enzio ranks sixth highest.

Choice E is correct, by process of elimination. You can also determine by examining the charts above that there is no situation in which Enzio ranks sixth highest. Choice A is incorrect. If the fourth condition is the case, you can see by examining the charts above that you created for that condition that it is possible for Capri to rank second highest. Choice B is incorrect. If the third condition is the case, you can see by examining charts 3A and 4A that it is possible for Gigi to rank third highest. Choice C is incorrect. If the fourth condition is the case, you can see by examining the charts above that you created for that condition that it is possible for Artisan to rank third highest. Choice D is incorrect. If the third condition is the case, you can see by examining charts 4C, 4D, and 4E that it is possible for Donato to rank fourth highest.

9

Practice Exam 3

SECTION I—Logical Reasoning

Time—35 minutes

24 Questions

Directions: The questions in this section are based on the reasoning contained in brief statements or passages. For some questions, more than one of the choices could conceivably answer the question. However, you are to choose the best answer—that is, the response that most accurately and completely answers the question. You should not make assumptions that are by commonsense standards implausible, superfluous, or incompatible with the passage. After you have chosen the best answer, blacken the corresponding space on your answer sheet.

1. Dottie says, "All donkeys bray. This animal does not bray. Therefore, it is not a donkey."

   Which one of the following, if true, most weakens Dottie's argument?

   ❑ A. You can train a dog to bray.
   ❑ B. Donkeys bray more than cows.
   ❑ C. Zebras also can bray.
   ❑ D. Some donkeys cannot bray.
   ❑ E. You cannot train a donkey to bray.

2. The Ace Foundation, which administers a college scholarship fund, provides potential applicants with the following information: To qualify for a scholarship, the applicant must have a 3.0 GPA and a score of 1600 on the SAT; a 3.5 GPA and a score of 1500 on the SAT; or a 3.75 GPA and a score of 1400 on the SAT. For GPAs and SAT scores between these milestones, a sliding scale is applied.

   Which one of the following is not consistent with preceding the facts?

   ❑ A. Most scholarship applicants had an SAT score in the range of 1400–1500.
   ❑ B. No scholarship applicant with an SAT score of less than 1400 and a GPA of less than 3.75 will qualify for the scholarship.
   ❑ C. The lower the GPA, the higher the SAT score required to qualify for the scholarship.
   ❑ D. Some applicants with an SAT score of less than 1500 and a GPA of less than 3.0 qualified for a scholarship.
   ❑ E. Nicholas qualified for a scholarship with a 3.7 GPA and a 1580 SAT score.

3. In equestrian instruction academies throughout the country, 90% of the students and instructors are female, and only 10% are male, but in professional equestrian competitions, 75% of the competitors are male.

   All of the following statements, if true, could help explain these statistics *except*:

   ❑ A. Many females stop riding once they reach adolescence.
   ❑ B. Male riders are more talented than female riders.
   ❑ C. Professional equestrian sports is not a socially acceptable profession for females.
   ❑ D. Males enjoy competition more than females.
   ❑ E. Males like horses as much as females.

4. The coach of the Croton Boys' U16 soccer team sent the following email to members of the team:

No one can play goalie in this week's game unless he has his own goalie gloves. If Christopher does not play goalie, Ryan will not play defense.

Which one of the following can reasonably be inferred from the preceding?

- ❑ A. If Christopher has goalie gloves, he will play goalie.
- ❑ B. If Christopher has goalie gloves, Ryan will play defense.
- ❑ C. If Christopher plays goalie, Ryan will play defense.
- ❑ D. If Ryan plays defense, Christopher has goalie gloves.
- ❑ E. If Christopher does not play goalie, Ryan will play offense.

5. The ring-tailed snipe normally thrives in an environment abundant in banyan trees. The lush greenery provided by the trees gives the animal enough nourishment to keep it healthy during its reproductive cycle. However, in the Cape Suzette region, which is known for its large number of banyan trees, the ring-tailed snipe is considered endangered.

Which of the following, if true, best explains the apparent discrepancy in the preceding argument?

- ❑ A. Many species of animals found in the Cape Suzette region, including the winkle bull-moose and the fuzzy polecat, are also considered endangered.
- ❑ B. The ring-tailed snipe is thought to be endangered in several other regions, such as Timbuktu and Kalamazoo.
- ❑ C. The bandersnatch, which is a natural predator of the ring-tailed snipe, is abundant in the Cape Suzette region.
- ❑ D. The Cape Suzette region is known for its harsh winters, where temperatures occasionally stunt the growth of the banyan trees.
- ❑ E. Ring-tailed snipes have a very rapid metabolism.

6. All women are confident, and all girls are poised. The team includes both women and girls. Every poised person is also confident, so every person on the team is confident.

Which one of the following statements is consistent with the preceding argument?

- ❑ A. There are no men or boys on the team.
- ❑ B. Only girls are confident.
- ❑ C. No member of the team is poised.
- ❑ D. No member of the team is confident.
- ❑ E. Only women are on the team.

7. The Florist's Shop on Grand Street was advertising a special on a dozen roses. However, when Jon went to the shop to order roses, he discovered that there were none left. The florist explained that the roses had already sold out.

   The florist's explanation is an example of which one of the following?

   ❑ A. Using evidence not relevant to a conclusion
   ❑ B. Attempting to change the grounds of an argument
   ❑ C. Failure to generalize from a specific case
   ❑ D. Rephrasing but not explaining a problem
   ❑ E. Euphemism

8. Politicians in the novels of D.H. Lawrence are often presented in a critical and uncomplimentary manner. As a result, many reviewers have concluded that Lawrence had a hostile attitude toward politicians.

   Which one of the following, if true, best supports the preceding conclusion?

   ❑ A. The observations about politicians are offered by characters in the novels with whom Lawrence clearly identifies.
   ❑ B. Lawrence's presentation of others in his novels is equally critical and uncomplimentary.
   ❑ C. The attitude toward politicians in Lawrence's novels is similar to that reflected in other novels written during the same period of time.
   ❑ D. Lawrence's novels are fictional.
   ❑ E. Lawrence was himself a politician.

9. Michael's answer to a question about an IRS regulation must be the best one because he is the only lawyer with a master's degree in taxation who answered the question.

   The preceing statement assumes which one of the following?

   ❑ A. Anyone who is a lawyer cannot be wrong.
   ❑ B. Any lawyer who has a master's degree in taxation must be correct about tax matters.
   ❑ C. A lawyer with a master's degree in taxation is a better judge of a tax matter than others.
   ❑ D. A lawyer with a master's degree in taxation is a better judge than other lawyers.
   ❑ E. A lawyer with a master's degree in taxation will usually give the best answer to a question.

10. I will probably have to put a new roof on my house this year. My next-door neighbor just put a new roof on his house, and my house and his house were built the same year and by the same construction firm.

Which of the following, if true, would most weaken the preceding argument?

❑ A. The next-door neighbor and the speaker both clean their roofs from debris after a storm.

❑ B. The next-door neighbor's roofing material is not the same as the speaker's.

❑ C. The construction firm that installed the roofs was known to never deviate in the materials it used or the quality of its installation.

❑ D. The speaker cannot afford to put on a new roof.

❑ E. The neighbor is a contractor himself, but the speaker is not.

11. Today, Darrell and I sat on my stoop, waiting for Noah. After a few minutes, Darrell got tired of waiting and left. I think the reason Darrell gets into trouble so frequently is that he is so impatient.

Which one of the following best describes the error in the speaker's reasoning?

❑ A. It bases the argument on unreliable evidence.

❑ B. It treats a dissimilar event as analogous to the present one.

❑ C. It reiterates its conclusion rather than supplying evidence to support it.

❑ D. It makes a claim by over-generalizing from specific evidence.

❑ E. It bases a generalization on claims that contradict one another.

QUESTIONS 12–13 RELATE TO THE FOLLOWING SCENARIO:

Newscaster: Senator Grogan, why have you been claiming that the vice-president has violated the law? He has not been charged with any crime.

Senator Grogan: The vice-president has indeed been charged with a crime. I have publicly alleged that he is guilty of the misuse of government funds.

12. From the exchange preceding, it is likely that Senator Grogan believes which of the following statements?

❑ A. Publicly alleging that someone has committed a crime is not the same as being charged with a crime.

❑ B. Misusing government funds is de facto evidence that someone has been charged with a crime.

❑ C. Publicly alleging that someone has committed a crime is de facto evidence that the person has misused government funds.

❑ D. Misusing government funds is not necessarily de facto evidence that someone has been charged with a crime.

❑ E. Publicly alleging that someone has committed a crime is the same as being charged with a crime.

13. Which of the following statements parallels Senator Grogan's reasoning most closely?

   ❑ A. According to the news, Congressman LeFoix lied under oath on the stand. Therefore, he must have already been convicted for perjury.

   ❑ B. The newspaper says that District Assemblyman Gerald stole money from his department. Therefore, he must be charged with embezzlement.

   ❑ C. Consumers allege that Cogswell Industries shortchanged them. Therefore, charges must be brought against all of the company officers.

   ❑ D. The secretary of energy has been tried for her sale of oil futures. Therefore, she must have been charged for insider trading.

   ❑ E. The district attorney alleged that Justice Granger improperly struck down the law. Therefore, the judge must be charged with assault.

14. Increasing the maximum speed limit from 55 MPH to 65 MPH will significantly increase the number of traffic accidents.

   Which one of the following, if true, most weakens the preceding argument?

   ❑ A. Prior to the increase, 95% of traffic accidents occurred when cars were traveling at between 55 and 65 MPH.

   ❑ B. Prior to the increase, 95% of traffic accidents occurred when cars were traveling at below 45 MPH.

   ❑ C. Few traffic accidents involve only one car.

   ❑ D. Most traffic accidents occur during the day.

   ❑ E. Most traffic accidents occurring when cars are traveling at speeds between 55 and 65 MPH do not result in injuries to the occupants of the vehicles.

15. There are 200 members of a country club. Club committee memberships have two terms: Fall/Winter and Spring/Summer. In Fall/Winter, 10 members were on the Finance Committee, 10 members were on the Entertainment Committee, and 15 members were on the Recruiting Committee. In Spring/Summer, all three of these committees had twice as many participants as in Fall/Winter. Therefore, during the entire year, all but 95 members of the country club were members of committees.

   All of the following, if true, would weaken the preceding conclusion *except*:

   ❑ A. Some members of the club joined more than one committee during both terms.

   ❑ B. Some members of the club never joined a committee.

   ❑ C. Some members of the club joined more than one committee during Fall/Winter.

   ❑ D. Some members of the club joined a committee during both Fall/Winter and Spring/Summer.

   ❑ E. Some members of the club joined more than one committee during Spring/Summer.

16. Scott says:

    When I was 16, I could get a driver's license, but I could not see an R-rated movie.

    When I was 18, I could vote, but I could not drink.

    Which one of the following expresses reasoning most similar to Scott's preceding?

    - ❑ A. When I was 62, I could retire, but I could not collect Social Security.
    - ❑ B. When I was 21, I could not smoke, but I could drink.
    - ❑ C. When I was 6, I could go to school, but I could also play outside by myself.
    - ❑ D. When I was 25, I graduated from law school, and I made a lot of money.
    - ❑ E. When I was 75, I could work, but I did not have to.

17. With its use of black tile, neon trim, and chevrons, Art Deco is known as the flamboyant architecture that spans the years "between the wars," roughly 1918 to 1941. Thanks to the explosion of interest in its unique flair, whole downtown sections of Miami, New York, and Los Angeles will forever retain a classic, timeless air.

    Assuming that the logic of the preceding argument is sound, which of the following buildings are least likely to be considered Art Deco in style?

    - ❑ A. A hotel in El Paso, Texas, with neon trim and chevrons
    - ❑ B. An apartment building in New York City with black tile
    - ❑ C. A motel in Nevada next to the neon-lit Las Vegas Strip
    - ❑ D. A residential home in Los Angeles built in 1919
    - ❑ E. A Palm Beach bungalow with black tile and neon-trimmed chevrons

18. Canadian musk oxen have a unique three-toed hoof and squared-off horns. Only Russian musk oxen have similar features. Because Canada and Russia are separated by the Bering Strait, this is clear evidence that at one time, a land bridge existed between the two areas at one point in time.

    The argument's conclusion is most weakened if which of the following statements are true?

    - ❑ A. The angle of Russian musk oxen's horns is not as squared off as that of Canadian musk oxen.
    - ❑ B. In 1650, a sea captain unloaded a herd of Russian musk oxen on the Canadian shore.
    - ❑ C. In the 1950s, soil samples dredged up from the Bering Strait show only a trace of marine sediments.
    - ❑ D. Canadian and Russian musk oxen are classified as distinctly separate species.
    - ❑ E. Some Canadian and Russian musk oxen are born with only two-toed hooves.

19. Prosecutor: A computer hacker that intercepts someone's online credit card information is committing theft. The fact that the theft is digital does not alter the fact that, like robbing a bank or breaking into someone's home, it is a theft of property. Therefore, the punishment that should be meted out to such a hacker should be no less stringent than that given to a bank robber or a burglar.

   Which one of the following most accurately describes the prosecutor's argument?

   ❑ A. It states a rule and then provides an exception to that rule.
   ❑ B. It bases a generalization upon a specific instance.
   ❑ C. It proposes a conclusion based on evidence.
   ❑ D. It uses analogy to strengthen the conclusion.
   ❑ E. It provides several points of view in support of a conclusion.

20. The ExFed Shipping Company is auditing its recent gasoline bills for its fleet of trucks. For the month of January, the average charge per gallon throughout the region was the same as it was in December. ExFed Shipping's total consumption of gasoline in January was higher than it was in December, but its total expenditure for January was less than its expenditure in December.

   Which one of the following, if true, best explains this finding?

   ❑ A. ExFed Shipping shut down for two weeks for vacation in January.
   ❑ B. During January, many ExFed Shipping vehicles were out of service.
   ❑ C. January was much more snowy than December.
   ❑ D. ExFed Shipping's vehicles used more regular unleaded gasoline than premium unleaded in January than December.
   ❑ E. During January, ExFed Shipping purchased new vehicles that get better mileage per gallon than its old vehicles.

21. Arthur Conan Doyle applied his substantial experience in multiple fields to make his fictional characters as real as possible. His most famous creation, Sherlock Holmes, possesses extensive knowledge of geology, physics, chemistry, and, of course, deductive logic. Similarly, it is clear that Doyle himself would be of an extremely sharp and quick wit, a man of even temperament shot through with flashes of arrogance and unearthly brilliance.

   Which one of the following is the strongest criticism of the preceding statement?

- ❑ A. The author never actually met Arthur Conan Doyle.
- ❑ B. The author does not offer a biographical sketch of Arthur Conan Doyle.
- ❑ C. Doyle's stories are considered to be lightweight fiction by today's literary critics.
- ❑ D. The author relies on secondhand sources only in coming to his conclusions.
- ❑ E. The author does not elucidate the details of each field that Doyle was conversant in.

22. The decision has been made to return the gargoyle statues to the Shrycler Building's facade. Newly uncovered photographs from the 1920s conclusively show that the building was originally crafted with these statues as part of the decoration. The statues were found in a local bank's vault, accompanied by a note reading "The owner disapproves of the design." Thus it appears likely that the statues were removed because of a disagreement as to their decorative function, not due to a structural defect.

The assertion that the statues were removed for a decorative reasons serves which one of the following functions in the argument?

- ❑ A. It clarifies the stakes involved at the base of the argument: form or function.
- ❑ B. It simply reiterates the main point for the sake of emphasis.
- ❑ C. It is the main point of the argument.
- ❑ D. It demonstrates by the use of an analogy.
- ❑ E. It is a subsidiary conclusion that supports the argument's main conclusion.

23. Barrel cacti may be fatter than any other cactus. Barrel cacti are never thinner than the thinnest organ pipe cacti, and some organ pipe cacti may even be fatter than some barrel cacti. Saguaro cacti are always fatter than organ pipe cacti. Prickly pear cacti are thinner than saguaro cacti but not thinner than organ pipe cacti.

Based on the preceding, which one of the following must be true?

- ❑ A. Prickly pear cacti may be thinner than barrel cacti.
- ❑ B. Saguaro cacti may be thinner than some prickly pear cacti.
- ❑ C. Every barrel cactus is fatter than every organ pipe cactus.
- ❑ D. A specific organ pipe cactus could not be fatter than a specific barrel cactus.
- ❑ E. Occasionally, a prickly pear cactus may be fatter than a saguaro cactus.

24. Some people have never tried blue spoo for dinner, but they don't know what they are missing. Blue spoo is creamier and has a richer "meat gelatin" flavor than traditional green or yellow spoo. If someone wants to have a truly delicious dish of spoo that is full of flavor, they must try blue spoo.

    If all of the preceding statements are true, which of the following must also be true?

    ❑ A. Flarn, which is a yellow spoo, cannot be truly delicious and full of flavor.

    ❑ B. Eating blue spoo will always be more pleasurable than eating any other kind of food.

    ❑ C. Green and yellow spoo are equally creamy and flavorful types of spoo.

    ❑ D. White wine is the beverage that best complements blue spoo.

    ❑ E. Gahk, which is a green spoo, can often be very flavorful and rich.

THIS IS THE END OF THE SECTION.

SECTION II—Reading Comprehension

Time—35 minutes

25 Questions

Directions: Each passage in this section is followed by a group of questions to be answered on the basis of what is stated or implied in the passage. For some of the questions, more than one of the choices could conceivably answer the question. However, you are to choose the best answer—that is, the response that most accurately and completely answers the question—and blacken the corresponding space on your answer sheet.

Mr. Chairman and members of the Subcommittee, I am delighted to be here this morning as a Federal Trade Commissioner. I appreciate your having this hearing today to address such an important topic. I will speak briefly about
5   children's online privacy.

As the Commission's June 1998 Report to Congress noted, children represent a large and rapidly growing segment of online consumers. I would guess that the numbers will only increase. Perhaps one of the most frightening facts the Report noted was
10   how many children's sites (89% of the 212 sites surveyed) collected personal information from them but appear not to obtain any kind of parental permission.

In the Commission's view, these practices raise especially troubling privacy and safety concerns because of the particular
15   vulnerability of children, the immediacy and ease with which information can be collected from them, and the ability of the online medium to circumvent the traditional gate-keeping role of the parent.

We are not alone in our concerns. A 1997 Louis Harris & Alan
20   Westin survey showed that 72% of parents whose children use the Internet object to a website's requesting a child's name and address when the child registers at the site, even if such information is used only internally. The Commission's goal is to put parents in control of commercial websites' collection of
25   personal information from their children.

The Commission's June report recommended that Congress
enact legislation to protect children's online privacy. The
Commission's recommended standards would enable parents to
make choices about when and how their children's information is
30   collected and used on the Web.

The recommended standards would require commercial websites to

➤ Provide for notice and parental consent before personal information is collected from children 12 and under, and

➤ Provide parents of children 13 and over with notice and an opportunity to
35   have their children's personal information removed from a website's data-
base after it has been collected.

We are encouraged that, in addition to Congressman Tauzin's
Data Privacy Act of 1997, Senators Bryan and McCain have just
introduced legislation that is fully compatible with our
40   recommendation.

Source: Excerpt from the Statement of Commissioner Sheila Anthony before the Subcommittee on
Telecommunications, Trade and Consumer Protection, July 21, 1998
http://www.ftc.gov/speeches/anthony/kidsst.htm

1. What is the purpose of the Congressional hearing referred to in this
passage?
- ❑ A. The growing use of children's time spent on the Internet
- ❑ B. The inability to restrict access to adult websites from children
- ❑ C. The lack of privacy of children's personal information on the Internet
- ❑ D. The parental consent forms used by most sites on the Internet
- ❑ E. The merits of the Data Privacy Act of 1997

2. What specific report is being referred to as the "Report" in line 9?
- ❑ A. The Congressional study on children's Internet usage
- ❑ B. The Federal Trade Commission Report of June 1998
- ❑ C. The 1997 Louis Harris & Alan Westin survey
- ❑ D. Congressman Tauzin's Data Privacy Act of 1997
- ❑ E. New legislation by Senators Bryan and McCain

3. The speaker is hoping to improve all these concerns *except*:
- ❑ A. The children's privacy
- ❑ B. The children's Internet access
- ❑ C. The children's safety
- ❑ D. The parents' ability to protect their child
- ❑ E. The parents' ability to regulate access

4. Who is the author intending to be the ultimate gate keeper for access and use of children's information gathered on the Web?

❑ A. Congress
❑ B. The FTC
❑ C. The websites
❑ D. The parents
❑ E. The children

5. What would weaken the proposal being made by the speaker in this passage?

❑ A. Examples of data abuse from popular children's websites
❑ B. The main children's websites volunteering to add parental consent forms
❑ C. A petition by the PTA and local organizations to improve privacy laws online
❑ D. Internet access providers mandating parental consent before surfing the Web
❑ E. The removal of address collection by children's websites

As I came to a halt before him, Tars Tarkas pointed over the incubator and said, "Sak." I saw that he wanted me to repeat my performance of yesterday for the edification of Lorquas Ptomel, and, as I must confess that my prowess gave me no

5   little satisfaction, I responded quickly, leaping entirely over the parked chariots on the far side of the incubator. As I returned, Lorquas Ptomel grunted something at me, and turning to his warriors gave a few words of command relative to the incubator. They paid no further attention to me and I was thus

10   permitted to remain close and watch their operations, which consisted in breaking an opening in the wall of the incubator large enough to permit of the exit of the young Martians.

On either side of this opening the women and the younger Martians, both male and female, formed two solid walls leading

15   out through the chariots and quite away into the plain beyond. Between these walls the little Martians scampered, wild as deer; being permitted to run the full length of the aisle, where they were captured one at a time by the women and older children; the last in the line capturing the first little one to reach the end

20   of the gauntlet, her opposite in the line capturing the second, and so on until all the little fellows had left the enclosure and been appropriated by some youth or female. As the women caught the young they fell out of line and returned to their respective chariots, while those who fell into the hands of the

25   young men were later turned over to some of the women.

I saw that the ceremony, if it could be dignified by such a name, was over, and seeking out Sola I found her in our chariot with a hideous little creature held tightly in her arms.

30 The work of rearing young, green Martians consists solely in teaching them to talk, and to use the weapons of warfare with which they are loaded down from the very first year of their lives. Coming from eggs in which they have lain for five years, the period of incubation, they step forth into the world perfectly developed except in size. Entirely unknown to their mothers,
35 who, in turn, would have difficulty in pointing out the fathers with any degree of accuracy, they are the common children of the community, and their education devolves upon the females who chance to capture them as they leave the incubator.

Their foster mothers may not even have had an egg in the
40 incubator, as was the case with Sola, who had not commenced to lay, until less than a year before she became the mother of another woman's offspring. But this counts for little among the green Martians, as parental and filial love is as unknown to them as it is common among us. I believe this horrible system which
45 has been carried on for ages is the direct cause of the loss of all the finer feelings and higher humanitarian instincts among these poor creatures.

From birth they know no father or mother love, they know not the meaning of the word home; they are taught that they are
50 only suffered to live until they can demonstrate by their physique and ferocity that they are fit to live. Should they prove deformed or defective in any way they are promptly shot; nor do they see a tear shed for a single one of the many cruel hardships they pass through from earliest infancy.

55 I do not mean that the adult Martians are unnecessarily or intentionally cruel to the young, but theirs is a hard and pitiless struggle for existence upon a dying planet, the natural resources of which have dwindled to a point where the support of each additional life means an added tax upon the community into
60 which it is thrown.

By careful selection they rear only the hardiest specimens of each species, and with almost supernatural foresight they regulate the birth rate to merely offset the loss by death.

Source: Excerpt from *A Princess of Mars*, Chapter 7 - "Child-Raising on Mars", by Edgar Rice Burroughs, 1912.
http://www.literature.org/authors/burroughs-edgar-rice/a-princess-of-mars/chapter-07.html

6. What is the main point that the passage tries to convey?

   ❑ A. The leaping abilities of the author

   ❑ B. The mating habits of Martians

   ❑ C. The selection and rearing of young Martians

   ❑ D. The evolution of Martians

   ❑ E. The operation of a Martian incubator

7. According to the author, what kind of development is stinted in the young Martians due to the current system of raising them?

   ❑ A. Physical

   ❑ B. Psychological

   ❑ C. Strategic

   ❑ D. Economic

   ❑ E. Primal instinct

8. Who is most likely one of the people that formed "two solid walls," as described in line 14?

   ❑ A. Tars Tarkas

   ❑ B. Sak

   ❑ C. Lorquas Ptomel

   ❑ D. Sola

   ❑ E. The author

9. According to the passage, everything about the Martian development process is carefully controlled *except*:

   ❑ A. The birth rate

   ❑ B. The military education of the young

   ❑ C. The language development skills

   ❑ D. The procreation of life

   ❑ E. The physical stature of young Martians

10. What do you think the author would recommend to improve the situation presented in this passage?

   ❑ A. Develop a way to assign Martian youth to their biological parents

   ❑ B. Have young Martians spend more time learning hunting techniques

   ❑ C. Recommend pre-birth testing to weed out any offspring with a known developmental disorder

   ❑ D. Build more incubators to produce more offspring

   ❑ E. Have the fathers select the young Martian as they leave the incubator

Good rococo ornamentation is rare abroad and even rarer in this country, which is essentially opposed in its tendencies and in its civilization to those luxurious days of the French kings who created the conditions under which this very delightful style
5   could flourish.

The Horticultural Palace is a great success as an interpretation of a style which rarely finds a sympathetic expression in this country. I do not feel at all that it ought, but in a case of this kind where a temporary purpose existed, it was happily chosen.

10   Of all isolated units, none causes greater admiration than the Fine Arts Palace. It presents the astounding spectacle of a building which violates the architectural conventions on more than one occasion, and in spite of it, or possibly for that very reason, it has a note of originality that is most conspicuous.
15   Everybody admits that it is most beautiful, and very few seem to know just how this was accomplished. Many of the "small fry" of the architectural profession enjoy themselves in picking out its faults, which are really, as suggested above, the reason for its supreme beauty.

20   Save for Mullgardt's court, it is the only building that seems to be based on the realization of a dream of a true artistic conception. With many other of the buildings one feels the process of their creation in the time-honored, pedantic way. They are paper-designed by the mechanical application of the
25   "T" square and the triangle. They do not show the advantage of having been experienced as a vision.

With Bernard Maybeck's Palace of Fine Arts, one has the feeling that this great temple is a realized dream; that it was imagined irrespective of time, cost, or demand. Like all of Maybeck's
30   buildings, it is thoroughly original. Of course the setting contributes much to the picturesque effect, but aside from that, the colonnades and the octagonal dome in the center of the semicircular embracing form of the main building present many interesting features.

35   There is a very fine development of vistas, which are so provided as to present different parts of the building in many ever-changing aspects. On entering the outer colonnade one forgets the proximity of everyday things; one is immediately in an atmosphere of religious devotion, which finds its noblest
40   expression in that delicate shrine of worship, by Ralph Stackpole, beneath the dome.

This spiritual quality puts the visitor into the proper frame of mind for the enjoyment of the other offerings of art within the building. Mr. Maybeck has demonstrated once again that his

45   talent is equal to any task in the field of architectural art. I wish
        we had more of his rare kind and more people to do justice to
        his genius.

Source: Excerpt from *The Art of the Exposition: Personal Impressions of the Architecture, Sculpture, Mural Decorations, Color Scheme & Other Aesthetic Aspects of the Panama-Pacific International Exposition*, by Eugen Neuhaus, 1915

11. What is the main point of this passage?
    - ❏ A. A comparison of different architectural styles
    - ❏ B. A history of the construction of the Palace of Fine Arts
    - ❏ C. An overview of the style of the Palace of Fine Arts
    - ❏ D. The evolution of rococo ornamentation
    - ❏ E. Symbols of religious freedom

12. Which of the following is *not* a feature of the Palace of Fine Arts?
    - ❏ A. Colonnades
    - ❏ B. Octagonal dome
    - ❏ C. Sweeping vistas
    - ❏ D. Worship shrine
    - ❏ E. Paper-designed

13. What best describes the author's opinion of the Palace of Fine Arts?
    - ❏ A. Routine
    - ❏ B. Inspiring
    - ❏ C. Pedantic
    - ❏ D. Cluttered
    - ❏ E. Sympathetic

14. What is another word or phrase that could be used for *spectacle* in line 11?
    - ❏ A. Glasses
    - ❏ B. Main event
    - ❏ C. Building
    - ❏ D. Important location
    - ❏ E. Visual accomplishment

15. What is the author of this passage hoping for at the end of the passage?
    - ❏ A. More shrines built by Ralph Stackpole
    - ❏ B. More access to the rest of the Palace of Fine Arts
    - ❏ C. More preservation efforts to keep the palace's original look
    - ❏ D. More people to build creations designed by Bernard Maybeck
    - ❏ E. More French-inspired buildings in this country

CDC Announces Rubella, Once a Major Cause of Birth Defects, Is No Longer a Health Threat in the U.S.

March 21, 2005

5
DR. GERBERDING: We are delighted to be here today to formally and officially declare that rubella has been eliminated from the United States. This is a major milestone in the path toward eliminating rubella in other parts of the world, including the Western Hemisphere and other regions that have committed to this very, very important health goal.

10
But what does it really mean to say we've eliminated rubella? What it means I think is very nicely illustrated on this graphic here. In the 1960s, many, many thousands of children in this country developed rubella. Rubella is the disease that many of us remember as children—the three-day measles or the soft
15
measles, usually not a particularly severe disease for young children, but a devastating disease if women acquire it during pregnancy because it is the cause of the Congenital Rubella Syndrome. That is a very, very serious condition that does result in birth defects, and death, and other complications for
20
unborn children.

So, in the 1960s in this country, we had very large outbreaks of rubella. I was one of those statistics, and I'm sure many people my age or older also remember outbreaks of rubella in their schools. The vaccine was introduced in the late part of the '60s
25
and, for a while, the vaccine was beginning to be used. We were seeing better and better control of rubella. But over time, as you can see in that red line on this graphic, we began to see fewer and fewer cases as immunization rates got higher and higher and higher.

30
And for the last several years in the United States, we have just had very few cases of rubella, and, recently, the cases that we do have are not cases that are being transmitted in the United States; they are cases that have been imported from other areas of the world where immunization rates are not as high as
35
they are here in the U.S.

So we feel it's very important, after the input of scientists and experts from a variety of reputable and scientific organizations, to make a clear statement that this is an achievement. We owe our success to the wonderful people in the immunization
40
communities across the United States who've been working hard to vaccinate children.

But the story is not done yet. There is amazing progress underway in other parts of the Western Hemisphere, which you'll hear about in a minute, but there are still parts of the
45
world where immunization is not common or not common enough to prevent children from developing Congenital Rubella Syndrome.

So, in this country, while we can celebrate this milestone, we
also have to remain vigilant because, as we say in public health,
50   our network is only as strong as the weakest link. And as long
as there is rubella anywhere in the world, there could be rubella
in our children, too. So we have to sustain our commitment to
immunization. We have to strengthen all of the links in the
network, and we have to do everything possible to protect the
55   health of children here within our country, as well as beyond.

Source: Excerpt from Telebriefing Transcript: CDC Announces Rubella, Once a Major Cause of Birth
Defects, Is No Longer a Health Threat in the U.S., Center for Disease Control – Office of
Communications/Media Relations, March 21, 2005
http://www.cdc.gov/od/oc/media/transcripts/t050321.htm

16. What is the main point of this passage?
   ❑ A. The spread of rubella throughout the world
   ❑ B. The origin of the rubella vaccine
   ❑ C. The complete elimination of rubella throughout the world
   ❑ D. The efforts of science to virtually eliminate rubella outbreaks in the
         United States and reduce outbreaks abroad
   ❑ E. Dr. Gerberding's actions as part of the CDC

17. What is most likely being represented in the "red line on the graphic,"
    referred to in line 27 of the passage?
   ❑ A. The number of rubella outbreaks
   ❑ B. The number of doses of rubella vaccine prepared
   ❑ C. The number of cases of newborns with Congenital Rubella Syndrome
   ❑ D. The number of countries immunizing against rubella
   ❑ E. The amount of money spent by the CDC for rubella vaccines

18. According to Dr. Gerberding, to what do we owe the success of rubella
    being eliminated in the United States?
   ❑ A. Education by parents
   ❑ B. Sanitation efforts
   ❑ C. Global cooperation
   ❑ D. Immunization
   ❑ E. Communication between nations

19. Where was this address by Dr. Gerberding likely to have been deliv-
    ered?
   ❑ A. The high school where the first vaccine was administered
   ❑ B. A global conference on rubella
   ❑ C. A Congressional hearing on the CDC's budget
   ❑ D. A local radio station's "science hour"
   ❑ E. The CDC Advisor's Monthly Board Meeting

20. All of the following are recommended by Dr. Gerberding *except*:
 ❏ A. Constant communication regarding future rubella outbreaks overseas
 ❏ B. Sharing of knowledge regarding rubella vaccine research
 ❏ C. Increasing immunizations around the world
 ❏ D. Monitoring children's health
 ❏ E. Improving the strength of the rubella vaccine

Originally the word *university* was applied to any aggregation of persons. In Rome, for instance, there were universities of priests and musicians. Tradesmen, too, formed themselves into universities, which probably were the ancient equivalent of the
5 more recent trade guilds. In the Middle Ages the term had fallen into desuetude, except in so far as it referred to study. Then we find the universitas magistrorum, doctorum, et scholorum. Probably the earliest founded was that of Salerno, about the year A.D. 875. This was primarily a school of medicine, and
10 attracted students from many lands.

It was, however, impossible as well as undesirable, to limit the range of study, and other branches were embraced, but it was not until almost the end of the twelfth century that a real university was founded at Bologna. Here the chief study was
15 law. The example of Bologna in founding schools was followed by Paris, where, early in the twelfth century, the idea of a "university" had been anticipated by William of Champeaux. He taught logic in Paris as early as 1109.

Many schools were aggregated, but it does not appear that they
20 acquired the name of university until the beginning of the thirteenth century. The University of Paris may be taken as the type of all modern ones, including our own at Oxford and Cambridge. Following upon the Paris model, which had attracted to itself students from every European country, universities
25 sprang into being all over Europe; Padua, Naples, Pavia, Rome, and Florence were probably among the most noted.

But it is to our English universities that we most directly turn our view. Doubtless, the oldest of these were influenced by, and formed upon, the plan of Paris. Oxford was an early centre of
30 scholastic life. Its first colleges were Balliol, Merton, and University, all of which were founded about the middle of the thirteenth century, and before the lapse of fifty years it had become recognized as an organized university throughout the world. Cambridge, as a university, was later than Oxford,
35 although her schools were contemporary. At Cambridge, as at Oxford, the central idea was the establishment of colleges, and their union by educational bonds into one whole.

The influence of these two universities on the life of England
cannot be over-estimated. Ever since their foundation a long,
40   extensive, and continuous list of eminent bishops, chancellors,
statesmen, and lawyers acknowledge one or other of them as
their alma mater. The extension of modern methods has,
fortunately, introduced to all these categories many who have
not enjoyed a university education, but the old institutions still
45   hold their own. Universities like Durham, London, Manchester,
Liverpool, and Leeds are the outcome of the last century, and,
together with the university extension work of the older
foundations, have very greatly aided the dissemination of
university ideas among aspirants to educational distinction.

Source: Excerpt from "A Short History of Education", by G. Benson Clough, 2nd ed., London 1904
http://www.socsci.kun.nl/ped/whp/histeduc/clough/

21. What would be a good title for this passage?
   ❏   A. The Origin of the University
   ❏   B. The Evolution of the University
   ❏   C. The Purpose of the University
   ❏   D. A Summary of European Universities
   ❏   E. The History of the University of Paris

22. According to the author, what is the main area affected by universities?
   ❏   A. Education
   ❏   B. Medicine
   ❏   C. Law
   ❏   D. Government
   ❏   E. Society

23. What is the meaning of the word *lapse* in line 32?
   ❏   A. Forgotten gap
   ❏   B. Passing of time
   ❏   C. Physical space between objects
   ❏   D. Distance
   ❏   E. Length of Oxford

24. What best describes the author's opinion about the influence of Oxford
and Cambridge on English life?
   ❏   A. Routine
   ❏   B. Static
   ❏   C. Antiquated
   ❏   D. Contemporary
   ❏   E. Meaningful

25. What would be a good topic for a new paragraph at the very end of this passage?

   ❑ A. The opening of a new building at Oxford

   ❑ B. Examples of how universities are affecting modern English life

   ❑ C. The current state of the University of Bologna

   ❑ D. An anniversary celebration at the University of Paris

   ❑ E. The teachings of Salerno in the United Kingdom

THIS IS THE END OF THE SECTION.

SECTION III—Analytical Reasoning

Time—35 minutes

24 Questions

Directions: Each group of questions in this section is based on a set of conditions. In answering some of the questions, it may be useful to draw a rough diagram. Choose the response that most accurately and completely answers each question and blacken the corresponding space on your answer sheet.

QUESTIONS 1–6 RELATE TO THE FOLLOWING LOGIC GAME:

A group of elementary school kids are making paper-link banners for an upcoming holiday party. They have five colors of paper to make these links: green, orange, purple, red, and yellow. They start by fixing one paper link to a hook and connecting each link in a sequential fashion. The teacher has given the following specifications for how to make each banner:

If a yellow link is adjacent to a purple link, any link that immediately precedes and any link that immediately follows those two links must be red.

You cannot put two links of the same color next to each other unless they are green-colored links.

No red link can be adjacent to any orange link.

Any portion of a banner containing eight consecutive links must include at least one link of each color.

1. If the banner has exactly eight links, which one of the following is an acceptable order, starting from the hook, for the eight links?
   - ❑ A. Green, red, purple, yellow, red, orange, green, purple
   - ❑ B. Orange, yellow, red, red, yellow, purple, red, green
   - ❑ C. Purple, yellow, red, green, green, orange, yellow, orange
   - ❑ D. Red, orange, red, yellow, purple, green, yellow, green
   - ❑ E. Red, yellow, purple, red, green, red, green, green

2. If an orange link is the fourth link from the hook, which one of the following is a pair that could be the second and third links, respectively?

- ❏ A. Green, orange
- ❏ B. Green, red
- ❏ C. Purple, purple
- ❏ D. Yellow, green
- ❏ E. Yellow, purple

3. If on an eight-link banner the second, third, and fourth links from the hook are red, green, and yellow, respectively, and the sixth and seventh links are purple and red, respectively, then which one of the following must be true?

- ❏ A. The first link is purple.
- ❏ B. The fifth link is green.
- ❏ C. The fifth link is orange.
- ❏ D. The eighth link is orange.
- ❏ E. The eighth link is yellow.

4. If on a six-link banner the first and second links from the hook are purple and yellow, respectively, then the fifth and sixth links *cannot* be

- ❏ A. Green and orange, respectively
- ❏ B. Orange and green, respectively
- ❏ C. Orange and yellow, respectively
- ❏ D. Purple and orange, respectively
- ❏ E. Yellow and purple, respectively

5. If on a nine-link banner the first and fourth links from the hook are purple, and the second and fifth links are yellow, which one of the following could be true?

- ❏ A. The seventh link is orange.
- ❏ B. The eighth link is green.
- ❏ C. The eighth link is red.
- ❏ D. The ninth link is red.
- ❏ E. The ninth link is yellow.

6. If on an eight-link banner the first four links from the hook are red, yellow, green, and red, respectively, then the fifth and sixth links *cannot* be

- ❏ A. Green and orange, respectively
- ❏ B. Green and purple, respectively
- ❏ C. Purple and orange, respectively
- ❏ D. Purple and yellow, respectively
- ❏ E. Yellow and orange, respectively

QUESTIONS 7–12 RELATE TO THE FOLLOWING LOGIC GAME:

Charles has to put together a roster for his company's annual softball game against the company's cross-town rival. He has eight healthy people who want to bat for the team: Cosmo, Dustin, Hal, Jordan, Ken, Peter, Roger, and Seth. He's allowed to submit five names for his roster. However, there are some things to take into consideration:

If Roger plays, Hal must play immediately after Roger on the roster.

Two of the three managers, Dustin, Ken, and Roger, have to be on the team.

Cosmo and Seth can't be next to each other on the roster.

If Ken is on the team, then Jordan can't be picked.

Peter has to play either first or second.

7. Which one of these rosters can be submitted?
   - ❑ A. Peter, Hal, Cosmo, Ken, Roger
   - ❑ B. Peter, Dustin, Ken, Cosmo, Seth
   - ❑ C. Dustin, Roger, Hal, Peter, Jordan
   - ❑ D. Dustin, Peter, Roger, Hal, Seth
   - ❑ E. Peter, Seth, Jordan, Roger, Hal

8. If the first three players are Peter, Ken, and Cosmo, respectively, then the fourth and fifth players, respectively, could be
   - ❑ A. Seth and Dustin
   - ❑ B. Roger and Hal
   - ❑ C. Seth and Roger
   - ❑ D. Dustin and Jordan
   - ❑ E. Hal and Seth

9. If Jordan has to play second in the roster, which of the following *must* be true?
   - ❑ A. Roger will play fourth.
   - ❑ B. Dustin will play fourth.
   - ❑ C. Dustin will play last.
   - ❑ D. Hal will play last.
   - ❑ E. Cosmo must not be playing.

10. If Dustin and Ken are playing, which one of these pairs of batters *cannot* play?
   - ❑ A. Cosmo and Seth
   - ❑ B. Hal and Jordan
   - ❑ C. Jordan and Roger
   - ❑ D. Roger and Seth
   - ❑ E. Roger and Hal

11. If Hal is not on the roster, which one of these rosters can be valid?

   ❑ A. Peter, Ken, Cosmo, Seth, Dustin

   ❑ B. Dustin, Peter, Seth, Ken, Cosmo

   ❑ C. Peter, Jordan, Dustin, Ken, Seth

   ❑ D. Peter, Roger, Cosmo, Dustin, Seth

   ❑ E. Ken, Cosmo, Peter, Dustin, Seth

12. If the fourth player is Seth, then the fifth player could be

   ❑ A. Roger

   ❑ B. Cosmo

   ❑ C. Jordan

   ❑ D. Peter

   ❑ E. Dustin

QUESTIONS 13–18 RELATE TO THE FOLLOWING LOGIC GAME:

Fran is planning a dinner party for six people at her house on Saturday evening. The six people will be seated around a circular table, equidistant from each other. Fran has invited her college friends: Gary, Hanna, Iris, James, and Kate. As Fran thinks about the seating arrangement for this party, she takes the following into account:

James and Gary must sit directly opposite from each other.

Fran and Kate cannot sit next to each other.

Iris should sit next to Hanna or James.

Gary and Kate must sit next to each other.

13. Which of the following is a possible seating arrangement for the table?

   ❑ A. Fran, Gary, Kate, Iris, James, Hanna

   ❑ B. Gary, Kate, James, Hanna, Iris, Fran

   ❑ C. Gary, Iris, Hanna, James, Fran, Kate

   ❑ D. James, Fran, Iris, Gary, Kate, Hanna

   ❑ E. James, Iris, Fran, Gary, Hanna, Kate

14. If Kate sits to the left of Gary, what is the full and complete list of people who could sit to the right of James?

   ❑ A. Iris

   ❑ B. Fran, Iris

   ❑ C. Fran, Hanna

   ❑ D. Hanna, Iris

   ❑ E. Fran, Hanna, Iris

15. If we know that Iris is only sitting next to James and not Hanna, who must be sitting across from Hanna?

- ❑ A. Fran
- ❑ B. Gary
- ❑ C. Iris
- ❑ D. James
- ❑ E. Kate

16. Which of the following must be true?

- ❑ A. Gary cannot sit next to Hanna.
- ❑ B. Hanna cannot sit next to Kate.
- ❑ C. James cannot sit next to Fran.
- ❑ D. Iris cannot sit next to Hanna.
- ❑ E. Kate cannot sit next to Iris.

17. If Fran and Iris sit opposite each other, all of the following could be true *except*:

- ❑ A. Gary sits to the right of Fran.
- ❑ B. Kate sits to the right of Iris.
- ❑ C. Hanna sits to the right of Iris.
- ❑ D. Fran sits between Gary and Hanna.
- ❑ E. Iris sits between James and Kate.

18. Fran and Kate talk on the phone that afternoon and settle their differences. In fact, Kate specifically requests to sit next to Fran for the dinner party. If Fran agrees, who could sit across the table from Fran?

- ❑ A. Hanna
- ❑ B. Iris
- ❑ C. James
- ❑ D. Hanna or Iris
- ❑ E. Hanna, Iris, or James

QUESTIONS 19–24 RELATE TO THE FOLLOWING LOGIC GAME:

The high school basketball team and its mascot are preparing to take their annual yearbook photo. The six people in the photo, from shortest to tallest, are Alex, Bob, Chris, Gary, Sam, and Willie. However, the label on the picture needs to include the person's position with his name. The six positions are center, mascot, point guard, power forward, shooting guard, and small forward. The photographer only remembers a few details from that photo shoot:

The center is not Sam and is taller than the point guard.

The mascot is taller than the shooting guard and the small forward.

The mascot is shorter than the power forward.

The point guard is taller than the small forward.

19. If we also knew that the point guard was shorter than the shooting guard, then who would the small forward have to be?

   - ❑ A. Alex
   - ❑ B. Bob
   - ❑ C. Chris
   - ❑ D. Gary
   - ❑ E. Sam

20. Going in order, which of the following could be a possible assignment for the list in the photo?

   - ❑ A. Shooting guard, point guard, small forward, center, mascot, power forward
   - ❑ B. Small forward, point guard, center, shooting guard, mascot, power forward
   - ❑ C. Small forward, point guard, center, mascot, shooting guard, power forward
   - ❑ D. Small forward, point guard, shooting guard, mascot, center, power forward
   - ❑ E. Small forward, shooting guard, point guard, mascot, center, power forward

21. If the center is Chris, the point guard must be which person?

   - ❑ A. Alex
   - ❑ B. Bob
   - ❑ C. Gary
   - ❑ D. Sam
   - ❑ E. Willie

22. Which of the following *cannot* be a possible arrangement of the team positions in the photo list, from shortest through tallest person?

   - ❑ A. Shooting guard, small forward, point guard, center, mascot, power forward
   - ❑ B. Shooting guard, small forward, point guard, mascot, power forward, center
   - ❑ C. Small forward, shooting guard, mascot, power forward, point guard, center
   - ❑ D. Small forward, shooting guard, point guard, center, mascot, power forward
   - ❑ E. Small forward, shooting guard, power forward, point guard, mascot, center

23. If Gary is the shooting guard, who could be the mascot?

- ❏ A. Alex
- ❏ B. Bob
- ❏ C. Chris
- ❏ D. Sam
- ❏ E. Willie

24. If Sam is the power forward, who could be the center?

- ❏ A. Chris
- ❏ B. Gary
- ❏ C. Bob
- ❏ D. Alex
- ❏ E. Willie

THIS IS THE END OF THE SECTION.

SECTION IV—Logical Reasoning

Time—35 minutes

24 Questions

Directions: The questions in this section are based on the reasoning contained in brief statements or passages. For some questions, more than one of the choices could conceivably answer the question. However, you are to choose the best answer—that is, the response that most accurately and completely answers the question. You should not make assumptions that are by commonsense standards implausible, superfluous, or incompatible with the passage. After you have chosen the best answer, blacken the corresponding space on your answer sheet.

1. Dr. Henderkoff: All cases of smallpox begin with a red rash.

   Dr. Zelasen: That's not just wrong, that's precisely wrong. There are at least 200 different diseases that begin with a red rash.

   Zelasen's reply to Henderkoff demonstrates that he believes Henderson's statement to mean which of the following?

   ❏ A. Every red rash is a precursor to a case of smallpox.
   ❏ B. A red rash means that a patient could be suffering from an illness, injury, or allergy.
   ❏ C. Every red rash is not a precursor to a case of smallpox.
   ❏ D. There is a correlation between red rashes and smallpox.
   ❏ E. A red rash means that a patient could have contracted one of up to 200 different diseases except for smallpox.

2. Olive oil is graded on texture, appearance, and taste. The first pressing of the olive fruit extracts oil that is bright green, flows smoothly, and has a strong olive taste. Oil with at least one of these characteristics is usually called extra virgin oil.

If this statement is true, then which of the following types of olive oils are least likely to be considered extra virgin?

❑ A. A virgin oil that flows smoothly

❑ B. A cold pressed oil that is bright green

❑ C. A super premium oil with a strong pepper taste

❑ D. A premium oil with a strong olive taste but syrupy texture

❑ E. An extra strong oil that is bright green but only has a mild olive taste

3. All interns are full time. All workers are paid. Some workers are interns.

If all of the preceding statements are true, which one of the following must also be true?

❑ A. All who are paid are full time.

❑ B. Some who are paid are interns.

❑ C. Some workers are full time but are not interns.

❑ D. All workers are interns.

❑ E. All interns are workers.

4. All lawyers are intelligent, and some investment bankers are intelligent. Therefore, some investment bankers are lawyers.

Which one of the following most closely parallels the reasoning used in the preceding argument?

❑ A. All cats have fur, and some dogs have fur. Therefore, dogs and cats are both mammals.

❑ B. All cars have four wheels. No motorcycles have four wheels. Therefore, no motorcycles are cars.

❑ C. All balls are round, and some toys are round. Therefore, some toys are balls.

❑ D. All infants cry, and all adults cry. Therefore, some adults are infants.

❑ E. All doctors are busy, and busy people are rich. Therefore, doctors are rich.

5. The El Nino global weather pattern is known to completely reverse typical weather patterns in Southern Europe. In the Italian principality of Chiriatti, the normally warm weather that predominates will give way to occasional frosts and cooler-than-average temperatures. This year all of the forecasts show El Nino conditions for the next few years. However, the director of agriculture is issuing advisories predicting that the local crop yield will show a large increase.

Which of the following statements, if true, most helps to resolve the apparent paradox in the preceding information?

- ❏ A. Blood oranges don't do well in frost, but fewer oranges mean that they will be sold at higher prices, increasing the money earned per orange.
- ❏ B. Arborio rice grows poorly in cold weather. Fewer pounds of rice grown means that rice will be sold at higher prices, increasing total amount of money farmers get for their crop yield.
- ❏ C. Chiriatti's main crop, the Festival tomato, flourishes in temperatures that are cooler than average.
- ❏ D. The El Nino cycle is not perfectly predictable.
- ❏ E. Cooler temperatures will mean that farmers will eventually switch to crops that grow in colder weather, like the Woolly eggplant. Thus, farmers will increase production.

6. Rather like a harried human commuter, the arctic tern is almost constantly in transit from Greenland to Antarctica and back. Until recently, arctic terns' poor sense of smell and average vision made it a minor mystery as to how they found their way. Surprisingly, the birds can follow magnetic headings to within a single degree, even accounting for the off-centeredness of the magnetic versus geographic pole.

The argument seeks to do which one of the following?

- ❏ A. Demonstrate that a specific rule applies to all subspecies of tern
- ❏ B. Derive a general conclusion about all members of a group from facts known about representative members of that group
- ❏ C. Establish the validity of one explanation for a phenomenon by excluding alternative explanations
- ❏ D. Support, by utilizing an analogy, how a certain phenomenon can occur
- ❏ E. Conclude that members of two groups of birds are likely to share certain abilities because of characteristics they share

7. By refusing to ban artificial blue dye #4 in our country's breakfast cereals, the Food and Drug Administration (FDA) has outsourced its sense of reason. It has accepted wholesale the claims of chemical corporations that the vitamins in the dye will actually improve the consumer's eyesight. No doubt the FDA would approve cancer-causing saccharine for our children if it were claimed that the chemical would also help them grow taller.

The author of this paragraph makes a case

- ❏ A. By drawing from analogy
- ❏ B. By citing multiple statistics and sources of research
- ❏ C. Through direct observation of the chemical corporation's policies
- ❏ D. Through long-term experience within the chemical industry
- ❏ E. By eliminating all alternative explanations

QUESTIONS 8–9 RELATE TO THE FOLLOWING SCENARIO:

Gem buyers were benefited this week when a new diamond mine was opened in Siberia. The very next day, the DeBeers diamond consortium held a sale on its mounted precious stones. It's safe to conclude that the reason DeBeers held their sale was because the new mine in Siberia opened.

8. What possible logical error is demonstrated in the preceding argument?

- ❏ A. This analogy does not hold up under close scrutiny.
- ❏ B. If A happened before B, then B will lead to C.
- ❏ C. If B follows A, then A and B are equal.
- ❏ D. If A happened before B, then A must have caused B.
- ❏ E. If A happened before B, then B must cause A.

9. Which one of the following contains flawed reasoning that most closely parallels that in the preceding argument?

- ❏ A. The last two World Wars were fought 18 months after a trade fair was held in Chicago. Therefore, holding trade fairs in Chicago causes World Wars.
- ❏ B. Sunspots were observed to increase in intensity after the Superbowls in 1980, 1982, 1984, 1988, and 2000. Therefore, holding Superbowls in even-numbered years causes sunspots to increase.
- ❏ C. The stock market has been known to plunge in value in October or when the price of palladium rises above $50. Therefore, the month or October or high palladium prices is a signal that the market will go down.
- ❏ D. Home mortgage interest rates will either move up, down, or remain constant, depending on whether the American League or the National League wins the World Series.
- ❏ E. Lunar eclipses take place after neap tides. Therefore, neap times must cause lunar eclipses.

10. I fully admit that tearing down the Paramount Theatre to make room for another FoodCo supermarket will bring more tax revenue to the township. Yet at what price? I fear that the homey, small-town atmosphere will be lost to yet more relentless, faceless hordes of big-city shoppers. And we will lose a priceless icon of Hollywood history. I urge all readers to sign the bill to protect this jewel of a building.

The advocate for protecting the Paramount Theatre makes a case via which of the following?

- ❏ A. Directly appealing to authority
- ❏ B. Drawing a conclusion from an analogy
- ❏ C. Deriving the conclusion from direct experience
- ❏ D. Deriving the conclusion from indirect observation
- ❏ E. Directly appealing to emotion and sentimentality

11. The claim that sharks never sleep is misguided. That notion is based on the simple observation that sharks always have their eyes open. Actually, sharks do not have eyelids, so in reality sharks are unable to close their eyes at all. Therefore, to a casual observer, sharks appear to be constantly awake.

Which of the following best identifies the conclusion of the preceding argument?

- ❏ A. Many common misconceptions about animals are made when we attribute human qualities to them.
- ❏ B. The fact that animals like cats have eyelids enables them to close their eyes and thus look like they are asleep when they are actually sleeping.
- ❏ C. It is more difficult for sharks to fall asleep than it is for humans because sharks do not have eyelids.
- ❏ D. Animals that lack eyelids are not necessarily always awake.
- ❏ E. While sharks cannot close their eyes, they do, in fact, sleep.

12. In Joe and Carol's family, everyone dislikes lima beans or spinach, or both, but Carol likes spinach.

Which one of the following statements cannot be true?

- ❏ A. Carol dislikes lima beans.
- ❏ B. Joe dislikes lima beans and spinach.
- ❏ C. Everyone in the family who likes lima beans dislikes spinach.
- ❏ D. No one in the family dislikes spinach.
- ❏ E. Joe likes lima beans and spinach.

13. Popular brand names often come about through oddball bits of chance. One example was the snack food Hacking's Crackers. Put off by the odd-sounding name, when Banisco Bakeries bought the Hacking Operation, it renamed the cracker as the Ritzy. During the Great Depression, it became the most popular snack in the United States. The name, which was picked to emphasize extreme luxury, has remained to this day.

Which of the following, if true, strengthens the conclusion of the passage?

- ❏ A. During the Depression, any brand name that connoted luxury sold well.
- ❏ B. During the Depression, any brand name that connoted luxury did not sell well.
- ❏ C. The daughter of the founder of Banisco Bakeries was named Ritzy.
- ❏ D. *Ritzy* was slang in the Depression for either *luxurious* or *trashy*.
- ❏ E. During the Depression, any crackers sold would do well because they were inexpensive, no matter the brand name.

14. Lilly and Lucy, two thoroughbred racehorses of equal ability, have run two match races (races in which only two horses compete), and Lilly has won both. Lilly and Lucy are now running in a third match race. Sam believes that it is highly unlikely that, given Lilly and Lucy's equal ability, Lilly will win the third match race.

Which one of the following best summarizes the assumption underlying Sam's reasoning?

❑ A. If A, B, and C are each improbable, then the joint occurrence of them all is improbable.

❑ B. If A and B are each improbable, then the occurrence of A, B, and C together is equally improbable.

❑ C. If the joint occurrence of A and B is probable, then the occurrence of C is also probable.

❑ D. If the joint occurrence of A, B, and C is improbable, then given that B and C have occurred, C is improbable.

❑ E. If the joint occurrence of A, B, and C is improbable, then each of A, B, and C is improbable.

15. Brazilian albino strawberries suffer from several distinct handicaps that normal strawberry plants do not. Their albino coloring is a disincentive for birds to eat them, meaning that the seeds in the berry get dispersed beyond their patch of plants less often than usual. They also spend more energy creating a bigger berry instead of growing more shoots and runners to spread along the forest floor. Native Brazilian jungle tribesmen, on the other hand, prize the albino berry plants for their extra-large fruit and sweetness. Therefore, when one finds a patch of albino berry plants in the Brazilian rainforest...

Which one of the following statements most logically concludes the argument?

❑ A. It is likely that the berries will be bigger than on regular plants.

❑ B. It is likely that native Brazilians have eradicated other local albino plants.

❑ C. It is likely that the berry plants are or were cultivated by native Brazilians.

❑ D. Other species of berries will soon take over the patch of ground.

❑ E. It is likely that you're simply extremely lucky, because the color doesn't imply anything.

16. Given that this animal has black-and-white polka dots, it must be a zorse.

    Which one of the following, if true, provides definitive support for the preceding conclusion?

    ❑ A. Zorses generally have black-and-white polka dots.

    ❑ B. Other black-and-white polka-dotted animals have proved to be zorses.

    ❑ C. Few types of animals other than zorses have black-and-white polka dots.

    ❑ D. All zorses have black-and-white polka dots

    ❑ E. Only zorses have black and white polka dots.

17. In a recent survey, three out of four veterinarians surveyed recommended Joint-Vite over Vitamin-Right for dogs over the age of 10.

    All of the following, if true, would weaken the weight of the preceding recommendation *except*:

    ❑ A. Only four veterinarians were surveyed.

    ❑ B. The veterinarians were paid to participate in the survey by the manufacturers of Joint-Vite.

    ❑ C. The veterinarians never actually used Joint-Vite.

    ❑ D. Joint-Vite has several negative side effects when used in dogs younger than 10.

    ❑ E. Joint-Vite is more expensive than Vitamin-Right.

18. Gini to Benjamin: I can't afford not to pay a babysitter $15 per hour to watch my child.

    Which one of the following offers the most logical interpretation of Gini's comments?

    ❑ A. Babysitting is worth at least $15 per hour to Gini.

    ❑ B. Gini believes $15 per hour is too much to pay a babysitter.

    ❑ C. Gini cannot afford a babysitter.

    ❑ D. Most babysitters earn more than $15 per hour.

    ❑ E. Gini believes Benjamin should pay the babysitter.

19. If you are a U.S. citizen and you want to enter the United States from Canada after December 31, 2006, you must have a passport.

    Which one of the following can be logically inferred from the preceding statement?

    ❑ A. All persons entering the United States after December 31, 2006, must have a passport.

    ❑ B. No one allowed to enter the United States before December 31, 2006, was required to have a passport.

    ❑ C. Before December 31, 2006, a passport was not required for U.S. citizens re-entering the United States from Canada.

    ❑ D. All persons who live in the United States after December 31, 2006, must have a passport to travel to Canada.

    ❑ E. Only U.S. citizens returning from Canada after December 31, 2006, must show a passport to enter the United States.

QUESTIONS 20–21 RELATE TO THE FOLLOWING SCENARIO:

Two thousand years of intensive farming in the Marchetti River Valley has taken a great toll on the land. Slash-and-burn agriculture, where peasants take a machete to cut down the tall palm trees and then set fire to the underbrush, rapidly depletes the thin layer of topsoil. Deprived of a dense network of plant roots to hold it in place, what soil is left washes into the sea.

20. Which one of the following, if true, most seriously strengthens the preceding argument?

  ❑ A. During the Roman Era in A.D. 100, the valley contained a large city, while today it consists of low-density suburbs.

  ❑ B. Slash-and-burn agriculture was an extremely primitive form of agriculture in medieval times and it remains so today.

  ❑ C. During the Roman era in A.D. 100, the Marchetti River Valley supported 100,000 people. Today, it can only support half of that.

  ❑ D. Slash-and-burn agriculture is considered the most destructive form of cultivation because it causes topsoil to wash into the sea.

  ❑ E. In Roman times, allowing peasants to cultivate the land led to the land's eventual degradation.

21. Which one of the following, if true, most seriously weakens the argument?

  ❑ A. Today, slash-and-burn agriculture is practiced in a much more sustainable manner that does not deplete the land.

  ❑ B. Modern fertilizers and soil buffers allow the valley to be as productive today as it was in Roman times.

  ❑ C. Soil washed into the sea is regularly dredged, transported by barge, and re-applied to the valley floor.

  ❑ D. The density and diversity of plant and animal life in the valley is as great now as it ever was.

  ❑ E. Since the Roman Era in A.D. 100, the valley has contained a large city. That city has the same population today as it did when the Romans were around.

22. Law school admissions officer: Our rules are very strict when it comes to admissions. Your grades must be all B's or better. Is that the case with you?

Law school applicant: I even exceed your requirements. The average of all my grades is even higher than a B.

Law school admissions officer: Excellent! I'll recommend that you be admitted to our school immediately.

From the preceding exchange, it is likely that the law school admissions officer believes which of the following statements?

- ❏ A. All of the applicant's grades justify admission if averaged.
- ❏ B. All of the applicant's grades average to a B or better.
- ❏ C. All of the applicant's grades are a B or better.
- ❏ D. All of the applicant's grades are high enough to justify admission.
- ❏ E. All of the applicant's grades average high enough to justify admission.

23. People who use tanning salons are generally vain. Narssica is a vain person. Therefore, Narssica's tan skin tone can't be natural.

   Which one of the following statements most closely parallels the reasoning in the preceding argument?

- ❏ A. Bushes with truncated leaves are usually big. The chokecherry is a very big bush. That bush over there is quite big, so it is probably a chokecherry.
- ❏ B. Anyone who likes French bread also likes bagels. Phil likes French bread, so he must also love bagels.
- ❏ C. Dawson is a vain person. His skin tone is artificial, so therefore he may be one of many people who visits tanning salons.
- ❏ D. Shaker chairs tend to be sturdy. The chair I bought yesterday is sturdy. That chair must be a Shaker chair.
- ❏ E. Squirrels with gray fur normally cannot fly. Because that squirrel has brown fur, it must be a flying squirrel.

24. It is widely thought that New Orleans, Louisiana, is the home of Cajun cooking. What few people recognize, however, is that the "home" of Cajun cooking includes all of the Deep South. Cajun cuisine is as much a part of the historical ways of preparing and flavoring food of the Carolinas and the Gulf states as anything that has ever come out of New Orleans. So-called Cajun cooking experts should acknowledge that what is currently popular in New Orleans stems in no small part from the cooking techniques and spices throughout the rest of the Deep South.

   Which of the following assumptions is central to the preceding argument?

- ❏ A. Currently, the only good Cajun cooking can be found in the South in general, not in New Orleans itself.
- ❏ B. If a cook is from the Gulf states or the Carolinas, then he or she directly influenced Cajun cuisine.
- ❏ C. Currently, the only good Cajun cooking can be found in New Orleans itself, not in the Deep South in general.
- ❏ D. Southern cooking techniques and spices have contributed to what makes Cajun cooking popular.
- ❏ E. Northern types of cooking cannot influence what cuisine is popular in the Deep South.

THIS IS THE END OF THE SECTION.

Answer Key for Practice Exam 3

SECTION I—Logical Reasoning

1. D	9. C	17. C
2. D	10. B	18. B
3. E	11. D	19. D
4. D	12. E	20. D
5. E	13. B	21. A
6. A	14. B	22. E
7. D	15. B	23. A
8. A	16. A	24. A

1. **Choice D** is correct. The fact that some donkeys cannot bray goes straight to the heart of the argument by contradicting the first statement that "all donkeys bray." Choice A is incorrect. Christopher's argument is not based on whether other animals can also bray. Whether you can train a dog to bray is irrelevant to whether a particular animal that cannot bray is or is not a donkey. Choice B is incorrect. This answer is a variation on Choice A. Christopher's argument is not based on whether other animals (cows) can also bray. Whether or not donkeys bray more than cows is irrelevant to whether a particular animal that cannot bray is or is not a donkey. Choice C is incorrect. This answer is also a variation on Choice A. Christopher's argument is not based on whether other animals (zebras) can also bray. Choice E is incorrect. Whether or not you can train a donkey to bray is irrelevant to whether a particular animal that cannot bray is or is not a donkey.

2. **Choice D** is correct. If some applicants with an SAT score of less than 1500 and a GPA of less than 3.0 qualified for a scholarship, this is inconsistent with the facts stated in the question, which require that applicants with SATs of 1500 must have GPAs of 3.0. Coupled with the sliding scale, an applicant with an SAT score of less than 1500 must have a GPA higher than 3.0 to qualify for a scholarship. Choice A is incorrect. You cannot definitely determine whether or not most scholarship applicants had an SAT score in the range of 1400–1500, so this statement is not necessarily inconsistent with facts stated in the question. Choice B is incorrect. The facts stated in the question provide that an applicant with an SAT of 1400 must have a GPA of at least 3.75 and vice versa. Therefore, it is true that no scholarship applicant with an SAT score of less than 1400 and a GPA of less than 3.75 will qualify for the scholarship. Choice C is incorrect. The facts stated in the question are consistent with the statement that the lower the GPA, the higher the SAT score required to qualify for the scholarship. Choice E is incorrect. Due to the use of the sliding scale, it is possible that Nicholas qualified for a scholarship with a 3.7 GPA and a 1580 SAT score.

3. **Choice E** is correct. The fact that males like horses as much as females does nothing to explain why more males than females are represented in professional equestrian competitions when females outnumber males at the instructional stage. Choice A is incorrect. The fact that many females stop riding once they reach adolescence, if true, could help explain why more males than females are represented in professional equestrian competitions when females outnumber males at the instructional stage. Choice B is incorrect. The fact that male riders are more talented than female riders, if true, could help explain why more males than females are represented in professional equestrian competitions

when females outnumber males at the instructional stage. Choice C is incorrect. The fact that professional equestrian sports is not a socially acceptable profession for females, if true, could help explain why more males than females are represented in professional equestrian competitions when females outnumber males at the instructional stage. Choice D is incorrect. The fact that males enjoy competition more than females, if true, could help explain why more males than females are represented in professional equestrian competitions when females outnumber males at the instructional stage.

4. **Choice D** is correct. If Ryan plays defense, then Christopher must be the goalie, and therefore Christopher must have his own goalie gloves. Choice A is incorrect. Choice A assumes that having goalie gloves is the only prerequisite for playing goalie. If Christopher has goalie gloves, he may play goalie, but not necessarily. Therefore, there is nothing in the statement that supports the inference that if Christopher has goalie gloves, he *will* play goalie. Choice B is incorrect. This choice makes the same sort of assumption as in choice A. The statement tells us only that if Christopher does not play goalie, Ryan will not play defense. It tells us nothing about the circumstances under which Ryan will play defense. Choice C is incorrect. This choice is very similar to choice B except that it removes the question as to whether Christopher is playing goalie or not. However, as noted previously in choice B, the statement tells us only that if Christopher does not play goalie, Ryan will not play defense. It tells us nothing about the circumstances under which Ryan will play defense. Therefore, whether or not Christopher plays goalie is irrelevant to whether Ryan will play defense. Choice E is incorrect. If Christopher does not play goalie, we know that Ryan will not play defense, but it does not necessarily follow that he will play offense instead (for instance, he might not play at all).

5. **Choice C** is correct. The ring-tailed snipe normally thrives in areas with abundant banyan trees. However, if a natural predator of the ring-tailed snipe is abundant in the Cape Suzette region, that could logically explain why the snipe is endangered in that area, where it would normally thrive. Choice A is incorrect because it talks about other endangered animals in the Cape Suzette region, but not the subject of this argument—the ring-tailed snipe. Choice B is incorrect because it talks about the ring-tailed snipe being endangered in areas outside the Cape Suzette region. Thus it is outside the argument's scope. Choice D is incorrect. While it could possibly explain why the animal fares worse there—the cold occasionally stunts the trees—it is a more indirect conclusion than choice C and thus not as strong. Choice E is incorrect because it is irrelevant to resolving the question.

6. **Choice A** is correct. The question states that the team includes both women and girls but does not state that it does not include men or boys. However, because every person on the team is confident, and because both women and girls, by definition in the statement, are confident, then the team must be comprised of just women and girls, and does not include men or boys. Choice B is incorrect. While girls may be confident (that is, all girls are poised and every poised person is confident), the question states specifically that all women are also confident. Choice C is incorrect. The question states that the team includes girls and that all girls are poised, so this statement is inconsistent with the argument. Choice D is incorrect. The question states that the team includes women and that all women are confident, so this statement is inconsistent with the argument. Choice E is incorrect. The question states that both women and girls are on the team, so this statement is inconsistent with the argument.

7. **Choice D** is correct. Telling Jon that the roses had "sold out" is an example of rephrasing the problem ("there were none left") without explaining it. Choice A is incorrect. The florist's explanation is not an example of using evidence not relevant to a conclusion. Choice B is incorrect. The florist's explanation is not an example of attempting to change the grounds of an argument. Choice C is incorrect. The florist's explanation is not an example of failing to generalize from a specific case. Choice E is incorrect. The florist's explanation is not an example of euphemism.

8. **Choice A** is correct. The fact that the observations about politicians are offered by characters in the novels with whom Lawrence clearly identifies, if true, provides a strong indication that the views expressed by those characters are similar to those held by Lawrence himself. Choice B is incorrect. The fact that Lawrence's presentation of others in his novels is equally critical and uncomplimentary, if true, does not necessarily provide support for the conclusion that Lawrence had a hostile attitude toward politicians. Choice C is incorrect. The fact that the attitude toward politicians in Lawrence's novels is similar to that reflected in other novels written during the same period of time, if true, does not necessarily provide support for the conclusion that Lawrence had a hostile attitude toward politicians. Choice D is incorrect. The fact that Lawrence's novels are fictional does not necessarily provide support for the conclusion that Lawrence had a hostile attitude toward politicians. Choice E is incorrect. The fact that Lawrence was himself a politician, if true, does not necessarily provide support for the conclusion that Lawrence had a hostile attitude toward politicians.

9. Choice C is correct. The statement assumes that a lawyer with a master's degree in taxation is a better judge of a tax matter than others. Choice A is incorrect. The statement does not assume that anyone who is a lawyer cannot be wrong. In fact, the statement says nothing about the correctness or incorrectness of the answer; rather just that the answer must be "the best one." Choice B is incorrect. As with choice A, the statement says nothing about the correctness or incorrectness of the answer; rather just that the answer must be "the best one." Choice D is incorrect. The answer choice does not indicate the subject matter of which a lawyer with a master's degree in taxation is a better judge and therefore is not as good a choice as choice C. Choice E is incorrect. Like choice D, the answer choice does not indicate the subject matter at issue.

10. The premise underlying the argument here is that if two entities have similar characteristics (that is, houses built in the same year by the same builder), then both will share other characteristics as well (that is, if one house needs a new roof, the other house will need a new roof).

Choice B is correct. This choice notes a dissimilarity between the two houses in a very relevant area (roofing material) that would cut against the assumption that because both houses were built in the same year and by the same builder, both roofs would need to be replaced at the same time. Choices A and C are incorrect. These choices focus on a similarity between both houses, and if anything, it would strengthen the argument rather than weaken it. Choice D is incorrect. Whether or not the speaker can afford to put on a new roof is irrelevant to the conclusion. Choice E is incorrect. The fact that the neighbor is a contractor and the speaker is not, while a difference between the two houses, is not relevant to whether both roofs would need to be replaced at the same time.

11. Choice D is correct. The speaker makes a claim by over-generalizing from specific evidence. In this instance, because Darrell exhibited the behavior of being impatient on one occasion, the speaker over-generalizes from this evidence to reach a much broader conclusion. Choice A is incorrect. In this instance, the speaker directly observed the evidence on which he is basing his conclusion (that is, Darrell got tired of waiting and left), and therefore the evidence cannot be characterized as unreliable. Choice B is incorrect. No other events are specifically described (only that "Darrell gets into trouble"), so there is no basis for assuming that such events are either similar or dissimilar to the present event. Choice C is incorrect. The speaker does supply evidence (albeit weak) for his/her conclusion. Choice E is incorrect, as there are no claims that conflict with one another in the speaker's statement.

12. **Choice E** is correct because the senator states that "of course" the vice president has been charged, because Senator Grogan publicly alleged the charge himself. Choice A is incorrect. This is the inverse of what Senator Grogan is saying. Choice B is incorrect because Grogan does not state that misuse of government funds is de facto evidence that a charge has been leveled. Choice C is incorrect. Grogan does not state that alleging that a crime has been committed is de facto evidence that funds have been misused. Choice D is incorrect because Grogan does not state this; he is claiming that because he alleged that the vice president has committed a crime, the vice president has actually been charged.

13. **Choice B** is correct because the news is alleging that a crime took place, which must mean that the accused person has been charged—the exact logical fallacy that is in Question 13. Choice A is incorrect. The statement says that because an alleged crime took place, the accused person has been convicted, not charged. Choice C is incorrect. The statement says that because an alleged crime took place, the accused person will be charged, not that he or she has already been charged. Choice D is incorrect. The statement says that a person has already been tried, thus the accused person must have been already charged. Choice E is incorrect. The statement says that because an alleged crime took place, the accused person has been charged with an unrelated crime. Choice B is a stronger answer.

14. **Choice B** is correct. If 95% of all traffic accidents occur when cars are traveling at below 45 MPH, then increasing the maximum speed limit from 55 MPH to 65 MPH should not significantly increase the number of traffic accidents. Choice A is incorrect. This choice, if true, strengthens the argument rather than weakening it. Choice C is incorrect. This fact, even if true, is not relevant to the argument. Choice D is incorrect. This fact, even if true, is not relevant to the argument. Choice E is incorrect. This fact, even if true, is not relevant to the argument.

15. **Choice B** is correct. This statement, if true, does not weaken the conclusion. The conclusion assumes that the members who joined the committees in Spring/Summer were entirely different from those who joined in Fall/Winter. This conclusion is therefore weakened by any fact that indicates that some or all members of the committees may have been the same during both time periods. Choice A is incorrect. The statement, if true, indicates that some or all members of the committees may have been the same during both time periods. Choice C is incorrect. The statement, if true, indicates that some or all members of the committees may have been the same during both time periods.

Choice D is incorrect. The statement, if true, indicates that some or all members of the committees may have been the same during both time periods. Choice E is incorrect. The statement, if true, indicates that some or all members of the committees may have been the same during both time periods.

16. The pattern that Christopher's reasoning follows is: "When I was X, I could do Y, but I could not do Z." The question requires you to pick the answer choice that most closely follows this line of reasoning.

    Choice A is correct. This answer choice follows the "When I was X, I could do Y, but I could not do Z" pattern. Choice B is incorrect. This answer choice does not follow the "When I was X, I could do Y, but I could not do Z" pattern. Instead, it follows a "When I was X, I could not do Y, but I could do Z" pattern. Choice C is incorrect. This answer choice does not follow the "When I was X, I could do Y, but I could not do Z" pattern. Instead, it follows a "When I was X, I could do Y, but I also could do Z" pattern. Choice D is incorrect. This answer choice does not follow the "When I was X, I could do Y, but I could not do Z" pattern. Instead, it follows a "When I was X, I did Y and I also did Z" pattern. Choice E is incorrect. This answer choice does not follow the "When I was X, I could do Y, but I could not do Z" pattern. Instead, it follows a "When I was X, I could do Y, but I did not have to do Y" pattern.

17. **Choice C** is correct because the building in question lacks a single one of the criteria that define an Art Deco building. Note that being "next to" a neon-lit area is not one of these criteria; an inattentive reader might miss that detail. Choice A is incorrect. The neon trim and chevrons qualify this building as Art Deco. Choice B is incorrect. The location and black tile mark the building as Art Deco. Choice D is incorrect because the location and the time built match the description of an Art Deco dwelling. Choice E is incorrect because the design fits that of an Art Deco building.

18. **Choice B** is correct because it shows an alternative way the similar-looking oxen could have crossed from Russia to Canada without a land bridge. Choice A is incorrect. The argument is not predicated on the two animals being exactly alike, only similar. Choice C is incorrect because it tends to strengthen the argument, not weaken it. Choice D is incorrect because it is irrelevant how the two are classified; it is the physical similarities that are the premise for the argument. Choice E is incorrect because it tends to strengthen the argument slightly by pointing out yet another physical similarity between Canadian and Russian musk oxen.

19. **Choice D** is correct. The prosecutor's argument uses analogy (computer hacking is like bank robbing or burglary) to strengthen the conclusion. Choice A is incorrect. The prosecutor's argument does not state a rule and then provide an exception to that rule. Choice B is incorrect. The prosecutor's argument does not base a generalization upon a specific instance. Choice C is incorrect. The prosecutor's argument does not provide any evidence upon which the conclusion is based. Choice E is incorrect. The prosecutor's argument does not provide several points of view in support of a conclusion.

20. **Choice D** is correct. If ExFed Shipping's vehicles used more regular unleaded gasoline (which is less expensively priced) than premium unleaded gasoline (which is more expensive) in January than December, this could explain how ExFed Shipping could have used more gasoline in January than December but paid less when the average price per gallon remained the same. Choice A is incorrect. Even if ExFed Shipping shut down for two weeks in January, because they used more fuel in January than December, this fact would not provide an adequate explanation. Choice B is incorrect. Even if many ExFed Shipping vehicles were out of service during January, because the company used more fuel in January than December, this fact would not provide an adequate explanation. Choice C is incorrect. Even if January was much more snowy than December, this fact is irrelevant and does not provide an adequate explanation. Choice E is incorrect. Even if ExFed Shipping purchased more fuel-efficient vehicles, because the company used more fuel in January than December, this fact would not provide an adequate explanation.

21. **Choice A** is correct. Given the conclusions drawn about Doyle's personality and the way he acted in personal relationships, the author would really only be able to drawn strong conclusions from meeting Doyle. Choice B is incorrect because it A is stronger. Given the author's assumptions as to Doyle's personality, the fact that they never met face-to-face is a stronger criticism than not relying on a secondhand account. Choice C is incorrect. Even if many critics think the book only worthy of light reading, it does not address the relevancy of the author's conclusions about Doyle. Choice D is incorrect because relying on secondhand accounts is superfluous to what the author is arguing. Choice E is incorrect. The specifics of what Doyle knows in each scientific field are superfluous to the core of the argument.

22. **Choice E** is correct because the reason for the removal of the statues is a subsidiary conclusion that bolsters the argument's conclusion that the

statues will be restored to the Shrycler Building's facade. Choice A is incorrect. The stakes do not have to be clarified. Choice B is incorrect. The point was not repeated. Choice C is incorrect because the conclusion as to why the statues had been removed is not the main point of the argument. Choice D is incorrect because no analogy was made.

23. From the information in the question you can determine the following:

> Barrel: In terms of fatness, nothing can be fatter; in terms of thinness, some barrels can be thinner than some organ pipes, saguaros, and prickly pears.

> Organ Pipe: In terms of fatness, can be fatter than some barrels, but not fatter than saguaros or prickly pears. In terms of thinness, can be equally thin as organ pipes and thinner than barrels and prickly pears.

> Saguaro: In terms of fatness, is fatter than all organ pipes and prickly pears; can also be fatter than some barrels. In terms of thinness, can be thinner than some barrels, but is never thinner than organ pipes or prickly pears.

> Prickly pear: In terms of fatness, can be fatter than some barrels, but not fatter than saguaros or prickly pears. In terms of thinness, can be equally thin as organ pipes and can be thinner than barrels and prickly pears.

Choice A is correct. See preceding explanation. Choice B is incorrect. See preceding explanation. Choice C is incorrect. See preceding explanation. Choice D is incorrect. See preceding explanation. Choice E is incorrect. See preceding explanation.

24. **Choice A** is correct. The conclusion of the argument is that if someone wants to try spoo that is truly delicious and full of flavor, he or she must try blue spoo. If someone must try blue spoo to try a spoo that is truly delicious and full of flavor, then flarn, a yellow spoo (that is, not blue) cannot be truly delicious and full of flavor. Choice A is logically inferable. Choice B is incorrect because it goes too far; the argument only concerns itself with the relative qualities of spoo, not with other kinds of food. Choices C and D are incorrect because they are both non sequiteurs to this argument; both statements could be completely accurate, but they do not relate directly to the argument, which focuses on blue versus other kinds of spoo. Choice E fails because the fact that green spoo can be very flavorful and rich does not necessarily have to be true for the conclusion—that having blue spoo is the way to have a truly delicious dish that is full of flavor.

SECTION II—Reading Comprehension

1. C	10. A	19. B
2. B	11. C	20. E
3. B	12. E	21. B
4. D	13. B	22. A
5. B	14. E	23. B
6. C	15. D	24. E
7. B	16. D	25. B
8. D	17. A	
9. E	18. D	

1. **Answer: C.** The key is to read the entire passage and understand the gist of what the author is conveying:

> While the Data Privacy Act is mentioned at the end of the passage, it's not the merits of that specific act that drive this passage, so we can eliminate choice E.

> While parental consent forms are an element of the discussion, they don't cover the main impact of this passage, so we can eliminate choice D.

> While the access of inappropriate content by children is a growing concern, that issue is not the specific concern addressed by this officer. Therefore, we can eliminate choice B.

> There is also no specific mention of the time a child spends on the Internet, just on the collection of that child's data without gaining parental consent. Therefore, we can eliminate choice A.

> Specifically, we can see that the author is a Federal Trade Commissioner talking to Congress about the privacy of children's data when they go online. Therefore, we would choose choice C.

2. **Answer: B.** When asked to refine the meaning of a particular phrase or word, it's helpful to step back and look at the larger context of the phrase or word in question. In this case, let's look at the second paragraph:

> As the Commission's June 1998 Report to Congress noted, children represent a large and rapidly growing segment of online consumers. I would guess that the numbers will only increase. Perhaps one of the most frightening facts the Report noted was how many children's sites (89% of the 212 sites surveyed) collected personal information from them but appear not to obtain any kind of parental permission.

It would appear that the report in question is in fact the "Commission's June 1998 Report to Congress." For further clarification, we know that the author of this passage is a member of the Federal Trade Commission, as identified in lines 2–3 of the passage. Therefore, we can conclude that choice B is the correct answer. We can look throughout the passage and find that the other four choices, while mentioned in the passage, have nothing to do with the Report in line 9 of this passage.

3. **Answer: B.** Whenever we're asked a question that asks something *except*, we can infer that four of the five answer choices would answer the question satisfactorily, but one answer choice would not do so, which makes it the choice we want! Therefore, we need to rule out the choices that make the question right, like so:

The paragraph starting on line 26 states:

> The Commission's June report recommended that Congress enact legislation to protect children's online privacy. The Commission's recommended standards would enable parents to make choices about when and how their children's information is collected and used on the Web.

This means that the speaker is hoping to improve the kids' privacy rights, as well as the parents' ability to regulate and protect their children. We also see that in lines 13–15 that:

> In the Commission's view, these practices raise especially troubling privacy and safety concerns because of the particular vulnerability of children...

Therefore, we can infer that the speaker sees the need to improve the kids' safety. So, we can eliminate choice C.

The key here is not how the child is accessing the Internet, but what the websites are doing with the child's information and how that information is being used. Choice B really isn't the issue, and therefore it's our best answer for this question.

4. Answer: D. The quick way to answer this question is if you spotted the specific mention starting in line 23:

> The Commission's goal is to put parents in control of commercial websites' collection of personal information from their children.

However, if you look at the recommendations or standards that the FTC is ultimately proposing to Congress:

> The recommended standards would require commercial websites to
>
> ➤ Provide for notice and parental consent before personal information is collected from children 12 and under, and
>
> ➤ Provide parents of children 13 and over with notice and an opportunity to have their children's personal information removed from a website's database after it has been collected.

You can see that the parents are required to act in both cases—not Congress, not the FTC itself, and not the individual websites.

5. Answer: B. The proposal being made by the speaker is to ask Congress to enact new standards enforcing parental consent forms and data removal, upon request, from these children's websites. Therefore, anything that would weaken that proposal would be something that would either prove this proposal isn't working or an alternative that would make this proposal less necessary. Looking through the answers, data abuse would only strengthen the speaker's case, so choice A isn't applicable. A petition drive to improve privacy laws would also strengthen the case and show the need and desire by the constituents to have this law in place. Choice C can be eliminated. Internet access providers are the gateway to these websites, but this doesn't solve the concern of what happens when the child registers at individual websites. Therefore, Choice D isn't enough to really weaken the proposal. Furthermore, the removal of the address collection is only a partial solution and wouldn't necessarily remove the need for these proposals. Choice E isn't the best answer. Self-regulation by the main children's websites would greatly reduce the need for Congress to step in, so choice B is the best bet in this scenario.

6. Answer: C. The key to solving the first question regarding the point or theme of an entire passage is to read the entire selection, without jumping to the first answer choice that you see within the text. In this case, choice A is the obvious "first paragraph" answer, included in the answer choices for anyone who assumes the point of the entire passage will be specifically mentioned in the first paragraph. Because this is the only place the leaping abilities of the author are discussed, we can eliminate this choice. While the Martian incubator is somewhat of the focus early on in this passage, further reading shows that the passage talks about the young Martians escaping from the incubator into the arms of their adoptive parent. Therefore, choice E doesn't truly cover the scope of the entire passage. We can eliminate choice E. Furthermore, while the mating habits dictate the process described in this passage, the development of the young Martian is also discussed, which makes choice B too narrow in scope as well. We should also eliminate that choice. This brings us to choices C and D. While it's true that the evolution of Martians is detailed somewhat in this process, especially near the end of the passage, this answer is almost too abstract. The specific selection and rearing habits are the true focus of this passage, and we should select choice C.

7. **Answer: B.** The key to solving this type of question is to understand the point of view the author is attempting to communicate regarding the point raised in the question and gain an opinion based on the author's presentation of the situation. In this case, the development of young Martians is best addressed in the end of paragraph 5:

> But this counts for little among the green Martians, as parental and filial love is as unknown to them as it is common among us. I believe this horrible system which has been carried on for ages is the direct cause of the loss of all the finer feelings and higher humanitarian instincts among these poor creatures.

The author is pointing out that, because the young Martians are randomly plucked from the incubator by an older Martian to be raised, there is no emotional bonding or development in the young Martian, which would contribute to their psychological development. We would then choose choice B. As further proof, we can consult the next paragraph:

> From birth they know no father or mother love, they know not the meaning of the word home; they are taught that they are only suffered to live until they can demonstrate by their physique and ferocity that they are fit to live. Should they prove deformed or defective in any way they are promptly shot; nor do they see a tear shed for a single one of the many cruel hardships they pass through from earliest infancy.

The author details the fact that this "cruel" method of raising the young actually refines their physical and strategic value, weeding out any of the "weak" or unfit for this society and training the survivors to fight on. This definitely isn't impacting their physical, strategic, or primal instinct development, so A, C, and E can be ruled out. The only discussion about the economic impact of this development practice comes late in the passage, where the author describes the lack of natural resources that has forced them to adopt this rigid procedure. Therefore, we can assume that this process actually *improves* or at least stabilizes the economic situation—it does not hurt it. Therefore, we should eliminate choice D.

8. **Answer: D.** When you're given a question that refers to a specific line number, the key is to review the larger scope of the sentence or phrase in question. In this case, let's look at parts of the second paragraph, starting with line 13:

   > On either side of this opening the women and the younger Martians, both male and female, formed two solid walls leading out through the chariots and quite away into the plain beyond. Between these walls the little Martians scampered…where they were captured one at a time by the women and older children…until all the little fellows had left the enclosure and been appropriated by some youth or female. As the women caught the young they fell out of line and returned to their respective chariots, while those who fell into the hands of the young men were later turned over to some of the women.

   Therefore, we know that we're looking for someone who would have participated in this process—namely, a woman or a younger Martian.

   We know from the first paragraph that Tars Tarkas and Lorquas Ptomel seem to be coordinating this event, and they are most likely not participating in the selection of a young Martian. Furthermore, we can see from the first sentence that Sak is actually not a person, but a command that Tarkas gives the author. So, now we're left with the author and his mate, Sola. To verify the right answer, we need to go down further in the passage to line 26, in the third paragraph:

   > I saw that the ceremony, if it could be dignified by such a name, was over, and seeking out Sola I found her in our chariot with a hideous little creature held tightly in her arms.

   Therefore, because the author finds Sola with a young Martian, we can assume that she was either part of this process or was handed a young

Martian from a younger male Martian who participated. Either way, she is our best answer for this question, and so you should select choice D.

9. **Answer: E.** There are clues throughout the passage that reference these individual answers and allow you to eliminate four of the five choices, in order to get the correct answer. In lines 61–63, the last paragraph tells us:

> By careful selection they rear only the hardiest specimens of each species, and with almost supernatural foresight they regulate the birth rate to merely offset the loss by death.

This tells us that the birth rate is carefully controlled, so we can eliminate choice A. In lines 29–32, we are told:

> The work of rearing young, green Martians consists solely in teaching them to talk, and to use the weapons of warfare with which they are loaded down from the very first year of their lives.

This tells us that the language and military education skills are controlled by the foster parents, so we can eliminate choices B and C. Lines 32–34 tell us:

> Coming from eggs in which they have lain for five years, the period of incubation, they step forth into the world perfectly developed except in size.

This sentence does two things for us, the readers. It tells us that the incubation process, which controls the procreation of life, seems to be predetermined, so we can rule out choice D. It also tells us that the one element not determined upon birth is the size of the young Martian. This tells us that the physical stature is not determined from birth, which leads us to believe that choice E is correct. Further reading shows us that the development process weeds out the inferior, as referenced in lines 51–52:

> Should they prove deformed or defective in any way they are promptly shot;…

While they eventually weed out the inferior, whose physical stature is not satisfactory, this is not something they can regulate in advance. This makes choice E our best choice for this question.

10. Answer: A. The author spends the end of the passage almost decrying the practice of how these young Martians are selected and raised. Specifically, this is pointed out:

> From birth they know no father or mother love, they know not the meaning of the word home; they are taught that they are only suffered to live until they can demonstrate by their physique and ferocity that they are fit to live. Should they prove deformed or defective in any way they are promptly shot; nor do they see a tear shed for a single one of the many cruel hardships they pass through from earliest infancy.

Because the young Martians are put through such a rigorous upbringing by arbitrary parents, there is not a correct amount of emotional development, no sense of family or home. Therefore, coming up with a system that would give parents a better connection to their offspring could offset this problem, and we would choose choice A. Coming at this question from the other perspective, we can look through the passage and rule out answers that wouldn't make sense in the eyes of the author. It's clear that the author feels this system produces the hardest, most vigorous people that can be. Therefore, they don't need to train the young better in hunting techniques, so there is no deficiency mentioned in that area. The birth rate seems to be "supernaturally controlled," so there's no need for more incubators. The selection process, if done by the fathers, wouldn't seem to give any new importance or provide a difference, so choice E doesn't help. While choice C would help the development of the Martian race, the author acknowledges that the weak and deformed are already ruled out, so that's not the emphasis here either.

11. Answer: C. When asked to summarize an entire passage into one sentence, it's important to make at least one pass-through of the reading, pick out the key points, and understand the flow and theme that ties it all together. While the rococo ornamentation is the subject of the first paragraph, it's meant as a lead-in to the information on the Palace of Fine Arts, so choice D is not reflective of the piece as a whole. As the author extols the beauty of the architecture of this palace, you see that the focus is on the palace, not on contrasting different architectural styles. This means that choice A would be an incorrect answer. While the author describes in some detail the different aspects of the Palace of Fine Arts, we are not given specific information as to when and how these aspects were created. This is *not* a history of the building, so choice B would be incorrect. Finally, while the "shrine of worship" in line 40 brings up notions of religious freedom, it's clear by now that choice E really has nothing to do with this particular passage, and we can eliminate it. This sweeping overview of the style of the Palace of Fine Arts is clearly defined in choice C, which is the correct answer.

12. **Answer: E.** The key here is to go through the passage and pick out the key descriptions of the palace, in order to find the one feature that is *not* linked to this building:

Lines 30–34:

> Of course the setting contributes much to the picturesque effect, but aside from that, the *colonnades and the octagonal dome* in the center of the semicircular embracing form of the main building present many interesting features.

Line 35:

> There is a very fine development of *vistas,*...

Lines 39–40:

> ...which finds its noblest expression in that delicate *shrine of worship*, by Ralph Stackpole, beneath the dome.

We also should note that this section about buildings *not* like the palace:

> Save for Mullgardt's court, *it is the only building* that seems to be based on the realization of a dream of a true artistic conception. With *many other of the buildings* one feels the process of their creation in the time-honored, pedantic way. *They are paper-designed* by the mechanical application of the "T" square and the triangle. They do not show the advantage of having been experienced as a vision.

In other words, the palace is the realization of the dream, while other buildings are paper-designed by mechanical applications. Choice E is the correct answer.

13. **Answer: B.** In order to pick out the tone of this piece, it's important to note the specific adjectives the author uses throughout this description. This question throws in a few words used verbatim in the passage in order to offer a "quick answer" to someone skimming the piece. Don't fall for this trick; rather, evaluate the entire passage based on the author's tone:

Line 6:

> The Horticultural Palace is a *great success* as an interpretation of a style…

Lines 10–14:

> Of all isolated units, none causes *greater admiration* than the Fine Arts Palace. It presents the *astounding spectacle* of a building which violates the architectural conventions on more than one occasion, and in spite of it, or possibly for that very reason, it has a *note of originality* that is most conspicuous.

Lines 27–28:

> With Bernard Maybeck's Palace of Fine Arts, one has the feeling that this *great temple is a realized dream*;…

These don't seem like instances of a "routine" building, nor a cluttered building. While there are different architectural styles and devices used, you never get the impression that it's too many pieces or too confusing. Now let's look at some of the traps:

Pedantic is used in lines 22–23 to describe *other* buildings:

> With many other of the buildings one feels the process of their creation in the time-honored, *pedantic* way.

Sympathetic is used in line 8 to say that the style used in the Palace *rarely* finds a sympathetic expression:

> The Horticultural Palace is a great success as an interpretation of a style which rarely finds a *sympathetic* expression in this country.

Hopefully, it's clear that the author is portraying a building he finds inspiring. Therefore, you should pick choice B for this question.

14. **Answer: E.** As with all questions asking to refine meaning, let's step back and take a look at the context of this word:

> Of all isolated units, none causes greater admiration than the Fine Arts Palace. It presents the astounding *spectacle* of a building which violates the architectural conventions on more than one occasion, and in spite of it, or possibly for that very reason, it has a note of originality that is most conspicuous. Everybody admits that it is most beautiful, and very few seem to know just how this was accomplished.

It's clear that the spectacle is referring to the building that violates the architectural conventions, or, more specifically, the Palace of Fine Arts. While *spectacles* can mean *glasses*, that's not the case here. The term is describing the building, so using the word *building* would be repetitive and incorrect. Because it's describing the building itself, and not a specific event at the palace, you can probably eliminate *main event* as well. That leaves two choices, *important location* and *visual accomplishment*. Going through the rest of the paragraph, you see that the author is describing it in other terms such as *originality* and *beautiful*. If you keep reading, you'll see for sure that the spectacle in this case is the amazing visual styles used in the architecture of this building. Therefore, you should choose choice E.

15. Answer: D. Let's take a look at the last paragraph of this passage:

> This spiritual quality puts the visitor into the proper frame of mind for the enjoyment of the other offerings of art within the building. Mr. Maybeck has demonstrated once again that his talent is equal to any task in the field of architectural art. I wish we had more of his rare kind and more people to do justice to his genius.

The author has concluded that the shrine of worship by Mr. Stackpole helps put the visitor in the right frame of mind to enjoy the other parts of the palace, and then credits Mr. Maybeck as a visionary talent. Most importantly, the author not only hopes for more visionary architects like Mr. Maybeck, but people who can construct buildings that convey Mr. Maybeck's style and genius. The author has carefully detailed some of the ingenious techniques used by Mr. Maybeck, such as the colonnades and dome, and is trying to project the importance of using that style in other situations. The best fit for the author's desires is expressed in choice D.

16. Answer: D. As we go through the passage, we see that Dr. Gerberding is outlining first the outbreak and then the eventual reduction of rubella outbreaks in the United States. She then goes on to detail the efforts to reduce rubella outbreaks, via increased immunization efforts, in other parts of the world. Therefore, we know that the point isn't about the spread of rubella, because the immunization efforts are the biggest part of this passage, so choice A can be ruled out. The origin of the rubella vaccine is mentioned in line 24, but this is simply the means to the end, which is eliminating rubella outbreaks, so Choice B isn't correct. We know from the passage that there are still outbreaks of rubella in other parts of the world, so choice C is factually incorrect. Finally, while Dr. Gerberding is presenting this report of rubella's reduction, the passage is not about her specific actions, but rather the CDC's efforts as a whole to reduce this larger problem. So choice E is not the best answer here. We are left with choice D, which truly conveys the entire passage most accurately.

17. **Answer: A.** It's important to pull back, on a question about refining meaning of a certain phrase, to get the full context of the situation. In this case, let's look at the third paragraph:

> So, in the 1960s in this country, we had very large outbreaks of rubella. I was one of those statistics, and I'm sure many people my age or older also remember outbreaks of rubella in their schools. The vaccine was introduced in the late part of the '60s and, for a while, the vaccine was beginning to be used. We were seeing better and better control of rubella. But over time, as you can see in that red line on this graphic, we began to see fewer and fewer cases as immunization rates got higher and higher and higher.

We can see that, at this point in the passage, the vaccine has been introduced, and it's being used to reduce the number of rubella outbreaks. As a corollary, this is occurring because the rate of immunization has been going up. Therefore, we can conclude that the line of the graphic that must've accompanied this article is tracking the declining rate of rubella outbreaks versus the increasing rate of rubella immunizations. Going through the answer choices, D and E aren't relevant, and nothing about the countries or CDC budget is mentioned in this paragraph. Likewise, the number of newborns with Congenital Rubella Syndrome hasn't been discussed here. The key to invalidating Choice B is the specific language used. That answer talks about doses *prepared*, not *delivered*. We are told that the immunization rate is going higher, but that is technically independent from the number of doses prepared. You can prepare millions of doses, but if they're not administered, that doesn't affect the immunization rate. Therefore, the best answer and our choice should be choice A. Other valid responses might be those representing an increasing immunization rate.

18. **Answer: D.** While some of the other answer choices no doubt helped the situation, it is clear from the passage that the effects of immunizing children with the rubella vaccine has been the main reason why there were declining rubella outbreaks until the point where the CDC could triumphantly announce that it has virtually eliminated it in the United

States. Remember, the question asks about the success of elimination in the United States, not the world. Therefore, choices C and E, while contributing to the worldwide reduction of rubella outbreaks, are not relevant in this question. Also, this disease was not assisted through education efforts, as rubella was attacking people indiscriminant of their activities. This was also not a disease brought about by poor sanitation—at least, there is no mention in this passage of that being the case. Remember, in answering these questions, the correct answers need to be a part of the passage. You should not draw *main* conclusions based on outside knowledge.

19. **Answer: B.** This question asks us to evaluate the passage and look for clues that give us an idea as to the setting where this speech was delivered. First, let's look at the beginning of the second paragraph:

> But what does it really mean to say we've eliminated rubella? What it means I think is very nicely illustrated on this graphic here.

Dr. Gerberding is using a visual aid, a graphic, to assist her in this presentation. Something like this doesn't lend well to a radio show, which is a pure audio format. We can eliminate choice D. The biggest clue probably comes in the paragraph, starting around line 42:

> But the story is not done yet. There is amazing progress underway in other parts of the Western Hemisphere, which you'll hear about in a minute, but there are still parts of the world where immunization is not common or not common enough to prevent children from developing Congenital Rubella Syndrome.

This should give us a better idea as to the nature of the setting. We're about to hear results about rubella immunizations and, most likely, reductions in rubella outbreaks in other parts of the Western Hemisphere. Furthermore, we're told about the needs to improve immunizations around the world. This is clearly outside the scope of a presentation being made at a high school. While the rubella vaccine made it possible to make this announcement, which would've made "ground zero," or the first high school to use the vaccine, a nice place to announce rubella's elimination, we're told about hearing evidence of progress in other parts of the world. This allows us to eliminate choice A. Furthermore, while the CDC's budget is an important driver for the CDC to participate in worldwide efforts to eliminate rubella, the specific analysis of rubella is a little too specific for a budget hearing. We should probably eliminate choice C as well. Given the global nature of the information to follow, this is probably outside the scope of a monthly board meeting as well. The focus of this entire speech is not about the CDC's specific efforts, but rather the outbreak and eventual containment of one specific disease, rubella. It would make sense to eliminate choice E and pick choice B as our correct answer.

20. **Answer: E.** When we're asked to draw conclusions about future activity after the passage, it's important to gain clues as to the main conclusions drawn by the author—or, in this case, the speaker—as to what the next steps should be and what is not covered. Because we're dealing with a question that list recommendations and are asked to find the *exception*, we can either rule out all the right answers or find proof that clearly invalidates one of these answer choices. The last paragraph deals with Dr. Gerberding's vision of future activities:

> So, in this country, while we can celebrate this milestone, we also have to remain vigilant because, as we say in public health, our network is only as strong as the weakest link. And as long as there is rubella anywhere in the world, there could be rubella in our children, too. So we have to sustain our commitment to immunization. We have to strengthen all of the links in the network, and we have to do everything possible to protect the health of children here within our country, as well as beyond.

First and foremost, she clearly states the need to "sustain our commitment to immunization." That rules out choice C. Next, she talks about strengthening "all the links in the network." This should be interpreted to mean that we need to communicate efforts with all other countries to contribute to a solution. That would rule out choices A and B. Finally, her last missive, "do everything possible to protect the health of children here within our country, as well as beyond" clearly states that we need to watch out for the kids, and one way to do that is to monitor their health. Nowhere does the passage state anything about improving the efficacy of the vaccine. We are led to believe that it's a good vaccine, with no major side effects, that has produced a wonderful thing: the virtual elimination of rubella in the United States. Choice E goes against the entire thrust and definition of this passage, and, therefore, should be the correct answer.

21. **Answer: B.** When we go through this passage, we see that in the first paragraph, we are given the definition and origin of the word *university*. As we move through the passage, we see the "traditional" sense of *university* established in Bologna and then Paris. As we move through history, we see how the University of Paris shaped the forming of other European universities. Specifically, our focus is shifted to two English universities—Cambridge and Oxford—and we learn about the specific impact they have on English life today. Now, you need to ask yourself:

> "Does this piece just focus on the origin of the university?" No, so choice A is wrong.

> "Does this piece just provide a summary of European universities?" No, so choice D is wrong.

> "Does this piece primarily focus on the University of Paris?" No, so choice E is wrong.

Does this piece better describe the evolution or purpose of the university? While the last paragraph shows us the purpose of Cambridge and Oxford, and how they've affected English life and society, that's not necessarily reflective of the passage as a whole. Instead, this passage shows us how the university has evolved, from Roman times to today, and choice B best reflects the entire passage.

22. **Answer: A.** While universities, especially Cambridge and Oxford, have impact throughout the land, the author focuses on how the universities are organized by education and their impact. Take this passage at the very end:

> *Universities* like Durham, London, Manchester, Liverpool, and Leeds are the outcome of the last century, and, together with the university extension work of the older foundations, *have very greatly aided the dissemination of university ideas among aspirants to educational distinction.*

While the author acknowledges other areas, especially in lines 39–42:

> …a long, extensive, and continuous list of eminent bishops, chancellors, statesmen and lawyers acknowledge one or other of them as their alma mater.

The passage simply acknowledges that these people attended one of these universities; it doesn't describe how their experience there shapes their activities in government, medicine, law, and so on. Therefore, our best answer is choice A.

23. **Answer: B.** Let's pull back and take a look at the paragraph where the word *lapse* is being used, in order to gain the context and understanding of the word's intent:

> But it is to our English universities that we most directly turn our view. Doubtless, the oldest of these were influenced by, and formed upon, the plan of Paris. Oxford was an early centre of scholastic life. Its first colleges were Balliol, Merton, and University, all of which were founded about the middle of the thirteenth century, and before the *lapse* of fifty years it had become recognized as an organized university throughout the world. Cambridge, as a university, was later than Oxford, although her schools were contemporary. At Cambridge, as at Oxford, the central idea was the establishment of colleges, and their union by educational bonds into one whole.

We can see from this paragraph that Oxford's first three colleges were Balliol, Merton, and University, and after the lapse of 50 years, people saw it as an organized university. Therefore, we can see that the lapse of 50 years is referring to time, not a forgotten gap or anything physical or related to distance. In the "passing" of those 50 years—or, in other words, "after 50 years"—people recognized Oxford as an organized university. This means that choice B, the passing of time, is our correct answer.

24. **Answer: E.** Because we're talking about the impact on English life, let's look at the example that covers the area mentioned in this question. Specifically, that's the last paragraph:

> *The influence* of these two universities on the life of England *cannot be over-estimated*. Ever since their foundation a long, extensive, and continuous list of eminent bishops, chancellors, statesmen, and lawyers acknowledge one or other of them as their alma mater. The extension of modern methods has, fortunately, introduced to all these categories many who have not enjoyed a university education, but the old institutions still hold their own. *Universities* like Durham, London, Manchester, Liverpool, and Leeds are the outcome of the last century, and, together with the university extension work of the older foundations, *have very greatly aided the dissemination of university ideas* among aspirants to educational distinction.

Here are a few key phrases to help gauge the author's opinion:

The influence...cannot be over-estimated.

Universities...have very greatly aided the dissemination of university ideas.

The extension of modern methods...introduced...many who have not enjoyed a university education.

We can see that the author places a great deal of importance on the university. Given the complexity and far-reaching nature of the university, as described throughout the passage, you should *not* conclude that these places of learning are simply routine. We see that universities from the last century have added with the "extension work" of their predecessors to help disseminate university ideas among the learned. That means they're ever-changing, evolving, and *not* static, nor are they antiquated. While the universities are described as contemporary, remember the language of the full question. We're looking for how the author sees the *impact* of the university, not the actual university itself. In that case, given the choice between contemporary and meaningful, with all the evidence presented, we should pick choice E, meaningful, as the correct answer.

25. **Answer: B.** Let's go through the passage and map out the key elements as they progress:

Early definition of *university*

Evolution into first University at Bologna

Development of University of Paris and model it inspired

Evolution of Oxford and Cambridge in the UK

Impact of Oxford and Cambridge in the UK

Given this flow of events, jumping back to something at Bologna or Paris would not provide a good flow for the entire passage. Therefore, you can rule out choices C and D. While Salerno is mentioned in the first paragraph, and another paragraph about him would give a "circular closure" to the entire piece, talking about his teachings without the context of the university would not make logical sense either. While the opening of a new building at Oxford is a future event that would move the piece forward, it's almost too specific and limiting, given the topics of the previous two paragraphs. Therefore, a further extension of universities as a part of modern English life would be the best topic for a new paragraph, and your answer should be choice B.

SECTION III—Analytical Reasoning

1. C	**9.** E	**17.** C
2. D	**10.** C	**18.** D
3. C	**11.** B	**19.** A
4. E	**12.** E	**20.** B
5. E	**13.** A	**21.** B
6. D	**14.** D	**22.** E
7. D	**15.** A	**23.** D
8. B	**16.** D	**24.** E

QUESTIONS 1–6 RELATE TO THE FOLLOWING LOGIC GAME:

A group of elementary school kids are making paper-link banners for an upcoming holiday party. They have five colors of paper to make these links: green, orange, purple, red, and yellow. They start by fixing one paper link to a hook and connecting each link in a sequential fashion. The teacher has given the following specifications for how to make each banner:

> If a yellow link is adjacent to a purple link, any link that immediately precedes and any link that immediately follows those two links must be red.

> You cannot put two links of the same color next to each other unless they are green-colored links.

> No red link can be adjacent to any orange link.

> Any portion of a banner containing eight consecutive links must include at least one link of each color.

ACTION:

Our job here is to build a banner chain from the hook until the last link specified. Note that in this game, we haven't set a specific size for the banner. There's no minimum and no maximum. However, the length of the banner is important because of the fourth rule specified. If we know the banner will be at least eight links long, then we consider the fourth rule in our calculations; otherwise, we ignore that rule.

SETUP:

The easiest way to represent this banner is through abbreviations of the color of each link to be used in the banner. For example, if we had a five-link banner with every color represented, in alphabetical order, we could represent it as so:

> HOOK: Green-Orange-Purple-Red-Yellow
>
> OR
>
> HOOK: G-O-P-R-Y

RULES:

It's hard to represent all the rules in shorthand, but we'll use the appropriate notations for each rule.

Rule 1: If P-Y or Y-P, then R-P-Y-R (or R-Y-P-R)

This means that if we have any adjacent pair of a purple link and a yellow link, the link before and the link after should be red links. Note, however, that the language specifies that they are red only if that link is there. What does this mean? If the first two links of a banner are purple and yellow, obviously there can't be a red link preceding the first link. In that case, we only add the red link after the pair:

> HOOK: P-Y becomes HOOK: P-Y-R

Rule 2: G-G okay and Not (O-O, P-P, R-R, Y-Y)

We can have two green links next to each other, but we can't have two of any other color being adjacent to each other.

Rule 3: Not (O-R) and Not (R-O)

We cannot have any orange link adjacent to any red link, period.

Rule 4: If length=8, at least 1 of each color per eight links.

As long as we have *at least* a banner of eight links, every sub-banner of eight links must contain at least one link of each possible color. For example, if we have a nine-link banner, the sub-banner of links 1–8 *and* the sub-banner of links 2–9 must contain at least one link of each color. This specific point will be important later, during one of the questions.

1. **Answer: C.** The typical thing to do with a question like this, since it's the first one of the game, is to use the individual rules to find combinations that are invalid and eliminate answer choices until we're left with the correct answer. Starting from the bottom, the fourth rule states that any banner with at least eight links must have one of each color within those eight links. Looking through the choices, choice E does not contain an orange link, which makes it is invalid. Choice E is incorrect. Rule 3 does not allow us to put a red link next to an orange link. However, choice A has a red link next to an orange link near the middle of the chain. Therefore, we can eliminate this one. Choice A is incorrect. Rule 2 states that you cannot put two colors next to each other unless that color is green. Going through the remaining answers, we see that choice B has two red links in the third and fourth positions, making this chain invalid. Choice B is incorrect. Rule 1 states that a pairing of yellow and purple links must have red links before and after this pair. Choice D has this yellow-purple pair in the fourth and fifth spots. While the previous link is red, the link after this pair is green, which violates the first rule. Therefore, we can eliminate this choice, too. Choice D is incorrect. The only answer choice left is C, which is correct.

2. **Answer: D.** As in the previous question, going through the individual rules can help us eliminate answer choices that cannot be right, so that we can find the one answer that could be valid. Let's start with the rules that directly pertain to the color of the link in question. Rule 3 states that you can't put a red link next to an orange link. If the fourth link is orange, the third link (or second choice in each answer pair) cannot be red. We see that choice B has a red link in the third position, so it's eliminated. Choice B is incorrect. Now let's look at the other rules that are indirectly related. Rule 2 states that no two adjacent links can be the same color unless that color is green. Choice C is invalid because it has two purple links next to each other. Choice C is incorrect. On that same tack, let's look at the remaining choices, given Rule 2. If we used choice A, the second through fourth links would look like this: green, orange, orange. Ah ha! We have an adjacent pair of orange links, which violates Rule 2. Choice A is incorrect. Let's look at the remaining two answers and see what the answer choices look like next to this orange link in the fourth position. Choice E gives us yellow-purple-orange. Yet Rule 1 clearly states that the link after any purple-yellow pair must be red. That means this choice can't be valid. Choice E is incorrect. We're left with one answer choice, D, which is correct.

3. **Answer: C.** The best way to figure out a question like this is to draw this banner and see which answer completes the banner properly. Given the information in the question, the banner must look like this:

HOOK: ?-R-G-Y-?-P-R-?

Remember, we're looking for an answer that *must* be true, not on that *could* be true, so we need to find a rule (or the only choice that doesn't violate any rules) that will tell us what to choose. Looking at the first location, the only thing we know for certain, so far, is that the link cannot be orange, because the second link is red. Therefore, we can't say that choice A must be true. Looking at the fifth location, we know that the link cannot be yellow or purple, for several reasons. First, a yellow or purple link would create an adjacent pair, and it would also create a purple-yellow pair *not* surrounded by red links. Looking at the eight locations, once again we know it can't be an orange link. So we know that choice D is incorrect. Now, let's look back at all our deductions. We know that the first link and the eighth link cannot be orange. However, Rule 4 states that, in an eight-link banner, we must have at least one of each color represented. Looking through the banner, we can see red, green, yellow, and purple, but no orange. If the orange link can't be in the first or eighth position, there's only one spot left—the fifth link. Therefore, the orange link *must* be in the fifth position. This means that choice C is correct.

4. **Answer: E.** As the questions get more involved, we need to sketch out the banner and use the rules to project "down the chain," if you will, and determine what can, must, and/or cannot be on the rest of the banner. Remember, we're looking for an answer choice that *cannot* be a possibility, so it must violate at least one of the rules. Remember to read the question carefully. This is only a six-link banner, so we don't have to worry about Rule 4. That rule requires at least an eight-link banner, so we can ignore it just for this question. Don't rule out an answer choice just because the choice would create a banner without all five colors. So far, our banner looks like this:

HOOK: P-Y-?-?-?-?

Rule 1 tells us that any links directly after a purple-yellow pair must be red. Therefore, the third link must be red:

HOOK: P-Y-R-?-?-?

Let's go through the answer choices and see what the banner would like hook:

Choice A, green and orange: HOOK: P-Y-R-?-G-O

If we put green in the fourth position, we have a valid banner, so this choice is possible.

Choice B, orange and green: HOOK: P-Y-R-?-O-G

We can't put orange or red in the fourth position, but any other color would produce a valid banner. This choice is possible.

Choice C, orange and yellow: HOOK: P-Y-R-?-O-Y

This is the same options as Choice B: anything but orange and red. This choice is possible.

Choice D, purple and orange: HOOK: P-Y-R-?-P-O

We can't put purple or red in the fourth position, but any other color would produce a valid banner. This choice is possible.

Choice E, yellow and purple: HOOK: P-Y-R-?-Y-P

Now we have more to work with in this case. Rule 1 states that any link preceding a yellow-purple pair *must* be red. That would mean we would have to put a red link in the fourth spot. However, doing so would create a red-red pair in spots 3 and 4, which is invalid according to Rule 2. Therefore, this combination is *not possible*, and we have our answer.

5. **Answer: E.** Like Questions 3 and 4, this one can best be answered by drawing the banner, based on the information in the question, filling in whatever links we can, based on the rules of the game, and then using the answers to find one option that is possible. From the information presented, we have a banner as follows:

    HOOK: P-Y-?-P-Y-?-?-?-?

We know from Rule 1 that any purple-yellow pair must be surrounded by red links. In this case, we have two pairs, so the third and sixth positions must be red, like this:

    HOOK: P-Y-R-P-Y-R-?-?-?

Now, remember that this banner is nine links long, so Rule 4 *does* apply to this banner. We need to have all five colors represented, and so far, we have only purple, yellow, and red. This means that within the seventh, eighth, and ninth positions, we need to have at least one green link and one orange link. Now, we could plug in answer choices and rule out possibilities or make further determinations about our banner. Let's see what we can rule out first:

> If we plug in choice A, the seventh link would be orange. But we know from our calculations that the sixth link is red, and we can't put an orange link next to a red link. Choice A is incorrect.

> If we plug in choice D, the eighth link would be red. This would mean that we couldn't put an orange link in the seventh position (as we already determined), *nor* could we put an orange link in the ninth position. But we know from Rule 4 that we *must* have an orange link in this banner. Choice D is incorrect.

> If we plug in choice C, the ninth link would be red. As in the previous answer, this would rule out orange from being in the only two spots left, the seventh and eighth links, and we must have at least one orange link on our banner. Choice D is incorrect.

> If we plug in choice B, the eighth link is green. This satisfies half of our needs to have each color on the banner. We know that we can't put the orange link in the seventh spot, so we would make it the ninth link, to look like this:

$$\text{HOOK: P-Y-R-P-Y-R-?-G-O}$$

However, we need to read the fourth rule *very* carefully. It states that "any portion" of a banner with eight links must have all five colors within that portion. If we take the first eight links out of this banner, we only have four colors; orange is cut off. Therefore, this option is not valid either. Choice B is incorrect. To preserve Rule 4, we would have to put green in the seventh position and orange in the eighth position, to look like this:

$$\text{HOOK: P-Y-R-P-Y-R-G-O-?}$$

As long as the ninth link isn't orange (Rule 2) or red (Rule 3), we have a valid banner. Choice E is possible, and it's our correct answer.

6. **Answer: D.** Because we're looking for an answer choice that *cannot* be possible, we need to find out which answer would violate one of the rules. Let's draw our banner as we know it so far:

HOOK: R-Y-G-R-?-?-?-?

We know from Rule 2 that the fifth link cannot be red. However, none of the answer choices have red in the fifth spot, so this doesn't help. We know from Rule 3 that the fifth link cannot be orange, but once again this doesn't help. Because we're dealing with an eight-link banner, we know that Rule 4 applies, and we must have one of each color present on our banner. We have red, yellow, and green, but no purple or orange yet. We could plug in all five options and see which ones produce an invalid banner. However, if you've gone through these steps, hopefully you'll pick the right one to start investigating: Choice D. Why? We haven't touched Rule 1 yet, and picking D would force us to do so. If we plug in choice D, purple and yellow, into our banner, we get this:

HOOK: R-Y-G-R-P-Y-?-?

So far so good. We needed the fourth link to be red, and it is. We know that the seventh link will also have to be red. We also know that we need an orange link, and we have one spot left, the eighth link. But there's a problem—a big problem. Rule 3 clearly states that you can't put an orange link next to a red one. But the seventh link has to be red, and the eighth link has to be orange. This option *cannot* be valid, and choice D is the correct answer.

QUESTIONS 7–12 RELATE TO THE FOLLOWING LOGIC GAME:

Charles has to put together a roster for his company's annual softball game against the company's cross-town rival. He has eight healthy people who want to bat for the team: Cosmo, Dustin, Hal, Jordan, Ken, Peter, Roger, and Seth. He's allowed to submit five names for his roster. However, there are some things to take into consideration:

If Roger plays, Hal must play immediately after Roger on the roster.

Two of the three managers, Dustin, Ken, and Roger, have to be on the team.

Cosmo and Seth can't be next to each other on the roster.

If Ken is on the team, then Jordan can't be picked.

Peter has to play either first or second.

ACTION:

In this game, we actually have to solve for two different things. First, we have to pick five people out of eight, so expect to get three basic questions:

> Who *can* be in the group?
>
> Who *must* be in the group?
>
> Who *cannot* be in the group?

Second, however, we have to pick a specific order of the team. This means we'll have to worry about positions, specifically:

> Who is first/second/third/fourth/last?
>
> Which of these rosters can be submitted?
>
> Which of these rosters is not possible?

SETUP:

We can represent your answer as a five-letter chain from left to right, signifying order. For example, if we choose Cosmo, Dustin, Hal, Jordan, and Ken to play in that specific order, we'd represent it as:

> C-D-H-J-K

If we're unsure of a certain spot in the roster, we just represent it with a question mark (?).

RULES:

We'll represent these rules as "sub-chains," or pieces of the puzzle, to help us determine our final solution.

> Rule 1: If R, then R-H.

If Roger plays, then we know two players on the roster: Roger and Hal, immediately after Roger.

> Rule 2: From set D, K, R, exactly two will play.

Basically, out of the set of three people Dustin, Ken, Roger, exactly two will play. Notice that this isn't *can* play; we know that two of these people *will* be on the roster.

> Rule 3: Not (C-S) and Not (S-C).

Basically, Cosmo and Seth cannot be immediately before or after each other, if they are to play on the team.

> Rule 4: If K, then not J.

This is simple: If Ken plays, then Jordan isn't playing. Of course, we can reverse this rule to come up with the corollary:

Rule 4 (reverse): If J, then not K.

If Jordan is on the team, then Ken can't be on the team because if he were, it would violate Rule 4.

Rule 5: P-?-?-?-? or ?-P-?-?-?.

We use the roster representation to show that Peter is in either the first or second position on the roster.

7. **Answer: D.** Because we're on the first question of the game, let's use the rules to go through and eliminate wrong answers, those that break one of the rules given to us, until we're left with one correct answer. Rule 1 states that Hal plays after Roger on the roster. If we go through the list, we see that in choice A, Hal plays way before Roger, so this roster is invalid. Choice A is incorrect. Rule 2 states that of the set Dustin, Ken, Roger, exactly two of those three people must be on the team. As we go through the remaining choices, we see that choice E only has Roger and not Dustin or Ken. Choice E is incorrect. Rule 3 states that Cosmo and Seth can't be next to each other in the roster. However, we can see that choice B has them batting fourth and fifth, which violates this rule. Choice B is incorrect. Rule 5 states that Peter must be first or second in the rotation. Going through the two remaining answer choices, we see that he's fourth in choice C, which makes this choice an invalid roster. Choice C is incorrect. We're left with one answer choice, D, which is the correct answer.

8. **Answer: B.** Once again, let's go through the existing rules and see if we can eliminate four of the five answers, leaving us with one possible answer. If we look at Rule 1, we see that if Roger is playing, Hal has to be the next player on the roster. This means that Roger cannot be the last member on the team, because that would mean Hal could not play next. Choice C is a clear violation of this rule. Choice C is incorrect. Let's look at Rule 2. We need to have two, and exactly two, of the three managers on the team. Ken is on the team by default, according to the question, so between the fourth and fifth players, one of them has to be either Dustin or Roger. We can see that choice E has neither Dustin nor Roger, so that violates the rule. Choice E is incorrect. Next, Rule 3 clearly states that Cosmo and Seth cannot be next to each other in the rotation. We see that, in choice A, if Seth is the fourth person on the roster, that means that Cosmo and Seth would be third and fourth, respectively, which violates Rule 3. (Choice C is also a violation of Rule 3, but we ruled that choice out already.) Choice A is

incorrect. Finally, Rule 4 states that if Ken is on the team, Jordan can't be on the roster. We see that Jordan is in choice D, which rules out that choice for us. Choice D is incorrect. We're left with one choice, B, which is the correct answer and follows Rule 1 perfectly.

9. **Answer: E.** In this case, we can take the information we are given in the question and build a potential roster. Then we can use the rules to determine who must fill any additional spots. After that, we can plug in the answer choices to see if it must be true or not. We're told that Jordan is playing second in the rotation. We know from Rule 5 that Peter must be either first or second, so by process of elimination, we know that Peter is playing first. So we can draw the roster as

P-J-?-?-?

We also know from the reverse of Rule 4 that, because Jordan is playing, Ken is not playing. However, we now use Rule 2 to determine that, because Ken is not playing, Dustin and Roger *must* be playing. Furthermore, by using Rule 1, because Roger is playing, we know that Hal is playing immediately after him. We now have our three remaining players on the roster: Dustin, Roger, and Hal. More importantly, however, because Roger and Hal have to play one after the other, we can devise two specific scenarios: either Roger plays third, Hal plays fourth (and Dustin plays fifth), or Roger plays fourth and Hal plays fifth. (leaving Dustin with third) Or, you can write it as

P-J-R-H-D or P-J-D-R-H

Going through the answer choices, we can make determinations:

A is incorrect because Roger could play third or fourth.

B is incorrect simply because Dustin *cannot* play fourth.

C is incorrect because Dustin could play third or last.

D is incorrect because Hal could play fourth or last.

E is therefore correct. Cosmo *cannot* play because the roster is set for the five players we have previously determined.

10. **Answer: C.** In this case, we use the pieces of information given to us to determine the one answer that definitely cannot be on the roster and pick it. Remember, we're looking for *cannot*, not *might not*. If Dustin and Ken are on the team, then Rule 2 tells us that we cannot include Roger on the team. Note, however, that this does *not* mean that Hal is an automatic exclusion by virtue of Rule 1. If you read that rule correctly, it's only in effect if Roger plays. It says nothing to

specifically exclude Hal if Roger is not playing. Next, Rule 4 specifically states that if Ken plays, Jordan does not play on the team. Therefore, we're looking for an answer that contains Roger and Jordan. Choice C is the answer we want.

11. **Answer: B.** In this case, let's take our new piece of information and use the rules to rule out choices we can prove to be invalid, to get down to our one possible correct choice. If Hal is not on the roster, then we can take the reverse of Rule 1 and say that Roger cannot be on the roster as well. After all, if Roger were on the roster, Hal would have to play after him, and this can't happen. We see that in choice D, Roger is on the roster without Hal, which cannot be valid. Choice D is incorrect. Next, we can use the fact that Roger is not on the roster to determine that Dustin and Ken *must* be on the roster. We can do a quick check here to see whether any of the answers only contain one or neither of these choices. In fact, all remaining choices contain both, so we can move on. Because we now know that Ken *must* be on the roster, we know from Rule 4 that since Ken is playing, Jordan cannot play. We see from choice C that Jordan is a member there, which makes that answer invalid. Choice C is incorrect. At this point, we can actually determine who must be on the team. Because we've ruled out Hal, Roger, and Jordan, and we know that Peter, Dustin, and Ken must play, the last two players we have, Cosmo and Seth, must be on the team as well. However, it's the order of the players that helps us determine the one correct answer. We know that Peter must play first or second, yet Choice E has him in the third slot, which makes this choice invalid. Choice E is incorrect. Finally, we know from Rule 3 that Cosmo and Seth cannot play next to each other, yet in Choice A, they are fourth and fifth, respectively, which makes this choice invalid. Choice A is incorrect. This leaves choice B as the correct answer, with the correct five players in a valid order.

12. **Answer: E.** Let's start with rules that pertain specifically to our newest piece of information. If Seth is playing in the fourth spot, we know that Cosmo cannot be playing next to Seth, so choice B is quickly eliminated. Choice B is incorrect. Let's go to other rules that pertain to our game. Rule 5 specifically states that Peter must play either first or second, so he cannot play in the fifth spot. Choice D is incorrect. Now, we don't know which of the three managers has to be eliminated, but the specific assignment of the fourth spot does tell us a couple things. First, because Roger could be playing, we know that he cannot play last, because if he plays, Hal would have to play after him. So we can

rule out choice A. Choice A is incorrect. We also know that we have to take two of the three managers, namely Dustin, Ken, and Roger. If we take Ken, then Rule 4 states that we can't take Jordan. However, if we pick Dustin and Roger, we could theoretically pick Jordan. But picking Dustin and Roger means we have to pick Hal, to play after Roger, as stated in Rule 1. In fact, in that scenario, Peter would have to play first, Roger and Hal would be second and third, respectively, and Dustin would take the last spot. So we couldn't pick Jordan in any circumstance, which rules out choice C. Choice C is incorrect. This leaves us with choice E, which we just showed to be possible in our last determination.

QUESTIONS 13–18 RELATE TO THE FOLLOWING LOGIC GAME:

Fran is planning a dinner party for six people at her house on Saturday evening. The six people will be seated around a circular table, equidistant from each other. Fran has invited her college friends: Gary, Hanna, Iris, James, and Kate. As Fran thinks about the seating arrangement for this party, she takes the following into account:

James and Gary must sit directly opposite from each other.

Fran and Kate cannot sit next to each other.

Iris should sit next to Hanna or James.

Gary and Kate must sit next to each other.

ACTION:

In this case, we have a fixed seating chart we have to arrange. Unlike in the paper link example, the first and last members of the "chain" are also adjacent, or next to each other. You can draw either a circle to represent the table or write out a chain of people, keeping in mind that the first and last members are next to each other, so you should make sure the people assigned at each end aren't violating the rules either.

SETUP:

We have six people and a six-seat table, so we don't have to worry about any empty chairs. We can write out the seating chart as so, for example, if people were sitting in alphabetical order based on first name:

F-G-H-I-J-K

In this case, we have Fran seated next to Gary, who is also seated to Hanna, and so on, until we get to Kate, who is sitting next to Fran.

We can also think of it as Seats 1–6, where Seats 1 and 6 are adjacent to each other.

RULES:

Rule 1: James and Gary must sit at opposite sides. This means that, for a six-person table, there must be two people between them on each side. Or, as a diagram, we will have one of the following 3 scenarios:

> S1: J-?-?-G-?-?
>
> S2: ?-J-?-?-G-?
>
> S3: ?-?-J-?-?-G

Rule 2: Fran and Kate cannot be in adjoining seats. The simplest way to express this is:

> Not (F-K) and Not (K-F) and Not (F in S1, K in S6) and Not (K in S1, F in S6)

This covers Fran and Kate being next to each other, especially in the case of Seats 1 and 6, which are adjacent.

Rule 3: Iris should sit next to Hanna or James, and we can write this as:

> ((I-H) or (H-I)) or ((I-J) or (J-I))

This covers all cases so that Iris is either sitting next to Hanna or she is sitting next to James.

Rule 4: Gary and Kate must sit next to each other. This is easy to express:

> G-K or K-G or (G in Seat 1, K in Seat 6) or (K in Seat 1, G in Seat 6)

13. **Answer: A.** Because we're on the first question, let's go through the various rules and see whether we can eliminate bad combinations until we're left with the one true combination. Rule 1 states that James and Gary must be seated opposite each other. So, let's look for scenarios where there are *not* two people separating the two. Scanning through the answers, we see that in choice B, only Kate separates the two, so we can rule that out. Choice B is incorrect. Rule 2 says that Fran and Kate can't sit next to each other. Going through the answer choices, we see in choice C that Fran and Kate are seated next to each other. Because that violates one of the rules, we can eliminate this choice. Choice C is incorrect. Rule 3 says that Iris must sit next to Hanna or James.

Remember, she doesn't have to sit next to *both* people to be valid. We only need one or the other, so let's analyze our three remaining choices. In choice D, Iris is sitting next to Fran and Gary, so this answer choice must be eliminated. Choice D is incorrect. Finally, Rule 4 states that Gary and Kate must sit next to each other. If we look at choices A and E, we see in choice E that Hanna separates Gary and Kate. We can rule out this selection. Choice E is incorrect. This leaves us with one potential answer choice, A, which is our correct answer.

14. **Answer: D.** In this case, we're asked to look at all possible scenarios and come up with the total list of people who could sit in the specified seat. Whenever we're asked to come up with a list like this, the handy thing to do is to use the rules to try to eliminate answers that we know *cannot* be true. In this case, we find someone who can't be on that list and rule out all instances with that person in the list. First, let's map out our scenario. We know that James and Gary must sit at opposite ends, so let's just assume that James is in Seat 1 and Gary is in Seat 4. (Because it's a circular table, this would work if we used a scenario with James in Seat 2, and so on. This one is easier to visualize.) We also know that Kate is in Seat 3, so our map looks like this:

    J-?-K-G-?-?

    Remember, we're trying to determine who *can* sit in Seat 2, the one to the right of James. Because Rules 1 and 4 have been satisfied, let's go through our other two rules. We know that Fran cannot sit next to Kate, so Fran *cannot* sit in Seat 2. This rules out choices B, C, and E. We are now left with choices A and D. Because both answer choices include Iris, we can safely assume that Iris is a possible candidate. With Iris in Seat 2, Fran and Hanna get Seats 5 and 6, in either order, and all four rules are safe. So, now, let's look at Hanna. If Hanna sits in Seat 2, Fran and Iris are left with Seats 5 and 6. However, we still have Rule 3 to consider. Iris must sit next to Hanna or James. Remember, however, that if Hanna is in Seat 6 (which leaves Fran in Seat 5), she is sitting next to James, who is in Seat 1. So Hanna could sit in Seat 2. Therefore, our answer choice is D, Hanna and Iris.

15. **Answer: A.** Let's start by identifying our new piece of information. We know that James and Iris are sitting next to each other, *and* the person also next to Iris is *not* Hanna. We know that Iris and James are a pair, like so:

    I-J

We also know that Gary and James must sit opposite each other, which means that two people separate them. If we have this solid pair of Iris and James, we can conclude that the sitting arrangement must look like this:

G-?-I-J-?-?

Now, we know that Hanna is *not* sitting in Seat 2, and we know that Kate is next to Gary, so she must be sitting in Seat 6, like so:

G-?-I-J-?-K

All we have left are Fran and Hanna. We can't have Fran in Seat 5, which would put her next to Kate (and put Hanna in Seat 2, next to Iris), so Fran must be in Seat 2 and Hanna in Seat 5, like so:

G-F-I-J-H-K

This is the only scenario that doesn't violate any of the rules, so there's only one option. (We can rule out choice E.) By looking at this seating arrangement, it is clear that Fran is sitting opposite Hanna, as two people separate them. Our answer is choice A.

16. **Answer: D.** For one of these answer choices to be true, we must *not* be able to violate the answer and come up with a valid scenario. So, for example, if choice A must be true, we must not come up with a valid solution where Gary is sitting next to Hanna. So, let's try to do that with each one.

    Choice A: G-H-?-?-?-?

We know that Gary must sit next to Kate and directly opposite James, so we get

G-H-?-J-?-K

If we put Fran in Seat 3 and Iris in Seat 5, we get this solution:

G-H-F-J-I-K

Iris is next to James, Fran and Kate are *not* next to each other, this works. Choice A is incorrect.

    Choice B: H-K-?-?-?-?

We know that Gary must sit next to Kate, so that puts him in Seat 3. According to Rule 1, James must be in Seat 6. Iris must be next to

James (because Hanna is surrounded by James and Kate), which leaves Fran in Seat 4. Graphically, it looks like this:

H-K-G-F-I-J

Choice B is incorrect.

Choice C: J-F-?-?-?-?

We know that Gary must be opposite James, which puts him in Seat 4. Kate is next to Gary in either Seat 3 or 5. However, putting Kate in Seat 3 would put her next to Fran, so let's put Kate in Seat 5. So now it looks like this:

J-F-?-G-K-?

We have Iris and Hanna left. If we put Iris in Seat 3, she's surrounded by Fran and Gary, which violates Rule 3. So, let's put Iris in Seat 6 and Hanna in Seat 3:

J-F-H-G-K-I

Choice C is incorrect.

Choice D: I-H-?-?-?-?

We know that James and Gary must be opposite each other, so in this scenario, let's place them like this:

I-H-G-?-?-J

Before we use Rule 4 to put Kate in Seat 4, let's look at something. The last two people to be assigned are Fran and Kate, and the only two seats left are adjoining ones. We cannot have Fran and Kate sitting next to each other, so we cannot come up with a valid scenario given this new rule. Therefore, we have found our answer: Choice D, Iris cannot sit next to Hanna. If we go through Choice E and put Kate next to Iris, we have Gary on Kate's left, and James on Iris's right (G-K-I-J-?-?), and Fran and Hanna take Seats 5 and 6, regardless.

17. **Answer: C.** Now that we have this extra information, let's use it, along with the existing rules, to see whether we can narrow down our scenarios and use those scenarios to determine our correct answer. Let's assume that Fran sits at Seat 1, which puts Iris at Seat 4. We know so far that our table looks like this:

F-?-?-I-?-?

But what else do we know? For starters, Kate can't be in either Seat 2 or Seat 6 because doing so would put her next to Fran. We also know that Kate *must* be next to Gary, so we can rule out some more options. If Kate can't be in Seat 2, Gary can't be in Seat 3. If Kate can't be in Seat 6, Gary can't be in Seat 5. This means that Gary *must* be either in Seat 2 or Seat 6. Given this option, we can draw out two scenarios. In the first scenario, if Gary is in Seat 2, Kate is next to him in Seat 3, James is opposite Gary, in Seat 5, and Hanna takes Seat 6. Iris is next to James, and all the rules are satisfied. In the second scenario, if Gary is in Seat 6, Kate is next to him in Seat 5, James is opposite Gary, in Seat 3, and Hanna takes Seat 2. Iris is next to James in this scenario, and all the rules are satisfied. If we draw out the two scenarios, they look like this:

F-G-K-I-J-H

F-H-J-I-K-G

Now, let's look at our answer choices:

We see that in Scenario 1, Gary sits to the right of Fran, so we can rule out choice A. We see that in Scenario 2, Kate sits to the right of Iris, so we can rule out choice B.

If we look at both scenarios together, we see that Fran is surrounded by Gary and Hanna, so we can rule out choice D. We also see that Iris is surrounded by James and Kate, so we can rule out choice E.

We're left with choice C, and both scenarios clearly show that Hanna does not and cannot sit to Iris's right (or left, for that matter).

James and Gary must sit directly opposite each other.

Fran and Kate cannot sit next to each other.

Iris should sit next to Hanna or James.

Gary and Kate must sit next to each other.

18. **Answer: D.** Sometimes, the last question of a logic game actually changes one of the rules (or adds a new rule completely) and has us solve the game with this changed/new rule. In this case, we simply need to draw out the particular scenarios by using this new rule and the other rules. If Kate sits next to Fran, we can write it as so:

K-F

But we still know that Gary sits next to Kate as well, so it looks like this:

G-K-F

We also know that James is still opposite Gary, so now the table looks like this:

G-K-F-J-?-?

Iris and Hanna fill the last two spots. Because they're next to each other, regardless of exact position, we've now satisfied all the remaining rules. So we have two scenarios:

G-K-F-J-H-I

G-K-F-J-I-H

Looking at these, either Hanna or Iris could be across from Fran. Our answer is choice D.

QUESTIONS 19–24 RELATE TO THE FOLLOWING LOGIC GAME:

The high school basketball team and its mascot are preparing to take their annual yearbook photo. The six people in the photo, from shortest to tallest, are Alex, Bob, Chris, Gary, Sam, and Willie. However, the label on the picture needs to include the person's position with his name. The six positions are center, mascot, point guard, power forward, shooting guard, and small forward. The photographer only remembers a few details from that photo shoot:

The center is not Sam and is taller than the point guard.

The mascot is taller than the shooting guard and the small forward.

The mascot is shorter than the power forward.

The point guard is taller than the small forward.

ACTION:

We are given an ordered list of six people, and we are to assign roles to each of the six names. We have rules that give us relationships between positions, and one rule regarding a person's name (the center is not Sam), and we have to use those to answer the questions in front of us. Whenever we have an ordered list and we have to assign something to each member of that list, we can expect questions such as

Which member of the list is position X?

Which member of the list *cannot* be position X?

Which is a valid list of positions for these members, in order?

Which is *not* a valid list of positions for these members, in order?

SETUP:

We have two chains here, the list of names from shortest to tallest, which can be written as follows:

A-B-C-G-S-W

Because we're talking about shortest to tallest, it would be useful to represent this with a list of < or > signs, to represent the differences between the players, like so:

A<B<C<G<S<W

Corresponding to this list, we have to assign one of six labels to each of the six players. For example, if we put the roles in alphabetical order, like the names, we would get:

A<B<C<G<S<W
C<M<PG<PF<SG<SF

As we work with our questions, let's define one shorthand method. If someone is "to the left of someone else," that means that "someone" is shorter than "someone else." Conversely, if someone is "to the right of someone else," that means that "someone" is taller than "someone else."

RULES:

We can convert each of our rules into "sub-chains" that we can string together, when possible, to form longer sub-chains. We know our maximum chain length is six people.

Rule 1: C<>Sam and C>PG

Rule 2: M>SG and M>SF

Rule 3: M<PF

Rule 4: PG>SF

Now, let's look for ways to combine rules:

Rule 1 + Rule 4: C>PG>SF
Rule 2 + Rule 3: PF>M>SG and PF>M>SF

We can also write them as < lists, as follows:

Rule 1 + Rule 4: SF<PG<C
Rule 2 + Rule 3: SG<M<PF and SF<M<PF

19. **Answer: A.** We know from our initial analysis that we have two sub-chains of the order of people:

    C>PG>SF and PF>M>SG (and PF>M>SF) or
    SF<PG<C and SG<M<PF (and SF<M<PF)

    With this new piece of information, we can now connect these chains to get a larger order of people:

    PG<SG<M<PF

    However, when we combine the SF<PG<C thread, we can see that four people are taller than the point guard, the center (PG<C), and the shooting guard, mascot, and power forward (PG<SG<M<PF). This means that the small forward is the only person shorter than the point guard, so it must be the first person, which is Alex. The correct answer is choice A.

20. **Answer: B.** Usually, the first question of a logic game involves eliminating wrong answer choices based on the rules given until we are left with a correct answer. In this case, it's the second question. Whenever we need to find one possible answer, the key is to rule out all the *impossible* answers. Therefore, let's go through the rules and rule out some answer choices:

    Rule 1: The center is not Sam and is taller than the point guard. What some people might not catch is that first part, that we can rule out Sam as the center. If we count through the list, we see that Sam is the fifth person on the list, from shortest to tallest. If we go through the answer choices, we can see that choices D and E both have center in the fifth spot. We know that cannot be possible, so we can eliminate those choices. Choices D and E are incorrect. Let's look at the second part of Rule 1. If the center is taller than the point guard, then the center must appear, on the list, to the *right* of the point guard. Let's look for instances where the center would be to the left of the point guard. Seeing none, we move on.

    Rule 2 states that the mascot is taller than the shooting guard and the small forward. Now, remember, this says *nothing* about the relationship between the shooting guard and the small forward. Therefore, we're looking for combinations where the mascot is to the *left* of either the shooting guard or the small forward because that instance would violate this rule. Going through our three remaining answers, choice C shows the mascot as shorter than the shooting guard, so we can rule out that choice. Choice C is incorrect.

Rule 3 states that the mascot is shorter than the power forward. In both our two remaining answers, the mascot is correctly put before the power forward, so there is no rule violation here.

Rule 4 states that the point guard is taller than the small forward. So, here, let's look at choices A and B and see whether either of them put the point guard before the small forward on the list. Choice A clearly does that, while B does not, so we can rule out choice A. Choice A is incorrect. This leaves us with our one correct answer, choice B.

21. **Answer: B.** Once again, we can use our new piece of information to enhance the rule sets we already know, to come up with the one correct answer. We know that the three shortest people are Alex, Bob, and Chris, or, in shorthand, A<B<C. We also know, from combining Rule 1 and Rule 4, that the small forward is shorter than the point guard, who is shorter than the center, or, in shorthand, SF<PG<C. Looking at them together, we see:

    A<B<C

    SF<PG<C

    If the center is Chris, as the question states, then the small forward has to be Alex, and the point guard has to be Bob. Therefore, our correct answer is choice B.

22. **Answer: E.** In this case, we're looking for one arrangement that *cannot* be true. Therefore, it's safe to assume that the other four answers can be true, so they don't violate any of the rules. Here, we're looking for *the first* arrangement we can find that violates at least one of the rules. So, let's go through the rules to see whether we can spot any "wrong" lists. Rule 1: PG<C. If we go through all five answers, we see that the point guard is to the left of the center in all cases, so there is *no* violation here. Rule 2. SG<M and SF<M. If we go through all five answers, we see that the shooting guard and small forward are to the left of the mascot in all cases, so there is *no* violation here. Rule 3: M<PF. If we go through all five answers here, we can see in choice E that the power forward is to the left of the mascot, which cannot be right. Therefore, we have found a combination that violates one of the rules, which is what we're looking for in this question. The correct answer for this question is choice E.

23. **Answer: D.** As in Question 21, we use this new assignment of data, and match it up to one of the sub-chains we've developed when combining applicable rules, to see what we can come up with here.

If we combine Rules 2 and 3, we devise the following order, which applies to this question:

SG<M<PF

That is, the shooting guard is shorter than the mascot, who is shorter than the power forward. We know that Gary is the shooting guard, and we also know that only two people are taller than Gary: Sam and Willie. We now also know that the mascot and the power forward are taller than the shooting guard, so we have our correlation:

SG<M<PF

G<S<W

The mascot should be Sam, so our correct answer is choice D.

24. **Answer: E.** In this case, we use the new piece of information in conjunction with the rules laid out before us to see how far we can define our order of people. We know that we have two sub-chains with one person in common, the small forward:

SF<PG<C

SF<M<PF

We also know that our order of players, by name, is as follows:

A<B<C<G<S<W

We know that the power forward is Sam, so we can make one assignment:

A<B<C<G<S<W

However, without more information, we cannot definitely assign people to the other positions. But we can place people within *ranges* of this chart and then see what we can rule out. Small forward: We know from the two sub-chains listed earlier that there are *four* people taller than the small forward: the point guard and center (SF<PG<C) and the mascot and power forward. For this to be true, the small forward must be Alex or Bob. Mascot: We know that the small forward is either Alex or Bob and the power forward is Sam. We also know that the mascot falls somewhere between the small forward and the power forward (SF<M<PF). Furthermore, we know that the mascot is taller than the shooting guard, so we cannot assume that the mascot is Bob, because that leaves only one person shorter than him (Alex), and we know from Rule 2 that there are two people shorter than the mascot. Therefore,

the mascot is either Chris or Gary. Shooting guard: Based on the last assumption that the mascot is either Chris or Gary, we know the shooting guard has to be shorter than the mascot, which means that the shooting guard can be Alex, Bob, or Chris. Point guard: We know that the point guard has to be taller than the small forward, and we've determined that the small forward has to be Alex or Bob. That means that, right now, the point guard could be Chris, Gary, or Willie, because Sam is already assigned. However, we know that the point guard is shorter than the center, so we can't offer Willie as an option for the point guard. That means the point guard must either be Chris or Gary. In summary:

Mascot: Chris or Gary

Point guard: Chris or Gary

Power forward: Sam

Shooting guard: Alex, Bob, or Chris

Small forward: Alex or Bob

It's pretty clear that the mascot and point guard are Chris and Gary, in either order, and the shooting guard and small forward are Alex and Bob, in either order. By process of elimination, we can now determine that the center is the only person *not* mentioned so far: Willie. Our answer is therefore choice E.

SECTION IV—Logical Reasoning

1. A	**9.** E	**17.** E
2. C	**10.** E	**18.** A
3. B	**11.** A	**19.** C
4. C	**12.** E	**20.** C
5. C	**13.** A	**21.** D
6. C	**14.** D	**22.** C
7. A	**15.** C	**23.** D
8. D	**16.** E	**24.** D

1. **Choice A** is correct. Zelaksen's reply indicates that he interpreted Henderkoff's remark to mean that the red rashes are indicators for only smallpox. Choice B is incorrect because it is too broad. Henderkoff made no reference to injuries or allergies in his statement, so Zelasen could not have referred to it. Choice C is incorrect. This is a logical inference from Zelasen's remark, not from Henderkoff's. Choice D is incorrect. This is a good answer, but it is not as strong as choice B because Zelasen isn't making his statement that a red rash equals smallpox. He is instead making the contention that a red rash can also be an indicator of other types of disease. Choice E is incorrect. Neither Zelasen's statement nor Henderkoff's excludes smallpox from the argument.

2. **Choice C** is correct because the oil in question lacks a single one of the criteria that defines an extra virgin olive oil. The "super premium" label on the oil does not make up for the lack of stated characteristics. Choice A is incorrect. The smooth flow of the oil qualifies this oil as extra virgin. Choice B is incorrect. The color of the oil qualifies this oil as extra virgin. Choice D is incorrect because the taste of the oil qualifies this oil as extra virgin. Choice E is incorrect because the color of the oil qualifies this oil as extra virgin.

3. **Choice B** is correct. Some workers are interns, and all workers are paid. Therefore, some who are paid are interns. Choice A is incorrect. For choice A to be true, all workers would have to be interns, which is not necessarily true. Choice C is incorrect. This statement, while it may be true, does not have to be true. Choice D is incorrect. The question specifically states that only some workers are interns. Choice E is incorrect. The fact that some workers are interns does not mean that all interns are workers, and nothing in the questions requires this to be true.

4. The reasoning used in the argument follows the pattern:

   All A = B

   Some C = B

   Therefore, some B = A

   Choice C is correct. This follows the pattern All A = B; some C = B; therefore, some B = A. Choice A is incorrect. This does not follow the pattern set forth previously. Choice B is incorrect. This does not follow the pattern set forth previously. Choice D is incorrect. This does not follow the pattern set forth previously. Choice E is incorrect. This does not follow the pattern set forth previously.

5. **Choice C** is correct. If Chiriatti's main crop flourishes in cool weather, then the local crop yield will increase. Choice A is incorrect. The director isn't claiming that the amount of money earned per crop will increase, only that the crop yield itself will increase. Choice B is incorrect because the director isn't claiming that the total amount of money earned will increase, only that the crop yield itself will increase. Choice D is incorrect as it is irrelevant that the cycle is not 100% predictable. Choice E is incorrect because it is purely speculative. Choice C is a stronger answer.

6. **Choice C** is correct because the argument excludes all explanations of how terns navigate except for magnetic fields. Choice A is incorrect. The argument does not seek to apply a rule to all subspecies of tern when it only talks about arctic terns. Choice B is incorrect as it does not pick out individual members of the group to draw conclusions about the entire arctic tern species. Choice D is incorrect. The article does not rely upon an analogy except for purposes of imagery at the start. Choice E is incorrect. There is no comparison being made between two groups of birds.

7. **Choice A** is correct because the author likens the FDA's acceptance of the claims of the chemical companies to additional claims involving saccharine. Choice B is incorrect because the author does not cite statistics and research to reach a conclusion. Choice C is incorrect. The article does not state that the author has observed the practices of the chemical industry. Choice D is incorrect. The article does not state that the author has worked with the chemical industry. Choice E is incorrect. The author does not explore alternative explanations and eliminate them.

8. **Choice D** is correct. The logical error is that if one event (the opening of a new mine) takes place before another event (the sale at DeBeers), that the mine opening caused the sale. It has not been proven that these events were necessarily related. Choice A is incorrect. No analogy is presented. Choice B is incorrect because there is no C event presented in the fact pattern. Choice C is incorrect because the two events are not equal; they differ in the type, nature, and location of the event. Choice E is incorrect. It is not implied that the DeBeers sale triggered the opening of the mine.

9. **Choice E** is correct because it most clearly demonstrates the logic in the original statement: that one event taking place triggers another event. Choice A is incorrect because it presupposes that one event takes place if another takes place, but only in a specific geographic

location. Choice E is stronger. Choice B is incorrect because it presupposes that one event takes place if another takes place, but only at specific times. Choice C is incorrect because it presupposes that one event takes place if one of two different events takes place. Choice E is still stronger. Choice D is incorrect because it really doesn't presuppose that anything changes at all!

10. **Choice E** is correct. The argument's conclusion admits that it is not based in objective facts (for example, higher tax revenue) but instead in emotion and sentimentality for small-town life and historic building design. Choice A is incorrect because the author does not appeal to any authority but directly to her readers. Choice B is incorrect because the advocate does not use analogy for her argument at all. Choice C is incorrect. The argument is not primarily drawn from direct experience with FoodCo, big-city shoppers, or Hollywood style. Choice D is incorrect. The argument is not drawn from indirect observation of any kind.

11. **Choice E** is correct. Although it was not presented up front, the argument's conclusion is simply that sharks really do sleep, even if they can't close their eyes. Choices A, B, and D are incorrect because the scope of the argument is specifically sharks, not animals in general. Choice C is incorrect. The argument doesn't focus on the difficulty of sleeping for sharks, only that they really do sleep, regardless of their lack of eyelids.

12. **Choice E** is correct. This statement could not be true. Because everyone in the family dislikes lima beans or spinach or both, if Joe likes lima beans, he must dislike spinach, and vice versa. Choice A is incorrect. This statement must be true. Because everyone in the family dislikes lima beans or spinach or both, if Carol likes spinach, she must dislike lima beans. Choice B is incorrect. Because everyone in the family dislikes lima beans or spinach or both, Joe could dislike both lima beans and spinach, and therefore this statement could be true. Choice C is incorrect. This statement must be true. Because everyone in the family dislikes lima beans or spinach or both, everyone in the family who likes lima beans must dislike spinach. Choice D is incorrect. It is possible that no one in the family dislikes spinach, so this statement could be true.

13. **Choice A** is correct because this bolsters the premise that the brand name was chosen to emphasize luxury. Choice B is incorrect as it would have provided a disincentive to name the cracker Ritzy to promote sales. Choice C is incorrect because it provides an alternate

explanation for the reason that Ritzy was chosen for the brand name. Choice D is incorrect because it shows that Ritzy connoted two terms, one positive and one negative. Choice A is a much stronger answer. Choice E is incorrect since it weakens the conclusion that the crackers acquired a new name to boost sales.

14. Your first task in answering this question is to identify the assumption underlying Sam's reasoning. The basic principle assumed by Sam is that in a series of races, where there are two horses of equal ability, each horse has a 50/50 chance of winning any given race, and therefore it is unlikely that the same horse will win three races in a row. In this question, Lilly winning the first race is represented by the letter *A*, Lilly winning the second race is represented by the letter *B*, and Lilly winning the third race is represented by the letter *C*.

 Choice D is correct. This statement best illustrates the assumptions underlying Sam's reasoning: That is, because it unlikely that Lilly win will three races in a row, given that Lilly has won the first two races, it is unlikely that she will win the third race. Choice A is incorrect. A (Lilly winning the first race) is not necessarily improbable, given that Sam assumes each horse has a 50/50 chance of winning any given race. Choice B is incorrect. As with respect to choice A, A (Lilly winning the first race) is not necessarily improbable, given that Sam assumes each horse has a 50/50 chance of winning any given race. Choice C is incorrect. This statement does not reflect the assumptions underlying Sam's reasoning. Choice E is incorrect. Although the first part of the answer ("if the joint occurrence of A, B, and C is improbable") correctly reflects the assumption underlying Sam's reasoning (that is, Sam thinks it unlikely that Lilly will win three races in a row), the second part of the answer ("then each of A, B, and C is improbable"; that is, it is unlikely that Lilly will win any of the three races) does not accurately reflect Sam's reasoning because, as noted earlier, Sam believes each horse has a 50/50 chance of winning any given race.

15. **Choice C** is correct. Because it is clear that the berries are prized by humans and are unlikely to be found in a wild patch of any size, this is a logical conclusion. Choice A is incorrect. The statement is true, but it simply restates a fact presented in the article. It does not force one to logically conclude anything. Thus choice C is a stronger answer. Choice B is incorrect. The opposite would be true because albino berries are prized. Choice D is incorrect because it is purely speculative. Choice E is incorrect because it is clear that the color does have meaning.

16. **Choice E is correct.** The fact that only zorses have black-and-white polka dots is definitive support for the conclusion stated in the question. Choice A is incorrect. The fact that zorses generally have black-and-white polka dots is not definitive support for the conclusion stated in the question. Choice B is incorrect. The fact that other black-and-white-polka-dotted animals have proved to be zorses is not definitive support for the conclusion stated in the question. Choice C is incorrect. The fact that few types of animals other than zorses have black-and-white polka dots is not definitive support for the conclusion stated in the question. Choice D is incorrect. The fact that all zorses have black-and-white polka dots is not definitive support for the conclusion stated in the question.

17. **Choice E is correct.** The fact that Joint-Vite is more expensive than Vitamin-Right, although perhaps a factor of concern to potential purchasers, does not weaken the weight of the veterinarians' recommendation. Choice A is incorrect. Only four veterinarians being surveyed would weaken the weight of the recommendation. Choice B is incorrect. If the veterinarians were paid to participate in the survey by the manufacturers of Joint-Vite, this would surely weaken the weight of the recommendation. Choice C is incorrect. If the veterinarians never actually used Joint-Vite, this would surely weaken the weight of the recommendations. Choice D is incorrect. If Joint-Vite has several negative side effects when used in dogs younger than 10, this would weaken the weight of the recommendation.

18. **Choice A is correct.** By saying "I can't afford not to pay...," Gini indicates that babysitting is worth at least $15 per hour to her. Choice B is incorrect. Nothing in the statement indicates that Gini believes $15 per hour is too much to pay a babysitter. Choice C is incorrect. Gini says "I can't afford not to hire," meaning that she feels she must hire. Nothing in the statement indicates whether Gini can or cannot afford to pay a babysitter. Choice D is incorrect. Nothing in the statement indicates that most babysitters earn more than $15 per hour. Choice E is incorrect. Nothing in the statement indicates that Gini believes Benjamin should pay for the babysitter.

19. **Choice C is correct.** You can logically infer from the statement that before December 31, 2006, a passport was not required for U.S. citizens re-entering the United States from Canada. Choice A is incorrect. The statement focuses solely on U.S. citizens entering the United States from Canada. This answer choice does not constitute a logical inference based on the statement. Choice B is incorrect. The statement focuses solely on U.S. citizens entering the United States from Canada.

This answer choice does not constitute a logical inference based on the statement. Choice D is incorrect. The statement focuses on reentry to the United States from Canada, not travel to Canada. As such, this answer choice does not constitute a logical inference based on the statement. Choice E is incorrect. The statement says nothing about the requirements for entry to the United States from countries other than Canada. As such, this answer choice does not constitute a logical inference based on the statement.

20. **Choice C** is correct. The fact that the valley can only support half as many people strengthens the conclusion that the land has been degraded. Choice A is incorrect because the conclusion that the land is degraded is not supported strongly by a change in population density. Choices B and D are incorrect. They strengthen the premise that slash-and-burn agriculture is bad in general, but they do not strengthen the overall conclusion that the land in the Marchetti Valley has been degraded for over 2,000 years. Choice E is incorrect because it only claims that peasants degraded the land in Roman times, not over 2,000 years.

21. **Choice D** is correct. If the density and diversity of life are the same as before, it is unlikely that the land has been degraded. Choice A is incorrect. The fact that a given cause is less destructive than before does not significantly weaken the overall conclusion. Choice B is incorrect because all it does is describe a corrective action that does little, if anything, to weaken the conclusion that the land has been degraded. Choice C is incorrect. That this corrective action has to be taken strengthens the conclusion that the land has been degraded because it proves that the soil is washing into the sea. Choice E is incorrect because it only specifies that the valley has the same number of people in it as before. It does not address the state of the land in the valley and so is a weaker answer than Choice D.

22. **Choice C** is correct because the admissions officer believes that when the applicant says his average grade is better than a B, it means that the applicant got only A's or B's. Choice A is incorrect. The admissions officer is aware that admission is justified only if each individual grade is B or better, not if the average is a B or better. Choice B is incorrect because the admissions officer is aware that admission is justified only if each individual grade is B or better. Choice D is incorrect. This choice is more vague than choice C because it is unclear whether the choice means that the admissions officer believes that all of the applicant's individual grades are better than a B or whether the average of the grades is better than a B. Choice C is a stronger answer. Choice E

is incorrect. As with Choices A and B, the admissions officer is aware that admission is justified only if each individual grade is B or better. Choice C remains the strongest answer.

23. **Choice D** is the correct answer. In choice D, Shaker chairs (a general group) tend to be sturdy (usually have a general quality), and the chair I bought yesterday (specific item) is sturdy (has the same general quality), so that chair (the specific item) must be a Shaker chair (a member of the general group). Thus D's reasoning parallels that of the initial argument most closely. Choice A is incorrect because the third sentence of the answer does not match the reasoning of the example argument. Choice B is incorrect because like and love are two different levels of preference. Choice C is incorrect because it does not parallel the reasoning of the initial argument, even though it involves similar subject matter. Choice E fails because the fact that the squirrel is not of the kind that normally can't fly doesn't mean that it can therefore fly.

24. **Choice D** is correct. The argument asserts that it is the other areas of the South (the Carolinas and Gulf states) that have contributed techniques to cook and flavor food that have been important in the rise of Cajun cooking's popularity. Choices A and C are incorrect. To say that the only good Cajun cooking currently found is in the South in general and not in New Orleans is too extreme. Choice B is incorrect because the assertions are about the history of the cuisines of these areas affecting Cajun cooking, not about chefs of the area in general. Also, it is an overreach to state that all chefs of the region directly affected the development of Cajun cooking or its current popularity. Choice E is incorrect because no assertions are made in the argument about Northern cooking.

Practice Exam 4

SECTION I—Analytical Reasoning

Time—35 minutes

24 Questions

Directions: Each group of questions in this section is based on a set of conditions. In answering some of the questions, it may be useful to draw a rough diagram. Choose the response that most accurately and completely answers each question and blacken the corresponding space on your answer sheet.

NOTE TO LSAT EXAM CRAM READERS

Several of the questions you'll find in this final practice test are considerably harder than what will be found on any actual LSAT. Do not be overly concerned if you run into difficulty, given the level of the challenge. Allowing you to practice with more difficult questions will prepare you for whatever the LSAT creators decide to do.

QUESTIONS 1–6 RELATE TO THE FOLLOWING SCENARIO:

Four greyhounds are assigned to four consecutive races—Races 1, 2, 3, and 4. Each greyhound has a number cloth of a different color, and each one is assigned to just one race. The greyhounds' names are Speedy, Bullet, Whitey, and Rocket. The colors of the number cloths are blue, red, yellow, and white. The following conditions apply:

Speedy is assigned to a lower-numbered race than is Bullet, and at least one race separates the two.

Whitey is assigned to Race 2.

Rocket's number cloth is white.

1. Which one of the following greyhound/number cloth pairs could be assigned to the first race?
   - ❑ A. Speedy, wearing a blue number cloth
   - ❑ B. Speedy wearing a white number cloth
   - ❑ C. Bullet, wearing a blue number cloth
   - ❑ D. Bullet, wearing a white number cloth
   - ❑ E. Rocket, wearing a yellow number cloth

2. If the greyhound wearing the blue-colored number cloth is assigned to a higher-numbered race than Rocket, which one of the following statements *cannot* be true?
   - ❑ A. Speedy is assigned to a lower-numbered race than is the greyhound wearing the red-colored number cloth.
   - ❑ B. Whitey is assigned to a lower-numbered race than is the greyhound wearing the blue-colored number cloth.
   - ❑ C. Whitey is assigned to a lower-numbered race than is the greyhound wearing the yellow-colored number cloth.
   - ❑ D. The greyhound wearing the red-colored number cloth is assigned to a lower-numbered race than is the greyhound wearing the blue-colored number cloth.
   - ❑ E. The greyhound wearing the yellow-colored number cloth is assigned to a lower-numbered race than is Whitey.

3. If Rocket is assigned to a lower-numbered race than is Bullet, which one of the following statements could be false?
   - ❑ A. Speedy is assigned to a lower-numbered race than is Rocket.
   - ❑ B. Bullet is assigned to Race 4.
   - ❑ C. Either the greyhound wearing the blue-colored number cloth or the greyhound wearing the yellow-colored number cloth is assigned to a lower-numbered race than Rocket.
   - ❑ D. The greyhound wearing the red-colored number cloth is assigned to a lower-numbered race than Rocket.
   - ❑ E. Rocket is assigned to Race 3.

4. What is the maximum possible number of different greyhounds and color combinations, any one of which could be assigned to Race 4?

❑ A. 2
❑ B. 3
❑ C. 4
❑ D. 5
❑ E. 6

5. If the greyhound wearing the red-colored number cloth is assigned to a higher-numbered race than is Rocket, then which one of the following statements could be false?

❑ A. Bullet is assigned to a higher-numbered race than is the greyhound wearing the blue-colored number cloth.

❑ B. Bullet is assigned to a higher-numbered race than is the greyhound wearing the yellow-colored number cloth.

❑ C. Rocket is assigned to a higher-numbered race than is the greyhound wearing the yellow-colored number cloth.

❑ D. The greyhound wearing the yellow-colored number cloth is assigned to a higher-numbered race than is the greyhound wearing the blue-colored number cloth.

❑ E. Rocket is assigned to a higher-numbered race than is the greyhound wearing the blue-colored number cloth.

6. If Whitey is wearing a red-colored number cloth, none of the following is a possible greyhound/number cloth color/race number combination *except*

❑ A. Speedy/yellow/Race 1; Whitey/red/Race 2; Bullet/blue/Race 3; Rocket/white/Race 4

❑ B. Whitey/red/Race 1; Speedy/blue/Race 2; Rocket/white/Race 3; Bullet/yellow/Race 4

❑ C. Speedy/yellow/Race 1; Whitey/white/Race 2; Rocket/red/Race 3; Bullet/yellow/Race 4

❑ D. Rocket/white/Race 1; Whitey/red/Race 2; Speedy/yellow/Race 3; Bullet/blue/Race 4

❑ E. Bullet/yellow/Race 1; Whitey/red/Race 2; Rocket/white/Race 3; Speedy/blue/Race 4

QUESTIONS 7–11 RELATE TO THE FOLLOWING SCENARIO:

At the Northeast Regional Club rally, each of eight members of the Garrison Club—Dee, Eve, Fran, Genevieve, Hannah, Irene, Jessica, and Kendall (known as the Garrison Club Kids)—will participate in two events, a potato race and an eating contest. For each of these events, the eight Garrison Club Kids are grouped into four two-person teams, subject to the following conditions:

If two Garrison Club Kids are teammates in the potato race, they cannot also be teammates in the eating contest.

Fran and Irene are teammates in the potato race.

Eve and Fran are teammates in the eating contest.

Jessica and Kendall are not teammates in either event.

7. Which one of the following is a pair of Garrison Club Kids who *cannot* be teammates in the eating contest but who could be teammates in the potato race?
   - ❑ A. Dee and Hannah
   - ❑ B. Eve and Jessica
   - ❑ C. Fran and Kendall
   - ❑ D. Hannah and Genevieve
   - ❑ E. Hannah and Irene

8. If Genevieve and Hannah are teammates in the potato race and Dee and Jessica are teammates in the eating contest, which one of the following is a pair that must be teammates in the potato race?
   - ❑ A. Dee and Eve
   - ❑ B. Dee and Kendall
   - ❑ C. Eve and Fran
   - ❑ D. Eve and Kendall
   - ❑ E. Irene and Kendall

9. Which one of the following could be a list of the four teams participating in the potato race?
   - ❑ A. Dee and Fran; Eve and Kendall; Genevieve and Irene; Hannah and Jessica
   - ❑ B. Dee and Genevieve, Eve and Hannah; Fran and Irene; Jessica and Kendall
   - ❑ C. Dee and Genevieve; Eve and Jessica; Fran and Kendall; Hannah and Irene
   - ❑ D. Dee and Genevieve; Eve and Kendall; Fran and Irene; Hannah and Jessica
   - ❑ E. Dee and Hannah; Eve and Fran; Genevieve and Jessica; Irene and Kendall

10. If Hannah and Eve are teammates in the potato race and Hannah and Irene are teammates in the eating contest, then each of the following lists a pair of Garrison Club Kids who must be teammates in one of the two events *except*
   - ❑ A. Dee and Genevieve
   - ❑ B. Dee and Jessica
   - ❑ C. Dee and Kendall
   - ❑ D. Genevieve and Jessica
   - ❑ E. Genevieve and Kendall

11. If Dee and Hannah are teammates in the potato race, then Genevieve could be the teammate of

   ❑ A. Eve in the potato race and Kendall in the eating contest

   ❑ B. Fran in the potato race and Kendall in the eating contest

   ❑ C. Jessica in the potato race and Fran in the eating contest

   ❑ D. Kendall in the potato race and Eve in the eating contest

   ❑ E. Kendall in the potato race and Hannah in the eating exercise

QUESTIONS 12–18 RELATE TO THE FOLLOWING SCENARIO:

The Thunderbolts U10 Boys' AYSO surfing team is having its team photo taken. Seven members of the team are present for the photo: Alex, Brian, Chris, Dylan, Evan, Frank, and Giles. The team photographer lines them up from left to right in a straight line in positions from 1 to 7, in accordance with the following conditions:

   Alex and Brian do not stand next to each other.

   Exactly two boys stand between Chris and Alex.

   Dylan and Alex stand next to each other.

   Frank and Brian do not stand next to each other.

   Chris's position is exactly two places to the left of Brian's position.

12. Which one of the following is an acceptable arrangement of Thunderbolts team members, from left to right?

   ❑ A. Alex, Dylan, Chris, Evan, Brian, Giles, Frank

   ❑ B. Alex, Dylan, Frank, Chris, Evan, Brian, Giles

   ❑ C. Alex, Frank, Dylan, Brian, Evan, Chris, Giles

   ❑ D. Evan, Alex, Dylan, Giles, Chris, Frank, Brian

   ❑ E. Frank, Evan, Dylan, Alex, Brian, Giles, Chris

13. If Giles stands in Position 1, then Evan must stand

   ❑ A. Between Brian and Chris

   ❑ B. Between Dylan and Giles

   ❑ C. Next to Alex

   ❑ D. Next to Frank

   ❑ E. In position 7

14. If Giles stands next to Alex, which one of the following *cannot* be true?

   ❑ A. Brian stands in position 7.

   ❑ B. Dylan stands in position 1.

   ❑ C. Dylan stands between Alex and Frank.

   ❑ D. Evan stands between Chris and Dylan.

   ❑ E. Giles stands between Alex and Frank.

15. If Evan stands in Position 7, how many boys stand between Evan and Giles?

- ❏ A. One
- ❏ B. Two
- ❏ C. Three
- ❏ D. Four
- ❏ E. Five

16. If Dylan and Evan stand next to each other, how many boys are standing between Giles and Frank?

- ❏ A. One
- ❏ B. Two
- ❏ C. Three
- ❏ D. Four
- ❏ E. Five

17. If Giles stands next to Frank, how many boys are standing between Brian and Evan?

- ❏ A. None
- ❏ B. One
- ❏ C. Two
- ❏ D. Three
- ❏ E. Four

18. Which one of the following *cannot* be true?

- ❏ A. Alex stands next to both Dylan and Giles.
- ❏ B. Brian stands next to both Evan and Giles.
- ❏ C. Evan stands next to both Brian and Chris.
- ❏ D. Frank stands next to both Alex and Giles.
- ❏ E. Giles stands next to both Alex and Evan.

QUESTIONS 19–24 RELATE TO THE FOLLOWING SCENARIO:

On Sunday afternoons, the Wine Cellar hosts a wine tasting. Customers are allowed to sample seven different varieties of wines: Ross Reserve, Simon Cabernet, Tivoli Shiraz, Umami Pinot Noir, Valerian Merlot, Wyatt Chardonnay, and Xaviar House Blend. Customers can select the order in which they will taste the different types of wine, according to the following conditions:

The Valerian Merlot must always be served some time after the Umami Pinot Noir.

The Simon Cabernet must be served exactly two tastings before the Tivoli Shiraz.

The Wyatt Chardonnay must be served some time before the Simon Cabernet.

The Valerian Merlot must be served either fifth for sixth.

The Ross Reserve must be served second.

19. Which one of the following sequences would be an acceptable order in which the wine is delivered?

- ❑ A. Umami Pinot Noir, Ross Reserve, Wyatt Chardonnay, Xaviar House Blend, Simon Cabernet, Valerian Merlot, Tivoli Shiraz
- ❑ B. Umami Pinot Noir, Ross Reserve, Xaviar House Blend, Simon Cabernet, Valerian Merlot, Tivoli Shiraz, Wyatt Chardonnay
- ❑ C. Wyatt Chardonnay, Ross Reserve, Simon Cabernet, Umami Pinot Noir, Valerian Merlot, Tivoli Shiraz, Xaviar House Blend
- ❑ D. Wyatt Chardonnay, Ross Reserve, Umami Pinot Noir, Valerian Merlot, Simon Cabernet, Xaviar House Blend, Tivoli Shiraz
- ❑ E. Wyatt Chardonnay, Simon Cabernet, Umami Pinot Noir, Tivoli Shiraz, Valerian Merlot, Ross Reserve, Xaviar House Blend

20. Which one of the following is a complete and accurate list of the order in which Tivoli Shiraz can be served?

- ❑ A. Fifth or sixth
- ❑ B. Fourth, fifth, or sixth
- ❑ C. Fifth, sixth, or seventh
- ❑ D. Third, fifth, sixth, or seventh
- ❑ E. Third, fourth, fifth, sixth, or seventh

21. If Valerian Merlot is served fifth, then which one of the following must be true?

- ❑ A. Simon Cabernet is served third.
- ❑ B. Tivoli Shiraz is served fourth.
- ❑ C. Umami Pinot Noir is served third.
- ❑ D. Wyatt Chardonnay is served first.
- ❑ E. Xaviar House Blend is served seventh.

22. Which one of the following conditions would make it possible to determine the exact ordering of the wines served?

- ❑ A. Simon Cabernet must be served fourth.
- ❑ B. Tivoli Shiraz must be served fifth.
- ❑ C. Valerian Merlot must be served sixth.
- ❑ D. Wyatt Chardonnay must be served first.
- ❑ E. Xaviar House Blend must be served seventh.

23. If Valerian Merlot is served sixth, then which one of the following *cannot* be true:

- ❑ A. Simon Cabernet is served fifth.
- ❑ B. Tivoli Shiraz is served seventh.
- ❑ C. Umami Pinot Noir is served fifth.
- ❑ D. Wyatt Chardonnay is served third.
- ❑ E. Xaviar House Blend is served first.

24. If Xaviar House Blend is served third, which one of the following must be true?

- ❑ A. Simon Cabernet is served fourth.
- ❑ B. Tivoli Shiraz is served seventh.
- ❑ C. Umami Pinot Noir is served first.
- ❑ D. Valerian Merlot is served fifth.
- ❑ E. Wyatt Chardonnay is served fourth.

THIS IS THE END OF THE SECTION.

SECTION II—Logical Reasoning

Time—35 minutes

24 Questions

Directions: The questions in this section are based on the reasoning contained in brief statements or passages. For some questions, more than one of the choices could conceivably answer the question. However, you are to choose the best answer—that is, the response that most accurately and completely answers the question. You should not make assumptions that are by commonsense standards implausible, superfluous, or incompatible with the passage. After you have chosen the best answer, blacken the corresponding space on your answer sheet.

1. Amtrak has recently announced that it is discontinuing its complimentary food. A survey of passengers on the Washington, D.C., to Boston route conducted during July asked passengers to rank various factors in order of importance to them in deciding whether to choose Amtrak or fly. The factors listed were complimentary food service, cost, frequent rider program discounts, on-time performance, and convenience of terminal location. Over 75% of those survey ranked on-time performance and cost as either the first, second, or third factors in their decisions. Fewer than 10% placed the complimentary food service above fifth. As a result, Amtrak management has determined that complimentary food service is not important to Amtrak customers and therefore has decided to eliminate it.

All of the following, if true, weaken the basis for management's conclusion *except*

   ❑ A. The passengers on the Washington, D.C., to Boston route are not representative of passengers on other Amtrak routes.

   ❑ B. The number of passengers who completed the survey was not statistically significant.

   ❑ C. Complimentary food service is not offered on the Washington, D.C., to Boston route.

   ❑ D. On the Washington, D.C., route, fares are lower than airline prices, and on-time performance is better than that of airlines that fly the same route.

   ❑ E. Of the 10% who placed complimentary food service above fifth, 9% placed it fourth.

2. Russell: To be a good lawyer, you have to be articulate.

Tamara: I don't agree. It takes much more than just being articulate to be a good lawyer.

Tamara has interpreted Russell's statement to mean which one of the following?

   ❑ A. If a person is articulate, he or she will be a good lawyer.

   ❑ B. Some good lawyers are articulate.

   ❑ C. Some articulate people make good lawyers.

   ❑ D. If a person is a good lawyer, he or she will be articulate.

   ❑ E. A person cannot be a good lawyer unless he or she is articulate.

3. Due to the prolonged heat wave being experienced in our region, the electricity company has had to institute rolling brownouts during daylight hours. Even still, the cost of electricity has risen significantly. The average electric bill has risen $50 a month for the past three months. Three months from now, our electricity bill will be enormous.

Which one of the following best states the flaw in the author's reasoning?

   ❑ A. It bases a conclusion on unreliable statistics.

   ❑ B. It fails to specify how much an enormous electricity bill would be.

   ❑ C. It assumes that the conditions experienced in the past three months will continue for the next three months.

   ❑ D. It fails to take into account the reasons why the electricity company has instituted rolling brownouts.

   ❑ E. It fails to define what constitutes a significant rise in the cost of electricity.

4. Tarik says: Every time I eat tofu, I get an upset stomach. Therefore, tofu is disgusting.

Which one of the following most closely parallels the logic of the preceding statement?

❑ A. All zorses are black and white. Therefore, zorses are zebras.

❑ B. I have been bitten three times by a shark. Therefore, sharks are dangerous.

❑ C. Every eighth-grade kid in the class is mean. Therefore, all kids in the eighth grade are mean.

❑ D. I smoke cigarettes, but I am healthy. Therefore, smoking cigarettes does not cause cancer.

❑ E. I made less money this year than last year. Therefore, the amount I will be required to pay in taxes will be lower.

5. Lions that eat fresh zebra meat every day have excellent manes and good teeth. Since the lion keepers at the Bronx Zoo feed their lions only dried food or cooked beef, they cannot have good teeth. Therefore, their teeth should be brushed every day to prevent decay.

Which one of the following contains reasoning most similar to that in the preceding statement?

❑ A. A woman who uses both Nexus shampoo and conditioner has shiny and healthy hair. Because Elizabeth uses Aprell shampoo and conditioner, she cannot have healthy hair. Therefore, she should visit the hair salon to have her hair cut.

❑ B. Soccer players who attend soccer summer camp generally make the school soccer team. Because Andrew has a private soccer coach, he is a better soccer player. Therefore, he will make the varsity team this year.

❑ C. Late-model sports cars in Westchester generally sell for over $25,000 if they are in excellent condition and have low miles. Jennifer's late-model sports car is in excellent condition and has low miles. Therefore, Jennifer's sports car will sell for more than $25,000.

❑ D. Hay that has been cut and baled after a rain is very susceptible to mold. Because Gail was not able to cut and bale her hay until after it rained, her hay is likely to get moldy.

❑ E. Fires that start during the night are often caused by arson, but fires that start during the day are often accidental. Because this fire started during the day, it is accidental.

6. If a student attends Varhard College, then he or she must be smart.

If the preceding statement is true, which one of the following statements can be reasonably inferred from it?

❑ A. The student in question attended Varhard College.

❑ B. The student in question is smart.

❑ C. The majority of students attending Varhard College are male.

❑ D. There are no students at Varhard College who are not smart.

❑ E. The majority of students attending Varhard College are smart females.

7. The electricity rates in Peekskill are high only for the first 100 kilo-watts used each month. The next 100 kilowatts cost half as much, and all electricity over 200 kilowatts costs one quarter as much as the first 100 kilowatts. Peekskill is in a moderate climate, and there is not very much variation in temperature between winter and summer. Electric heaters and air conditioners are equally efficient from an electricity standpoint. To heat an average-size home in the winter with electricity is not very expensive, but it is more expensive than using gas or oil heat.

All of the following are logical conclusions based upon the above *except*

❑ A. It takes about as much electricity to heat a house in Peekskill during the winter as it does to cool it during the summer.

❑ B. More residents of Peekskill use oil or gas to heat their homes than electricity.

❑ C. A resident of Peekskill who uses more than 200 kilowatts of electricity a month may have a lower average per-kilowatt rate than a resident who uses only 90 kilowatts per month.

❑ D. More residents of Peekskill use electricity to cool their homes than use electricity to heat their homes.

❑ E. A resident of Peekskill who uses 200 kilowatts of electricity in a month pays less for that electricity than a resident of Peekskill who uses only 100 kilowatts in a month.

8. To do well on the LSAT, you should take a practice exam every day and keep track of the questions that you do not answer correctly.

Which one of the following best summarizes the assumption on which the preceding conclusion is based?

❑ A. Everyone makes mistakes.

❑ B. The more you practice, the better you do.

❑ C. To err is human, to forgive divine.

❑ D. Practicing enables you to identify what you do not know and learn from your mistakes.

❑ E. Prep courses are necessary to do well on the LSAT.

9. Most hit movies are of low intellectual value; therefore, *Cutthroat Island*, a very unpopular movie, is probably of high intellectual quality.

Which one of the following is most parallel to the logic expressed in the preceding statement?

❑ A. Most polar bears are found in cold climates; therefore, all cold climates probably have polar bears.

❑ B. Most people who go on the South Beach Diet stop smoking. If Caroline does not go on the South Beach Diet, she will probably continue smoking.

❑ C. Most new cars have a built-in DVD player in the back seat. Tina's car is new, but it does not have a built-in DVD player.

❑ D. Most types of spam have declined since the passage of the CAN-SPAM Act; therefore, the CAN-SPAM Act probably has been effective in deterring spam.

❑ E. Most countries that are run by dictators experience rampant corruption. Therefore, the country of Abuc, which is run by a dictator, probably experiences rampant corruption.

10. Ralph: My son Brian is taking the bar exam in California this week. I'm a little bit worried because I checked the statistics and found that out only 50% passed the last time the exam was given.

Bonnie: You shouldn't worry so much. Your son went to the law school at Extremely Good University, and I just read an article in *American Lawyer* that 80% of the students from Extremely Good University Law School passed the California bar exam the first time they took it.

Which one of the following is most likely to be the most reliable estimate of Brian's chances of passing the California bar exam, based on the preceding information?

❑ A. 30%

❑ B. 40%

❑ C. 50%

❑ D. 65%

❑ E. 80%

11. A recent book I read examines claims that some dogs can understand human speech at a level equal to that of a typical human five-year-old. According to the book, few of these claims are backed up by impartial scientific experiments. The few tests that were conducted indicated that dogs were responding to nonverbal cues rather than actually understanding human language.

Which one of the following can be inferred from the preceding statement?

❑ A. No dog can understand human speech.

❑ B. All dogs respond to nonverbal cues.

❑ C. A typical dog has a better vocabulary than a three-year-old boy.

❑ D. No dog has been scientifically proven to understand human language.

❑ E. Dogs have been conclusively shown to be capable of understanding human speech.

12. Bienecke, a lobbyist, has criticized the proposal that government should subsidize health care costs for the working poor. Yet investigation reveals that Beinecke's own health care costs have been subsidized by the government. Therefore, we should ignore Bienecke's criticism.

Which one of the following expresses erroneous reasoning most similar to that expressed in the preceding statement?

- ❑ A. Simon, a kindergarten teacher, has suggested that that soda should not be sold in elementary schools. But Simon drinks soda during lunch at the school all the time, so we shouldn't pay any attention to his suggestion.
- ❑ B. Dubois, a state senator, is the sponsor of legislation to reduce taxes on oil refineries. Dubois owns an oil refinery. Therefore, we shouldn't vote for that legislation.
- ❑ C. Smith, an architect, recommends that the architectural drawings be redone. Smith is an excellent architect, so we should heed his advice.
- ❑ D. Canter, a baseball player, has lied before, so we should discount his testimony before the Congressional committee.
- ❑ E. Squire, an employee, is not a very productive worker, so we shouldn't grant Squire's request for a raise.

13. A recent study reveals that Internet advertising does not significantly affect consumer preferences with respect to caffeinated versus decaffeinated energy drinks. The study compared two groups of male adults, ages 21–30. One group went online regularly and was frequently exposed to Internet advertising. The other group never used the Internet. Both groups strongly preferred caffeinated energy drinks, which are frequently advertised on the Internet.

Which one of the following, if true, most weakens the preceding conclusion?

- ❑ A. The preference for caffeine can be influenced by factors such as advertising.
- ❑ B. The preferences of males ages 21–30 who do not use the Internet are influenced by the preferences of males ages 21–30 who do use the Internet.
- ❑ C. Most of the members of the group that used the Internet were already familiar with the advertisements for caffeinated energy drinks.
- ❑ D. Both groups rejected decaffeinated energy drinks even though these were also heavily advertised on the Internet.
- ❑ E. Energy drink preferences of children who use the Internet are known to be very different from the energy drink preferences of children who do not use the Internet.

14. Kittens ordinarily prefer moist food to dry food. However, if one feeds a six-month-old kitten dry food rather than moist food, over a period of about six months, it will develop a preference for dry food and refuse to eat moist food. Therefore, a cat's eating habits can be affected by the type of food to which it has been exposed as a kitten.

The preceding conclusion is based on which one of the following assumptions?

- ❏ A. One-year-old cats do not naturally prefer dry food to moist food.
- ❏ B. A cat's eating habits naturally change as it gets older.
- ❏ C. The dry food fed to kittens must taste good.
- ❏ D. Moist food is better for kittens than dry food.
- ❏ E. Cats naturally prefer dry food to moist food.

15. Babies during their first six months spend much of their time sleeping. They seem to awaken only to eat and cry. Yet babies develop so much during their first six months.

Which one of the following, if true, most helps to explain the preceding situation?

- ❏ A. Babies have a greater need to sleep than older children.
- ❏ B. Babies of all species sleep a lot during the first six months.
- ❏ C. Babies do not have to be awake to develop.
- ❏ D. A baby's need to eat is greater than the need to sleep.
- ❏ E. Babies who cry a lot develop more quickly than babies who do not.

16. Options R Us is the financial services firm you should use to trade stock options. People who trade stock options using Options R Us make twice as much money as people who don't trade stock options using Options R Us.

Which one of the following patterns of reasoning is most similar to that in the preceding statement?

- ❏ A. Peanut oil is the best oil for stir-frying Chinese food. If you don't use peanut oil, the food won't taste good.
- ❏ B. Breath Clean is the gargle of choice for those people who want clean-smelling breath. People who gargle with Breath Clean have much cleaner-smelling breath than people who are unconcerned about the way their breath smells.
- ❏ C. If you're looking for a washing machine, the Wash'm Good Washer is the one to choose. The latest issue of *Washing Machine Manufacturer* magazine rates them No. 1 in terms of efficiency and cost.
- ❏ D. When grilling hamburgers, you should not add salt until after the hamburgers have already cooked. Otherwise, the hamburgers will be dry.
- ❏ E. Diet-Rite for Dogs is the best dog food for dogs who are overweight. Dogs that eat Diet-Right for Dogs lose twice as much weight as dogs that eat Lo-Cal for Dogs.

17. Matthew: The WMB brand of car is the best car. In *Car Magazine* tests, it lasted the longest and generally required the fewest repairs of any other type of car.

    Allison: That can't be right. I used to own a WMB, and that car needed more repairs than any of the other types of cars I've ever owned.

    Which one of the following best illustrates why the reasoning in Allison's response to Matthew is flawed?

    ❏ A. Allison's response contradicts Matthew's claim, based on unreliable evidence.

    ❏ B. Allison's response rejects a reasonable generalization, based on the experience of a single person.

    ❏ C. Allison's response offers an unfounded claim of expertise.

    ❏ D. Allison's response does not attempt to refute Matthew's claim.

    ❏ E. Allison's response is not based on the same grounds as Matthew's claims.

18. Five hundred high school students were asked to read a short story (Story A) during first period. Later that day, during seventh period, they reread Story A and then read a second short story (Story B), and they were asked which one they liked better. The survey found that more than 400 students reported that they liked Story B better. These results support the theory that people prefer reading something that is new to them compared to reading it more than once.

    Which one of the following, if true, most supports the preceding theory?

    ❏ A. Two-thirds of a group of high school students who read only Story A in the morning and then read both Story A and Story B later in the same day preferred Story A.

    ❏ B. Seventy-five percent of a group of high school students who read Story A and Story B (having read both previously) preferred Story A.

    ❏ C. The 500 high school students who read Story A in the morning and both Story A and Story B in the afternoon were members of the high school reading club.

    ❏ D. Of 300 students who read both Story A and Story B in the morning and read Story B in the afternoon, 250 students preferred Story A.

    ❏ E. Many of the high school students who read Story A in the morning said afterward that they found it boring.

19. In a recent referendum, the citizens of Uoush voted to repeal all property taxes. However, the cost of providing public education is financed entirely out of property taxes. Uoush wishes to continue to provide a public education for its children. Therefore, if property taxes are eliminated, the entire cost of financing public education will have to be paid for out of an increase in state income taxes.

The preceding conclusion is based on which one of the following assumptions?

❑ A. If property taxes are not eliminated, there will be no need to increase state income taxes.

❑ B. The cost of providing a public education will be less if it is financed by property taxes rather than state income taxes.

❑ C. If property taxes are eliminated and state income taxes are increased, there will be less emphasis on quality education.

❑ D. The referendum in which the voters of Uoush voted to repeal property taxes was unconstitutional.

❑ E. There are no other sources of fund available to pay for the financing of public education other than an increase in state income taxes.

20. Because the building has more children than apartments, and every child lives in an apartment, it must be true that at least one of the apartments contains more than one child.

Which one of the following most closely parallels the pattern of reasoning in the preceding statement?

❑ A. Because in Rarum there are more cars than garages, and every car must be parked off the street, it must be true that at least one of the garages must be a two-car garage.

❑ B. At least one of the pens in the chicken coop must contain more than one chicken, because the chicken coop has more chickens than pens, and every chicken lives in a pen.

❑ C. Because puppies outnumber kittens, and every family has at least one pet, it must be true that every family has puppies.

❑ D. Because every year the number of college graduates has increased, it must be true that the number of college graduates will also increase.

❑ E. Every car has at least four wheels, and every motorcycle has two wheels, so it must be true that cars have more wheels than motorcycles.

21. Chuck: The profit we made this year should only be used for research and development of new products.

Angela: I disagree. We should use the profit to expand our marketing efforts with respect to our existing product line.

On the basis of the preceding, about which one of the following issues do Chuck and Angela disagree?

❑ A. Using the profit for research and development is a waste of resources.

❑ B. Unless new products are developed, there will be no future profits.

❑ C. There is a better way to use the profit than using it for research and development for new products.

❑ D. Expanded marketing efforts with respect to the existing product line will lead to future profits.

❑ E. The profit should be saved, not spent.

22. The Gagemort Real Estate company experienced difficulties with its largest real estate development project, and it lost quite a bit of money in the process. Therefore, I am advising Big to focus on developing several smaller projects instead.

Which one of the following, if true, provides the most support for the preceding conclusion?

❑ A. Large real estate development projects are much more financially lucrative than small development projects.

❑ B. Large real estate development projects require more resources and are more complex than smaller projects, and they therefore present a higher level of risk.

❑ C. Small real estate development projects are more inherently satisfying on a personal level than large real estate projects.

❑ D. The cost of completing all types of real estate development projects is increasing.

❑ E. Several smaller projects are equivalent in every way to one big project.

23. Anthony will agree to join the baseball team only if Dylan also joins the baseball team and the other members of the team promise to make Dylan the captain. However, although Dylan is willing to join the team, the other team members are not willing to promise to make Dylan the captain of the team. Therefore, Anthony will not agree to join the team.

Which one of the following most closely parallels the logic expressed in the preceding?

❑ A. Patty will work with Steve on the report only if Kim also works on the report. However, Kim will not work on the report, so neither will Patty.

❑ B. Lilly will go outside with Lucy only if the weather is above 60 degrees and it is not raining. However, although it is not raining, it is only 50 degrees, so Lilly will stay inside.

❑ C. Sam and Jana will bake the cake if Jana returns home from work by 8:00. If Jana does not return home by then, Sam will bake the cake with Dean.

❑ D. Peter was supposed to do the presentation, but he is not feeling well. Because Peter cannot make the presentation, either Thomas or Andrew will do it.

❑ E. James will buy a Corvette if Samuel lends him the money and he can find a red one in excellent condition for less than $25,000. However, although Samuel is willing to lend him the money, and although James was able to find a red Corvette, it was not in excellent condition, and it was not less than $25,000. Therefore, James will not buy it.

24. A study was recently conducted to determine the impact, if any, of the current aggressive police enforcement of laws against using a cell phone while driving on accident rates. Since the police began their campaign last month, accident rates have decreased by 15% from the previous month. Therefore, the decrease in the number of people who drive while using their cell phones has reduced the number of accidents.

Which one of the following, if true, most seriously weakens the preceding conclusion?

❏   A. The police campaign was heavily reported in the local news and in local newspapers.
❏   B. The cost of a ticket for using a cell phone while driving is $500.
❏   C. The police campaign focused on the most heavily traveled highways in the city.
❏   D. Police also stopped drivers if they were not wearing seat belts.
❏   E. Police only stopped drivers if they were using cell phones and also speeding.

THIS IS THE END OF THE SECTION.

SECTION III—Logical Reasoning

Time—35 minutes

24 Questions

Directions: The questions in this section are based on the reasoning contained in brief statements or passages. For some questions, more than one of the choices could conceivably answer the question. However, you are to choose the best answer—that is, the response that most accurately and completely answers the question. You should not make assumptions that are by commonsense standards implausible, superfluous, or incompatible with the passage. After you have chosen the best answer, blacken the corresponding space on your answer sheet.

1. The mast on *Magic*, a Santa Cruz 52 sailboat, was too long to be stored in the Viking Boatyard's boathouse. Fortunately, the mast can now be stored in the boathouse, thanks to the efforts of the mastmaker, who has figured out a way to disassemble the mast into two parts for storage while allowing it to be reassembled later without any impact on its functionality.

   The preceding argument depends on which one of the following assumptions?

   ❑ A. The mast can be separated into two equal-sized parts.
   ❑ B. Neither of the two separated parts of the mast is too big to fit into the boathouse.
   ❑ C. The cost of separating the mast into two parts will not be more than the cost of replacing the mast in the event that it breaks.
   ❑ D. Nothing in the boathouse will have to be removed in order to make room for the mast.
   ❑ E. It is imperative that the mast be stored in the boathouse.

2. The best-tasting carpaccio requires beef from cows that have been fed solely on grass. When beef is obtained from cows that have eaten food other than grass, chefs are unable to ensure that their products do not contain antibiotics, and taste tests have shown that only carpaccio that is free of antibiotics gets top marks on taste tests.

The claim that only carpaccio that is free of antibiotics can get top marks on taste tests plays which one of the following roles in the argument?

❑ A. It constitutes the argument's conclusion.

❑ B. It is a statement that must be negated in order to support the conclusion.

❑ C. It is an assumption upon which the argument depends.

❑ D. It is a logical inference based on the conclusion.

❑ E. It serves to support the argument's conclusion.

3. Ann: Once we get the new HVAC system fully installed, we will be able to heat, cool, and ventilate the building much more easily and efficiently. So I recommend that, if necessary, we borrow funds in order to install the system as soon as possible.

Jane: I think we should keep our current HVAC system for as long as possible. I don't believe the time and money spent to install the new system would be worth it at this point.

Ann and Jane disagree about which one of the following issues?

❑ A. Whether it is possible to install a new HVAC system

❑ B. When the new HVAC system should be installed

❑ C. Whether the current HVAC system works adequately

❑ D. Whether borrowing money to install the new HVAC system is advisable

❑ E. Whether the new HVAC system will be as efficient as advertised

4. Nurse: I disagree with Dr. Collins's evaluation of Tina Johnson. Dr. Collins has advised that Tina should have cosmetic surgery on her nose because it will make her feel better about herself. I don't think that Tina's parents can't afford to pay Dr. Collins for the procedure, let alone the cost of the hospital stay.

Which one of the following best describes the flaw in the reasoning of the conclusion?

❑ A. The evidence on which the conclusion is based is derived solely from personal knowledge.

❑ B. The conclusion fails to consider the best interests of the patient.

❑ C. The conclusion is based solely on the assumption that the patient's family cannot afford the treatment.

❑ D. The conclusion constitutes a personal attack.

❑ E. The conclusion is based on a claim that has been contradicted by the evidence.

5. KP Tweedy, a leading thoroughbred racehorse trainer, relies heavily on income from his major clients, and he would have been forced to shut down his stable this year if any of his major clients left the stable. However, KP not only has been able to keep his stable going, but he has just announced that he has purchased a new farm in Ocala, Florida, to provide a base of operations for the winter.

If this statement is true, which one of the following must also be true?

- ❑ A. KP Tweedy won the lottery this year.
- ❑ B. None of KP Tweedy's major clients left his stable this year.
- ❑ C. KP Tweedy's racehorses were very successful this year.
- ❑ D. KP Tweedy added additional clients this year.
- ❑ E. All of KP Tweedy's major clients were pleased with his performance this year.

6. The New York Yankees have announced that henceforth they will hire only former major league baseball players as coaches, based on the principle that those who instruct must thoroughly understand the subject matter and only a person who has actual experience in a subject matter can thoroughly understand it.

Which one of the following is most applicable to the principle relied upon in the preceding argument?

- ❑ A. New York Medical College announces that it will hire only professors with Ph.D.s.
- ❑ B. Julliard College announces that it will hire as a theater instructor only someone who has appeared in a Broadway show.
- ❑ C. The Nantock Public School superintendent announces that she will hire only male gym instructors.
- ❑ D. IBM announces that it will hire only graduates with M.B.A.s.
- ❑ E. The IRS announces that it will hire only taxpaying U.S. citizens as tax examiners.

7. If book revenues have increased at Phoenix Press in August, then either book prices or the number of books sold have increased for the month, but not both. If the number of books sold has increased in August, the marketing director of Phoenix Press will receive a bonus. If book revenues have not increased in August, then the marketing director will not receive a bonus.

If all of the preceding statements are true, which one of the following can be concluded from the fact that the marketing director of Phoenix Press did not receive a bonus?

- ❑ A. Book prices have increased in August.
- ❑ B. Book revenues have increased in August.
- ❑ C. Book revenues have not increased in August.
- ❑ D. The number of books sold has increased in August
- ❑ E. The number of books sold has not increased in August.

8. For the last five years, it has been illegal to drive a motorcycle without a helmet in the state of Wyoming. All of the members of the Freedom Riders Motorcycle Club must live in Wyoming and have ridden a motorcycle without a helmet at least once in the last year. The Freedom Riders Motorcycle Club is currently considering several new members.

Which one of the following can be logically inferred from the preceding information?

 ❑ A. The current members of the Freedom Riders Motorcycle Club have ridden their motorcycles illegally at least once during the past year.

 ❑ B. Every current member of the Freedom Riders Motorcycle Club has ridden his or her motorcycle without a helmet outside of Wyoming.

 ❑ C. No one under consideration for membership in the Freedom Riders Motorcycle Club has legally ridden a motorcycle without a helmet within Wyoming.

 ❑ D. Current members of the Freedom Riders Motorcycle Club who have never ridden their motorcycle without a helmet outside of Wyoming have broken the law at least once.

 ❑ E. The Freedom Riders Motorcycle Club does not include members who have ridden a motorcycle without a helmet legally within Wyoming.

9. The south region in the country of Renzsuela has been experiencing a recession. When asked about the economic condition of the region's York County, the premier of finance in Renzsuela asserted that its stagnant economy reflected the inescapable effects of the recession for all counties in the region. But that cannot be true because nearby Duke County's economy is as healthy as ever, despite the overall current economic issues plaguing the region.

Which one of the following, if true, most helps to explain why the economy of York County is experiencing difficulties while the economy of Duke Country is not.

 ❑ A. Several small financial services firms have moved from York County to Duke County since the recession began.

 ❑ B. The economy of York County generates more revenue than the economy of Duke County, even during a recession.

 ❑ C. York County's economy relies primarily on manufacturing, which has been particularly affected by the recession, while Duke County's economy relies primarily on tourism, which has been largely unaffected.

 ❑ D. The economic recession in the south region has been more severe than the recession in the west region of Renszuela.

 ❑ E. York County and Duke County both have similar population levels.

10. Companies that use a rotating three-shift program hope to maximize production, but this program causes employees to be feel tired all the time. Employees are able to work efficiently only if they do not feel tired all the time. Therefore, the rotating three-shift program does not increase production and should be discontinued.

Which one of the following arguments offers reasoning most similar to that of the preceding argument?

- ❏ A. New York imposes a state income tax to increase state revenues, but some people who do not like taxes move away rather than pay taxes to the state. Despite this, New York's state revenues are usually higher than those of states that do not have a state income tax, and therefore state incomes taxes are worthwhile.

- ❏ B. Environmental laws are intended to protect the environment, but in many cases they are not enforced. Laws must be enforced in order to be effective. Therefore, in order to be effective, environmental laws must be enforced.

- ❏ C. Regulations that require that all equestrians wear a safety helmet while mounted are aimed at those riders who are not sufficiently safety conscious. However, such regulations infringe on freedom of choice and therefore should be ignored.

- ❏ D. The DARE (Drug Abuse Resistance Education) program aims to convince children to avoid drugs but causes many children to feel as if the adults are lecturing to them. Children will listen to advice only if they feel they are not being lectured to. Therefore, the DARE program is not effective and should be abandoned.

- ❏ E. Car alarms are supposed to prevent burglaries, but often they just end up annoying the people who must listen to them. People should pay more attention when a car alarm goes off.

11. A car that is not aerodynamic and does not get good gas mileage cannot be considered a good car. A car with an efficient engine will get good gas mileage, so the presence of an efficient engine in a car ensures that it is a good car.

The preceding argument can be faulted for which one of the following errors of reasoning?

- ❏ A. It fails to establish that the presence of an efficient engine means that the car is aerodynamic.

- ❏ B. It fails to establish that some cars without efficient engines can be considered good cars.

- ❏ C. It fails to establish that a car can be aerodynamic only if it has an efficient engine.

- ❏ D. It fails to establish that good gas mileage means the car has an efficient engine

- ❏ E. It fails to establish that some cars that are aerodynamic and get good gas mileage may not be good cars.

12. Last year, Carol and Ken agreed that they would take on a new book project only when they were both prepared to devote themselves fully to the project. At the beginning of last month, Carol assumed that Ken was ready to do so, but it now appears that she was mistaken: Ken just agreed to assume a visiting professorship at Big College University for the year, and that will take up most of his time and energy.

Which one of the following is a logical conclusion for the preceding argument?

- ❏ A. Ken was never really interested in taking on a new book project with Carol.
- ❏ B. Taking on a new book project involves even longer hours than Ken would be required to devote to the visiting professorship.
- ❏ C. Carol is prepared to take on a new book project this year.
- ❏ D. Ken and Carol will not take on a new book project this year.
- ❏ E. Carol was wrong when she assumed that Ken was ready to commit himself to a new book project.

13. Medical device manufacturers have recently been testing a new form of stent that will widen the arteries of patients suffering from heart disease. The manufacturers announced their confident belief that patients who are suffering from heart disease will be cured through the use of such stents.

The preceding conclusion is based on which of the following assumptions?

- ❏ A. Using stents is the safest way to help patients suffering from heart disease.
- ❏ B. Doctors who learn of the tests will implant the stents in patients suffering from heart disease.
- ❏ C. There are no methods of alleviating heart disease other than using stents.
- ❏ D. Manufacturing the stents will be financially lucrative for medical device manufacturers.
- ❏ E. Medical device manufacturers need to adequately test devices before marketing them.

14. A magazine that wants to increase the productivity of its magazine authors should pay them for each article they write rather than pay them an annual salary. Magazine authors who are paid $1,000 per article, for example, will have more incentive to write as many articles as possible, compared to magazine authors who know they will receive the same annual salary no matter how many articles they write.

The preceding conclusion assumes which one of the following?

- [ ] A. Most magazines pay their authors an annual salary.
- [ ] B. Most magazines want to increase the productivity of their authors.
- [ ] C. Magazine authors who know they will receive an annual salary have less incentive to write articles than do magazine authors who are paid on a per-article basis.
- [ ] D. Magazine authors prefer their pay to be based on the number of articles they write.
- [ ] E. Magazine authors can be motivated to increase their productivity through monetary rewards.

15. A bill to ban the hunting of foxes with dogs has recently been introduced before the New Jersey State legislature. Fran, a fervent believer in animal welfare, recently sent the following email to those members of the legislature who have announced their opposition to the bill: "Before you cast a negative vote on the Fox Hunting Bill, consider what it would feel like to be chased for miles and miles, until you could no longer breathe, and then ripped to shreds by a pack of dogs."

Which one of the following best describes Fran's method of argument?

- [ ] A. She provides evidence to undercut the rationale of her opponents.
- [ ] B. She makes an emotional appeal.
- [ ] C. She makes a personal attack on her opponents.
- [ ] D. She presents a conclusion supported by specific evidence.
- [ ] E. She derides the viewpoint of her opponents.

16. On Block Island, Rhode Island, deer have greatly proliferated, stripping the land of the pine firs that form the majority of their diet. Many of the deer appear to be affected with chronic wasting disease. To stabilize the ecology of the area without having to shoot the deer, scientists have suggested introducing a natural predator, such as the gray wolf.

Which one of the following, if true, is most damaging to the argument?

- [ ] A. Gray wolves have never been known to live on Block Island.
- [ ] B. The deer on Block Island are habituated to dogs and do not fear them.
- [ ] C. Residents of Block Island oppose the introduction of the gray wolf.
- [ ] D. Gray wolves will not hunt prey that is diseased.
- [ ] E. Gray wolves are themselves endangered.

17. Simon to Theodore: If you voluntarily take an action that you know creates a risk, you are responsible for the consequences of that action.

If Simon applies the preceding principle to Theodore's behavior, which one of the following statements is true?

❑ A. Theodore is responsible for his dog getting loose because even though his sister left the door open, Theodore knew that his dog might run outside.

❑ B. Theodore is responsible for his father's flat tire because even though his father ran over the nails, Theodore left them on the driveway, knowing that the nails were sharp.

❑ C. Theodore is not responsible for getting sick because even though he went to visit his sick aunt, he tried to take precautions.

❑ D. Theodore is responsible for losing his bike because even though he thought it safe in his garage, someone stole it.

❑ E. Theodore is responsible for getting good grades in school because that's his job.

18. A poll of members of the American Yacht Club showed that a majority of those polled believed that the club was spending an appropriate percentage of its budget on food services. Therefore, any increase in the amount of the club's budget should not be spent on food services.

Which one of the following best describes the flaw in the preceding reasoning?

❑ A. The conclusion fails to take into account the total amount of the club's budget.

❑ B. The evidence cited in the argument cannot be considered to be reliable.

❑ C. The conclusion confuses amount spent with percentage spent.

❑ D. The conclusion fails to consider other possibly valid alternatives.

❑ E. The conclusion is based on a generalization that is contradicted by the evidence.

19. All golfers have excellent hand–eye coordination. Alex is a major league baseball player. Therefore, Alex should be a good golfer.

Which one of the following is most similar to the preceding erroneous pattern of reasoning?

❑ A. Anyone who can ride a bicycle can, with practice, learn to ride a horse. John rides a bicycle very well. Therefore, he should be able to learn how to ride a horse very quickly.

❑ B. People with long fingers are well suited to playing the piano. Everyone in Stephanie's family has long fingers. Therefore, Stephanie would be well suited to playing the piano.

❑ C. People who are good at playing the trumpet must have excellent lung capacity. Ian is a very good glassblower. Therefore, Ian would make a good trumpet player.

❑ D. All people in the book industry love books. Alice loves books. Therefore, she must be in the book industry.

❑ E. All professors must be articulate. Ken is a professor. Therefore, he must be articulate.

20. Angela has won the M & S Bowling Finals for three years straight. But this year, Linda beat Angela. You can conclude from this fact that Linda trained very hard.

    The preceding conclusion follows logically if which one of the following is assumed?

    ❏ A. Angela is usually a better bowler than Linda.

    ❏ B. If Angela trained harder, she would have won the bowling finals.

    ❏ C. Linda won because Angela did not bowl in the bowling final.

    ❏ D. Angela did not train as hard as Linda trained.

    ❏ E. Linda could beat Angela only if she trained very hard.

21. Due to the wide number of U2 songs being downloaded off the Internet, sales of U2 CDs have decreased precipitously.

    Which one of the following most closely parallels the preceding reasoning?

    ❏ A. Due to the wide variety of DVDs now available, sales of DVD players have increased.

    ❏ B. Due to the introduction of its new low-fare brand Delta Song, many seats on regular Delta flights are empty.

    ❏ C. Due to the cheaper cost of labor overseas, many companies are now outsourcing American jobs.

    ❏ D. Due to the competition between Pepsi and Coke, neither brand has dominated market share.

    ❏ E. Due to the decreased availability of oranges, sales of orange juice have decreased.

22. Edith: The only way to get a Supreme Court clerkship is to be editor-in-chief of the Law Review or number one in the class ranking at one of the top five law schools in the country.

    Lisa: You're wrong. My friend Mary is a clerk for one of the justices on the U.S. Supreme Court, and she didn't even go to a top-five law school. She told me she got the clerkship because of her political connections.

    Lisa uses which one of the following techniques to counter Edith's argument?

    ❏ A. She attempts to change the grounds of the argument.

    ❏ B. She offers a counterexample to Edith's claim.

    ❏ C. She offers a counterclaim supported by an analogy.

    ❏ D. She attempts to undermine Edith's argument by making a personal attack on Edith's character.

    ❏ E. She offers an unsupported generalization as an alternative to Edith's claim.

23. Last month, as a result of a mad pig scare, all pigs in the province of Atrebla were destroyed, eliminating the province's pork supply. Since then, the only meat available for consumption in Atrebla are beef, mutton/lamb, and poultry products.

If the preceding is true, which one of the following statements must also be true?

❏ A. Most of the residents of Atrebla are poultry eaters.

❏ B. Before the mad pig scare, the residents of Atrebla ate less pork than any other kind of meat.

❏ C. Residents of Atrebla prefer mutton and beef to pork.

❏ D. No pork has been imported to Atrebla for consumption since the pigs in Atrebla were destroyed.

❏ E. The destruction of all pigs in the province of Atrebla severely impacted Atrebla's economy.

24. Foozeball fans don't know how much pain a varsity foozeball player endures. Injuries such as sprained thumbs and jammed fingers might normally warrant a player leaving the game. But as a point of professional pride, players never show pain, and many varsity foozeball players live with serious pain on a daily basis. It is also an unspoken rule that they never leave buddies to fend for themselves on the field. Because of these pressures, it is highly unlikely that varsity players will miss a single play when they get hurt, let alone a game.

Which of the following, if true, gives the most support to the preceding argument?

❏ A. Varsity foozeball teams remove injured players rather than let them continue to play.

❏ B. Foozeball referees are required by rule to call an extended timeout if any player is injured on the field.

❏ C. Given the money that most varsity foozeball players make, they would be wise to just sit out of the game when they get hurt.

❏ D. The average fan suffers just as many serious injuries as the average foozeball player.

❏ E. Most varsity foozeball players who are injured during a game do not leave that particular game for any extended period of time.

THIS IS THE END OF THE SECTION.

SECTION IV—Reading Comprehension

Time—35 minutes

27 Questions

Directions: Each passage in this section is followed by a group of questions to be answered on the basis of what is stated or implied in the passage. For some of the questions, more than one of the choices could conceivably answer the question. However, you are to choose the best answer—that is, the response that most accurately and completely answers the question—and blacken the corresponding space on your answer sheet.

With one notable exception, no therapeutic effects have been achieved in gene therapy trials to date. The first successful gene therapy occurred in a recent French study in which a therapeutic transgene for correcting X-linked severe combined immune deficiency was
5　introduced into the bone marrow cells of children, resulting in improved function of their immune systems and correction of the disease. This encouraging success aside, the generally disappointing results are due, in part, to the inherent limitations of adult and cord blood stem cells. In principle at least, the use of human embryonic
10　stem cells might overcome some of these limitations, but further research will be needed to determine whether embryonic stem cells are better suited to meet the needs of gene therapy applications than are adult stem cells.

One important feature of the optimal cell for delivering a therapeutic
15　transgene would be its ability to retain the therapeutic transgene even as it proliferates or differentiates into specialized cells. Most of the cell-based gene therapies attempted so far have used viral vehicles to introduce the transgene into the hematopoietic stem cell. One way to accomplish this is to insert the therapeutic transgene into the one of
20　the chromosomes of the stem cell. Retroviruses are able to do this, and for this reason, they are often used as the vehicle for infecting the stem cell and introducing the therapeutic transgene into the chromosomal DNA. However, mouse retroviruses are only efficient at infecting cells that are actively dividing. Unfortunately, hematopoietic
25　stem cells are quiescent. The percentage of stem cells that actually receive the therapeutic transgene has usually been too low to attain a

therapeutic effect. Because of this problem, investigators have been exploring the use of viral vehicles that can infect nondividing cells, such as lentiviruses (e.g., HIV) or adeno-associated viruses. This

30   approach has not been entirely successful, however, because of problems relating to the fact that the cells themselves are not in an active state.

One approach to improving the introduction of transgenes into hematopoietic stem cells has been to stimulate the cells to divide so

35   that the viral vehicles can infect them and insert the therapeutic transgene. Inder Verma of the Salk Institute has noted, however, that this manipulation can change other important properties of the hematopoietic stem cells, such as plasticity, self-renewal, and the ability to survive and grow when introduced into the patient. This

40   possibility might be overcome with the use of embryonic stem cells if they require less manipulation. And, in fact, some preliminary data suggest that retroviral vectors may work more efficiently with embryonic stem cells than with the more mature adult stem cells. For example, researchers have noted that retroviral vectors introduce

45   transgenes into human fetal cord blood stem cells more efficiently than into cord blood stem cells from newborns, and that the fetal cord blood stem cells also had a higher proliferative capacity. This suggests that fetal cord blood stem cells might be useful in cell-based, in-utero gene therapy to correct hematopoietic disorders before birth.

50   In some cases—such as a treatment of a chronic disease—achieving continued production of the therapeutic transgene over the life of the patient will be very important. Generally, however, gene therapies using hematopoietic stem cells have encountered a phenomenon known as "gene silencing," where, over

55   time, the therapeutic transgene gets "turned off" due to cellular mechanisms that alter the structure of the area of the chromosome where the therapeutic gene has been inserted. Whether the use of embryonic stem cells in gene therapy could overcome this problem is unknown, although preliminary evidence suggests that this

60   phenomenon may occur in these cells as well.

Source: Excerpt from Stem Cells: Scientific Progress and Future Research Directions. Department of Health and Human Services. June 2001. http://stemcells.nih.gov/info/scireport.

1. Which one of the following would be the best title for the passage?
   - ❏ A. "The Failure of Gene Therapy"
   - ❏ B. "The Successes of Gene Therapy"
   - ❏ C. "Challenges in Effectively Delivering Gene Therapy"
   - ❏ D. "The Uses of Retroviruses in Gene Therapy"
   - ❏ E. "The Use of Embryonic Stem Cells in Gene Therapy"

2. Which one of the following best describes the author's attitude toward the use of human embryonic stem cells in gene therapy?
- ❑ A. Judgmental
- ❑ B. Neutral
- ❑ C. Diffident
- ❑ D. Disdainful
- ❑ E. Incredulous

3. From the passage, you can infer that all of the following are true about hematopoietic stem cells *except*:
- ❑ A. It has proven difficult to introduce transgenes into hematopoietic stem cells.
- ❑ B. It is possible to change the properties of hematopoietic stem cells.
- ❑ C. Hematopoietic stem cells normally actively divide.
- ❑ D. Mouse retroviruses cannot be effectively used to insert therapeutic transgenes into the chromosomes of a hematopoietic stem cell.
- ❑ E. Gene silencing makes using hematopoietic stem cells for gene therapy problematic.

4. The author of the passage is likely to agree with all of the following statements *except*:
- ❑ A. Initial attempts at actually implementing gene therapy have been disappointing.
- ❑ B. It is not clear whether embryonic stem cells are any better suited for gene therapy than adult stem cells.
- ❑ C. The use of cord blood stem cells for gene therapy is problematic.
- ❑ D. The viruses that cause HIV are too dangerous to be used in gene therapy.
- ❑ E. Treatment of chronic diseases is likely to require continued production of the therapeutic transgene over the life of the patient.

5. According to the passage, which of the following is the most promising?
- ❑ A. The use of retroviral vectors with embryonic stem cells
- ❑ B. The use of mouse retroviruses to infect hematopoietic stem cells
- ❑ C. The use of embryonic cells to combat gene silencing
- ❑ D. The use of adeno-associated viruses to infect non-dividing cells
- ❑ E. Simulating hematopoietic stems cells to divide

6. Which one of the following best expresses the meaning of the word *quiescent* as it is used in line 25 of the passage?
- ❑ A. Inactive
- ❑ B. Mobile
- ❑ C. Lifeless
- ❑ D. Active
- ❑ E. Proliferative

7. According to the passage, all of the following are limitations on the use of adult and newborn cord blood stem cells in gene therapy *except*:

☐ A. The inability of the stem cells to retain the therapeutic transgene as it proliferates or differentiates into specialized cells

☐ B. The inability of the stem cells to actually receive the therapeutic transgene

☐ C. The fact that the stem cells themselves are not in an active state

☐ D. The "gene-silencing phenomenon"

☐ E. The failure of stem cells to contain chromosomal DNA

While the Constitution of the United States divides all power conferred upon the Federal Government into "legislative powers," the "executive power," and the "judicial power," it does not attempt to define those terms. To be sure, it limits the jurisdiction of federal courts to "cases"

5   and "controversies," but an executive inquiry can bear the name "case" and a legislative dispute can bear the name "controversy." Obviously, then, the Constitution's central mechanism of separation of powers depends largely upon common understanding of what activities are appropriate to legislatures, to executives, and to courts. One of

10   those landmarks is the doctrine of standing. Though some of its elements express merely prudential considerations that are part of judicial self-government, the core component of standing is an essential and unchanging part of the case or controversy requirement of Article III.

15   Over the years, our cases have established that the irreducible constitutional minimum of standing contains three elements: First, the plaintiff must have suffered an "injury in fact"—an invasion of a legally protected interest which is (a) concrete and particularized, and (b) "actual or imminent, not 'conjectural' or 'hypothetical.' Second,

20   there must be a causal connection between the injury and the conduct complained of. Third, it must be "likely," as opposed to merely "speculative," that the injury will be "redressed by a favorable decision."

The party invoking federal jurisdiction bears the burden of establishing

25   these elements. Because they are not mere pleading requirements but rather an indispensable part of the plaintiff's case, each element must be supported in the same way as any other matter on which the plaintiff bears the burden of proof, *i.e.*, with the manner and degree of evidence required at the successive stages of the litigation. At the

30   pleading stage, general factual allegations of injury resulting from the defendant's conduct may suffice. In response to a summary judgment motion, however, the plaintiff can no longer rest on such "mere allegations," but must "set forth" by affidavit or other evidence "specific facts," which for purposes of the summary judgment motion

35   will be taken to be true. And at the final stage, those facts (if controverted) must be "supported adequately by the evidence adduced at trial."

40   When the suit is one challenging the legality of government action or inaction, the nature and extent of facts that must be averred (at the summary judgment stage) or proved (at the trial stage) in order to establish standing depends considerably upon whether the plaintiff is himself an object of the action (or forgone action) at issue. If he is, there is ordinarily little question that the action or inaction has caused him injury, and that a judgment preventing or requiring the action will

45   redress it. When, however, as in this case, a plaintiff's asserted injury arises from the government's allegedly unlawful regulation (or lack of regulation) of someone else, much more is needed. In that circumstance, causation and redressability ordinarily hinge on the response of the regulated (or regulable) third party to the government

50   action or inaction—and perhaps on the response of others as well. The existence of one or more of the essential elements of standing "depends on the unfettered choices made by independent actors not before the courts and whose exercise of broad and legitimate discretion the courts cannot presume either to control or to predict"

55   and it becomes the burden of the plaintiff to adduce facts showing that those choices have been or will be made in such manner as to produce causation and permit redressability of injury. Thus, when the plaintiff is not himself the object of the government action or inaction he challenges, standing is not precluded, but it is ordinarily "substantially

60   more difficult" to establish.

Source: Excerpt from Manuel Lujan, Jr., Secretary of the Interior, Petitioner v. Defenders of Wildlife et al. (United States Supreme Court opinion, No. 90-1424, June 12, 1992)

8. Which one of the following most accurately expresses the main idea of the passage?
   ❑ A. Standing is an essential component of federal jurisdiction.
   ❑ B. Federal courts only have jurisdiction over cases and controversies.
   ❑ C. Plaintiffs seeking federal jurisdiction bear the burden of proof.
   ❑ D. It is hard to establish standing when a suit is challenging the legality of government action or inaction.
   ❑ E. Summary judgment motions require a higher burden of proof.

9. According to the passage, all of the following are elements of establishing standing *except*:
   ❑ A. A legally protected interest
   ❑ B. An interest that is concrete and particularized
   ❑ C. An actual, imminent, or hypothetical invasion of the interest
   ❑ D. The conduct complained of being a causative factor in the injury
   ❑ E. An injury that is likely to be corrected by a decision in favor of the plaintiff

10. The author is likely to disagree with all of the following statements *except*:

- ❏ A. The Constitution clearly defines what constitutes legislative powers, executive power, and judicial power.
- ❏ B. The doctrine of standing is unrelated to the issue of separation of powers.
- ❏ C. In order to establish standing, a plaintiff need only make general factual allegations of its various elements without having to prove any of them.
- ❏ D. When the plaintiff is the object of a government action or inaction, standing is more difficult to establish.
- ❏ E. Separation of powers depends in major part on a common understanding of what activities are appropriate to each of the three branches of government.

11. Which one of the following best expresses the meaning of the word *adduce* as it is used in line 55 of the passage?

- ❏ A. Withhold
- ❏ B. Dispute
- ❏ C. Cite
- ❏ D. Gainsay
- ❏ E. Controvert

12. The case described in the passage involves which one of the following?

- ❏ A. A suit challenging the legality of a government action in which the plaintiff is an object of the action
- ❏ B. A suit challenging the legality of a government inaction in which the plaintiff is an object of the foregone action
- ❏ C. A suit challenging the legality of a government's regulation of someone other than the plaintiff
- ❏ D. A suit challenging the constitutional minimum of standing
- ❏ E. A suit between two private parties

13. According to the passage, all of the following are true with respect to standing *except*:

- ❏ A. Every element of the doctrine of standing is an essential part of the case and controversy requirement of the Constitution.
- ❏ B. There is an irreducible constitutional minimum of standing.
- ❏ C. The requirements to establish standing change, depending on the type of case involved.
- ❏ D. The requirements to establish standing change, depending on the phase of the case.
- ❏ E. The doctrine of standing helps to define the separation of powers.

A social and political e-commerce issue likely to persist into the foreseeable future is Microsoft's dominance (which some characterize as monopolistic) of the computer software platform market and the potential extension of that dominance into various areas of e-commerce.

5 Monopolies can have many social and economic benefits. For instance, consumers and societies benefit from network economies, which occur when there is a single set of system standards that everyone uses, such as a single telephone standard, a single electricity standard, and a single railroad standard. Monopolies can also have social costs, and

10 in the United States they have been officially frowned upon since the Sherman Anti-Trust Act of 1890 broke up the steel monopoly of J.P. Morgan and later the oil monopoly of John Rockefeller. Monopolies can engage in predatory pricing behavior to drive competitors out of business, threaten new entrants to the marketplace, and raise prices

15 above what a competitive marketplace would produce. As a result, they can stifle innovation. The Sherman Anti-Trust Act does not declare monopolies illegal, but it does proscribe monopolistic anticompetitive behavior intended to either create or sustain a monopoly.

20 Since the early 1990s, the U.S. Department of Justice has been monitoring Microsoft's market behavior. It has found a consistent pattern of monopolistic and anticompetitive behavior. For instance, in 1994, Microsoft consented to a Justice Department decree that it stop tying the purchase of one product to that of another, such as the

25 operating system to an office productivity suite. In 1996, the Justice Department began investigating Microsoft's dominance of the operating system and browser markets, and in particular the tying together of the operating system and the browser. In October 1997, the Justice Department filed a petition against Microsoft, alleging it was

30 violating the 1994 consent decree by forcing PC manufacturers to install the Internet Explorer browser as a condition of offering Windows. In May 1998, the Justice Department and various state attorneys filed an antitrust lawsuit against Microsoft, claiming it was engaging in illegal, anticompetitive practices to destroy competition. In

35 June 2000, a U.S. District Judge found Microsoft guilty of violating antitrust laws in the operating system and browser markets, and recommended breaking up the company into two parts. Microsoft has recently abandoned its anticompetitive licensing practices that forced PC manufacturers to display Microsoft icons on the desktop and

40 discarded plans for the Windows XP operating system to use SmartTags to link users of Microsoft Office tools to Microsoft websites and services.

The question is: Do we, as a society, want Microsoft to dominate the e-commerce environment just as it has dominated the operating

45 system and browser marketplace? If .NET and .NET MyServices succeed, Microsoft will not only supply the operating system of all your devices, the browser, and office productivity tools, but will also supply

all the vital e-commerce and personal information management tools
required to lead a digital life. The centerpiece of these
50   strategies—Passport—will supply your digital ID and will handle
the payment process as well for much of B2C e-commerce. Microsoft
will become the centralized repository of personal identifiable
information for tens of millions of e-commerce consumers.

Some extraordinary consumer benefits will result from these services.
55   Many of the digital information silos will disappear, e-commerce
transaction costs will fall, and consumers will have greater control over
their personal information.

However, .NET and .NET MyServices raise some very interesting
questions. If .NET and .NET MyServices succeed, it is likely that other
60   firms will not be able to compete with Microsoft in providing similar
services because Microsoft already controls the operating system and
the browser. Microsoft may, as it has in the past, engage in
monopolistic anticompetitive behavior through its licensing process.
For instance, it may refuse to license .NET and .NET MyServices to
65   websites that also use competing services.

Do we want a single company to dominate e-commerce authentication
and payment services? Passport stores your vital personal and
payment information on Microsoft servers, but who watches over
Microsoft? Can market forces and consumer opinion work by
70   themselves to keep Microsoft in check?

Source: Excerpt from "There's a Hailstorm in Your Future," in E-commerce.
business.technology.society, First Edition, © Kenneth C. Laudon and Carol Guercio Traver, 2002;
permission granted

14. Which one of the following best expresses the main point of the
passage?
- ❑ A. Monopolies have social and economic benefits as well as costs.
- ❑ B. Microsoft's past market behavior raises concerns about the potential impact of its .NET and .NET MyServices strategies.
- ❑ C. Microsoft's market behavior is anti-competitive.
- ❑ D. Extraordinary consumer benefits may result if .NET and .NET MyServices are successful.
- ❑ E. Microsoft dominates the e-commerce environment.

15. Which of the following best describes the function of the third paragraph of the passage?
- ❑ A. It provides evidence in support of a contention.
- ❑ B. It contradicts the thesis of the passage.
- ❑ C. It attempts to reconcile two conflicting schools of thought.
- ❑ D. It presents a viewpoint different from that of the author.
- ❑ E. It provides possible explanations for a paradox.

16. According to the passage, all of the following are potentially negative impacts of monopolies *except*:
   - ❏ A. Driving competitors out of business
   - ❏ B. Threatening new entrants to the marketplace
   - ❏ C. Raising prices above what a competitive marketplace would produce
   - ❏ D. Stifling innovation
   - ❏ E. Network economies

17. The author is likely to agree with all of the following statements *except*:
   - ❏ A. Microsoft dominates the computer software platform market.
   - ❏ B. Passport is the centerpiece of Microsoft's .NET and .NET MyServices strategies.
   - ❏ C. If .NET and .NET MyServices succeed, Microsoft may engage in monopolistic anticompetitive behavior.
   - ❏ D. Market forces and consumer opinion are enough in and of themselves to check Microsoft's market behavior.
   - ❏ E. If .NET and .NET MyServices succeed, extraordinary consumer benefits will result.

18. Which one of the following best describes the author's attitude toward Microsoft?
   - ❏ A. Condemnatory
   - ❏ B. Skeptical
   - ❏ C. Encomiastic
   - ❏ D. Unctuous
   - ❏ E. Disparaging

19. All of the following are facts stated in the passage *except*:
   - ❏ A. Microsoft has engaged in monopolistic anticompetitive behavior through its licensing process.
   - ❏ B. Monopolies are illegal under the Sherman Anti-Trust Act.
   - ❏ C. Passport stores personal and payment information on Microsoft servers.
   - ❏ D. PC manufacturers are no longer required to display Microsoft icons on the desktop.
   - ❏ E. The U.S. Department of Justice has been monitoring Microsoft's market behavior for at least four years.

20. From the context of the passage, you can infer that the phrase "digital information silos" refers to which one of the following?
   - ❏ A. Isolated collections of personal information
   - ❏ B. Vendors who are Microsoft competitors
   - ❏ C. Personal information management tools
   - ❏ D. Anticompetitive licensing practices
   - ❏ E. Microsoft's dominance of the computer software platform market

America's national security and economic well-being have long rested on its technological and industrial prowess. Over the four-decade-long Cold War, the nation's defense technology and industrial base (DTIB) became isolated from the commercial base. That isolation raised the
5   cost of defense goods and services, reduced the Department of Defense's access to commercial technologies with potential defense application, and made it difficult for commercial firms to exploit the results of the nation's extensive defense science and technology investments.

10   The integration of defense and commercial technology and industry (often termed civil–military integration—CMI) has been advocated as a means to preserve the U.S. defense capability in the face of budget reductions. Under CMI, common technologies, processes, labor, equipment, material, and/or facilities are used to
15   meet both defense and commercial needs.

Despite several previous initiatives to promote integration, much of the U.S. DTIB remains isolated. Concerns over possible costs and risks to modifying government acquisition to implement CMI have hindered change. Some technologies, industrial sectors and product tiers are
20   more amenable to integration than others, and indeed, integration is already occurring in many of the tiers and technologies most amenable to CMI. Increasing CMI will depend in part on the product, process, and tier involved. Prime contractors performing systems integration are less able to integrate their products and processes with commercial
25   counterparts than are producers of components and subcomponents. On the other hand, services appear particularly amenable to commercial purchases.

There are clear benefits to increasing CMI. Analysis indicates significant cost savings will result from increased use of commercial
30   items and integrating R&D, production, and maintenance processes. Even greater savings might come from changes in military systems design. Further, CMI may improve defense access to new technology in the future.

There are, however, obstacles to further CMI. One major obstacle is
35   the sheer complexity involved. In most instances, the barriers to CMI are sufficiently intertwined to demand a comprehensive (and complex) set of policies if projected benefits are to accrue. Efforts to promote integration therefore carry costs and risks as well; one of the most discussed risks is that commercial goods and services may fail in
40   military operations. Increased CMI may also result in greater dependence on foreign goods and services. Changes in oversight might result in increased instances of fraud and abuse. Alternatives exist to deal with such risks, but efforts to increase CMI must carefully balance expected benefits to the DTIB and the economy with potential pitfalls
45   resulting from those same policies.

There are three possible strategies for increasing CMI: a readjustment strategy, a reform strategy and a restructuring strategy. A

50 readjustment strategy involves the least risk but may generate the fewest benefits. It seeks to increase CMI modestly while retaining many of the current procedures for oversight of defense expenditures. It includes increasing commercial purchases for defense needs. A reform strategy, building on a readjustment strategy, seeks to foster CMI more actively; changing rules to promote the integration of both R&D and production of defense and commercial products. Finally, a

55 restructuring strategy that incorporates the two earlier strategies might gain the maximum potential CMI benefits, but would demand major changes in future military acquisition policy, system design, and force structure. This strategy would present correspondingly greater risks.

60 Successful implementation of CMI requires a long-term commitment. It involves careful design and planning of systems, components, and subcomponents, and extends to all tiers and throughout the planning and production process. While the potential benefits are significant, they will take time to accrue. Patience and a steady effort are

65 paramount requirements for successful CMI.

Source: U.S. Congress, Office of Technology Assessment, Other Approaches to Civil-Military Integration: The Chinese and Japanese Arms Industries, BP-ISS-143 (March 1995). http://www.wws.princeton.edu/~ota/ns20/year_f.html

21. Which one of the following would be the best title for the passage?

 ❑ A. "America's DTIB"
 ❑ B. "Using CMI to Meet America's Defense Needs"
 ❑ C. "The Benefits of CMI"
 ❑ D. "CMI Barriers"
 ❑ E. "Strategies for Increasing CMI"

22. According to the passage, all of the following are barriers to the successful implementation of CMI or risks associated with CMI *except*:

 ❑ A. Commercial goods and services may fail in military operations.
 ❑ B. Increased CMI may result in greater dependence on foreign goods and services.
 ❑ C. Increased instances of fraud and abuse may result.
 ❑ D. There is complexity involved in implementation.
 ❑ E. Commercial firms are unwilling to exploit the results of the nation's defense investments.

23. Which one of the following best describes the general organization of the passage?

   ❑ A. The passage states a thesis, provides examples in support of the thesis, presents opposing viewpoints, and then restates the thesis.

   ❑ B. The passage provides the historical context surrounding an issue, presents both sides of a controversy, and then concludes with a statement of support for one of the sides.

   ❑ C. The passage states a thesis, presents viewpoints that oppose the thesis, provides examples in support of both viewpoints, and concludes with a question.

   ❑ D. The passage identifies a problem, followed by a list of obstacles to solving the problem, discusses concrete examples of the obstacles, proposes various alternatives to solve the problem, and concludes with an endorsement of a particular alternative.

   ❑ E. The passage identifies a problem, offers a solution to the problem, identifies various issues with respect to the solution, and describes some possible strategies for implementing the solution.

24. The tone of this passage can best be described as

   ❑ A. Condescending and ironic

   ❑ B. Judgmental and analytical

   ❑ C. Balanced and objective

   ❑ D. Didactic and pedantic

   ❑ E. Hostile and argumentative

25. The primary purpose of the passage is to

   ❑ A. Describe the issues surrounding, and possible methods of implementing, a CMI program to support the United States's defense in an era of budget cuts

   ❑ B. Explain why commercial firms have found it difficult to exploit the results of the nation's defense science and technology investments

   ❑ C. Examine why much of the U.S. DTIB remains isolated

   ❑ D. Discuss strategies for increasing CMI

   ❑ E. Assess the potential costs and benefits of CMI

26. The author of the passage is likely to agree with all of the following *except*:

   ❑ A. Attempting to implement CMI is not a worthwhile endeavor.

   ❑ B. The isolation of the nation's DTIB from its commercial base has negative consequences that should be addressed.

   ❑ C. Some sectors will be more successful in implementing CMI than others.

   ❑ D. CMI can create significant cost savings.

   ❑ E. Efforts to increase CMI are not risk free.

27. You can infer from the passage that all of the following statements are false *except*:

   ❏ A. Increasing CMI is not expected to impact the nation's economy.

   ❏ B. CMI has never been tried.

   ❏ C. A reform strategy for increasing CMI poses the least risk.

   ❏ D. A restructuring strategy is an incremental approach to increasing CMI.

   ❏ E. CMI cannot be implemented successfully overnight.

THIS IS THE END OF THE SECTION.

Answer Key for Practice Exam 4

SECTION I—Analytical Reasoning

1. A	9. D	17. A
2. C	10. A	18. E
3. D	11. E	19. A
4. C	12. B	20. C
5. D	13. A	21. E
6. A	14. D	22. B
7. B	15. B	23. C
8. B	16. D	24. B

QUESTIONS 1–6 RELATE TO THE FOLLOWING SCENARIO:

Four greyhounds are assigned to four consecutive races—Races 1, 2, 3, and 4. Each greyhound has a number cloth of a different color, and each one is assigned to just one race. The greyhounds' names are Speedy, Bullet, Whitey, and Rocket. The colors of the number cloths are blue, red, yellow, and white. The following conditions apply:

Speedy is assigned to a lower-numbered race than is Bullet, and at least one race separates the two.

Whitey is assigned to Race 2.

Rocket's number cloth is white.

1. **Answer: A.** From examining the conditions, we can derive the following possibilities as to which greyhound is assigned to which race. The second condition tells us that Whitey is assigned to Race 2. The first condition tells us that Speedy is assigned to a lower-numbered race than is Bullet, and at least one race separates the two. Therefore, we know that Speedy must be assigned to Race 1 because assigning Speedy to either Race 3 or 4 would violate the first condition. With respect to the colors of the number cloths of the various greyhounds, the third condition tells us that Rocket's number cloth is white. From this information, we can create the following chart:

Race 1	Race 2	Race 3	Race 4
Speedy	Whitey	Bullet or Rocket (white)	Rocket (white) or Bullet

   We can therefore immediately eliminate choices B, D, and E as violating the third condition. We can also eliminate choice C because, as we can see from the preceding chart, Bullet cannot be assigned to the first race without violating the first condition. Therefore, by process of elimination, we see that the correct choice must be choice A. Choice A is correct (see preceding discussion). Choice B is incorrect (see preceding discussion). Choice C is incorrect (see preceding discussion). Choice D is incorrect (see preceding discussion). Choice E is incorrect (see preceding discussion).

2. **Answer: C.** In this problem, the incorrect choices are those choices that could be or that definitely are true. The scenario for this question tells us that the greyhound wearing the blue-colored number is assigned to a higher-numbered race than Rocket. From looking at the chart that we created to answer Question 1, we can see that the only possible races for Rocket are Races 3 and 4. For a greyhound wearing the blue-colored cloth to be assigned to a higher-numbered race than

Rocket, this must mean that Rocket is in the third race and that Bullet must be the greyhound wearing the blue-colored number cloth, and that he is in the fourth race. There is no way for us to tell what color number cloth (red or yellow) Speedy or Whitey is wearing. With this information in hand, we can create the following chart:

Race 1	Race 2	Race 3	Race 4
Speedy (red or yellow)	Whitey (yellow or red)	Rocket (white)	Bullet (blue)

We are now ready to answer the question.

Choice C is correct. Whitey is assigned to Race 2, and the greyhound wearing the yellow-numbered cloth must be either Speedy (in Race 1) or Whitey himself (in Race 2). If it is Whitey himself, he obviously cannot be assigned to a lower-numbered race than he is already in, and if it is Speedy, Whitey cannot be assigned to a lower-numbered race than Speedy because Speedy is in Race 1 and Whitey is in Race 2. Therefore, this statement cannot be true and so choice C is the correct choice. Choice A is incorrect. If Rocket (wearing the white-colored number cloth) is in the third race and Bullet (wearing the blue-colored number cloth) is in the fourth race, then it is possible that Speedy is assigned to a lower-numbered race (Race 1) than Whitey (who is in Race 2, and who may be wearing a red-colored number cloth). Choice B is incorrect. As we can see from the chart, Whitey is, in fact, assigned to a lower-numbered race (Race 2) than is the greyhound wearing the blue-numbered cloth (Bullet, in Race 4). Choice D is incorrect. This statement must be true because Bullet, wearing the blue-colored number cloth, is in Race 4, the highest-numbered race. The greyhound wearing the red-colored number cloth must be in a lower-numbered race. Choice E is incorrect. As we can see from the chart, this statement might be true if Speedy is wearing the yellow-colored number cloth.

3. **Answer: D.** Once again, the incorrect choices are those choices that could be or definitely are true. We can create the following chart to help answer this question:

Race 1	Race 2	Race 3	Race 4
Speedy	Whitey	Rocket (white)	Bullet

Choice D is correct. Bullet could be wearing a red-colored number cloth, and he is assigned to a higher-numbered race than Rocket, so the statement in choice D could be false and is therefore the correct choice.

Choice A is incorrect. We can see from the chart that Speedy must be assigned to Race 1. Choice B is incorrect. We can see from the chart that Bullet must be assigned to Race 4. Choice C is incorrect. This answer must be true because Rocket is in Race 3. No matter what color number cloth Bullet is wearing (red, yellow, or blue), either Speedy or Whitey must be wearing blue or yellow, and both of them are assigned to a lower-numbered race than Rocket. Choice E is incorrect. We can see from the chart that Rocket must be assigned to Race 3.

4. **Answer: C.** To answer this question, we can refer to the chart we created to answer Question 1:

Race 1	Race 2	Race 3	Race 4
Speedy	Whitey	Bullet (color unknown) or Rocket (white)	Rocket (white) or Bullet (color unknown)

From this chart, we can see that the maximum possible number of different greyhounds and color combinations that could be assigned to Race 4 is four, as follows:

Rocket (white)

Bullet (red)

Bullet (blue)

Bullet (yellow)

Choice C is correct (see preceding discussion). Choice A is incorrect (see preceding discussion). Choice B is incorrect (see preceding discussion). Choice D is incorrect (see preceding discussion). Choice E is incorrect (see preceding discussion).

5. **Answer: D.** To answer this question, we can refer once again to the chart we prepared for Question 1. From the scenario for this question, we know that the only greyhound that can be assigned a higher-numbered race than Rocket is Bullet and that therefore Rocket must be in Race 3 and Bullet must be in Race 4 and therefore wearing a red-colored number cloth. This information allows us to create the following chart:

Race 1	Race 2	Race 3	Race 4
Speedy (yellow or blue)	Whitey (blue or yellow)	Rocket (white)	Bullet (red)

We can now easily answer the question.

Choice D is correct. This statement could be false. It is possible for the greyhound wearing the yellow-colored number cloth (which could be Speedy) to be is assigned to a lower-numbered race (Race 1) than is the greyhound wearing the blue-colored number cloth (which could be Whitey in Race 2). Choice A is incorrect. This statement is true. Because Bullet is assigned to Race 4 and is wearing a red-colored number cloth, he must be in a higher-numbered race than is the greyhound wearing the blue-colored number cloth. Choice B is incorrect. This statement is true. Because Bullet is assigned to Race 4 and is wearing a red-colored number cloth, he must be in a higher-numbered race than is the greyhound wearing the yellow-colored number cloth. Choice C is incorrect. This statement is true. Because Rocket is assigned to Race 3, and we know that Bullet in Race 4 is wearing a red-colored number cloth, Rocket must be assigned to a higher-numbered race than is the greyhound wearing the yellow-colored number cloth. Choice E is incorrect. This statement could be true. Rocket (assigned to Race 3) could be assigned to a higher-numbered race than is the greyhound wearing the blue-colored number cloth (which could be Speedy in Race 1 or Whitey in Race 2).

6. **Answer: A.** We can create the following chart to represent the possibilities required by the conditions and the information provided in the scenario for the question:

Race 1	Race 2	Race 3	Race 4
Speedy (blue or yellow)	Whitey (red)	Bullet (yellow or blue) or Rocket (white)	Rocket (white) or Bullet (yellow or blue)

Using this chart, we can see that we can immediately eliminate choices B, C, D, and E as failing to meet one or more of the conditions set forth, leaving Choice A as the correct choice by process of elimination.

Choice A is correct. From examining the earlier chart, we can see that this combination of greyhounds/number cloth color and race number is possible without violating any of the conditions of the scenario. Choice B is incorrect. It is not possible for Whitey to be assigned to Race 1 without violating the second condition. Choice C is incorrect. It is not possible for Rocket's number cloth to be red without violating the third condition. Choice D is incorrect. It is not possible for Speedy to be in Race 3 and Bullet to be in Race 4 without violating the first condition. Choice E is incorrect. It is not possible for Bullet to be in Race 1 and Speedy to be in Race 4 without violating the first condition.

QUESTIONS 7–11 RELATE TO THE FOLLOWING SCENARIO:

At the Northeast Regional Club rally, each of eight members of the Garrison Club—Dee, Eve, Fran, Genevieve, Hannah, Irene, Jessica, and Kendall (known as the Garrison Club Kids)—will participate in two events, a potato race and an eating contest. For each of these events, the eight Garrison Club Kids are grouped into four two-person teams, subject to the following conditions:

> If two Garrison Club Kids are teammates in the potato race, they cannot also be teammates in the eating contest.
>
> Fran and Irene are teammates in the potato race.
>
> Eve and Fran are teammates in the eating contest.
>
> Jessica and Kendall are not teammates in either event.

7. **Answer: B.** In this question, we are looking for a pairing that cannot participate in the eating contest but could participate in the potato race. From examining the conditions, we can see that Eve and Fran are teammates in the eating contest. Therefore, neither choice B nor choice C can be a pair without violating the conditions. None of the other pairings A, D, or E appear to violate any conditions, so it is possible that they could be pairings that participate in the eating contest and therefore are most likely incorrect. Focusing on B and C, we can see that under the second condition, Fran is already a partner in the potato race with Irene, so it is not possible for Fran to be a partner with Kendall, thereby allowing us to eliminate choice C as a possible correct choice. By process of elimination, we are left with choice B, Eve and Jessica. Choice B is correct (see earlier discussion). Choice A is incorrect (see earlier discussion). Choice C is incorrect (see earlier discussion). Choice D is incorrect (see earlier discussion). Choice E is incorrect (see earlier discussion).

8. **Answer: B.** From the information provided in the conditions and the scenario for the question, we know the following:

   Eating contest pairs:

   Eve and Fran

   Dee and Jessica

   Potato race pairs:

   Fran and Irene

   Genevieve and Hannah

We know from the fourth condition that Jessica and Kendall are not teammates in either event; and because we know from the scenario that Dee and Jessica are paired in the eating contest (and therefore cannot be paired in the potato race under the first condition), the other possible potato race pairs are:

Jessica and Eve

Kendall and Dee

Examining the possible choices, we can see that choice B is the only possible correct choice.

Choice B is correct (see earlier discussion). Choice A is incorrect (see earlier discussion). Choice C is incorrect (see earlier discussion). Choice D is incorrect (see earlier discussion). Choice E is incorrect (see earlier discussion).

9. **Answer: D.** The second condition tells us that Fran and Irene are teammates in the potato race. Therefore, we can immediately eliminate choices A, C, and E, which violate this condition. We are then left with choosing between choices B and D, both of which show Fran and Irene as teammates. However, in choice B, Jessica and Kendall are teammates, which violates the fourth condition. Therefore, by process of elimination, choice D is the correct choice. Choice D is correct (see earlier discussion). Choice A is incorrect (see earlier discussion). Choice B is incorrect (see earlier discussion). Choice C is incorrect (see earlier discussion). Choice E is incorrect (see earlier discussion).

10. **Answer: A.** From the information provided in the conditions and the scenario for the question, we know the following:

Eating contest pairs:

Eve and Fran

Hannah and Irene

Jessica and Dee or Genevieve

Kendall and Genevieve or Dee

Potato race pairs:

Fran and Irene

Eve and Hannah

Jessica and Dee or Genevieve

Kendall and Genevieve or Dee

This question requires us to pick the pairing that *cannot* be teammates. From looking at these possible pairings, we can immediately rule out choices B, C, D, and E because all of these represent possible pairings. We know that choice A, therefore, is the correct choice, not only by process of elimination but also because, as we can see, a pairing of Dee and Genevieve is not possible without violating the conditions and the scenario given in the question.

Choice A is correct (see earlier discussion). Choice B is incorrect (see earlier discussion). Choice B is incorrect (see earlier discussion). Choice D is incorrect (see earlier discussion). Choice E is incorrect (see earlier discussion).

11. **Answer: E.** From the information provided in the conditions and the scenario for the question, we know the following:

Potato race pairs:

> Fran and Irene
>
> Dee and Hannah
>
> Jessica and Eve or Genevieve
>
> Kendall and Genevieve or Eve

Eating contest pairs:

> Eve and Fran

This information enables us to eliminate choices A and B. Because Jessica and Kendall can't be partners together under the fourth condition, one of them must be a partner with Eve, and therefore Genevieve cannot be a partner with Eve (choice A). And because Fran is partners with Irene in the potato race, she cannot be partners with Genevieve (choice B). We can also eliminate choices C and D. Genevieve cannot be a partner with either Fran (choice C) or Eve (choice D) in the eating contest because under the third condition, Fran and Eve are partners together in that eating contest. Therefore, by process of elimination, we find that choice E is the correct choice. Choice A is incorrect (see earlier discussion). Choice B is incorrect (see earlier discussion). Choice C is incorrect (see earlier discussion). Choice D is incorrect (see earlier discussion).

QUESTIONS 12–18 RELATE TO THE FOLLOWING SCENARIO:

The Thunderbolts U10 Boys' AYSO surfing team is having its team photo taken. Seven members of the team are present for the photo: Alex, Brian,

Chris, Dylan, Evan, Frank, and Giles. The team photographer lines them up from left to right in a straight line in positions from 1 to 7, in accordance with the following conditions:

> Alex and Brian do not stand next to each other.
>
> Exactly two boys stand between Chris and Alex.
>
> Dylan and Alex stand next to each other.
>
> Frank and Brian do not stand next to each other.
>
> Chris's position is exactly two places to the left of Brian's position.

12. **Answer: B.** From examining the conditions, we can immediately eliminate choice E as violating the first condition (Alex and Brian cannot stand next to each other); choice A as violating the second condition (there must be two boys standing between Chris and Alex); choice C as violating the third condition (Chris must be to the left of Brian, not the right); and choice D as violating the fourth condition (Frank and Brian cannot stand next to each other). By process of elimination, we can quickly arrive at choice B as the correct choice. Choice B is correct. It does not violate any of the conditions (see preceding discussion). Choice A is incorrect. It violates the second condition (see preceding discussion). Choice C is incorrect. It violates the third condition (see preceding discussion). Choice D is incorrect. It violates the fourth condition (see preceding discussion). Choice E is incorrect. It violates the first condition (see preceding discussion).

13. **Answer: A.** To tackle this question, we need to first consider what the conditions tell us about the relative placements of the various boys. Under the second condition, we know that two boys stand between Chris and Alex; therefore, one of the following two possibilities is the case:

> Chris-?-?-Alex
>
> Or
>
> Alex-?-?-Chris

We also know from the fifth condition that Chris's position is exactly two places to the left of Brian's position. Therefore, there are again two possibilities:

> Chris-?-Brian-Alex
>
> Or
>
> Alex-?-?-Chris-?-Brian

However, the first of these two possibilities (Chris-?-Brian-Alex) violates the first condition, which provides that Alex and Brian do not stand next to each other. Therefore, we know that only the second of the two possibilities (Alex-?-?-Chris-Brian) complies with the conditions. We also know that under the third condition, Dylan and Alex stand next to each other. This offers the following possibilities:

Dylan-Alex-?-?-Chris-?-Brian

Or

Alex-Dylan-?-Chris-?-Brian

In this latter case, the missing sixth spot may be either at the front or end of the line. Because under the fourth condition Frank and Brian do not stand next to each, we now have the following possibilities:

1. Dylan-Alex-Frank-?-Chris-?-Brian

2. Dylan-Alex-?-Frank-Chris-?-Brian

3. Dylan-Alex-Frank-Chris-?-Brian-?

4. Frank-Alex-Dylan-?-Chris-?-Brian

5. ?-Alex-Dylan-Frank-Chris-?-Brian

6. Alex-Dylan-Frank-Chris-?-Brian-?

Now we add into this mix the requirement that Giles stand in Position 1. Only Option 5 has Position 1 open. We can see by examining this options that Evan would be between Brian and Chris; therefore, Choice A is the correct answer.

14. **Answer: D.** By examining the earlier listing, we can see that Giles can stand next to Alex in both Options 2 and 5. Examining these options, we can see that all of the choices are true except choice D, so therefore choice D is the correct choice. Choice D is correct. In both Options 2 and 5, Evan stands between Chris and Brian. Therefore, the statement that if Giles stands next to Alex, Evan stands between Chris and Dylan cannot be true (see earlier discussion). Choice A is incorrect. In both Options 2 and 5, Brian stands in Position 7 (see earlier discussion). Choice B is incorrect. In Option 2, Dylan stands in Position 1 (see earlier discussion). Choice C is incorrect. In Option 5, Dylan stands between Alex and Frank (see earlier discussion). Choice E is incorrect. In Option 2, Giles stands between Alex and Frank (see earlier discussion).

15. **Answer: B.** Examining the list of options that we created for Question 13, we see that there are two options in which Evan could stand in Position 7 (Options 3 and 6). In both of these options, Giles must be in Position 5, one position to the left of Giles. Therefore, choice A is correct.

16. **Answer: D.** Examining the list of options that we created for Question 13, we can see that the only option in which Evan could stand next to Dylan is Option 4, which would then place Giles in Position 6. Because in this option Frank is in Position 1, there are four boys standing between Giles and Frank, and therefore choice D is correct.

17. **Answer: A.** Examining the list of options that we created for Question 13, we can see that Giles can stand next to Frank in two of these options, Options 1 and 2. In both of these options, Evan must therefore stand next to Brian, and therefore there are no boys standing between Evan and Brian. Therefore, choice A is the correct choice.

18. Answer: E. By examining the list of options we created for Question 13, we can see that under no circumstances in any of the options does Giles ever stand next to Evan. Therefore, choice E is the correct choice.

QUESTIONS 19–24 RELATE TO THE FOLLOWING SCENARIO:

On Sunday afternoons, the Wine Cellar hosts a wine tasting. Customers are allowed to sample seven different varieties of wines: Ross Reserve, Simon Cabernet, Tivoli Shiraz, Umami Pinot Noir, Valerian Merlot, Wyatt Chardonnay, and Xaviar House Blend. Customers can select the order in which they will taste the different types of wine, according to the following conditions:

The Valerian Merlot must always be served some time after the Umami Pinot Noir.

The Simon Cabernet must be served exactly two tastings before the Tivoli Shiraz.

The Wyatt Chardonnay must be served some time before the Simon Cabernet.

The Valerian Merlot must be served either fifth or sixth.

The Ross Reserve must be served second.

19. Answer: A. By examining the conditions, we can eliminate choice B because it violates the third condition, choice C because it violates the second condition, choice D because it violates the fourth condition, and choice E because it violates the fifth condition. Therefore, by process of elimination, we find that choice A is the correct choice.

20. **Answer: C.** In Question 19, we saw that in choice A, Tivoli Shiraz was served seventh. Therefore, we can immediately eliminate choices A and B as incorrect because neither of these choices have Tivoli Shiraz being served seventh. We now must choose between choices C, D, and E. Looking at various conditions, we can derive the following information:

Under the fifth condition, the Ross Reserve must be served second, and under the fourth condition, the Valerian Merlot must be served either fifth or sixth, providing two possibilities:

?-Ross Reserve-?-?-Valerian Merlot-?-?

Or

?-Ross Reserve-?-?-?-Valerian-Merlot-?

Because under the first condition, the Valerian Merlot must always be served sometime after the Umami Pinot Noir, we know that the Umami Pinot Noir must be served either first, third, fourth, or fifth. Because under the second condition the Simon Cabernet must be served exactly two tastings before the Tivoli Shiraz, and we know that the Tivoli Shiraz could be served seventh, the *latest* the Simon Cabernet could be served would be fifth (that is, the Simon Cabernet could not be served either sixth or seventh). We know from the third condition that the Wyatt Chardonnay must be served sometime before the Simon Cabernet. Because Ross Reserve must be served second, the *earliest* Simon Cabernet could be served would be third (if Ross Reserve is served first). Given the second condition, therefore, the earliest Tivoli Shiraz could be served is fifth. The third condition also tells us that the Wyatt Chardonnay could be served either first, third, fourth, or fifth. Given these conditions, either Tivoli Shiraz or Xaviar House Blend must be served seventh. We can summarize these findings as follows:

Ross Reserve: Served second

Simon Cabernet: Served not earlier than third, not later than fifth

Tivoli Shiraz: Served not earlier than fifth, not later than seventh; always follows serving of Simon Cabernet by two

Umami Pinot Noir: Served either first, third, fourth, or fifth

Valerian Merlot: Served either fifth or sixth

Wyatt Chardonnay: Served either first, third, fourth, or fifth

Xaviar House Blend: Could be served seventh but does not have to be

Looking at this summary, we can see that Tivoli Shiraz cannot be served earlier than fifth. This information allows us to cross off choices A, B, and D, thereby leaving choice C as the correct choice by process of elimination. Choice C is correct. Tivoli Shiraz can be served fifth, sixth, or seventh (see earlier discussion). Choice A is incorrect. Tivoli Shiraz can be served seventh (see discussion above). Choice B is incorrect. Tivoli Shiraz cannot be served any earlier than fifth (see earlier discussion). Choice D is incorrect. Tivoli Shiraz cannot be served any earlier than fifth (see earlier discussion). Choice E is incorrect. Tivoli Shiraz cannot be served any earlier than fifth (see earlier discussion).

21. **Answer: E.** From looking at the conditions and the list of possible serving orders we created to help answer Question 19, we know the following:

Ross Reserve: Served second.

Simon Cabernet: Served not earlier than third, not later than fifth. Here, because Valerian Merlot is served fifth, Simon Cabernet must be served third or fourth. If Simon Cabernet were served third, then Tivoli Shiraz must be served fifth, but that is not possible because Valerian Merlot is served fifth. Therefore, Simon Cabernet must be served fourth, and therefore Tivoli Shiraz is served sixth.

Tivoli Shiraz: Served sixth (see the preceding).

Umami Pinot Noir: Served either first or third.

Valerian Merlot: Served fifth.

Wyatt Chardonnay: Served either first or third.

Xaviar House Blend: Must be served seventh.

From this analysis, we can see immediately that the only choice listed that must be true is choice E. Choice E is correct. If Valerian Merlot is served fight, Xaviar House Blend must be served seventh (see earlier discussion). Choice A is incorrect. If Valerian Merlot is served fifth, Simon Cabernet is served fourth (see earlier discussion). Choice B is incorrect. If Valerian Merlot is served fifth, Tivoli Shiraz is served sixth (see earlier discussion). Choice C is incorrect. If Valerian Merlot is served fifth, Umami Pinot Noir can be served first (see earlier discussion). Choice D is incorrect. If Valerian Merlot is served fifth, Wyatt Chardonnay can be served third (see earlier discussion).

22. **Answer: B.** To answer this question, we must determine which choice provides a condition that leads to only one possible ordering. In the previous question, Simon Cabernet was served fourth, and Xaviar House Blend was served seventh, but the order of serving Umami Pinot Noir and Wyatt Chardonnay was still open (each could have been served either first or third), so from this information we know that we can eliminate choices A and E as not providing a sufficient condition to fix the order. We must now choose among B, C, and D.

Examining choice B, we can see that if Tivoli Shiraz must be served fifth, the following order develops:

Ross Reserve: Served second (fifth condition)

Simon Cabernet: Served third (because Tivoli Shiraz is served fifth; second condition)

Tivoli Shiraz: Served fifth (condition posited by choice B)

Umami Pinot Noir: Served fourth (because the conditions require that it be served first, third, fourth, or fifth, and first, third, and fifth are otherwise occupied under the various conditions)

Valerian Merlot: Served sixth (fourth condition)

Wyatt Chardonnay: Served first (because it must be before Simon Cabernet under the third condition, and with Ross Reserve served second, first is the only spot open)

Xaviar House Blend: Served seventh (only spot left open)

Therefore, because the condition expressed in choice B leads to a definitive ordering, we can immediately stop, as this must be the correct answer. Choice B is correct (see earlier discussion). Choice A is incorrect (see earlier discussion). Choice C is incorrect (see earlier discussion). Choice D is incorrect (see earlier discussion). Choice E is incorrect (see earlier discussion).

23. **Answer: C.** From looking at the conditions and the list of possible serving orders that we created to help answer Question 19, we know the following:

Ross Reserve: Must be served second.

Simon Cabernet: Could be served not earlier than third, not later than fifth. Here, because Valerian Merlot is served sixth, Simon Cabernet could be served third or fifth. (It cannot be served fourth because then Tivoli Shiraz must be served sixth, but Valerian Merlot already occupies that place.)

Tivoli Shiraz: Could be served fifth or seventh.

Umami Pinot Noir: Could be served first, third, or fourth. Cannot be served fifth because that would push Simon Cabernet into third and require Tivoli Shiraz to be served fifth, but fifth would be occupied by Umami Pinot Noir.

Valerian Merlot: Must be served sixth.

Wyatt Chardonnay: Could be served first, third, or fourth. Cannot be served fifth (same as Umami Pinot Noir).

Xaviar House Blend: Could be served first, fourth, or seventh.

Looking at the list of choices, we can see that under these conditions, the only one that cannot be true is choice C. Therefore, choice C is the correct answer. Choice C is correct. If Valerian Merlot is served sixth, it is not possible for Umami Pinot Noir to be served fifth without violating the conditions (see earlier discussion). Choice A is incorrect. If Valerian Merlot is served sixth, it is possible for Simon Cabernet to be served fifth without violating any of the conditions (see earlier discussion). Choice B is incorrect. If Valerian Merlot is served sixth, it is possible for Tivoli Shiraz to be served seventh without violating any of the conditions (see earlier discussion). Choice D is incorrect. If Valerian Merlot is served sixth, it is possible for Wyatt Chardonnay to be served third without violating any of the conditions (see earlier discussion). Choice E is incorrect. If Valerian Merlot is served sixth, it is possible for Xaviar House Blend to be served first without violating any of the conditions (see earlier discussion).

24. **Answer: B.** From looking at the conditions and the list of possible serving orders that we created to help answer Question 19, we know that the only two wines that could be served seventh are Xaviar House Blend or Tivoli Shiraz. If Xaviar House Blend is served third, then Tivoli Shiraz must be served seventh. As soon as we see that this is one of the choices (choice B), we need go no further, as this must be the correct answer.

SECTION II—Logical Reasoning

1. E	**9.** B	**17.** B
2. A	**10.** E	**18.** D
3. C	**11.** D	**19.** E
4. B	**12.** A	**20.** B
5. A	**13.** B	**21.** C
6. D	**14.** A	**22.** B
7. E	**15.** C	**23.** B
8. D	**16.** B	**24.** E

1. **Choice E** is correct. If, of the 10% who placed complimentary food service above fifth, 9% placed it fourth, this fact would not weaken the basis for management's conclusion. Choice A is incorrect. If the passengers on the Washington, D.C., to Boston route are not representative of other passengers on other Amtrak routes, then this would weaken management's conclusion that all passengers on all Amtrak trains believe that complimentary food service is not important. Choice B is incorrect. If the number of passengers who completed the survey is not statistically significant, then this would weaken management's conclusion that all passengers on Amtrak trains believe that complimentary food service is not important. Choice C is incorrect. If complimentary food service is not offered on the Washington, D.C., to Boston route, this would weaken management's conclusion because those passengers, not having experienced complimentary food service, might not value it as highly as those who had experienced such service. This answer choice is a variation on answer choice A. Choice D is incorrect. If, on the Washington, D.C., route, fares are lower than airline prices, and on-time performance is better than that of airlines that fly the same route, then it is reasonable to assume that those factors may be more valuable to those passengers who chose to take the train (and who were therefore surveyed) than other factors, compared to other areas of the country in which train fares and on-time performance are comparable to those of airlines. In such a situation, other factors are more likely to be determinants in the choice.

2. **Choice A** is correct. Tamara's response indicates that she believes that Russell has said that being articulate is all that is required in order to

be a good lawyer. Choice B is incorrect. This is not what Tamara's response indicates. Choice C is incorrect. This is not what Tamara's response indicates. Choice D is incorrect. Although this accurately restates what Russell meant, this is not what Tamara understood him to say. Choice E is incorrect. As with choice D, while this accurately restates what Russell meant, this is not what Tamara understood him to say.

3. **Choice C** is correct. The author mistakenly assumes that the conditions experienced in the past three months will continue. Choice A is incorrect. The author's conclusion is not based on unreliable statistics. Choice B is incorrect. The author's failure to specify how big an "enormous" electricity bill would be does not detract from the reasoning underlying the author's conclusion. Choice D is incorrect. The reasons the electricity company instituted rolling brownout are not relevant to the author's conclusion. Choice E is incorrect. The author, in fact, does define what he/she considers a significant rise in the cost of electricity (that is, $50 a month)

4. **Choice B** is correct. The statement in this answer choice parallels the logic used in the statement in the question. The logic in the statement makes an overly broad characterization based on specific occurrences experienced by a particular individual. For instance, in the statement, Tarik gets an upset stomach after eating tofu and therefore concludes that tofu is disgusting. However, it may not be disgusting to others. In choice B the speaker is bitten three times by a shark and concludes that sharks are dangerous. However, others may not view sharks as dangerous. Choice A is incorrect. The statement in this answer choice does not in any way parallel the logic used in the statement in the question. Choice C is incorrect. The statement in this answer choice does not parallel the logic used in the statement in the question. The statement in this answer choice does not include an allusion to the specific experience of the speaker that is present in the statement in the question and choice B. Choice D is incorrect. While the logic of the statement in this answer choice parallels the logic used in the statement in the question to a certain extent, it does so in the negative and is therefore not as good a choice as choice B. Choice E is incorrect. The statement in this answer choice does not in any way parallel the logic used in the statement in the question.

5. The logic is this statement is as follows: If X (lions eat fresh zebra every day), then Y (they have excellent manes and good teeth). But if not X (lions eat dried food and cooked beef), then not Y (cannot have good teeth).

Choice A is correct. The statement in this answer choice follows the same logic as in the statement in the question. If X (woman uses Nexus shampoo and conditioner) then Y (has shiny and healthy hair). But if not X (woman uses Aprell shampoo and conditioner), then not Y (cannot have healthy hair). Choice B is incorrect. The statement in this answer choice does not follow the same logic as the statement in the question. It does not parallel the "if not X, then not Y" portion of the reasoning. Choice C is incorrect. The statement in this answer choice does not follow the same logic as the statement in the question. It does not parallel the "if not X, then not Y" portion of the reasoning. Choice D is incorrect. The statement in this answer choice does not follow the same logic as the statement in the question. It does not parallel the "if not X, then not Y" portion of the reasoning. Choice E is incorrect. The statement in this answer choice does not follow the same logic as the statement in the question. It does not parallel the "if not X, then not Y" portion of the reasoning.

6. **Choice D** is correct. If the statement in the question is true, we can logically infer that there are no students at Varhard College who are not smart (that is, all students at Varhard College are smart). Choice A is incorrect. The statement in the question does not presuppose that the student in question attended Varhard College since it begins with "If the student attended Harvard College...." Choice B is incorrect. The statement in the question does not presuppose that the student in question is smart because the statement begins with a conditional phrase. Choice C is incorrect. The statement in the question does not provide any support for this inference. Choice E is incorrect. The statement in the question does not provide any support for this inference (that is, the majority of students attending Varhard College could be smart males).

7. **Choice E** is correct. A resident of Peekskill who uses 200 kilowatts of electricity will always pay more in absolute dollars than a resident of Peekskill who uses only 100 kilowatts. Choice A is incorrect. It is likely that, because of Peekskill's moderate climate that does not vary much between winter and summer, and because electric heaters and air conditioners are equally efficient, it takes about as much electricity to heat a house during the winter with electricity as it does to cool it during the summer. Choice B is incorrect. It is likely that more residents of Peekskill use oil and gas than electricity to heat their homes because although it is not very expensive to heat an average-size home in the winter with electricity, it still is more expensive than using gas or oil heat. Choice C is incorrect. It is likely due to the sliding scale for electricity that a resident of Peekskill who uses more than 200 kilowatts of

electricity a month may have a lower average per-kilowatt hour rate than a resident who uses only 90 kilowatts per month. Choice D is incorrect. It is likely that more residents of Peekskill use electricity to cool their homes than use electricity to heat their homes because oil and gas provide options for heating, but not for cooling.

8. **Choice D** is correct. This answer choice best summarizes the assumption on which the conclusion in the question is based. Choice A is incorrect. This answer choice focuses only on the "mistakes" part of the conclusion without reflecting the "practice" part. Choice B is incorrect. This answer choice does not reflect the concept in the conclusion that one learns from one's mistakes. Choice C is incorrect. The conclusion is not based on the assumption that "to err is human, to forgive divine." Choice E is incorrect. The conclusion is not based on an assumption that prep courses are necessary to do well on the LSAT.

9. The logic expressed in the statement is as follows: If X (popular), then Y (low intellectual value); if not X (if not popular), then not Y (high intellectual value).

   Choice B is correct. The logic expressed in this answer choice parallels the logic expressed in the statement: If X (people on South Beach Diet), then Y (stop smoking); if not X (not on South Beach diet), then not Y (continue smoking). Choice A is incorrect. The logic expressed in this answer choice does not parallel the logic expressed in the second part of the statement (if not X, then not Y). Choice C is incorrect. The logic expressed in this answer choice does not parallel the logic expressed in the second part of the statement. Instead, the logic expressed in this answer choice is as follows: If X, then Y; if X, but not Y. Choice D is incorrect. The logic expressed in this answer choice does not parallel the logic expressed in the statement. Choice E is incorrect. The logic expressed in this answer choice does not parallel the logic expressed in the statement. Instead, the logic expressed in this answer choice is as follows: If X, then Y; if X, then Y.

10. **Choice E** is correct. This estimate, which is based on statistics that are more specific to the matter at issue than those cited by Ralph, is most likely to be the most reliable estimate. Choice A is incorrect. This estimate is not based on any information supplied. Choice B is incorrect. This estimate (which represents the result of multiplying the two estimates) is not relevant. Choice C is incorrect. This estimate is based on general information (passage rate of all taking the bar exam the last time). The information provided by Bonnie provides statistics that are more specific to the matter at issue here, and it is therefore likely to provide a more reliable estimate than this. Choice D is incorrect. This

estimate (which represents the average of the two different estimates) is not relevant.

11. **Choice D** is correct. We can logically infer from the statement that no dog has been scientifically proven to understand human language. Choice A is incorrect. Nothing in the statement specifically refutes that some dogs may be able to understand human speech. Choice B is incorrect. Nothing in the statement supports the broad inference that all dogs respond to nonverbal clues. Choice C is incorrect. Nothing in the statement supports the inference that a typical dog has a better vocabulary than a three-year-old boy. Choice E is incorrect. Nothing in the statement supports the inference that dogs have been conclusively shown to be capable of understanding human speech.

12. **Choice A** is correct. In the statement, Bienecke's criticism of a program is erroneously considered invalid because Bienecke has himself partaken of/benefited from the very program that he has criticized. In this answer choice, Simon's suggestion is erroneously considered invalid because Simon himself has engaged in the very behavior that he is suggesting be eliminated. Choice B is incorrect. In this answer choice, Dubois would benefit from the proposal, and this provides a valid reason for recommending against it. Choice C is incorrect. In this answer choice, the reasoning is not erroneous, nor does it parallel the reasoning expressed in the statement. Choice D is incorrect. In this answer choice, the reasoning is not erroneous, nor does it parallel the reasoning expressed in the statement. Choice E is incorrect. In this answer choice, the reasoning is not erroneous, nor does it parallel the reasoning expressed in the statement.

13. **Choice B** is correct. The fact that the preferences of males ages 21–30 who do not use the Internet are influenced by the preferences of males 21–30 who do use the Internet significantly weakens the argument in the statement. If Internet advertising of caffeinated energy drinks influenced the group that used the Internet, and then that group influenced the group that did not use the Internet, this could explain why both groups preferred the same thing although one was exposed to advertising and the other not, which directly undercuts the conclusion of the study. Choice A is incorrect. The fact that the preference for caffeine *can* be influenced by factors such as advertising is not necessarily relevant to the conclusion of this particular study that a particular type of advertising did not have an impact on consumer preferences. Choice C is incorrect. The fact that most members of the group that used the Internet were already familiar with the advertisements for caffeinated energy drinks is irrelevant to the conclusion. Choice D is incorrect.

The fact that both groups rejected decaffeinated energy drinks even though they were heavily advertised on the Internet supports the conclusion rather than weakens it. Choice E is incorrect. The fact that energy drink preferences of children who use the Internet are known to be very different from the energy drink preferences of children who do not use the Internet is irrelevant to the conclusion.

14. **Choice A** is correct. The conclusion that a cat's eating habits can be affected by the type of food to which it has been exposed as a kitten is based on the assumption that one-year-old cats do not naturally prefer dry food to moist food. If this assumption were incorrect (that is, if one-year-old cats do naturally prefer dry food to moist food), this would totally obviate the conclusion. Choice B is incorrect. This assumption does not support the conclusion but instead weakens it. Choice C is incorrect. This assumption is irrelevant to the conclusion. Choice D is incorrect. This assumption is irrelevant to the conclusion. Choice E is incorrect. As noted with respect to Choice A, this assumption obviates the conclusion rather than supports it.

15. **Choice C** is correct. The fact that babies do not have to be awake to develop explains why babies develop so much during the first six months even though they are only infrequently awake. Choice A is incorrect. The fact that babies have a greater need to sleep than older children does not explain the situation. Choice B is incorrect. The fact that babies of all species sleep a lot during the first six months does not explain the situation. Choice D is incorrect. The fact that a baby's need to eat is greater than his or her need to sleep does not explain the situation. Choice E is incorrect. The fact that babies who cry a lot develop more quickly than babies who do not does not explain the situation.

16. The pattern of reasoning in the first part of the statement of the question is that X (which is a form of Y) is the best form of Y for Z. Implicit in this statement is that X is better than other forms of Y at Z. In the comparison that forms the second part of the statement, we would normally expect to see X's results compared to other forms of Y. However, instead, the statement makes an erroneous comparison of X's results at Z with those who do not even engage in Z.

Choice B is correct. This answer choice follows the same erroneous pattern of reasoning as the statement X (Breath Clean) is the best Y (gargle) for Z (want clean-smelling breath). The statement and this answer choice then compare the results of people who use X for Z with people who do not even do Z. Choice A is incorrect. While this answer choice follows the pattern of reasoning in the first part of the statement (X is the best Y for Z), it does not follow the pattern in the second part of the statement. Choice C is incorrect. While this answer choice follows the same pattern of reasoning as the first part of the statement, it does not follow the pattern of reasoning in the second part of the statement. Choice D is incorrect. This answer choice does not follow the same pattern of reasoning as the statement at all. Choice D is incorrect. This answer choice follows the same pattern of reasoning as the first part of the statement but does not follow the erroneous pattern of reasoning in the second part of the statement. Instead, it makes an appropriate comparison.

17. **Choice B** is correct. Matthew's claim is a reasonable generalization, given that it is based on *Car Magazine* testing reports which found that the car generally required the fewest repairs of any other type of car. Allison attempts to refute that generalization with a specific instance of her personal experience. Choice A is incorrect. Allison's response is based on personal experience, so the evidence cannot be characterized as unreliable. Choice C is incorrect. Allison does not claim to be an expert. Choice D is incorrect. Allison's response does attempt to refute Matthew's claim. Choice E is incorrect. Allison's response is based on the same grounds (frequency of repairs) as Matthew's claim.

18. **Choice D** is correct. This fact, if true, supports the theory, because a majority of the respondents preferred the story they read only once. Choice A is incorrect. This fact, if true, weakens the theory rather than supports it because a majority of respondents preferred the story that they had read twice. Choice B is incorrect. This fact, if true, weakens the theory rather than supports it because a majority of the respondents preferred the story that they had read twice. Choice C is incorrect. This fact, even if true, is irrelevant to the theory. Choice E is incorrect. This fact, if true, weakens the theory rather than supports it because it provides an alternative rationale for why students preferred Story B to Story A.

19. **Choice E** is correct. The conclusion is based on the assumption that there are no other sources of funds available to pay for the financing of public education other than an increase in state income taxes. Choice A is incorrect. The conclusion is not based on the assumption that if property taxes are not eliminated, there will be no need to increase state income taxes. Choice B is incorrect. The conclusion is not based on the assumption that the cost of providing a public education will be lower if it is financed by property taxes rather than by state income taxes. Choice C is incorrect. The conclusion is not based on the assumption that if property taxes are eliminated and state income taxes are increased, there will be less emphasis on quality education. Choice

D is incorrect. The conclusion is not based on the assumption that the referendum in which Uoush voted to repeal property taxes was unconstitutional.

20. **Choice B** is correct. The reasoning in this answer choice most closely parallels the pattern of reasoning in the statement. Here, building/coop has more children/chickens than apartment/pens, and every child/chicken lives in an apartment/pen, so it must be true that at least one apartment/pen contains more than one child/chicken. Choice A is incorrect. Although at first glance, the reasoning in this answer choice appears to parallel the reasoning of the statement, there is a critical difference. The statement specifies that every child lives in an apartment, and therefore because there are more children than apartments, at least one apartment must contain more than one child. This answer choice, however, specifies that every car must be parked off the street, which is not necessarily synonymous with being parked in a garage. Therefore, it does not necessarily have to be true that at least one of the garages must be a two-car garage. Choice C is incorrect. The reasoning in this answer choice does not parallel the pattern of reasoning in the statement. Choice D is incorrect. The reasoning in this answer choice does not parallel the pattern of reasoning in the statement. Choice E is incorrect. The reasoning in this answer choice does not parallel the pattern of reasoning in the statement.

21. **Choice C** is correct. This is the issue as to which Chuck and Angela disagree. Chuck believes that the profit should *only* be used for research and design; therefore, he cannot believe that there is a better way to use the profit. We can infer from Angela's statement that she believes, however, that there is a better way to use the profit—to expand marketing efforts with respect to the existing product line. This is the crux of the disagreement between Chuck and Angela. Choice A is incorrect. We know that Chuck does not think that using the profit for research and development would be a waste of resources. However, Angela does not necessarily think that doing so *would* be a waste of resources (only that there is a better way to use the money), so Chuck and Angela do not necessarily disagree about this issue. Choice B is incorrect. Neither Chuck nor Angela expresses any opinion as to whether the development of new products is required for future profits. Choice D is incorrect. Neither Angela nor Chuck expresses any opinion as to whether expanded marketing efforts with respect to the existing product line will lead to future profits. Choice E is incorrect. From their statements, we can infer that both Chuck and Angela agree that the profit should be spent, not saved.

22. **Choice B** is correct. If large real estate development projects require more resources and are more complex than smaller projects, and therefore present a higher level of risk, this supports the author's conclusion that given Big's losses, it should focus on small development projects that require less resources, are less complex, and therefore are of lower risk. Choice A is incorrect. If large real estate development projects are much more financially lucrative than small development projects, this weakens the conclusion rather than supports it. Choice C is incorrect. Even if small real estate development projects are more inherently satisfying on a personal level than large real estate projects, this is irrelevant to a conclusion about what action a business entity should take. Choice D is incorrect. The fact that the cost of completing all types of real estate development projects is increasing neither supports nor detracts from the conclusion. Choice E is incorrect. This fact, if true, weakens the conclusion because there would be no difference between the two activities.

23. The logic of the statement is as follows: X (Anthony) will do Y (join the baseball team) if two conditions, A and B, are met. However, only one condition of the two conditions is not met, so X will not do Y.

    Choice B is correct. This answer choice most closely parallels the logic set forth in the statement. X (Lilly) will do Y (go outside) if two conditions, A (above 60 degrees) and B (not raining), are met. However, only one condition of the two conditions is not met, so X (Lilly) will not do Y (go outside). Choice A is incorrect. This answer choice does not parallel the logic set forth in the statement. Choice C is incorrect. This answer choice does not parallel the logic set forth in the statement. Choice D is incorrect. This answer choice does not parallel the logic set forth in the statement. Choice E is incorrect. Although this answer choice is fairly close to the logic set forth in the statement, it sets up more than two conditions (Samuel lending money, red color, excellent condition, less than $25,000) to be met. Therefore, Choice B more closely parallels the logic of the statement and therefore is a better choice than this.

24. **Choice E** is correct. The conclusion in the statement is based on several assumptions. The first assumption is that cell phone usage while driving is correlated with accidents. The second assumption is that the police campaign decreased this activity, therefore leading to a decrease in the number of accidents. This answer choice offers the possibility that it is the action of speeding, rather than cell phone usage, that is correlated with accidents, thereby weakening the validity of the conclusion. Choice A is incorrect. The fact that the police campaign was

heavily reported in the local news and in local newspapers does not weaken the conclusion. The conclusion is based on two assumptions. The first assumption is that cell phone usage while driving is correlated with accidents. The second assumption is that the police campaign decreased this activity, therefore leading to a decrease in the number of accidents. This answer choice does not detract from either of those assumptions. Choice B is incorrect. If anything, the fact that the cost of a ticket for using a cell phone while driving is $500 provides support for the second assumption, making it more likely that the police campaign decreased the number of people driving while using cell phones. Choice C is incorrect. The fact that the police campaign focused on the most heavily traveled highways in the city does not weaken the conclusion because it does not detract from either of the assumptions on which the conclusion is based. Choice D is incorrect. The fact that the police also stopped drivers if they were not wearing seat belts does not weaken the conclusion. Although wearing a seat belt protects a person if an accident occurs, the failure to wear a seat belt is not likely to be a causative factor in the occurrence of an accident.

SECTION III—Logical Reasoning

1. B	**9.** C	**17.** C
2. E	**10.** D	**18.** B
3. B	**11.** A	**19.** C
4. C	**12.** D	**20.** B
5. B	**13.** B	**21.** B
6. B	**14.** E	**22.** B
7. E	**15.** B	**23.** D
8. D	**16.** D	**24.** E

1. **Choice B** is correct. The argument requires that we assume that neither of the two separated parts of the mast is too big to fit in the boathouse. Choice A is incorrect. Nothing in the argument requires that we assume that the mast must be separated into two equal-sized parts. Choice C is incorrect. The cost of separating the mast into two parts is irrelevant to the argument. Choice D is incorrect. The assumption that nothing in the boathouse would have to be removed in order to make room for the mast is irrelevant to the argument. Choice E is incorrect.

Although one can assume that the owner of the mast would like the mast to be stored in the boathouse (otherwise, why go to the trouble of figuring out how to separate it?), nothing in the argument indicates that anyone considered this to be imperative.

2. **Choice E** is correct. The claim that only carpaccio that is free of antibiotics can get top marks on taste tests serves to support the argument's conclusion. Choice A is incorrect. The claim that only carpaccio that is free of antibiotics can get top marks on taste tests is not the argument's conclusion. The argument's conclusion is that the best-tasting carpaccio requires beef from cows that have been fed solely on grass. Choice B is incorrect. The claim that only carpaccio that is free of antibiotics can get top marks on taste tests is not a statement that must be negated in order to support the conclusion. Choice C is incorrect. The claim that only carpaccio that is free of antibiotics can get top marks on taste tests is specifically stated in the argument; therefore, it cannot be an assumption. Choice D is incorrect. The claim that only carpaccio that is free of antibiotics can get top marks on taste tests is specifically stated in the argument; therefore, it cannot be an inference.

3. **Choice B** is correct. Ann and Jane disagree as to when the new HVAC system should be installed. Ann thinks it should happen as soon as possible, and Jane believes they should wait as long as possible. Choice A is incorrect. Ann and Jane do not disagree about whether it is possible to install a new HVAC system. Choice C is incorrect. Ann and Jane do not necessarily disagree about whether the current HVAC system works adequately. Ann may think that it is adequate but just prefer to install the new system. Jane may believe that it is inadequate but still prefer to wait to install the new system. Choice D is incorrect. Although Jane doesn't think the "money spent" to install the new system would be worth it at this point, she doesn't express any opinion on the advisability of borrowing money versus some other method of funding the installation. Choice E is incorrect. Jane does not necessarily believe that the new HVAC system will not be as efficient as advertised; she just doesn't think that its benefits will outweigh its costs at this point in time.

4. **Choice C** is correct. The conclusion is based solely on the assumption that the patient's family cannot afford the treatment. However, this is not a valid basis for attacking the underlying rationale for the action. Choice A is incorrect. The fact that the evidence on which the conclusion is based is derived solely from personal knowledge is not necessarily a flaw in the reasoning of the conclusion. Choice B is incorrect. The person drawing the conclusion is not obligated to consider the

best interests of the patient. Furthermore, what constitutes the best interests of the patient is not decipherable from the information conveyed by the statement. Choice D is incorrect. The conclusion does not constitute a personal attack. Choice E is incorrect. The conclusion is not based on a claim that has been contradicted by the evidence.

5. **Choice B** is correct. If the statement is true, the one thing one can say with certainty is that it must be true that none of KP Tweedy's major clients left his stable this year because KP Tweedy was not forced to shut it down. Choice A is incorrect. Although one may wonder where KP Tweedy got the money to purchase a new farm, it is not necessarily true that he won the lottery. Choice C is incorrect. Although one might assume that KP Tweedy's racehorses were successful this year, this is not necessarily true, as the statement indicates that his income comes from his clients, not from the racehorses. Choice D is incorrect. There is nothing in the statement that requires that KP Tweedy have added additional clients this year. Choice E is incorrect. Although some or all of KP Tweedy's clients may have been pleased with his performance this year (after all, they did not leave him), this is not necessarily true (some may have been displeased but still chosen to stay, for instance).

6. **Choice B** is correct. This answer choice most aptly applies the principle relied upon in the argument—an instructor with actual experience (Broadway) in the subject matter (theater). Choice A is incorrect. The principle in the statement says that only a person who has actual experience in the subject matter can be an instructor. Because New York Medical College is a medical school, then if this principle is being appropriately replied, all of its professors should be M.D.'s, not Ph.D.'s. Choice C is incorrect. If the subject matter is gym, the quality being "male" does not constitute "actual experience" in that subject matter. Choice D is incorrect. This answer choice does not include either the element of instruction or specific subject matter experience. Choice E is incorrect. This answer choice does not include the element of instruction.

7. **Choice E** is correct. If the marketing director did not get a bonus, then the number of books sold did not increase in August. Choice A is incorrect. We cannot conclude that book prices have increased based on the statements in the argument. Choice B is incorrect. In order for the marketing director to receive a bonus, book revenues must increase, and the increase must be a result of an increase in the number of books sold. We know only that the marketing director did not get a bonus. It is possible that the reason for this is that book revenues

decreased. Therefore, we cannot definitely conclude that book revenues increased based on the statements in the argument. Choice C is incorrect. As noted previously, in order for the marketing director to receive a bonus, book revenues must increase, and the increase must be a result of an increase in the number of books sold. If book revenues increase as a result of the increase in book price, then the marketing director does not get a bonus. We know only that the marketing director did not get a bonus. It is possible that the reason for this is that book revenues increased, but the increase was a result of an increase in book price, not number of books sold. Therefore, we cannot definitely conclude that book revenues did not increase based on the statements in the argument. Choice D is incorrect. The argument specifically states that if the number of books sold increased in August, then the marketing director would get a bonus. Because the marketing director did not get a bonus, the number of books could not have increased.

8. **Choice D** is correct. From the information in the statement, we can logically infer that current members of the Freedom Riders Motorcycle Club who have never ridden their motorcycle without a helmet outside of Wyoming have broken the law at least once. Choice A is incorrect. Because it is possible that one or all of the current members of the Freedom Riders Motorcycle Club have ridden their motorcycles without a helmet in a state in which such activity is allowed, we cannot logically infer that they have ridden their motorcycles illegally at least once during the past year. Choice B is incorrect. We cannot logically infer that every current member of the Freedom Riders Motorcycle Club has ridden his or her motorcycle without a helmet outside of Wyoming because some of the members may have chosen to break the law and do so within the state of Wyoming. Choice C is incorrect. No information in the statement is provided with respect to the persons under consideration for membership in the Freedom Riders Motorcycle Club, so we cannot logically infer anything about their behavior. Choice E is incorrect. From the information in the statement, we cannot logically infer that the Freedom Riders Motorcycle Club does not include members who have ridden a motorcycle without a helmet legally within Wyoming. Some of the members may have done so previous to the ban on such activity five years ago.

9. **Choice C** is correct. If true, this statement most helps to explain why the economy of York County is experiencing difficulties while the economy of Duke Country is not. Choice A is incorrect. It is unlikely that the relocation of several small financial services firms from York County to Duke County was significant enough to impact the overall

financial conditions of the two counties. Choice B is incorrect. This, if anything, would seem to indicate that York County's economy was better situated to handle a recession than Duke County's. Choice D is incorrect. This fact is irrelevant because we are concerned with the performance of two counties within the south region, not how the south region is faring vis-a-vis other regions of Renszuela. Choice E is incorrect. This fact does not provide any help in explaining why the economy of York County is experiencing difficulties while the economy of Duke County is not.

10. **Choice D** is correct. This answer choice offers reasoning that is most similar to that of the argument. It describes a program with a goal and a negative side effect of the program that prevents it from being effective, and it concludes that as a result the program should be abandoned. Choice A is incorrect. The reasoning used by the argument is as follows: It sets forth the aim of a particular program (maximize production) and then notes a negative side effect that prevents the goal of the program from being realized, concluding that as a result, the program does not fulfill its goal and therefore should be discontinued. In this answer choice, the aim of the program and then a negative side effect are mentioned, but the negative side effect does not prevent the goal of the program from being realized, and the conclusion does not state that the program should be abandoned. Choice B is incorrect. See the discussion of the reasoning in choice A. Choice B does not conclude that the "program" (laws) should be abandoned, but rather that the laws should be enforced. Choice C is incorrect. Although this answer choice discusses a program with a goal and concludes that the program should be abandoned (regulations ignored), it does not include a negative side effect of the program that leads to the conclusion. Choice E is incorrect. This answer choice does not conclude that the "program" (car alarms) should be abandoned.

11. **Choice A** is correct. The argument identifies two qualities that must be present in order for a car to be considered a good car—it must be aerodynamic, and it must get good gas mileage. But the argument then proceeds to discuss only the relationship of an efficient engine (which the conclusion states ensures that the car is good) to the second of the two elements (good gas mileage), ignoring the first element (aerodynamics). It fails, as this answer choice notes, to establish that the presence of an efficient engine means that the car also satisfies the first element. Choice B is incorrect. This answer choice is not really relevant to the argument in the statement because the argument is concerned with a car that has an efficient engine. Choice C is incorrect. This

answer choice is too broad because the argument need not establish that a car can be aerodynamic *only* if it has an efficient engine but merely that having an efficient engine means that a car is aerodynamic. Choice D is incorrect. This answer choice contradicts what is explicitly stated in the argument (that a car with an efficient engine will get good gas mileage). Choice E is incorrect. This answer choice also contradicts what is explicitly stated in the argument (that a car that is aerodynamic and gets good gas mileage can be considered a good car).

12. **Choice D** is correct. This is the most logical conclusion to the argument. Because Ken is not prepared to devote himself fully to a new book project, and because this is a prerequisite to Ken and Carol taking on a new book project, one can logical conclude that Ken and Carol will not take on a new book project this year. Choice A is incorrect. This is not necessarily a logical conclusion for the argument in the statement. Just because Ken is not ready to take on a new book project now does not mean that he was never really interested in doing so. Choice B is incorrect. There is nothing in the argument that provides evidence for such a conclusion. Choice C is incorrect. Although one might assume this is true, it is not necessarily so. Nothing in the argument indicates Carol's stance on taking on a new book project. The evidence in the argument only relates to Carol's views on Ken's position. Choice E is incorrect. This answer choice merely restates evidence already set forth in the argument.

13. **Choice B** is correct. The manufacturers conclude that the stents will cure heart disease. However, in order for them to do so, doctors must first implant the stents in patients suffering from heart disease. Choice A is incorrect. Whether or not the stents are the safest way is not relevant to the conclusion, which addresses only efficacy, not safety. Choice C is incorrect. Whether there are other methods of alleviating heart disease is irrelevant to the conclusion. Choice D is incorrect. While one might assume that manufacturing the stents will be financially lucrative for medical device manufacturers, this is not necessarily so, and even if it were, the conclusion is not based on this assumption. Choice E is incorrect. While one might assume that medical device manufacturers in fact need to adequately test devices before marketing them, this assumption is not related to the conclusion that patients who are suffering from heart disease will have their conditions cured through the use of stents.

14. **Choice E** is correct. The conclusion assumes that magazine authors can be motivated to increase their productivity through monetary rewards. Choice A is incorrect. There is no evidence in the argument

or conclusion on which to base such an assumption. Choice B is incorrect. There is no evidence in the argument or conclusion as to what "most" magazines want. Choice C is incorrect. This answer choice merely restates an element that is specifically stated in the argument. Choice D is incorrect. There is no evidence in the argument or conclusion on which to base such an assumption.

15. **Choice B** is correct. Fran makes an emotional appeal to her opponents. Choice A is incorrect. Fran does not provide any evidence or attempt to undercut the rationale of her opponents. Choice C is incorrect. Fran does not make a personal attack on her opponents. Choice D is incorrect. Fran does not present a conclusion supported by evidence. Choice E is incorrect. Fran does not deride the viewpoint of her opponents.

16. **Choice D** is correct. If true, the fact that gray wolves will not hunt prey that is diseased damages the argument because it suggests that gray wolves will not eliminate the many deer that are suffering from chronic wasting disease and that therefore the ecology of the area will remain unstable. Choice A is incorrect. The fact that the gray wolf has never been known to live on Block Island does not invalidate the fact that it is a natural predator of deer. Choice B is incorrect. The fact that deer on Block Island are habituated to dogs and do not fear them does not damage the argument that introducing a natural predator such as the gray wolf to Block Island could stabilize the ecology of the area without requiring the shooting of deer. Choice C is incorrect. The fact that residents of Block Island oppose the introduction of gray wolves does not damage the argument that introducing a natural predator such as the gray wolf to Block Island could stabilize the ecology of the area without requiring the shooting of deer. Choice E is incorrect. The fact that gray wolves are themselves endangered is irrelevant to the argument.

17. **Choice B** is correct. Theodore is responsible for his father's flat because he voluntarily took an action (left nails on the driveway), knowing that because they were sharp, the nails created risk. Choice C is incorrect. Theodore is responsible for getting sick because he voluntarily took an action (visited his sick aunt) that he knew posed a risk. Choice A is incorrect. Theodore is not responsible for the dog getting loose because the dog did not get loose from any action that Theodore voluntarily took. Choice D is incorrect. Theodore is not responsible for losing his bike because although he voluntarily took an action (left it in his garage), he did not know this action created a risk (he thought it was safe). Choice E is incorrect. Although Simon may believe that

Theodore should be held responsible for getting good grades in school, that belief is unrelated to the principle cited by Simon.

18. **Choice C** is correct. The conclusion confuses amount spent with percentage spent. Choice B is incorrect. The evidence cited in the argument can be considered reliable. Choice A is incorrect. The total amount of the club's budget is irrelevant to the conclusion. Choice D is incorrect. The conclusion is not required to consider other possible alternatives, so its failure to do so cannot be deemed a flaw. Choice E is incorrect. The conclusion is not based on a generalization that is contradicted by the evidence.

19. **Choice C** is correct. This answer choice is most similar to the erroneous pattern of reasoning set forth in the statement. It states that members of certain professions have a certain quality and that someone who is a member of a second profession that one may infer also requires that same quality would therefore be good at the first profession. Choice A is incorrect. The erroneous pattern of reasoning set forth in the argument is as follows: Members of a certain profession have a certain quality. Someone who is a member of a second profession that one may infer also requires the same quality should therefore also be good at the first profession. This answer choice does not follow that erroneous pattern of reasoning. Instead, it posits that because someone who can do something should be able to do a second thing, that a person who can do the first thing should also be able to do the second thing. Choice B is incorrect. This answer choice does not follow the erroneous pattern of reasoning set forth in the statement. Instead, it posits that someone with a certain quality can do well at a certain thing and that therefore if someone has that quality, he or she should also be able to well at that certain thing. Choice D is incorrect. This answer choice does not follow the erroneous pattern of reasoning set forth in the statement. Instead, it posits that all members of a certain profession have a certain quality and that if someone has that quality, that person must be a member of that profession. Choice E is incorrect. This answer choice does not follow the erroneous pattern of reasoning set forth in the statement. Instead, it posits that all members of a certain profession have a certain quality and that if someone is a member of that profession, that person must have that quality.

20. **Choice E** is correct. If Angela has won three years straight, but this year Linda beat Angela, if we assume that Linda could beat Angela only if she trained very hard, then it is logical to conclude based on this assumption that Linda trained very hard. Choice B is incorrect. The conclusion is about Linda, so an assumption about Angela is irrelevant.

Choice A is incorrect. The conclusion is about Linda, so an assumption about Angela is irrelevant. Choice C is incorrect. This assumption contradicts the facts stated in the argument. Choice D is incorrect. The conclusion is about Linda, so an assumption about Angela is irrelevant.

21. **Choice B** is correct. Competition between two products of the same type (flights on Delta Song, flights on regular Delta) has resulted in the first type cannibalizing sales of the second type. Choice A is incorrect. The principle being expressed by the argument is that competition between two products of the same type (U2 songs on the Internet, U2 songs on CD) has resulted in the first type cannibalizing sales of the second type. In this answer choice, availability of one type of product (DVDs) has increased sales of a different type of product (DVD players). Choice C is incorrect. This answer choice does not feature explicit competition between products (only perhaps implied competition between labor in the United States versus labor overseas) and as such does not parallel the reasoning expressed in the statement. Choice D is incorrect. Although this answer choice features explicit competition between two products, they are of different brands rather than the same brand. Choice E is incorrect. This answer choice does not feature competition between two products of the same type.

22. **Choice B** is correct. Lisa offers a counterexample to Edith's claim. Choice A is incorrect. Lisa does not attempt to change the grounds of the argument. Her response focuses on the evidence cited by Edith for her claim. Choice C is incorrect. Lisa does not offer a counterclaim nor any analogies. Choice D is incorrect. Lisa does not attempt to undermine Edith's argument by making a personal attack on Edith's character. Choice E is incorrect. Lisa does not offer an unsupported generalization as an alternative to Edith's claim.

23. **Choice D** is correct. If the only meats available for consumption in Atrebla are beef, mutton/lamb, and poultry products, then it must be true that no pork has been imported to Atrebla for consumption because the pigs in Atrebla were destroyed. Choice A is incorrect. There is nothing in the statement that requires the statement in this answer choice to be true. Choice B is incorrect. There is nothing in the statement that requires the statement in this answer choice to be true. Choice C is incorrect. There is nothing in the statement that requires the statement in this answer choice to be true. Choice E is incorrect. While this might very well be true, it does not have to necessarily be true.

24. **Choice E** is correct. The argument's conclusion is that even when foozeball players are hurt during a game, they usually continue to play. Because Choice E shows that most foozeball players who are injured during a game do not miss any significant playing time, it supports the conclusion. Choices A and B are incorrect because they undermine the conclusion—that even when foozeball players are hurt during a game, they continue to play. Choice C is incorrect. Although it may be sound advice, it doesn't come out and support the argument's conclusion that players continue to play even with an injury. Choice D fails because the fact that fans may suffer the same rate of injuries is irrelevant to the contention that the players will simple ignore the injury and return to the game.

SECTION IV—Reading Comprehension

1. C	10. E	19. B
2. B	11. C	20. A
3. C	12. C	21. B
4. D	13. A	22. E
5. A	14. B	23. E
6. A	15. A	24. C
7. E	16. E	25. A
8. A	17. D	26. A
9. C	18. B	27. E

1. **Choice C** is correct. "Challenges in Effectively Delivering Gene Therapy" would be the best choice for the title of the passage because that is the primary focus of the passage. Choice A is incorrect. "The Failure of Gene Therapy" would not be the best choice for the title of the passage. While the passage notes in the first paragraph that the results achieved in gene therapy trials to date have been disappointing, the passage does not focus on the failures of gene therapy; rather, it focuses on the challenges facing researchers. Choice B is incorrect. "The Successes of Gene Therapy" would not be the best choice for the title of the passage. As noted in the first paragraph of the passage,

there had been only one successful gene therapy trial at the date the passage was written. The passage does not focus on the success of that particular trial but rather on the challenges facing researchers in delivering gene therapy. Choice D is incorrect. "The Uses of Retroviruses in Gene Therapy" would not be the best choice for the title of the passage. While the second paragraph of the passage mentions the uses of retroviruses in gene therapy, this is not the primary focus of the passage. Choice E is incorrect. "The Use of Embryonic Stem Cells in Gene Therapy" would not be the best choice for the title of the passage. While the passage does discuss the use of embryonic stem cells as a possible alternative to adult and cord blood stem cells, the passage primarily focuses on the challenges and difficulties attendant to using adult and cord blood stem cells, and not on the use of embryonic stem cells.

2. **Choice B** is correct. The author's attitude toward the use of human embryonic stem cells in gene therapy can best be described as neutral (see the explanation for choice A in Question 1). Choice A is incorrect. Nothing in the passage indicates that the author has formed a particular judgment with respect to the use of embryonic stem cells. In the last sentence of the first paragraph, the author notes that the use of embryonic stem cells might overcome some of the limitations of using adult and cord blood stem cells but that further research will be needed to determine this. In lines 39–41 of the passage, the author notes that that there is a "possibility" that one of the limitations of adult hematopoietic stem sells might be overcome with the use of embryonic stem cells "if" they require less manipulation. Later, in lines 47–49, the author notes that certain research findings "suggest" that fetal cord blood stem cells might be useful." The final sentence of the passage notes, "whether the use of embryonic stem cells in gene therapy could overcome [the problem of gene silencing] is unknown." Choice C is incorrect. Nothing in the passage indicates that the author has a diffident (shy or timid) attitude with respect to use of embryonic stem cells. Choice D is incorrect. Nothing in the passage indicates that the author has a disdainful attitude with respect to use of embryonic stem cells. Choice E is incorrect. Nothing in the passage indicates that the author has an incredulous (disbelieving) attitude with respect to use of embryonic stem cells.

3. **Choice C** is correct. We can infer that it is not true that hematopoietic stem cells normally are actively dividing from the juxtaposition of the following two sentences: "[M]ouse retroviruses are only efficient at infecting cells that are actively dividing. Unfortunately, hematopoietic stems cells are quiescent" (lines 23–25). From this sentence construction, we should be able to determine that *quiescent* means inactive, or

not actively dividing. Further support for this inference can be garnered from the next sentence, in lines 27–28, which states, "because of this problem, investigators have been exploring the use of viral vehicles that can infect *nondividing* cells." Choice A is incorrect. We can infer that it is true that it is difficult to introduce transgenes into hematopoietic stem cells because the second paragraph of the passage focuses on these difficulties, and the third paragraph focuses on approaches to improving this process. Choice B is incorrect. We can infer from the third paragraph of the passage that it is true that it is possible to change the properties of hematopoietic stem cells because lines 37–38 note that one of the approaches to improving the introduction of transgenes into hematopoietic stem cells can "change other important properties" of such cells. Choice D is incorrect. We can infer that is it is true that mouse retroviruses cannot be effectively used to insert therapeutic transgenes into the chromosomes of a hematopoietic stem cell because in lines 20–25, the passage states that while retroviruses are often used as a vehicle for introducing the therapeutic transgene into chromosomal DNA, mouse retroviruses are only efficient at infecting cells that are actively dividing, and hematopoietic stem cells are quiescent (not actively dividing). Choice E is incorrect. We can infer from the last paragraph of the passage that it is true that gene silencing makes using hematopoietic stem cells for gene therapy problematic.

4. **Choice D** is correct. The author of the passage is likely to disagree that the viruses that causes HIV are too dangerous to be used in gene therapy. In lines 27–29, the author notes that investigators have been exploring the use of viral vehicles that can infect nondividing cells, such as lentiviruses (for example, HIV). Choice A is incorrect. Based on the first paragraph of the passage, the author of the passage is likely to agree that initial attempts at actually implementing gene therapy have been disappointing. In line 1, the author notes that "with one notable exception, no therapeutic effects have been achieved in gene therapy trials to date" and in line 7, characterizes these results as "generally disappointing." Choice B is incorrect. The author of the passage is likely to agree that it is not clear whether embryonic stem cells are any better suited for gene therapy than adult stem cells. In lines 10–11, the author notes that "further research will be needed" to determine this. Choice C is incorrect. The author of the passage is likely to agree that the use of cord blood stem cells for gene therapy is problematic. In lines 7–9 of the passage, the author notes that "the generally disappointing results are due, in part, to the inherent limitations of adult and cord blood stem cells." Choice E is incorrect. The author of the passage is likely to agree that treatment of chronic diseases is likely to

require continuous production of the therapeutic transgene over the life of the patient. In lines 50–52 of the passage, the author notes that in the treatment of chronic disease, achieving continued production of the therapeutic transgene over the life of the patient will be very important.

5. **Choice A** is correct. In the third paragraph of the passage, the author notes that preliminary data suggests that retroviral vectors work more efficiently with embryonic stem cells than with the more mature adult stem cells. Choice B is incorrect. In the second paragraph of the passage, the author notes that mouse retroviruses are not efficient at infecting hematopoietic stem cells. Choice C is incorrect. In the last sentence of the passage, the author notes that preliminary evidence suggests that the phenomenon of gene silencing may also occur in embryonic stem cells. Choice D is incorrect. In lines 29–32, the author notes that the approach of using adeno-associated viruses has not been entirely successful. Choice E is incorrect. In lines 36–38, the author notes that Inder Verma of the Salk Institute has found that stimulating hematopoietic stems cells to divide can change other important properties of the cell.

6. **Choice A** is correct. "Inactive" (with respect to cell division) is the best choice for the meaning of the word *quiescent* as it is used in the context of the passage. Choice B is incorrect. *Quiescent* means to be inactive or dormant. It does not mean to be mobile. Choice C is incorrect. *Quiescent* means to be inactive or dormant. It does not mean to be lifeless. Choice D is incorrect. *Quiescent* means to be inactive or dormant. It does not mean to be active. Choice E is incorrect. *Quiescent* means to be inactive or dormant. It does not mean to be proliferative.

7. **Choice E** is correct. As noted in line 23 of the passage, stem cells in fact do contain chromosomal DNA. Therefore, this could not be a limitation on the use of adult and newborn cord blood stem cells in gene therapy. Choice A is incorrect. As noted in the second paragraph of the passage, the inability of the stem cells to retain the therapeutic transgene as it proliferates or differentiates into specialized cells is a limitation on the use of adult and newborn cord blood stem cells in gene therapy. Choice B is incorrect. As noted in lines 25–27 of the passage, the inability of the stem cells to actually receive the therapeutic transgene is a limitation on the use of adult and newborn cord blood stem cells in gene therapy. Choice C is incorrect. As noted in lines 29–32 of the passage, the fact that the stem cells themselves are not in an active state is a limitation on the use of adult and newborn cord blood stem cells in gene therapy. Choice D is incorrect. As noted in lines 53–57 of

the passage, the "gene-silencing" phenomenon is a limitation on the use of adult and newborn cord blood stem cells in gene therapy.

8. **Choice A** is correct. The main idea of the passage is that standing is an essential component of federal jurisdiction. This idea is introduced in the first paragraph of the passage, and the remainder of the passage is devoted to defining what constitutes standing. Choice B is incorrect. While it true that the passage notes in the first paragraph that under Article III of the U.S. Constitution, federal courts have jurisdiction over cases and controversies, this is not the primary focus of the passage. Choice C is incorrect. While it is true that the passage notes in lines 24–25 that plaintiffs seeking federal jurisdiction bear the burden of proof, this is not the primary focus of the passage. Choice D is incorrect. The passage does not comment on the ease or difficulty of establishing standing when a suit is challenging the legality of government action or inaction. Choice E is incorrect. While it is true that the passage notes in lines 31–35 that summary judgment motions require a higher burden of proof than the pleading stage, this is not the focus of the passage.

9. **Choice C** is correct. As stated in line 17 of the passage, an actual or imminent invasion of the interest at issue is a required element of standard. The passage specifically states that the invasion may *not* be hypothetical. Choice A is incorrect. As stated in line 18 of the passage, a legally protected interest is an element of establishing standing. Choice B is incorrect. As stated in lines 18–19 of the passage, the interest at issue must be concrete and particularized in order to establish standing. Choice D is incorrect. As stated in lines 19–21 of the passage, in order to establish standing, the conduct complained of must be a causative factor in the injury. Choice E is incorrect. As stated in lines 21–23 of the passage, in order to establish standing, the injury must be one that is likely to be corrected by a decision in favor of the plaintiff.

10. **Choice E** is correct. Based on the first paragraph of the passage, the author would agree with the statement that separation of powers depends in major part on a common understanding of what activities are appropriate to the three branches of government. Choice A is incorrect. Line 3 of the passage states that the Constitution does not attempt to define the terms *legislative powers*, *executive power*, and *judicial power*. Choice B is incorrect. In lines 7–9, the author notes that the Constitution's central mechanism of separation of powers depends largely upon common understanding, and in lines 9–10 the passage states that one of those landmarks is the doctrine of standing. Choice

C is incorrect. While it is true that at the pleading stage, general factual allegations may suffice, the passage goes on to note in lines 31–35 that the plaintiff can no longer rest on such mere allegations. Choice D is incorrect. In lines 57–60, the author notes that when the plaintiff is not himself the object of the government action or inaction challenged, standing is ordinarily substantially more difficult to establish.

11. **Choice C** is correct. *To adduce*, as used in the context of the passage, means to cite. Choice A is incorrect. *Adduce* does not mean to withhold. Choice B is incorrect. *Adduce* does not mean to dispute. Choice D is incorrect. *Adduce* does not mean to gainsay. Choice E is incorrect. *Adduce* does not mean to controvert.

12. **Choice C** is correct. In line 30 of the passage, the author refers to the case as involving an injury that rises from the government's regulation of someone other than the plaintiff. Choice A is incorrect. In line 30 of the passage, the author refers to the case as involving an injury that rises from the government's regulation of someone other than the plaintiff. Choice B is incorrect. In line 30 of the passage, the author refers to the case as involving an injury that rises from the government's regulation of someone other than the plaintiff. Choice D is incorrect. In line 30 of the passage, the author refers to the case as involving an injury that rises from the government's regulation of someone other than the plaintiff. Choice E is incorrect. In line 30 of the passage, the author refers to the case as involving an injury that rises from the government's regulation of someone other than the plaintiff.

13. **Choice A** is correct. In lines 10–14 of the passage, the author notes that some of standing's elements express merely prudential considerations that are part of judicial self-government but that its core component is an essential and unchanging part of the case or controversy requirement of Article III. From this, one may infer that there are elements of the doctrine of standing that are not essential parts of the case or controversy requirement. Choice B is incorrect. In lines 15–16, the author states, "our cases have established that the irreducible constitutional minimum of standing contains three elements." Choice C is incorrect. In the fourth paragraph of the passage, the author discusses how the type of suit affects the requirements of establishing standing. Choice D is incorrect. In the third and fourth paragraphs of the passage, the author discusses how the stage of the suit affects the requirements of establishing standing. Choice E is incorrect. In the first paragraph, the author discusses how the doctrine of standing helps define the separation of powers.

14. **Choice B** is correct. The concerns that Microsoft's past market behavior raises about the potential impact of its .NET and .NET MyServices strategies are the primary focus of the passage. Choice A is incorrect. While it is true that the passage states in the second paragraph (line 5 and lines 9–10, respectively) that monopolies can have social and economic benefits as well as costs, this is not the focus of the passage. For instance, the passage only briefly mentions the social/economic benefits of markets (network economies). Choice C is incorrect. While it is true that the passage describes Microsoft's market behavior as anti-competitive, and while this behavior is a focus of the passage, unlike Choice B, this answer choice fails to mention .NET and .NET MyServices, which are of primary importance in the passage. Choice D is incorrect. While it is true that the passage mentions in line 54 that extraordinary consumer benefits may result if .NET and .NET MyServices are successful, this is not the primary focus of the passage Choice E is incorrect. The passage does not state that Microsoft dominates the e-commerce environment, but rather that it has the potential to extend its dominance of the computer software platform market into the e-commerce arena (lines 3–4).

15. **Choice A** is correct. The third paragraph of the passage provides evidence in support of the contention that Microsoft has acted in a monopolistic and anticompetitive manner by citing various Justice Department decrees, investigations, and lawsuits. Choice B is incorrect. The third paragraph does not contradict the thesis of the passage. Choice C is incorrect. The third paragraph of the passage does not attempt to reconcile two conflicting schools of thought. Choice D is incorrect. It cannot be stated with certainty that the third paragraph of the passage presents a viewpoint different from that of the author. Choice E is incorrect. The third paragraph of the passage does not provide possible explanations for a paradox.

16. **Choice E** is correct. Line 6 of the passage identifies network economies as a benefit of monopolies. Choice A is incorrect. Lines 12–14 of the passage note that "monopolies can engage in predatory pricing behavior to drive competitors out of business." Choice B is incorrect. Lines 12–14 of the passage note that monopolies can engage in predatory pricing behavior to threaten new entrants to the marketplace. Choice C is incorrect. Lines 14–15 of the passage note that monopolies raise prices above what a competitive marketplace would produce. Choice D is incorrect. Line 16 of the passage notes that monopolies can stifle innovation.

17. **Choice D** is correct. Given the questioning tone of the article and its emphasis on Microsoft's previous monopolistic and anti-competitive market behavior that required intervention by the U.S. Justice Department, the U.S. District Court, and various state attorneys general, it is not likely that the author believes that market forces and consumer opinion are enough in and of themselves to check Microsoft's market behavior. Choice A is incorrect. Line 2 of the passage refers to Microsoft's dominance of the computer software platform market, which the author notes is likely to persist into the foreseeable future. Choice B is incorrect. Line 50 of the passage indicates that the author believes that Passport is the centerpiece of Microsoft's .NET and .NET MyServices strategies. Choice C is incorrect. Lines 62–63 indicate that the author believes that if .NET and .NET MyServices succeed, Microsoft may, as it has in the past, engage in monopolistic anticompetitive behavior. Choice E is incorrect. Line 54 of the passage indicates that the author believes that if .NET and .NET MyServices succeed, extraordinary consumer benefits will result from these services.

18. **Choice B** is correct. The author's attitude toward Microsoft can best be described as skeptical and questioning. For instance, in lines 43–44, the author wonders whether "we, as a society, want Microsoft to dominate the e-commerce environment just as it has dominated the operating system and browser marketplace." In line 58, the passage notes that ".NET and .NET MyServices raise some very interesting questions." And in the concluding paragraph, the passage questions "who watches over Microsoft" and whether market forces and consumer opinion can work by themselves to keep Microsoft in check. Choice A is incorrect. While the author evidences a somewhat critical attitude toward Microsoft, the attitude cannot be described as condemnatory, given the potential benefits that the author cites as a possibility if .NET and .NET MyServices succeed. Choice C is incorrect. Nothing in the passage indicates that the author has an encomiastic (congratulatory) attitude toward Microsoft. Choice D is incorrect. Nothing in the passage indicates that the author has an unctuous (insincerely earnest) attitude toward Microsoft. Choice E is incorrect. Nothing in the passage indicates that the author is attempting to disparage (belittle) Microsoft.

19. **Choice B** is correct. As stated in lines 16–17 of the passage, Sherman Anti-Trust Act did not make monopolies illegal. Choice A is incorrect. Lines 62–63 of the passage indicate that Microsoft has engaged in monopolistic anticompetitive behavior through its licensing process. Choice C is incorrect. Lines 67–68 of the passage state that Passport

stores personal and payment information on Microsoft servers. Choice D is incorrect. Lines 37–39 of the passage states that PC manufacturers are no longer required to display Microsoft icons on the desktop. Choice E is incorrect. Although the date on which the passage was written is not indicated, from the third paragraph of the passage, we know that "since the early 1990s" the U.S. Department of Justice has been monitoring Microsoft's market behavior, and we can confirm that it has been doing so for at least four years, because according to the passage, in 1994 Microsoft consented to a Justice Department decree; in 1996, it began investigating Microsoft's dominance of the operating system and browser markets; in 1997 it filed a petition against Microsoft; and in 1998, it filed an antitrust lawsuit against Microsoft.

20. **Choice A** is correct. The reference to "digital information silos" states that "many of the digital information silos will disappear" (lines 55–56 of the passage). Although this phrase is not explicitly defined, by reading the previous paragraph, which talks about Microsoft supplying all the vital e-commerce and personal information management tools required to lead a digital life, the reference to Passport supplying a digital ID and handling the payment process for much of B2C e-commerce, as well as the reference to Microsoft becoming the "centralized repository" of personal identifiable information, we can deduce that what the author believes is going to disappear are isolated collections of personal information. Instead, Microsoft will hold all our information and supply it to those who need it. Choice B is incorrect. There is nothing in the passage that would lead one to infer that the phrase "digital information silos" refers to vendors who are Microsoft competitors. Choice C is incorrect. There is nothing in the passage that would lead one to infer that the phrase "digital information silos" refers to personal information management tools. Choice D is incorrect. There is nothing in the passage that would lead one to infer that the phrase "digital information silos" refers to anticompetitive licensing practices. Choice E is incorrect. There is nothing in the passage that would lead one to infer that the phrase "digital information silos" refers to Microsoft's dominance of the computer software platform market.

21. **Choice B** is correct. "Using CMI to Meet America's Defense Needs" would be the best choice for the title of the passage because that is the primary focus of the passage. Choice A is incorrect. "America's DTIB" is not the best choice for the title of the passage. Although the nation's DTIB is a subject of the passage, this title is too generic and is not descriptive of the primary focus of the passage. Choice C is incorrect. "The Benefits of CMI" would not be the best choice for the title of the passage. Although the benefits of CMI are mentioned in the fourth

paragraph of the passage, this title is too narrow and is not descriptive of the primary focus of the passage. Choice D is incorrect. "CMI Barriers" is not the best choice for the title of the passage. While obstacles to the successful implementation of CMI are discussed in the fifth paragraph of the passage, this title is too narrow and is not descriptive of the primary focus of the passage. Choice E is incorrect. "Strategies for Increasing CMI" is not the best choice for the title of the passage. While strategies for increasing CMI are discussed in the sixth paragraph of the passage, this title is too narrow and is not descriptive of the primary focus of the passage.

22. **Choice E is correct.** The passage does not report that the unwillingness of commercial firms to exploit the results of the nation's defense investments is a barrier to successful implementation of CMI or a risk associated with CMI. Rather, the passage notes that the isolation of the DTIB is what makes it difficult for commercial firms to exploit the results of the nation's defense investments (lines 4–9). Choice A is incorrect. The passage states in lines 38–40 that one of the greatest risks of CMI is that commercial goods and services may fail in military operations. Choice B is incorrect. The passage states in lines 40–41 that increased CMI may result in greater dependence on foreign goods and services. Choice C is incorrect. The passage states in lines 41–42 that another risk of CMI is that increased instances of fraud and abuse may result. Choice D is incorrect. The passage states in lines 34–35 that one of the major obstacles to CMI is its sheer complexity.

23. **Choice E is correct.** The general organization of the passage can be best described as follows: The passage identifies a problem, offers a solution to the problem, identifies various issues with respect to the solution, and describes some possible strategies for implementing the solution. Choice A is incorrect. The passage does not begin with the statement of a thesis, and then provide examples in support of the thesis, present opposing viewpoints, and then restate the thesis. Choice B is incorrect. While the passage does begin by providing some historical context for the development of the isolation of the nation's DTIB, it does not then present both sides of a controversy or conclude with a statement of support for one of the sides. Choice C is incorrect. The passage does not state a thesis, present viewpoints that oppose that thesis, provide examples in support of both viewpoints, and then conclude with a question. Choice D is incorrect. While the passage does begin by identifying a problem, it does not follow with a list of obstacles to solve the problem, discuss concrete examples of the obstacles, propose various alternatives to solve the problem, and conclude with an endorsement of a particular alternative.

24. **Choice C** is correct. The tone of the passage can best be described as balanced and objective. As noted with respect to answer Choice B, the author dispassionately examines the issues surrounding CMI, discussing both its positive attributes and its risks, without overtly taking sides. Choice A is incorrect. The passage does not evince a condescending and ironic tone. Choice B is incorrect. While the tone of the passage might be characterized as analytical, it cannot also be characterized as judgmental. Instead, the author dispassionately examines the issues surrounding CMI, discussing both its positive attributes and its risks, without overtly taking sides. Choice D is incorrect. The passage does not evince a didactic (excessively moralizing) and pedantic (bookish) tone. Choice E is incorrect. The tone of the passage cannot be described as hostile and argumentative. As noted with respect to Choice B, the author dispassionately examines the issues surrounding CMI, discussing both its positive attributes and its risks, without overtly taking sides.

25. **Choice A** is correct. The primary purpose of the passage is to describe the issues surrounding and possible methods of implementing a CMI program to support the United States's defense in an era of budget cuts. Choice B is incorrect. Explaining why commercial firms have found it difficult to exploit the results of the nation's defense science and technology investments is not the primary purpose of the passage. This issue is addressed only briefly in the first paragraph of the passage. Choice C is incorrect. Examining why much of the U.S. DTIB remains isolated is not the primary purpose of the passage. This fact is only briefly noted at the beginning of the third paragraph (lines 16–17). Choice D is incorrect. Discussing strategies for increasing CMI is not the primary purpose of the passage. This is merely one aspect of the passage, whose larger purpose, as noted in the explanation for choice A, is to describe the issues surrounding and possible methods of implementing a CMI program to support the United States's defense in an era of budget cuts. Choice E is incorrect. Assessing the potential costs and benefits of CMI is not the primary purpose of the passage. It is merely one aspect of the passage, whose larger purpose, as noted in the explanation for choice A, is to describe the issues surrounding and possible methods of implementing a CMI program to support the United States's defense in an era of budget cuts.

26. **Choice A** is correct. The author is likely to disagree that attempting to implement CMI is not a worthwhile endeavor. Given the author's identification of the isolation of the nation's DTIB from its commercial base as a factor in the increase of the cost of defense goods and services, the reduction of the Defense Department's access to commercial

technologies and the difficulties of commercial firms in exploiting the results of the nation's defense investments, and presentation of CMI as a potential solution to this problem that has "clear benefits," the author likely believes that implementing CMI is a worthwhile, although not risk-free, endeavor. Choice B is incorrect. In the first paragraph of the passage, the author describes the isolation of the nation's DTIB from its commercial base as having a variety of negative consequences, and we can infer that the author believes that these consequences should be addressed because the second paragraph of the passage identifies a potential solution to the problem. Choice C is incorrect. The author is likely to agree that some sectors will be more successful in implementing CMI than others. Lines 26–27 of the passage, for instance, specifically state that services appear particularly amenable to commercial purchases. Choice D is incorrect. The author is likely to agree that CMI can create significant cost savings. Lines 28–29 of the passage report that "analysis indicates significant cost savings will result." Choice E is incorrect. The author is likely to agree that efforts to increase CMI are not risk free. For instance, the fifth paragraph of the passage is devoted to a description of the various risks posed by increased CMI.

27. **Choice E** is correct. We can infer from the passage that the statement that "CMI cannot be implemented successfully overnight" is true, not false, because the last paragraph of the passage describes successful implementation of CMI as requiring a long-term commitment, mentions that potential benefits will "take time to accrue," and mentions "patience and steady effort." Choice A is incorrect. We can infer from the passage that the statement "Increasing CMI is not expected to impact the nation's economy" is false because in line 44 of the passage, the author notes that "expected benefits to…the economy" from increasing CMI must be balanced against potential pitfalls. Choice B is incorrect. We can infer from the passage that the statement "CMI has never been tried" is false because line 16 of the passage refers to "several previous initiatives to promote integration" and then further speaks of "increasing CMI" (line 22), which implies that it already exists. Choice C is incorrect. We can infer from the passage that the statement "A reform strategy for increasing CMI poses the least risk" is false because line 48 of the passage describes the readjustment strategy as involving the least risk. Choice D is incorrect. We can infer from the passage that the statement "A restructuring strategy is an incremental approach to increasing CMI" is false because in lines 56–57 of the passage, the restructuring strategy is described as demanding major changes, which is the opposite of an incremental approach.

CD Contents and Installation Instructions

The CD features a state-of-the-art exam preparation engine from ExamForce. This uniquely powerful program will identify gaps in your knowledge and help you turn them into strengths. In addition to the ExamForce software, the CD includes an electronic version of this book in Portable Document Format (PDF) format, a "Need to Know More?" PDF file of useful resources, and the Adobe Acrobat Reader used to display these files.

Also included on the CD-ROM is an audio version of portions of the Self-Assessment and the chapters on Logical Reasoning, Analytical Reasoning, and Reading Comprehension. To play it, you can use the disc with your computer's CD-ROM drive, Walkman, or home stereo.

The audio presentation offers another avenue for learning. Some retain more material in a simple visual presentation; others prefer a hands-on, or "kinesthetic" approach. Still others prefer to listen to the material in order to concentrate on what is being said.

Even if you're primarily a visual learner, consider listening to the CD on the car stereo or when you're working on other tasks at hand. You may find that you pick up on different bits of information or that arguments (which are verbal to begin with) are easier to understand and dissect when listened to and then read. Whichever way promotes the best retention and learning of the proper technique, continue using it for your best LSAT exam result.

The CramMaster Engine

This innovative exam engine systematically prepares you for a successful test. Working your way through CramMaster is the fastest, surest route to a successful exam. The presentation of questions is weighted according to your unique requirements. Your answer history determines which questions you'll see next. It determines what you don't know and forces you to overcome those shortcomings. You won't waste time answering easy questions about things you already know.

Multiple Test Modes

The CramMaster test engine, from ExamForce, has three unique testing modes to systematically prepare you for a successful exam.

Pretest Mode

Pretest mode is used to establish your baseline skill set. Train CramMaster by taking two or three pretests. There is no review or feedback on answers in this mode. View your topic-by-topic skill levels from the History menu on the main screen. Then, effective exam preparation begins by attacking your weakest topics first in Adaptive Drill mode.

Adaptive Drill Mode

Adaptive Drill mode enables you to focus on specific exam objectives. CramMaster learns the questions you find difficult and drills you until you master them. As you gain proficiency in one area, it seeks out the next with which to challenge you. Even the most complex concepts of the exam are mastered in this mode.

Simulated Exam Mode

Simulated Exam mode approximates the real LSAT exam. By the time you reach this level, you've already mastered the exam material. This is your opportunity to exercise those skills while building your mental and physical stamina.

Installing CramMaster for the LSAT Exam

The following are the minimum system requirements for installation:

➤ Windows 98, Me, NT4, 2000, or XP

➤ 128MB of RAM

➤ 38MB of disk space

> If you need technical support, please contact ExamForce at 1-800-845-8569 or email support@examforce.com. Additional product support can be found at www.examforce.com.

To install the CramMaster CD-ROM, follow these instructions:

1. Close all applications before beginning this installation.

2. Insert the CD into your CD-ROM drive. If the setup starts automatically, go to step 6. If the setup does not start automatically, continue with step 3.

3. From the Start menu, select Run.

4. Click Browse to locate the CramMaster CD. From the Look In drop-down list in the Browse dialog box, select the CD-ROM drive.

5. In the Browse dialog box, double-click Setup.exe. In the Run dialog box, click OK to begin the installation.

6. On the Welcome screen, click Next.

7. Select "I Agree" to the End User License Agreement (EULA); click Next.

8. The CramMaster setup will run a system check to determine whether required files are installed on your system. If it detects missing files, it will install them on your system. Save any restart requests until the CramMaster installation is finished.

9. Enter your registered user information and click Next.

10. On the Choose Destination Location screen, click Next to install the software to C:\Program Files\CramMaster.

11. On the Select Program Manager Group screen, verify that the Program Manager group is set to CramMaster, and click Next.

12. On the Start Installation screen, click Next.

13. On the Installation Complete screen, click Finish.

14. For your convenience, a shortcut to CramMaster will be created automatically on your desktop.

Using CramMaster for the LSAT Exam

An introductory slide show will start when CramMaster first launches. It will teach you how to get the most out of this uniquely powerful program. Uncheck the Show on Startup box to suppress the introduction from showing each time the application is launched. You may review it at any time from the Help menu on the main screen. Tips on using other CramMaster features can be found there as well.

Customer Support

If you encounter problems installing or using CramMaster for the LSAT exam, please contact ExamForce at 1-800-845-8569 or email support@ examforce.com. Support hours are from 8:30 a.m. to 5:30 p.m. EST Monday through Friday. Additional product support can be found at www. examforce.com.

If you would like to purchase additional ExamForce products, call 1-800-845-8569 or visit www.examforce.com.

Need to Know More?

If you feel that you need additional information, there are three areas that you'll want to know more about.

General LSAT Information

You can pick up copies of the LSAT Information or Law School Application guides at your local college's career or career counseling office. Because applying to law school requires attaining a four-year degree, your best bet is to visit a local four-year college or university as opposed to a community college that grants two-year degrees.

Additionally, you can get information directly off the Internet at the Law School Admission Council's website: http://www.lsac.org.

Additional LSAT Preparation via Practice Exams

The lsac.org site provides links to at least one free practice exam (if you have Adobe Reader, which is available free online). Note that this exam does not come with explanations to the answers.

The LSAC also provides links to additional books that contain practice exams. In order to get more practice taking the LSAT, it's highly worthwhile to order additional tests online or purchase books with additional LSAT tests at your local bookstore.

Additional LSAT Preparation via Coursework

The two most well-known LSAT "prep" courses are offered by the Princeton Review and Stanley-Kaplan. Given the competitive world of test prep, there are many, many other providers out there today. While we can't give specific endorsements for one firm over another, we can offer the advice that you should pick whichever firm offers the style of learning you feel most comfortable with and is able to match your price point and schedule.

Glossary

Author Bias or "Attitude"
An author's viewpoints in a given passage color the material to provide evidence of how the author wishes to portray events or selected facts to subtly persuade you.

Argument Components
Arguments consist of two basic parts: *premises* and *conclusions*. Premises are the statements that are supposed to—but do not always—lead to a conclusion.

Conditions
Conditions follow a premise in a logic game by imposing series of rules or conditions that determine the relationships among the subjects.

Conclusions
The part of an argument that is arrived at from the premises to an argument.

Drawing Conclusions
A type of question where you'll be asked to draw a specific point out of the reading passage. These facts or arguments typically are used to do one of two things to the passage: strengthen the main argument, or weaken it.

Furthering Implications
This is a variation on "Drawing Conclusions." In this instance, you'll be asked to draw out the specific point of the reading passage and take it one step further to a conclusion.

Logic Games

A particular type of question that you will only find in the Analytical Reasoning portion of the LSAT. Each logic game has three separate components: the premise, the conditions, and the questions. The premise establishes the subjects (objects or people) and setting for the game. Conditions follow the premise by imposing series of rules or conditions that determine the relationships among the subjects.

Logic Versus Truth

In the context of the LSAT, "logical" does not equal "true." Logical arguments are only a series of statements that must properly follow in order to establish a given proposition.

Premise (Logic Game)

The premise establishes the subjects (objects or people) and setting for a logic game.

Premise (Logical Reasoning)

Premises are the statements that are supposed to—but do not always—lead to a conclusion.

Primary Idea(s)

The most accurate summary of a passage's central idea. This is the most common of all questions on the LSAT's Reading Comprehension section.

Refining Meaning

Clarifying an ambiguous passage, narrowing the meaning of a word, or supplying a definition for an expression or local colloquialism.

Index

F - G

L

Q - R

S - T - U

How can we make this index more useful? Email us at indexes@quepublishing.com